The Project Manager's Guide to Software Engineering's Best Practices

Mark J. Christensen and Richard H. Thayer

IEEE
**COMPUTER
SOCIETY**
http://computer.org

Los Alamitos, California

Washington • Brussels • Tokyo

```
        Library of Congress Cataloging-in-Publication Data

Christensen, M.J.   (Mark J.), 1947-
      The project manager's guide to software engineering's best
      practices
/  Mark J. Christensen and Richard H. Thayer.
      p. cm.
      Includes bibliographical references and index.
      ISBN 0-7695-1199-6
      1. Software engineering.   I. Thayer, Richard H.   II. Title
      005.1--dc21

                                                      2001005658
```

IEEE Computer Society Press Order Number BP01199
Library of Congress Number 2001005658
ISBN 0-7695-1199-6

Additional copies may be ordered from:

IEEE Computer Society	IEEE Service Center	IEEE Computer Society
Customer Service Center	445 Hoes Lane	Asia/Pacific Office
10662 Los Vaqueros Circle	P.O. Box 1331	Watanabe Bldg., 1-4-2
P.O. Box 3014	Piscataway, NJ 08855-1331	Minami-Aoyama
Los Alamitos, CA 90720-1314	Tel: + 1-732-981-0060	Minato-ku, Tokyo 107-0062
Tel: + 1-714-821-8380	Fax: + 1-732-981-9667	JAPAN
Fax: + 1-714-821-4641	http://shop.ieee.org/store/	Tel: + 81-3-3408-3118
E-mail: cs.books@computer.org	customer-service@ieee.org	Fax: + 81-3-3408-3553
		tokyo.ofc@computer.org

Publisher: Angela Burgess
Group Managing Editor, CS Press: Deborah Plummer
Advertising/Promotions: Tom Fink
Printed in the United States of America

Contents

Foreword

We, as a community of millions of software developers, have now expended more effort writing software than was expended building all the monuments that have ever existed in the history of the world. In the course of all this activity, much of it frenetic to say the least, we have built up collective knowledge that I like to call the Best Practices of software engineering. Some of this knowledge has been captured in folklore based on experience, some in professional publications documenting research and case studies. Many of the most important of these best practices are captured in the software engineering standards published by the IEEE Computer Society.

The problem faced by most practitioners of software development, and most especially those practitioners who find themselves responsible for the management of software projects, is how to apply this knowledge. Helping to bridge the gaps between practice, research, and the standards is the purpose of the current book written by Mark Christensen and Richard Thayer.

They have merged the spirit and form of the standards with practical lessons learned in applying the standards and in managing software engineering projects. They have focused on those standards that have the most direct and broadest application to software projects, spanning the full range of activities, starting with the initial concept and ending with the maintenance and support of a software product. They have enriched their discussion of the standards with practical, useful advice, drawn from their own experience and that of the community of software development professionals. I heartily endorse this book to the reader, whether they are currently involved in managing software projects today or simply desire to have a better understanding of the full scope of software development.

Leonard L. Tripp
1999 President of the IEEE Computer Society
December 2001

Preface

Since the earliest days of the computer industry, experience has shown that managing a software projects is a complex and demanding activity. Repeated studies have shown that management problems remain one of the top two or three causes of difficulties in, or even outright failure of, software development projects. This fact has remained unchanged as the technology used to design, implement, and deploy software systems has undergone rapid and widespread evolution. Likewise, the importance of software project management has been unaffected by changes in the business and structural models employed by both industries and individual companies. Thus, while the fundamental issues of software project management have consistently exerted an influence on the success of product developments, the same mistakes continue to be made:

- Requirements are unclear at the beginning of projects and are not managed during the project.

- Project planning is incomplete or not done at all.

- Management of the project is weak or arbitrary.

- Underlying and supporting processes needed to perform the technical work are often ignored.

It seems individual companies and software managers have had to re-learn these same lessons. Yet, the profession as a whole has recognized that certain issues are of fundamental importance and has made various attempts to capture the 'best practices' that can be used to address these problems. Many books have been published by experts. Seminars and training materials have been offered. The most widely based of these attempts to infuse software engineering best practices is the series of Software Engineering Standards developed by the IEEE Computer Society. These standards have been developed over many years by large and diverse groups of dedicated volunteers. Yet their influence on the profession is not as great as it should be, in large part, the authors believe, because each standard addresses an individual topic in a very formal manner.

This book is dedicated to the proposition that the standards capture many of the 'best practices' of the profession. The goal of this book is to assist the reader in applying those standards to their projects and organization. The editors and authors of the present volume have attempted to illuminate and elaborate upon those standards that bear on the three key areas of:

- Software Systems Engineering and the higher-level view of the product that it provides.

- Processes and their use in supporting and controlling the development of software.

- Planning and control of the activities of software project by adopting a systems view of the product and a process-oriented view of its development.

While from time-to-time the authors have referred to specific technologies used to perform the management activities of a software project, this has been done to illustrate the issues involved in managing projects, not to endorse any particular approach. In the same vein, issues specific to any implementation technology have been avoided. Thus, the pros and cons of object-oriented design, or automated testing methods are not debated. This is consistent with the spirit and intent of the relevant standards themselves.

The body of the book is organized into three Parts:

- Software Systems Engineering, which argues that software development projects are most successful when the development of products is approached from a systems level viewpoint, ranging from the specification of the products, through their test, installation, maintenance, and use by customers.

- Process Management and Control, which describes the key activities needed to define, support, and manage projects software development processes. In addition to discussing the key topics of life-cycle processes definition, product and process reviews, configuration management, and quality assurance and the applicable IEEE Standards, it also treats the important topic of Software Process Improvement.

- Project Planning and Management completes the book, integrating the elements of cost and schedule estimation and control, risk management, and the role metrics play in performing those tasks.

The authors and editors believe that the contents of this book, together with the underlying IEEE Standards, will aid our colleagues in their continuing quest to improve the predictability with which quality products are produced by our profession.

Mark J. Christensen

Richard H. Thayer

Acknowledgements

This book was initiated as a series of project reports by a team of graduate students from the California State University at Sacramento, California. Each team member worked on three to four knowledge areas, and, like this book, based this outline on the appropriate IEEE Software Engineering Standard. Like many graduate students studying software engineering these students had years of experience in the development and maintenance of software systems, and in a few cases, a few were managers of projects

The authors would like to acknowledge their efforts and to thank them.

Student	Responsible for Knowledge Area:
Karma Guinn	Concept of Operations Document Software Cost and Scheduling Modeling Software Requirements Engineering
Ed Perillo	Software Documentation and Users' Manual Software Maintenance Software Testing
Tim Schoenhardt	Lifecycle Process Management and Overview Software Engineering Project Management
Kathryn Wendt	Software Configuration Management Software Cost and Scheduling Modeling Software Metrics
Jon Wilhelmsen	Software Quality Assurance Software Reviews and Audits Software Verification and Validation

Dr. Robin B. Hunter is the acknowledged author of the chapter on Software Process Improvement. Hunter is a world renowned researcher in software process improvement and a member of the SPICE committee.

The chapter on Risk Management was originally developed by Dr. Richard H. Thayer, one of the authors of this book.

Reviewers

Because of the importance of this book to the Computer Society, a decision was made to have each knowledge area (book chapter) reviewed by one or more experts in the area to insure the book is technically correct and current. This was done over the fall of 2000 and the spring of 2001. To give credit, the following is a list of reviewers that contributed to the accuracy of this book.

	Knowledge Area	Standards	Reviewers
1.	Software Systems Engineering	IEEE Std. 1220-1998 IEEE Std. 1233-1998	Dr. Merlin Dorfman
2.	Concept of Operations	IEEE Std 1362-1998	Dr. Richard E. Fairley
3.	Software Requirements Specification	IEEE Std 830-1998	Dr. Stuart R. Faulk Dr. Allan M. Davis
4.	Software User Documentation	IEEE Std 1063-2001	Mr. Ian Sommerville
5.	Software Verification and Validation	IEEE Std 1012-1998	Ms. Delores R. Wallace
6.	Software Maintenance	IEEE Std 1219-1998	Mr. Thomas M. Pigoski
7.	Software Life Cycle Process Management	IEEE Std 1074-1997 IEEE/EIA Std 12207.0-1996	Mr. James W. Moore
8.	Software Process Improvement	ISO 9000-3:1991 ISO 9001:1991 ISO/IEC 15504:1998 ISO/IEC 12207:1995 ISO/IEC 9126:1995	Mr. Mark C. Paulk
9.	Software Configuration Management	IEEE Std 828-1998	(none)
10.	Software Quality Assurance	IEEE Std 730-1998	Dr. John W. Horch
11.	Software Reviews	IEEE Std 1028-1997	Mr. John J. Marciniak
12.	Software Cost and Schedule	IEEE Std 1058-1998	Dr. Richard E. Stutzke
13.	Software Engineering Project Management	IEEE Std 1058-1998	Dr. Thomas E. Tomayko Dr. Richard H. Thayer
14.	Software Risk Management	IEEE Std P1540-2001	Mr. James W. Moore
15.	Software Metrics	IEEE Std 1045-1992 IEEE Std 1061-1998	Mr. J. Dennis Lawrence

Part I

Software Systems Engineering

Part I, Chapters 1–6, covers the key activities of software systems engineering. Performing these activities in an effective manner requires that the project staff, and above all the software engineering project manager, adopt a systems level view of the product and project. This means that the product should be treated as an entity and should be regarded from the viewpoint of the user, the operator, and the maintainer. Thus the systems team must specify and evaluate the products of the development team in a more-or-less independent manner depending on the nature of the product, the contract, and the relationship with the customer. At the same time, in order to be effective, the systems team must develop technical insights into the product far beyond those of a typical user or customer. The major tasks and products of these system-level activities are described in the following chapters.

Chapter 1, *Software Systems Engineering*, presents an overview of the system-level activities and processes involved in developing, managing, testing, and delivering the software items of projects. These activities are most intensely performed at the beginning and the end of programs, first as the requirements are being developed, the top level software (and hardware, as required) architecture is laid out, and then later as the user documents are developed and the system is tested. The material of the chapter is based on a combination of several IEEE software standards, other references, and the experience of the authors in the development of information, avionics, factory support, and networking systems. The subsequent chapters of this part describe the most important technical activities required to perform these system level tasks, together with what should be done to plan and manage them.

Chapters 2 and 3 describe the processes, activities, and products involved in performing the early activities of software systems engineering, namely the development of the software requirements of systems. In Chapter 2, *Concept of Operations*, the tasks required to develop a user-level view of the system are described, including how the system will be used and also how it will be operated and maintained. These activities result in a concept of operations (ConOps) document, the format and content of which is documented in IEEE Standard 1362-1998. This document, together with other technical (usually performance-based) specifications, is used to develop the software requirements specification (SRS) described in Chapter 3. In addition to describing a selection of the methods available for developing requirements, this chapter discusses the most important management issues that often arise when developing the SRS. Finally, the chapter describes the format and typical content that should included in a SRS, as described in IEEE Standard 830-1998. The SRS is the key document upon which the software design is based.

While the software products specified in the SRS are being designed, the ConOps and requirements documents should be used to develop the documents needed by the user to use, operate, and maintain the software components of the system. The range of documents needed, together with the activities needed to develop them, are described in Chapter 4, *Software User Documentation*. This chapter is based upon the content of IEEE Standard 1063-1987, which provides a description of the content and form of the documents that should be developed in a typical software development project. In addition to the content of the standard the chapter also describes how the development of the user documents should be planned and managed, like any other item being developed by the project.

As the project proceeds through its developmental activities, as described in subsequent chapters of this book, there is a continuing need for technical and managerial oversight. Chapter 5, *Software Verification and Validation*, describes the planning and management of the activities needed to evaluate that the software products conform to their requirements. Derived from IEEE Standard 1012-1998, Chapter 5 also describes some of the technical, contractual, and business considerations that must be considered when determining the scope of the verification and validation (V&V) effort. In addition, the chapter describes the format of an IEEE-compliant V&V plan, the content of the plan, and how it should be developed and managed. When properly and appropriately planned, the V&V activities can be invaluable to the management team, as well as to the developers.

Finally, after all other activities associated with a project have been completed, the product must be supported and maintained for many years. Typically, more than half the costs associated with an application are incurred after it is delivered. It can be further argued that the maintenance activities of a project begin with the integration of the product. Chapter 6, following the guidelines of IEEE Standard 1219-1998 describes the form and content of the software maintenance plan (SMP), which should be initially developed during the project planning phase and then revised as the product matures during development.

Chapter 1

Software Systems Engineering

1.1   Introduction

This chapter describes the application of systems engineering principles to the development of a computer software system. The activities, tasks, and procedures that make up these principles are known as *software systems engineering* (SwSE). The purpose of this chapter is to identify SwSE processes and tools, describe them, and reflect on their contribution to the software development process.

Systems have become larger and more complex than ever before. The hardware and software that makes up those systems have, correspondingly, grown in capacity and complexity at nearly an exponential rate. In some cases, the physical and logical boundaries of systems are no longer clear-cut (witness the increasing interdependencies of internet-based systems), and other classes of systems having clear boundaries are growing in their complexity as well (witness the increasing functionality and integration of modern aircraft and automotive systems). The workstation sitting on virtually everyone's desk or the wireless device in their pockets reflects this trend: Microsoft Word has grown in size from a product that would fit on a 360-Kbyte diskette to a product that will only fit on a 600-Mbyte CD, and desktop operating systems have grown from requiring a few tens of thousands of bytes of memory to well over 8 million.

Hardware capacity has grown to the point where the size and capability of a software program are no longer determined by the capabilities of the computing platforms. Likewise, efficiency of implementation no longer ranks among the primary design goals for most development projects. This has fueled demand for larger and larger systems, of which the software is often the most critical component. The trend is, and will continue to be for some time, to develop extremely large and complex software systems.

The majority of these large software systems are not delivered on the desired date for the expected cost. All too often, when they are delivered, they do not completely satisfy the customer's desires or the producer's promises. This phenomenon, when combined with the shortage of adequately skilled software engineers, has come to be regarded as the "software crisis" [Gibbs 1994, Royce 1991]. In response to this so-called crisis, engineering practices have been increasingly introduced into software development efforts. Some of these practices are straightforward adaptations of engineering practices that have been used to develop nonsoftware products for some time, whereas others are more novel.

As these practices are applied during the development of a product, it is not sufficient to simply mechanically track project status. Monitoring the resources used, the schedules met, or the milestones accomplished will not provide sufficient feedback as to the health of the project. The technical processes and products must be actively managed. Systems engineering provides the tools needed to perform the technical management of systems under development.

Engineering practices applied to software products consist primarily of (1) processes for the systematic development of the software elements of the system and (2) representation methods and tools, used to describe the products and their attributes. Examples include the following:

- *Life cycle development processes*—These divide the project into phases.

- *Managing software as a distinct and separate element of a project*—Ensures that adequate support and oversight are applied to the effort.

- *Use of intermediate products (specifications and descriptions)*—Takes advantage of, for example, requirements specifications and design descriptions.

- *Software-specific analysis, representation methods, and design tools*—Makes use of, for example, structured and object-oriented techniques.

- *Reviews and audits*—Used to provide visibility to the ongoing development activities and their products.

- *Verification, validation, and testing*—Confirms that the products of the development effort conform to their requirements.

- *Configuration management and quality assurance*—Provides confidence that the developmental activities are being conducted as planned and that the results are available and reproducible.

- *Prototyping*—Explores requirements, evaluates alternative approaches, and determines the feasibility of proposed solutions.

- *Use of off-the-shelf components*—Leverages existing technologies and improves interoperability with other products used in the application domain.

This chapter is not based on any single IEEE software engineering standard but instead is derived from a collection of standards that support software systems engineering. This chapter also supports IEEE Standard 1220-1998, *IEEE Standard for the Application and Management of the Systems Engineering Process*, and IEEE Standard 1233-1998, *IEEE Guide for Developing System Requirements Specifications*.

1.2   Objectives

In this chapter you will learn:

- How the software systems engineering process is used to manage the technical effort of a project.

- How software systems engineering affects all phases of the development life cycle.

- The relationship between product systems engineering and software systems engineering.

- The relationship between software systems engineering and project management.

- The activities that make up software systems engineering.

- The role of software systems engineering in the software requirements analysis process.

- The role of software systems engineering in the software design process.

- The activities of software systems engineering that support the planning of the project.

- The activities of software systems engineering that support control of the project.

- How software systems engineering supports verification, validation, and testing.

1.3   Systems Engineering Concepts

1.3.1   Overview of Systems

Before describing the processes and methods that make up systems engineering, the term system should be defined. The IEEE standards define a system as:

> *A collection of components organized to accomplish a specific function or set of functions. [IEEE Standard 610.12-1990]*

Equivalently, a *system* is a collection of related or associated entities that together accomplish of one or more specific objectives. The key words are *related, together*, and *specific* objectives. A mere assemblage of isolated entities or elements with no common objective would not be a system. They might, instead be parts of other systems or completely autonomous items. This concept is illustrated in Figure 1.1.

A *man-made system* is a collection of hardware, software, people, facilities, procedures, and other factors organized to accomplish a common objective. A *software system* is, therefore, a man-made system or subsystem made up of a collection of programs and documents that together accomplish some specific requirements. Thus, one software system may operate entirely on a conventional desktop or data processing environment, whereas another might in fact be a subsystem of a larger system composed of sensors, mechanical and optical devices, and computers.

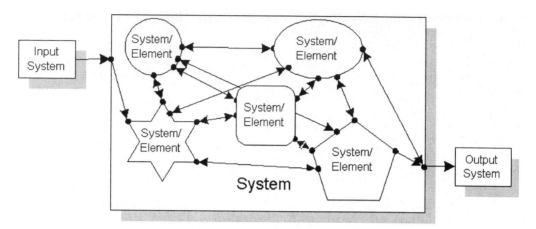

A system is a collection of related elements related in a way that allows the accomplishment of some tangible objective.
...Pressman 1982

Figure 1.1: A System Interacting with Two Others [Pressman 1982]

1.3.2   Systems Engineering

Systems engineering (SE) is the practical application of the scientific, engineering, and management skills required to transform a user's need into a description of a system configuration that best satisfies that need in an effective and efficient way. The products of SE activities are largely documents, not physical artifacts. The single product that is not a document is the final system itself. The document products are used to ensure that the system is developed in an orderly, technically sound manner and is acceptable to the customer. Examples of such documents include these:

- The top-level architecture of the system, identifying its topology, its subsystems, and their interactions;

- Specifications for the system and its subsystems;

- The logistical and maintenance concepts needed to sustain the system;

- Trade studies and analyses used to select between different design and implementation approaches for the system and subsystems;

- Evaluations of intermediate products of the subsequent development activities;

- Integration of the subsystems to form a whole;

- System-level test plans, execution of those tests (which results in the final system), and reports of actual performance;

- Assessments and interpretation of technical anomalies uncovered as the project evolves; and

- Technical oversight of the various suppliers, both internal and external, producing subsystems, or components that will be integrated into the product.

According to H. C. Alberts [Alberts 1988], a professor at the Defense System Management College in Fort Belvoir, Virginia, who teaches SE, the term SE was first proposed in 1956 by H. Hitch, chairman of the Aeronautical Engineering Department at Penn State University. Based on experience gained during the Second World War while developing large, complex systems, such as high-altitude bombers, surface ships, submarines, tanks, and their attendant manufacturing and support systems, Hitch was trying to develop an engineering discipline that could concentrate on the development of large systems that used many diverse engineering disciplines to develop a system with an expected long life. In 1961 the first formal educational program in systems engineering was established at the University of Arizona, followed by a select group of other universities. These principles were first systematically applied to large systems developments in the 1960s and 1970s, such as the Apollo moon program [Chapman et al. 1992] and the USAF/USN Ballistic Missile Program [Dorfman 2001].

Systems engineering provides the overall technical management of a system development project. IEEE Standard 1220-1998 defines the environment and processes that comprise systems engineering. A variety of definitions can be given for systems engineering, all of which contain the same essential features:

> Systems engineering is the management function that controls the total system development effort for the purpose of achieving an optimum balance of all system elements. It is a process that transforms an operational need into a description of system parameters and integrates those parameters to optimize the overall system effectiveness. [DSMC 1989]

> The systems engineering process is the integrated sequence of activities and decisions that transforms a defined need into an operational, life-cycle-optimized system that achieves an integrated and optimal balance of its components. [USAF 1985]

> The principle top-level function of systems engineering is to ensure that the system satisfies its requirements throughout its life cycle. Everything else follows from this function. [Wymore 1993]

Thus, SE is a generic problem-solving process that provides mechanisms for defining, describing, and evolving both the product and the processes needed to build the product. This process should be applied throughout the system life cycle to all activities associated with product development, verification/test, manufacturing, training, operation and use, support, distribution, and disposal [IEEE 1220-1998].

Systems engineering defines the plan to be followed in managing a project's technical activities. It identifies the system life cycle model for the project, along with the necessary processes. Likewise, systems engineering defines the environment or framework within which those processes will operate, together with the interfaces between them, the products, and the approach used to manage risk throughout the development of the project. Finally, systems engineering produces the technical baseline for all development, both software and hardware. The requirements specified for the system must be divided into those allocated to the software subsystem and those allocated to the hardware subsystem (or both or neither). Based on the requirements allocated to each subsystem it must be designed, implemented, and tested using the applicable software and hardware engineering processes and, ultimately, integrated with the other subsystems to create the system.

The emphasis of the systems engineering effort for a given project is determined by the nature of the product and what phase of the product life cycle is currently ongoing. Thus the generic systems engineering effort would be intense in the early stages of the product development life cycle as the concept of operations document, system architecture, software requirements specification, hardware requirements specification, and draft acceptance test plans were being first created. Concurrently the maintenance and support concepts would be elaborated. As the hardware and software items are actually being designed and implemented, the systems engineering effort would consist primarily of the verification and validation that the items being produced will satisfy their intended requirements and use. Later, as the items are integrated, the systems effort would be dominated by the integration of the items and, ultimately, by the system-level testing that will lead to acceptance.

Figure 1.2 presents a conceptual view of the relative systems engineering effort applied during a typical program.

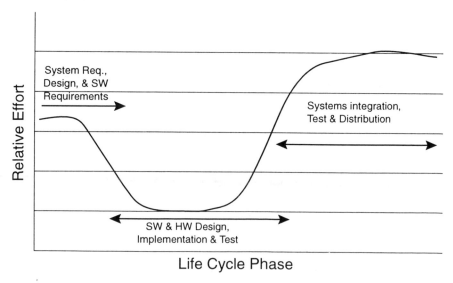

Figure 1.2: Relative Systems Engineering Effort Over a Typical Development Lifecycle

1.3.3   Functions of Systems Engineering

Systems engineering includes the following functions:

- *Problem definition*—Determine the product expectations, needs, and constraints by collecting and analyzing requirements. Work closely with the customer to establish the operational needs.

- *Solution analysis*—Determine what options exist to satisfy the requirements and constraints; study and analyze the possible solutions. Select the optimum one, balancing immediate needs, implementation options, long-term suitability, and operational utility.

- *Process planning*—Determine the major technical tasks to be accomplished, the effort required to perform those tasks, the priority of tasks, and the potential risks to the project.

- *Process control*—Determine the methods for controlling the technical activities of the project and the process, measure progress, review intermediate products, and take corrective action when necessary.

- *Product evaluation*—Determine the quality and quantity of delivered products through evaluations consisting of, but not limited to, testing, demonstration, analysis, examination, and inspection.

At this point it is important to distinguish between systems engineering and project management. First, systems engineering is fundamentally a *capability* that an organization does or does not possess. It may or may not be a specific, identifiable entity within a company. Depending on the product being developed there may or may not be a group with the term "Systems Engineering" in its title. Likewise, for a particular project, there may or may not be someone with the title "project system engineer." The functions listed above are often performed by a combination of the system architect, the lead designer, and the process architect.

This is not the case with project management: Every project should have someone with the title "project manager" or "software engineering project manager" whose primary functions are described in Chapter 12. Some of the functions listed above also appear on the list of tasks to be performed by software engineering project management. This is especially true for those functions associated with process planning and control. The distinction is that project management is concerned with the process planning (e.g., scheduling) and control for all of the activities of the project, whereas systems engineering is concerned with the technical activities of the product development and sustainment. In this sense systems engineering is an agent of project management in this area of activity. However, systems engineering is primarily concerned with the methods that will be applied to accomplishing those tasks. In that sense systems engineering goes beyond the traditional concerns of project management.

A similar distinction should be made with the functions of systems engineering and those of the software or hardware engineering disciplines. Each group performs similar functions but on different scales and breadth of application. While the overall systems engineering function is concerned with the technical processes, methods, and tasks of a project at the architectural and operational level, the software or hardware engineering functions are concerned with the technical processes, methods, and tasks needed to develop and deliver their components to the systems engineering function for evaluation and, ultimately, integration. As a result, the systems viewpoint must be carried forward into the software and hardware specialties.

For projects developing products with both hardware and software components, the software and hardware functions should have representatives on the *systems engineering team*. The role of these individuals will be both to support the systems engineering effort with their specific skills and to carry the systems viewpoint forward into the activities of their specialized functions as the components are developed. In the event that the project is developing only software items and has no other organization with suitable technical background, the software organization itself must adopt the systems role. Thus, either scenario requires that individuals or groups be available to perform the software systems engineering function.

1.4   Software Systems Engineering

As discussed above, software systems engineering, like systems engineering itself, is both a technical and management process. The *technical process* of SwSE is the analytical effort necessary to transform an operational need into a description of a software system; a software design of the proper size, configuration, and quality; its successive elaboration in requirements and design specifications; the procedures needed to verify, test, and accept the finished product; and the documentation necessary to use, operate, and maintain the system.

SwSE is not a job description—it is a process and a mind-set that should be adopted when approaching software engineering at the highest levels. Many organizations and people can and do practice SwSE: system engineers, managers, software engineers, and programmers, as well as customers and users. Many practitioners consider SwSE to be a special case of SE. Others consider SwSE to be part of software engineering. But what really matters is that it be done, not what organizational arrangements are made to do it.

SE and SwSE are often overlooked in software development projects. Systems that are composed entirely of software or run on commercial, off-the-shelf computers are often considered "just" software projects, not system projects, and no effort is expended to develop a systems engineering approach. This results in a *code-centric* approach to product development that ignores many important customer requirements, commonly known as *hacking*. The lack of a systems engineering approach to projects often results in software that will not run on the hardware selected, or will not integrate with hardware and other software systems, or that is not suitable for long-term usage. This neglect of the systems aspects of product development has contributed to the aforementioned long-running software

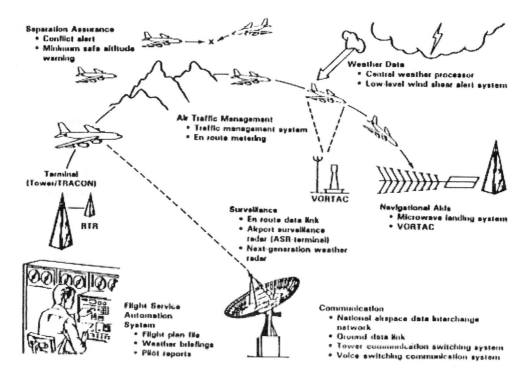

Figure 1.3: Software Integrates the System (Courtesy Northrop Grumman Information Technology, formerly Logicon, Inc.).

crisis [Gibbs 1994, Royce 1991].

Dr. Winston W. Royce, an early leader in software engineering, is credited with introducing the term *software systems engineering*, in the early 1980s [Royce 1988].

1.4.1 Role of Software in Modern Systems

The dominant technology in many modern technical products is software. Software often provides the cohesiveness, control, and functionality that enable products to deliver solutions to customers. Figure 1.3 [Fujii 1989] illustrates the concept that software is the unifying element of modern systems. Software also provides the flexibility needed to work around limitations or problems encountered when integrating other items into the system. This is especially true for problems discovered late in the development cycle, such as in integration. Fixing a hardware/software interface anomaly in software can save, literally, hundreds of thousands or even millions of dollars compared to a solution implemented in hardware. "Software is easy to change, but hard to change correctly" (an anonymous project manager).

As a result, software is usually the most complex part of any system and its development often becomes the greatest technical challenge as the system is created. In the air traffic control system, for example, software integrates people, radar, airplanes, communications, and other equipment to provide an effective air traffic control system. Software also provides the functionality needed to integrate modern business in the form of *enterprise information systems* or *enterprise resource planning* systems, as well as supporting the creation of virtual communities and interest groups on the Internet.

1.4.2   Application of Systems Engineering to Software Systems

As described earlier, systems engineering defines the product at the highest level. The systems engineering approach focuses on the operation and use of the product throughout its life cycle and applies this viewpoint to the specification of the essential features that all solutions to the problem should possess. This is done prior to decomposing the solution into specific hardware and software subsystems. Applying this same philosophy to software subsystems, or to systems composed purely of software, results in the description of the software in terms of its essential features and how those features relate to the use and operation of the system throughout its life cycle. Later, as the software is decomposed into specific software subsystems, explicit design decisions are applied to the design. These, in turn, become constraints during the next steps of the implementation process.

The concept of deferring design decisions until the proper time is a generalization of the practice of avoiding the application of constraints for as long as possible in the development process. The further into the development process a project gets before a constraint is defined, the more flexible the implemented solution will be. The designer, whether a systems or software designer, must, of course, exercise good judgment in applying this rule, because design decisions cannot be delayed to the point where the implementation is affected. In addition, some constraints are so fundamental that they can virtually dictate some aspects of the solution. The trick is to know the difference: the motto "Write no code before its time" applies equally well to design.

1.4.3   The Necessity of Software Systems Engineering

The rate at which new, complex products are being developed is continuously accelerating, and the proper operation of many of these new systems is highly dependent on software systems and subsystems. *Thus, software systems are larger and more complex now than at any time in history.* This trend is caused by a number of factors, acting separately and together:

- Inexpensive computer hardware is available, which allows users to specify more sophisticated and complex requirements.

- Software is providing an ever-increasing percentage of many systems' functionality.

- Increased software complexity is driven by increased system complexity.

- Customers are demanding more reliable and usable software systems.

- Customers want the flexibility offered by software-based solutions.

As a result, software development costs are growing in both absolute and relative terms; it is not uncommon for the cost of the software of a system to be several times that of the hardware. As the cost of developing the software grows, so does the schedule. If the project is conducted properly, the schedule growth is not as severe as that of the cost,[1] but if the project is not managed properly the schedule can more than double. As software projects grow in size and complexity, so does the risk that problems will occur. Such large and complex systems require the technical system management provided by the systems engineering approach. Without such a systems engineering approach the following problems often result:

- Complex software systems development projects become unmanageable.

- Costs are overrun and schedules are missed.

- Unacceptable risks are not recognized and, as a result, the project takes the risk unknowingly.

- Unacceptable engineering procedures (or none at all) are used.

- Erroneous decisions are made early in the life cycle that are often not detected until late in the project when they are very costly to correct.

- Subsystems and components are developed without proper coordination. The result is that they will not integrate readily—or at all.

- Some parts and components are never specified or built. Requirements, even if captured in the software requirements specification, are ignored and, as a result, not met.

- The delivered system fails to work properly.

- Parts of the system must be reworked after delivery— repeatedly.

A consistently applied software systems engineering approach is necessary if the software community is to build and deliver the "new order" of computer-dependent systems now being sought by governments, industry, and the public.

1.4.4   Role of Software Systems Engineering

For software only projects, the software systems engineering function is responsible for the overall technical management of the system and the verification of the final products. It is responsible for the activities and tasks listed in Table 1.1. This is not meant to be an all-inclusive list but to give insight into the types of tasks and responsibilities comprising SwSE.

---

[1]For an explanation of this phenomena, see the discussion of parametric models in the chapter on cost and schedule estimation, Chapter 12.

Interface technically with the customer.
Support systems engineering at the product level for hybrid hardware/software systems.
Determine project software effort and schedule.
Determine and manage software technical risk.
Define and document software requirements.
Perform functional analysis of requirements and flowdown.
Determine system data throughput and storage.
Perform trade-off studies and time-line analyses.
Develop prototypes.
Design and document top-level software system architecture.
Define and document software technical interfaces.
Manage software interface control working group.
Develop verification and validation procedures and plans.
Develop software systems test plans, procedures, and cases.
Define standards, practices, and methodologies.
Conduct external and internal reviews.
Verify and audit technical products.
Manage software system configuration and change.
Identify technology needs.
Provide subcontractor software technical direction and oversight.

Table 1.1: Activities and Tasks of Software Systems Engineering

In projects developing both hardware and software items, the software systems engineering effort will either perform these functions entirely or will play a significant role in performing them as part of an overarching systems engineering activity.

1.4.5   Relationship to Software Engineering

Some areas of overlap are seen with the preceding discussion of software systems engineering and the activities of software engineering as usually conceived. Significant differences do, however, exist. In particular, as usually defined, software engineering is principally concerned with the implementation of software requirements. More fully, software engineering is:

- The practical application of computer science, management, and other sciences to the analysis, design, construction, and maintenance of software and its associated documentation;

- An engineering science that applies the concepts of analysis, design, coding, testing, documentation, and management to the successful completion of large, custom-built computer programs under constraints of time and budget; and

- The systematic application of methods, tools, and techniques to achieve a stated requirement or objective for an effective and efficient software system.

These definitions would imply that software systems engineering is partly a subset of software engineering. However, the above definitions do not focus on the needs of users, nor do they explicitly encompass the full life cycle of support that is the dominant feature in the definitions of systems engineering presented earlier.

Figure 1.4 illustrates the relationships between systems engineering, software systems engineering, and software engineering functions. In this view, the systems engineering function performs initial analysis and design and final system integration and testing. During the initial stages of software development, the software systems engineering function is responsible for software requirements analysis and architectural design. Software systems engineering is also responsible for the final testing of the software system and its delivery to the systems function. Actual component engineering, implementation, and testing are the dominion of software engineering in this view. A similar diagram can be drawn for any hardware items of a system, if such items are being developed or procured. This diagram should be contrasted with Figure 1.1, which shows the notional distribution of effort for systems engineering during the development process.

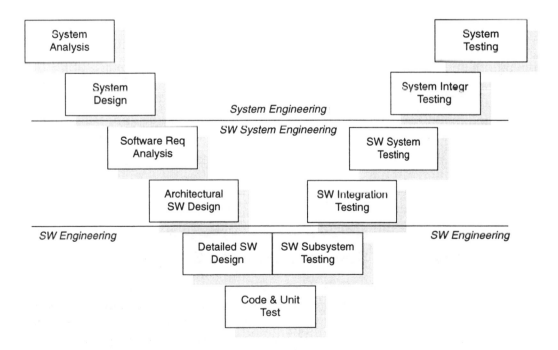

Figure 1.4: Engineering Activities and Product Flow

1.4.6   Relationship to Project Management

The *project management (PM) process* assesses the risks and costs of the software system, establishes the program master schedule, managerially integrates the various engineering specialties and design groups, maintains configuration control, and continuously audits the effort to ensure that cost and schedule are met and technical requirements objectives are satisfied. Many of these functions are performed by other organizations operating under direction from project management. For example, the configuration control function is typically performed by a group of that name, not by PM.

Figure 1.5 illustrates the relationships between PM, SwSE, and software engineering. PM has overall management responsibility for the project and the authority to commit resources. SwSE determines the "big picture" technical approach, interfaces with the technical customer, and approves and accepts the final software product. Software engineering is responsible for developing the software design, coding, and testing the design and, in general, developing the software configuration items (subsystems).

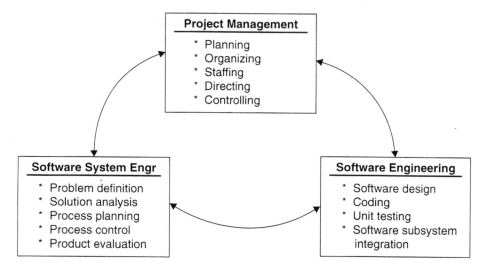

Figure 1.5: Management Relationships

1.4.7   Activities of Software Systems Engineering

The major activities of software systems engineering are listed next. Notice the parallels between these tasks and those performed by systems engineering in hybrid hardware/software developments (see Section 1.3.3). The terms in parentheses are the names commonly used when these functions are performed as part of an overall systems engineering effort.

- *Requirements analysis (problem definition)*—Determine the needs and constraints by analyzing the system requirements that have been allocated to software.

- *Architectural software design (solution analysis)*—Determine the set of solutions to the software requirements and constraints, conduct trade studies, perform analysis of possible solutions, and select the optimum one.

- *Process planning*—Determine the tasks to be done, the scope and the effort necessary to perform the tasks, the precedence between tasks, and the potential risks to the project.

- *Process control*—Determine the methods to be used in technically controlling the project and the processes, measure progress, review intermediate products, and take corrective action when necessary.

- *Verification, validation, and testing (product evaluation)*— Evaluate the final product and documentation through testing, demonstrations, analysis, and inspections. This includes any necessary software system integration activities.

The following sections of this chapter discuss these activities on a summary basis in order to illustrate their relationships. They are also discussed in more detail in separate chapters of this volume.

1.5 Software Requirements Analysis

Software requirements are (1) software capabilities needed by a user to solve a problem or achieve an objective and/or (2) capabilities that must be provided or possessed by a software system or software system component to satisfy a contract, standard, specification, or other formally imposed document [IEEE 610.12-1990].

The IEEE standard for software requirements specifications [IEEE 830-1998] partitions software requirements into the following categories:

- *Functional requirements*—Specify the functions that a system or system component must be capable of performing.

- *Performance requirements*—Specify performance characteristics that a system or system component must possess, such as speed, accuracy, frequency.

- *External interface requirements*—Specify hardware, software, or database elements with which a system or system component must interface; sets forth constraints on formats, timing, or other factors caused by such an interface.

- *Design constraints*—Affect or limit the design of a software system or software system component, for example, language requirements, physical hardware requirements, software development standards, and software quality assurance standards.

- *Quality attributes*—Specify the quality features, such as correctness, reliability, maintainability, and portability, that the product must possess.

The first step in any software development activity is to investigate, determine, and document the system requirements in a system requirements specification and/or software requirements in a software requirements specification (SRS).

Software requirements analysis is initiated when:

- Customer and user system requirements have been identified adequate to the needs of the development model;

- A system architectural design (sometimes called a top-level design) has been completed;

- A corresponding set of software subsystems has been identified;

- All customer/user requirements have been properly allocated (assigned) to one or more of these subsystems (*Note:* This process may reveal problems with the system documents such as the system requirements specifications, system architecture design, or system testing planning documents.); and

- If appropriate, a systems requirements review (SRR) should have been completed.

Software requirements analysis is complete when:

- A concept of operations document is complete (if not already furnished by the customer or developed during the system requirements phase);

- The software requirements of the system and subsystems have been identified;

- An SRS is written for each of the software subsystems. An SRS identifies "what" each software subsystem must do (without describing "how" it will be implemented);

- The SRS has been verified;

- A requirements trace is completed;

- A preliminary user manual is written;

- A test compliance matrix is finished;

- A preliminary test specification is finished;

- The software specification reviews are complete; and

- A requirements (sometimes called allocated) baseline is established in the configuration management system.

The purpose of the SRS is to define the software requirements in sufficient detail to allow the software designer to design a product that satisfies those requirements unambiguously. Some sections of the SRS may need to reference external specifications, in which case the relevant portions of the specific version of those documents must be placed under the same regime of configuration management as the SRS itself. An example of such a class of documents is interface control documents (ICDs), which describe the interfaces between software and hardware items or systems. Chapter 3, on software requirements specifications, gives more detail on the processes used to develop the software requirements.

1.5.1 Concept Analysis and the ConOps Document

Software system analysis is an engineering process used to clearly and explicitly identify software requirements. It consists of "translating" the system requirements allocated to software into measurable technical software requirements or, depending on the nature of the product, directly translating the customer's operational requirements into software requirements. *Software requirements specifications* are the documented form of the requirements identified during requirements analysis. Software requirements come from many sources. Each particular project will have different sources, one of the most important of which should be the concept of operations document.

The *concept analysis* process identifies the overall systems characteristics from the viewpoint of an operator or user. Concept analysis is used by the systems engineers to clarify the operational needs of users. It is used to facilitate communications between users, the buyer, and developers. Development of a *concept of operations* (ConOps) document to record the results of concept analysis provides a bridge from user needs into the system and software development process. The ConOps document may be done during the SE engineering process or at any time prior to the development of the software requirements. See Chapter 2 for more detail on concept of operations.

1.5.2 Software Requirements Analysis and Specifications

Software requirements analysis is the process of studying the customer's system needs and operational environment to arrive at a definition of system or software requirements. Numerous tools and techniques have been developed during the past 25 years that can be used to (1) analyze the requirements and (2) represent the requirements. The general categories of such methods are natural language, semiformal notations, and formal notations. These representation methods are discussed in Chapter 3.

1.5.3 Prototyping

A *prototype* is a limited working model of the software system or a part of the system. A prototype is used to stimulate feedback from users that is used for improving and specifying a complex human interface, for establishing the feasibility of requirements studies, or for identifying further requirements. If the user is involved in the prototyping process, care must be exercised to ensure that the user realizes that the prototype is indeed a limited concept demonstrator with specific objectives and is not a fully capable, maintainable system. Failure to clearly communicate this fact can result in unmet expectations.

1.5.4   Traceability

Software requirements are said to be *traceable* if it is possible to follow the requirement from its point of origin as a system or ConOps requirement, to its allocation in an SRS, to its implementation in a design and code, and ultimately to its test criteria in a test specification. Tracing is a very effective tool (sometimes used by independent verification and validation teams) for checking that all of the system and software requirements have been addressed.

1.5.5   Preliminary User's Manual

User's manuals are prepared by the developer and used to provide the customer and/or user personnel with the information needed to use and operate the software system. The manual content and format are specifically designed to meet the needs of the intended users. Chapter 4, Software User Documentation, should be consulted for more details on the format, content, and processes that should be applied when developing such documents.

The preliminary user's manual should be developed early in the software development process to assist in the verification of the software requirements. The user's manual is prepared from the SRS because the requirements specifications describe the finished system. If the SRS contains errors of omission, incompleteness, or incorrectness, these errors may be discovered by the users during their review of the user's manual.

1.5.6   Preliminary Test Specification

A *preliminary test specification* is a test document that specifies the test approach for a software feature or combination of software features and identifies the associated tests.

Preliminary versions of acceptance and system test specifications should be developed early in the software development process to provide a means of verifying the software requirements. The test documents are prepared from the requirements specifications because those documents are intended to describe the system when implemented.

If the SRS contains errors of omission or is incomplete, incorrect, or inconsistent, the test developers are likely to discover it early in the life cycle. No requirement can be viewed as being finalized until its testability has been demonstrated in an appropriate software test document. For details on the software test process, the reader should consult the testing chapter in this book.

1.5.7　Test Compliance Matrix

A *test compliance matrix* is used to represent what methods will be used to verify (test) each software requirement. It is a useful tool, not only for planning subsequent testing efforts, but also to verify the realism of the requirements themselves. This matrix is often embodied in the preliminary test specification.

1.5.8　Software Specification Review

The *software specification review* (SSR) is conducted to allow customers, users, and management to evaluate the software requirements specification and other applicable documents. The objective is to assess the progress of the software requirements activities. The SSR is sometimes a contractually required event. Chapter 11, Software Reviews, should be consulted for more details on how to conduct such reviews.

The SSR is a joint acquirer-supplier review (sometimes called a milestone review) conducted to finalize software requirements so that the software developer can initiate top-level or architectural software design. The SSR is conducted when software requirements have been sufficiently defined to allow the evaluation of the developer's responsiveness to and interpretation of the system or customer technical requirements. The customer's and developer's determination that the SRS and interface specifications form a satisfactory basis for proceeding into the top-level design phase will be the primary result of a successful SSR.

1.5.9　Software Requirements Verification

Verification techniques should be used to evaluate how accurately and faithfully the SRS responds to the system-level requirements and architectural design. The verification process evaluates the software requirements by looking for incorrect, incomplete, ambiguous, or untestable requirements, as well as for any noncompliance with the system functional and nonfunctional requirements. For a general discussion of the methods of validation and verification, see Chapter 5.

Some of the tools and procedures used to perform verification and validation of the software requirements include traceability analysis, evaluation, interface analysis, and test planning [IEEE 1012-1998]. Specific tools include control flow analysis, data flow analysis, algorithm analysis, simulation analysis, in-process audits, and requirements walkthroughs.

1.5.10　Requirements Baseline

The *requirements baseline* is a specific, formal description of the requirements of a product that has been accepted and agreed on by all parties concerned at a specific point in time.

The *software requirements baseline* is the software configuration established at the end of the software requirements development phase. This baseline is embodied in an approved software requirements and interface specification. It should be placed under formal configuration control by joint agreement between the developer and the customer. This is commonly referred to as the *allocated baseline*. For a further discussion of the concept of baselines and the role they play in managing the software process, see Chapter 9.

1.6   Software Design

Software design is the process of decomposing, selecting, and documenting the most effective and efficient elements and topology that will implement the software system requirements. Software design is traditionally partitioned into two phases: *architectural* (or top-level) design and *detailed* design.

Software architectural design (sometimes called preliminary or top-level design) is similar to system design in that the structure of the software is designed and the software requirements are allocated to components of the structure. The fundamental approach to the flow of control and data between the components is determined in this phase as well. This may require that the operating or run-time system be selected in the event it is not predetermined by requirements.

Software detailed design (sometimes called critical design) typically includes definition and structuring of computer program components and data, definition of the interfaces, and preparation of timing and sizing estimates. Software detailed design is equivalent to component engineering from the systems viewpoint and is considered part of software engineering. The components in this case are independent software modules and artifacts. This chapter allocates software architectural design to the systems software engineering process and software detailed design to software engineering, irrespective of organizational arrangements.

Software system design is initiated when:

- The software requirements have been identified, documented, and reviewed.

- The draft user's manual and draft test documents have been developed.

Software system design is completed when:

- The "how" question is answered (conceptual design).

- The software architectural description is completed.

- An architectural design review (often called a preliminary design review) is completed and all relevant parties have accepted the design description.

- The preliminary operator's and maintenance manuals are written.

- The design trace is completed.

- The architectural design is reviewed.

- The architectural design is verified.

- The software integration test plan is written.

- The resulting product baseline is established.

Software system design is the engineering process used to create the software architectural design. The objective of design is to translate the software requirements into a software architecture that will implement them effectively.

1.6.1 Architectural Design Description

The *architectural design description* typically consists of these items:

- An overall description of the software processing architecture showing the major subsystems, data items, and their topology;

- Functions allocated to the lowest level identified in the architecture, together with any class hierarchies;

- Data flow, database, and associated processes;

- Control of processing;

- System utilities and operating system interfaces;

- External and internal interfaces; and

- Allocated storage and throughput.

The design must logically and specifically satisfy all of the requirements identified in the allocated baseline. The design should be elaborated to a level of detail adequate to demonstrate that the requirements are satisfied and to support the next phase of the selected development life cycle—and no more.

1.6.2 Preliminary Operator's and Maintenance Manuals

The preliminary operator's and maintenance manuals are initial versions of two of the three deliverable documents used to support a software system. The user's manual, whose preliminary version was created earlier, is the third. These items are described in more detail in the chapter on user documentation, Chapter 4.

An *operator's manual* is used by the system's operators (in contrast to the users) to support the users and operate the system. On some systems, particularly modern desktop computers, the operator and the user are the same individuals or organizations and, as a result, the operator and user's manuals are combined.

The *maintenance manual* is intended to support the efforts of future software engineers in maintaining the system. A maintenance manual (sometimes called a *software maintenance document*) should describe the internals of the system software in sufficient clarity and detail to allow software engineers and programmers to perform corrective, perfective, and adaptive changes to the software after it has been delivered. See the chapter on software maintenance of this book, Chapter 6.

Creating the preliminary versions at this time provides several benefits:

- Just as with the preliminary version of the user's manual, creation and review of these documents can assist in validating the software design.

- The information is current and hence more likely to be accurate. Of course, the documents must be maintained if material changes are made to the software design during subsequent phases of development.

- The documents can be used by the test and integration teams as they familiarize themselves with the system's expected behavior.

- The development organization can use the documents to educate new engineers in both the operation of the system and its design.

1.6.3   Traceability of the Design

Applying the same techniques used to trace the requirements from the user needs to the SRS, the software requirements should be traced forward and backward through the design. The results should be documented in a requirements tracing report that is presented during the architectural design review. This particular effort typically calls for a *requirements tracing tool*. The objective of this activity is to ensure that the design satisfies all requirements (the forward trace) and that the design contains no features not present in the requirements (the backward or reverse trace).

1.6.4   Architectural Design Review

The *architectural design description* and other products of the software architecture design are reviewed by an appropriate review team composed of the developers, customers, and potential users of the system. This is a major joint acquirer-supplier review called the *preliminary design review* (PDR) in earlier periods. If the architectural design and other products of the current phases of development are judged acceptable, the developers are permitted to proceed to the detailed design phase. The chapter on software reviews (Chapter 11) should be consulted for details on how to prepare for and conduct such reviews.

The term *architectural design* has gradually replaced the early term *preliminary design* as being more appropriate for the activities involved. The acronym for the appropriate review (architectural design review, ADR) was not widely adopted, so the term *preliminary design review* (PDR) remains in wide use at this time.

1.6.5 Architectural Design Verification

The software design specifications should be verified against the software requirements and the top-level system design. The verification process looks for incomplete or incorrect design, inefficient and unmaintainable design, poor user interfaces, and poor documentation.

The minimum verification tasks are design traceability analysis, design evaluation, interface analysis, and updating of the verification and validation (V&V) test plan and test design specifications for component testing, software systems integration testing, system testing, and acceptance testing [IEEE 829-1998, IEEE 1028-1997]. The V&V activity then reports any discrepancies found between these levels of life cycle documents and any other major problems detected in the course of the verification process.

1.6.6 Architectural Design Baseline

In contrast to the allocated baseline, which consists largely of the approved requirements describing what the system is to do, the *architectural design baseline* is the first level of the configuration that describes how the system will satisfy its requirements. This baseline is established when the software architectural design and interface specification are approved and placed under formal configuration control. Depending on the contract this may be a developer-only decision or customer concurrence may be required.

Many projects do not formally establish this baseline. This often leads to serious problems because the lack of such an intermediate milestone often means traceability from the requirements to the design is lost. That is, the representational gap between the requirements and the implementation in code cannot be bridged.

1.7 Process Planning

Planning consists of specifying the *goals* and *objectives* for a project and the *strategies*, *policies*, *plans*, and *procedures* to be followed to achieve them. Phrased slightly differently, planning is made up of deciding in advance what to do, how to do it, when to do it, and who will do it.

Planning a software engineering project is composed of the SwSE and management activities that lead to selection from several alternatives of the future course of action for the project and an explicit approach for completing those actions.

The planning process is initiated when a decision has been made to develop a software system. Planning is a continuous effort. Software system planning is completed when the project is finished. For more details on planning activities, the chapters on software engineering project management and cost and schedule estimation of this book should be consulted. The following sections provide a brief outline of the major planning activities.

Software Systems Engineering Determines:	Project Management Determines:
The tasks to be done	The skills necessary to do the task
The order of precedence between tasks	The schedule for completing the project
The size of the effort (in staff time)	The cost of the effort
The technical approach to solving the problem	The managerial approach to monitoring the project's status
The analysis and design tools to use	The planning tools to use
The technical risks	The management risks
The process model to be used	The process model to be used
Updates to the plans when the requirements or development environment changes	Updates to the plans when the managerial conditions and environment changes

Table 1.2: Partitioning of the Planning Effort

1.7.1   Plan Workload

Project planning should be split into two separate but related components: planning done by the project management function and planning done by software systems engineering.

It is a natural but erroneous assumption to believe that only PM plans the project. In reality PM, while serving as the central coordination point for planning and executing the project, only does part of the project planning directly. In most software projects, in fact, the bulk of the planning is done by the SwSE function. Of course, in some projects, the project manager functions as the software/systems engineering project manager and may well do both. The exact split of planning tasks will depend on the size and nature of the project, the customers' planning, and reporting requirements, and the culture of the developing organization. Thus, a given organization might choose to partition the planning of a software system development project along the lines shown in Table 1.2.

1.7.2   Determine Tasks

A *work breakdown structure* (WBS) is a method of representing, in a hierarchical manner, the parts of a process or product. It can be used for representing a process (for example, requirements analysis, design, coding, or testing), a product (for example, applications program, utility program, or system software), or both. The WBS is a major systems engineering tool that can be used by both software engineers and project managers.

The WBS is used by SwSE to partition the software project into elementary tasks to be done. Figure 1.6 shows a generic example of a WBS. A more detailed discussion of the concept of the WBS can be found in Chapter 12, Software Cost and Schedule.

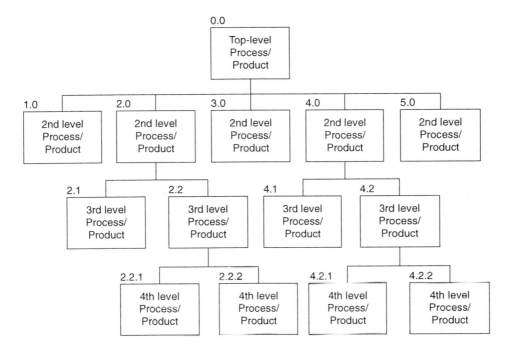

Figure 1.6: Generic Work Breakdown Structure (WBS)

1.7.3   Determine Effort and Schedule

The software systems engineering function, working with and as part of an estimation team, next determines the effort (normally in labor hours) and precedence relationships between tasks. PM will then assemble the tasks into a precedence activity network and determine a schedule and the critical path (see Figure 1.7). The critical path is the longest (in time) logically possible path through the schedule network, and it is used to highlight critical tasks and task-to-task relationships.

1.7.4   Determine Risks

A *risk* is something undesirable that may happen. For example, the project's schedule might overrun, or the project might exceed its budget, or it might deliver an unsuitable product. Usually these problems have some technical content and hence can be best identified and planned for by applying a systems engineering approach.

Risks are characterized by three factors:

1. Uncertainty is involved, often expressed as a probability.

2. A loss is associated with it (life, money, property, reputation, and so forth).

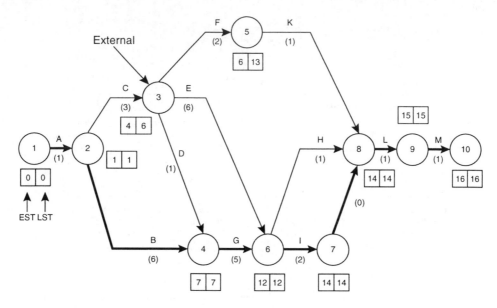

Figure 1.7: Activity Network

3. The problems are manageable—in the sense that human action can be applied to change its form and degree.

A *problem* is a risk that has materialized. Selecting and evaluating risks requires considerable knowledge, experience, and skill. Persons having these attributes are often found performing systems engineering (software or not) functions. They also usually have visibility into the factors that cause problems to arise. For details on the risk management process, see Chapter 14.

1.8   Process Control

Controlling is the collection of management activities used to ensure that a project is executed according to its plan. Actual performance of tasks and their results are measured against plans, deviations are noted, and corrective actions are taken to ensure conformance of plans and actual results.

A *process control system* is a feedback system that monitors the state of the entity being controlled using specific properties and metrics that are used to determine how well the project is progressing and responding to problems. Process control asks these questions: Are there any potential problems that will cause delays in meeting the requirement within the budget and schedule? Have any of the risks materialized as problems? Are the design and implementation approaches still viable?

Control must lead to corrective action—either to bring the actual status back to the plan, to change the plan, or to terminate the activity.

Software Systems Engineering	Project Management
Determines the requirements to be met	Determines the project plan to be followed
Selects technical standards to be followed, e.g., IEEE Standard 830	Selects managerial standards to be followed, e.g., IEEE Standard 1058
Establishes technical metrics to control e.g., progress, requirements growth, errors reported, rework	Establishes management metrics to control, e.g., progress, cost growth, schedule slippage, staffing shortage
Uses peer reviews, in-process reviews, SQA, V&V, and audits to determine adherence to requirements and design	Uses joint acquirer-supplier (milestone) reviews and SCM to determine adherence to cost, schedule, and progress
Reengineers the software requirements when necessary	Replans the project plan when necessary

Table 1.3: Partitioning of the Control Effort

1.8.1 Control the Workload

Similar to planning, control is also partitioned into two separate but related components: (1) those aspects of control performed by PM and (2) those aspects performed by software systems engineering acting as the technical agent. As with planning, the nature and size of the product, the relationship with the customer, and the culture of the developing organization will determine the exact nature of the work split. Table 1.3 shows one example of how the control responsibilities of a software system project might be partitioned.

1.8.2 Standards of Performance

Goals for each task must be defined and must be measurable. The goals will be achieved when tasks are correctly accomplished. A *performance standard* is a documented set of criteria used to specify and determine if the task was indeed accomplished. Such a standard is usually a set of procedures that defines the process for developing a software product and/or specifies the quality of a software product. For example, the coding standard should be used when performing code inspections or walkthroughs. Compliance with the standard would be one measure (among many) of completeness for coding. In another example, projects should adopt a test coverage standard that can be used to determine the adequacy of testing.

In many organizations today, the software systems engineering function can draw on a software process improvement organization for assistance in establishing such standards. For a discussion of the role of process improvement, see Chapter 8.

1.8.3   Monitoring and Reporting

Monitoring and reporting systems should be used to objectively determine project status. These systems determine what data are necessary, who will receive the data, when they will receive the data, and what they will do with the data to control the project. Software systems engineering and project management must have feedback on the progress of the project and the quality of the products if they are to properly control the project. The type, frequency, originator, and recipient of project reports must be specified. Status reporting tools must provide visibility into actual progress, and not just resources used or time passed. A few of the more prominent monitoring and reporting systems are discussed in the following subsections. For more information on monitoring and reporting systems, see the related chapters on software engineering project management, cost and schedule estimation, metrics, reviews, and software quality assurance and configuration management.

1.8.3.1   Software Quality Assurance

Software quality assurance (SQA) is "a planned and systematic pattern of all actions necessary to provide adequate confidence that the item or product conforms to established technical requirements" [IEEE 730-1998]. Specifically, the SQA function is used to monitor the performance of tasks to ensure that they are performed in accordance with the project process requirements and performance standards. Thus, SQA should be used to establish confidence that when a task is said to be completed, in fact, it was completed consistent with expectations.

1.8.3.2   Software Configuration Management

Software configuration management (SCM) is used to control the status of selected software items. SCM is the discipline of identifying and recreating the configuration of an item at specific points in time. This allows changes to the configuration to be applied in a systematic manner, thereby maintaining the integrity and traceability of changes to the software items throughout the system life cycle [IEEE 828-1998].

1.8.3.3   Earned Value and Work Package Specifications

A *work package specification* is a description of the work to be accomplished in completing a function, activity, or task. A *work package* specifies the objectives of the work, staffing, the expected duration, the resources, the results, incremental milestones within the package, and any other special considerations. Work packages are normally small tasks that can be assigned to two or three individuals to be completed in 2 to 3 weeks. A series of work packages organized into a schedule, as shown earlier in Figure 1.6, makes up a software project schedule.

Earned value systems are used to integrate the planned and actual status of each work package in a project schedule, producing an assessment of how closely the actual task completion dates and costs conform to those of the original plan. This information is then used to plan and monitor corrective actions, as well as to determine new delivery dates and final project costs. Earned value provides "visibility of progress." An earned value system can be used, for example, to generate program-wide predictions for cost and schedule performance. This book's chapter on Software Cost and Schedule (Chapter 12) should be consulted for more details.

1.8.3.4 Walkthroughs and Inspections

Walkthroughs and *inspections* (frequently called peer reviews) are reviews of a software product (design specifications, code, test procedures, etc.) conducted by the peers of the group whose work is being reviewed. Walkthroughs and inspections are a critique of a software product by the producer's peers for the sole purpose of finding errors.

The inspection system was developed by Michael Fagan of IBM in 1976, and are typically more structured than walkthroughs. The results of such walkthroughs and inspections, together with how closely the actual dates when the reviews occurred adhered to the plan, will give insight into the progress of the project.

1.8.3.5 Independent Audits

A *software project audit* is an independent review of a software project to determine compliance with software requirements, specifications, baselines, standards, policies, and SQA plans. Such audits can be used to verify the accuracy and fidelity of the normal status and monitoring systems. The software systems engineering and project management functions may be the initiators of such audits or their activities may fall within the scope of an audit commissioned by upper management or the customer. Audits are not part of the normal monitoring function.

1.8.4   Applying Corrective Action

Corrective action brings requirements and plans into conformance with actual project status. This might involve obtaining a larger budget, splitting work packages to introduce more parallelism into the schedule, adding key people, redesigning a specific module, introducing a multiphase delivery approach, or providing more time on the development computer for testing. Other corrective actions might include slipping the schedule or postponing compliance with some requirements to later deliveries.

1.9   Verification, Validation, and Testing

The purpose of the *verification, validation,* and *testing* (VV&T) effort is to determine that the engineering process is correct and the products are in compliance with their requirements. The three components of VV&T are defined as follows:

1. *Verification*—The process of determining whether the products of a given phase of the software development cycle fulfill the requirements established during the previous phase. Verification answers the question "Am I building the product right?"

2. *Validation*—Determination of the correctness of the final program or software produced from a development project with respect to the user's needs and requirements. Validation answers the question "Am I building the right product?"

3. *Testing*—The execution of a complete or partial program, with known inputs and outputs that are both predicted and observed, for the purpose of finding errors. Testing is frequently considered part of validation.

The VV&T process is thus used to evaluate the interim and final products of the project. Examples of interim products would be requirement specifications, design descriptions, test plans, and review results. Typical final products would be the product software and the final user's and training manuals. For a detailed discussion of software VV&T activities please consult Chapter 5.

Any individual or functional group within a software development project can be assigned V&V tasks. Software systems engineering should make use of V&V techniques and tools to evaluate requirements specifications, design descriptions, and other interim products of the design process. SwSE makes use of testing to determine if the final product meets the project requirements specifications.

The last step in any software development activity is to validate and test the final software product against the SRS and to validate and test the final system product against the SysRS.

Software validation (including testing) is initiated when:

- The implementation (coding) of the software is completed.

- Unit tests are completed.

Software validation (including testing) is completed when:

- Software integration testing is completed.

- Software system testing is completed.

Several strategies exist for performing software integration testing, as the following section illustrates.

1.9.1   Integration Test

Software integration testing combines or integrates components of the software system and tests the resulting configuration to determine if it works as required and expected. Integration testing can be either incremental or nonincremental. Incremental testing is performed by testing a small part of the system and then incrementally adding components to the configuration, performing specific tests on each increment. Nonincremental testing involves assembling all components of the system and then testing them all at once. Hardware engineers call this the smoke test; that is, "Let's test it all at once and see where the smoke rises." Because software failures don't smoke, it is often difficult to tell where a system has failed when all components are being tested at one time. This strategy is also commonly known as the "Big Bang Theory of Integration"—for predictable reasons.

Incremental testing has proven to be a more successful approach. Three main strategies are used to integrate a system incrementally: top-down, bottom-up, and data flow. These are shown in Figures 1.8 and 1.9. *Top-down testing* is the process of integrating the system under test, progressively, from top to bottom, using simulations of low-level components (called *stubs*) during testing to complete the system. This is in contrast to *bottom-up testing*, in which the system under test is built up progressively, from bottom to top, using software drivers to simulate top-level components during testing. *Flow testing* is performed by identifying the components that will execute in response to a specific stimulus and then adding those components to the configuration incrementally. This often results in a hybrid of the bottom-up and top-down strategies with the stimulus occurring near the bottom of one leg of the tree, with data and control flowing up the tree (the upward leg) and then progressing down one or more branches of the tree (the downward leg). This approach is especially attractive when integrating multithreaded systems, where each thread is, in turn, integrated using the operating system as the flow control mechanism.

Each of these strategies has a number of advantages and disadvantages, some of which are listed in Table 1.4. At first glance, bottom-up testing appears to have the most advantages and least disadvantages. However, advantage 3 under top-down testing and disadvantage 2 under bottom-up testing provide significant management advantages through increased customer visibility into the integration progress, so that top-down testing is often the preferred method. However, flow testing offers similar advantages for multithread systems and has some of the technical advantages of bottom-up testing. At the same time, it can be more challenging to manage. The choice of integration strategy should be made carefully and should be largely determined by the architecture and nature of the system.

1.9.2 Systems and Acceptance Testing

In this activity, the integrated software system is tested to verify that it satisfies the software requirements. Tests are conducted in conformance with formal test documents and the test compliance matrix. Systems and acceptance testing are usually the ultimate and final tests used to determine if the product should be released to its users. Systems tests are often performed in the supplier's facilities using contrived data designed to evaluate the system. In some cases this is followed by acceptance testing, which may be conducted at the acquirer's or user's facility but may be performed at that of the supplier, depending on the logistics and contract. The ultimate distinction between the two is that system testing is largely technical in nature, marking the end of the development process, whereas acceptance

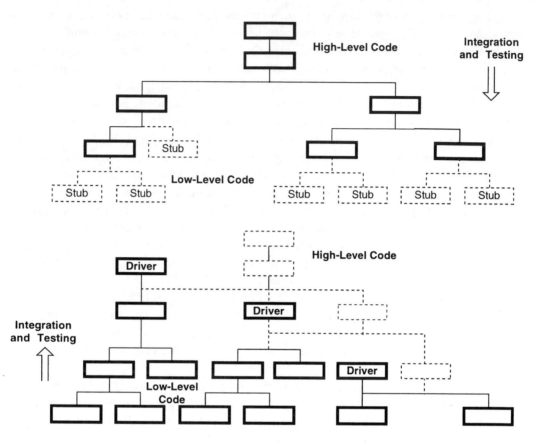

Figure 1.8: Top-Down Testing versus Bottom-Up Testing

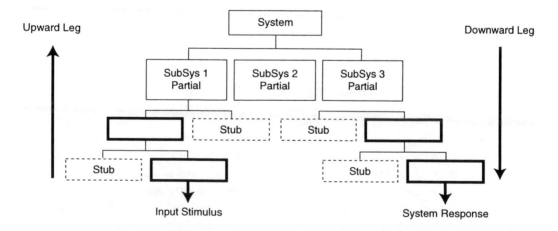

Figure 1.9: Data or Control Flow Testing

Top-Down Testing	
Advantages	**Disadvantages**
(1) Is more productive if major flaws occur toward the top of the program.	(1) Stub modules must be produced.
(2) Representation of test cases is easier.	(2) Stub modules are often complicated.
(3) Earlier skeletal programs allow demonstration (and improve morale).	(3) Representation of test cases in stubs can be difficult.
	(4) Observation of test output is more difficult.
Bottom-Up Testing	
Advantages	**Disadvantages**
(1) Is more productive if major flaws occur toward the bottom of the program.	(1) Driver modules must be produced.
(2) Test conditions are easier to create.	(2) The program as an entity does not exist until the last module is added.
(3) Observation of test results is easier.	
Flow Testing	
Advantages	**Disadvantages**
(1) Is more productive if major flaws occur along a flow of control or data. Best at finding flaws in architecture.	(1) Flows and impacted modules may be difficult to separate or recognize.
(2) Test conditions relate directly to system operations/input requirements; hence, are easily understood and created.	(2) Modules from multiple groups may be needed to complete any individual flow, increasing planning burden.
(3) Test results can be easily interpreted and related to system output requirements.	(3) Partial versions of intervening modules may be needed.

Table 1.4: Comparisons of Top-Down, Bottom-Up, and Flow Testing

testing usually occurs immediately before contractual delivery.

As described earlier, *verification* is the process of determining whether or not the products of a given phase of the software development cycle fulfill the requirements established during the previous phase. *Validation* is the process of ensuring that what is built corresponds to what was actually required; it is concerned with the completeness, consistency, and correctness of the requirements.

During the software systems testing phase, the software system is verified against the design baseline to determine if the final program properly implements the design. This process is commonly performed by an audit of the *as-built configuration* (that is, the code) and the *as-designed configuration* (that is, the documents). At roughly the same time, the software system is tested and validated against the original system and software requirements specification to see if the product implements the specified requirements. These activities are often performed during a functional configuration audit/physical configuration audit (FCA/PCA). The chapter on reviews (Chapter 11) discusses this concept in more detail.

1.10   Summary

Conducting a software engineering project without adopting a systems engineering perspective puts a project in jeopardy of being incomplete or having components that do not work together or that exceed the project's schedule and budget.

The disciplines of systems and software systems engineering are most actively used during the early phases of the system life cycle, establishing the fundamental objectives and technical plans and then, at the later parts of the life cycle, verifying whether the objectives have been achieved. A review of the emphasis in this chapter will show that much of the work of software systems engineering is performed during the top-level requirements analysis and top-level design phases. The other major activity of software systems engineering is the final validation and testing of the completed system.

Systems engineering principles, activities, tasks, and procedures can be applied to software development. This chapter has summarized, in broad steps, what is necessary to implement a program of software systems engineering for either a hardware/software system or for a system composed totally of software.

Software systems engineering is not easy, it is not cheap, but it is cost effective.

Applicable Standards

IEEE Std 610.12-1990. *IEEE Standard Glossary of Software Engineering Terminology*, IEEE, New York.

IEEE Std 730-1998. *IEEE Standard for Software Quality Assurance Plans*, IEEE, New York.

IEEE Std 828-1998. *IEEE Standard for Software Configuration Management Plans*, IEEE, New York.

IEEE Std 829-1998. *IEEE Standard for Software Test Documentation*, IEEE, New York.

IEEE Std 830-1998. *IEEE Recommended Practice for Software Requirements Specifications*, IEEE, New York.

IEEE Std 1008-1987 (R1993). *IEEE Standard for Software Unit Testing*, IEEE, New York.

IEEE Std 1012-1998. *IEEE Standard for Software Verification and Validation*, IEEE, New York.

IEEE Std 1016-1998, *IEEE Recommended Practice for Software Design Descriptions*, IEEE, New York.

IEEE Std 1028-1997. *IEEE Standard for Software Reviews*, IEEE, New York.

IEEE Std 1058-1998. *IEEE Standard for Software Project Management Plans*, IEEE, New York.

IEEE Std 1063-1987 (R1993). *IEEE Standard for Software User Documentation*, IEEE, New York.

IEEE Std 1220-1998. *IEEE Standard for the Application and Management of the Systems Engineering Process*, IEEE, New York.

IEEE Std 1233, 1998 Edition. *IEEE Guide for Developing System Requirements Specifications (including IEEE Standard 1233a)*, IEEE, New York.

IEEE Std 1362-1998. *IEEE Guide for Information Technology—System Definition-Concept of Operation Document*, IEEE, New York.

IEEE Std 12207.2-1997. *IEEE/EIA Standard: Industry Implementation of International Standard ISO/IEC 12207:1995 Standard for Information Technology—Software Life Cycle Processes—Implementation Considerations*, IEEE, New York.

Additional References

[Alberts 1988]   Alberts, H. C. (1988). "System Engineering—Managing the Gestalt." *System Engineering Management Course Syllabus*, The Defense System Management College, Fort Belvoir, VA.

[Bersoff 1984]   Bersoff, E. H. (1984). "Elements of Software Configuration Management." *IEEE Trans. Software Engineering*, vol. SE-10, no. 1, January, pp. 79–87. Reprinted in *Software Engineering Project*

Management, R. H. Thayer, ed. IEEE Computer Society Press, Los Alamitos, CA, 1997.

[Chapman et al. 1992]   Chapman, W. L., Bahill, A. T., and Wymore, A. W. (1992). *Engineering Modeling and Design*, CRC Press, Boca Raton, FL.

[DSMC 1989]   Defense System Management College. (1989). *System Engineering Management Course Syllabus*, Ft. Belvoir, VA.

[Dorfman 2001]   Dorfman, M. (2001). Personal correspondence with Dr. Merlin Dorfman who worked on the U.S. missile program during 1960–1970.

[Fujii 1989]   Fujii, R. (1989). Speaker at IEEE Seminar on Software Verification and Validation, two-day public seminar presented by the IEEE Standards Board, Munich, July 13–14, 1989.

[Gibbs 1994]   Gibbs, W. W. (1994). "Software's Chronic Crisis." *Scientific American*, September, pp. 86–95.

[Howes 1989]   Howes, N. R. (1989). "On Using the Users' Manual as the Requirements Specification II." *System and Software Engineering Requirements*, R. H. Thayer and M. Dorfman, eds. IEEE Computer Society Press, Los Alamitos, CA, 1990.

[Myers 1979]   Myers, G.J. (1979). *The Art of Software Testing*. John Wiley & Sons, New York.

[Pressman 1982]   Pressman, R. S. (1982). *Software Engineering: A Practitioner's Approach*. McGraw-Hill, New York.

[Royce 1988]   Royce, W. W. (1988). "Software Systems Engineering." Seminar presented during the Management of Software Acquisition Course. Defense Systems Management College, 1981–1988, Fort Belvoir, VA.

[Royce 1991]   Royce, W. W. (1991). "Current Problems." *Aerospace Software Engineering: A Collection of Concepts*, C. Anderson and M. Dorfman, eds. American Institute of Aeronautics, Washington, DC.

[USAF 1985]   U.S. Air Force. (1985). *Technical Reviews and Audits for Systems, Equipment, and Computer programs*, MIL-STD 1521B (USAF), proposed revision. Joint Policy Coordination Group on Computer Resource Management, Washington, DC.

[Wymore 1993]   Wymore, A. W. (1993). *Model-Based Systems Engineering*. CRC Press, Boca Raton, FL.

Chapter 2

Concept of Operations

2.1 Introduction

The primary objective of a software development project is to deliver to a customer a product that meets the customer's needs today and allows for growth in the future. During the last 30 years, the software engineering community has learned that to accomplish this, a consistent and repeatable set of processes is required. One of the most important of these processes, because it occurs earliest in any engineering project and hence establishes the foundation on which all other activities are based, is the development and documentation of the user's requirements. For many projects, a significant source of requirements should be the indexconcept of operations document*concept of operations document* or the *ConOps*.

Depending on the nature of the product and the relationship between the user's and the developer's organizations, the ConOps may be viewed as either a source of requirements or an actual requirements document. In either case, it is an important but not necessarily the sole source of requirements. IEEE Standard 1362-1998, *IEEE Guide for Information Technology System Definition—Concept of Operation Document*, describes the format and content of the ConOps and is the basis for this chapter. Chapter 3 and 830-1998, *IEEE Recommended Practice for Software Requirements Specifications*, describes the objectives and form of the complete software requirements specifications (SRS) document, for which the ConOps is often a critical source. To clarify this relationship, we briefly describe the role the ConOps plays in the development of the full SRS. Specifically, the process of developing the ConOps focuses on understanding the major features of the user's operational requirements. This includes the user's normal, day-to-day operational usage patterns and modes of the system together with issues associated with installing and maintaining the system. Other sources of requirements beyond the operational ones described in the ConOps are present in most development projects. These can be found in a separate performance specification, or in industrial or statutory standards with which the project and product must comply. Next, the requirements analysis process will integrate, correlate, reduce, expand, and ultimately translate these combined user needs and expectations into the software requirements specification (SRS), as described in Chapter 3 of this book, as well as in IEEE Standard 830-1998. Verification and validation processes should then be applied to the SRS. The requirements verification checks to ensure that the specifications are complete and consistent, that is, that we are "building the product right." The requirements validation checks to ensure that the specifications are correct and reflect the user's operational requirements, that is, that we are "building the right product." The full verification and validation processes that encompass these and other activities are described in Chapter 5.

The requirements engineering process has three interrelated perspectives: that of the acquirer, the individual or organization who is responsible for acquiring (as distinct from using or developing) the desired system; that of the actual users; and that of the developer. The acquirer is the representative of the users in the development process and usually is the contractual point of contact for the developing organization. In this chapter, we focus on developing the operational requirements from the user's perspectives and documenting those requirements with a ConOps document. The chapter on developing the SRS will focus on developing the requirements from the developer's perspective using the ConOps as one of several sources. The next section describes the purposes, roles, and general content and format of an IEEE Standard 1362-compliant ConOps. Subsequent sections describe the detailed structure of the ConOps, who can and should write the ConOps, some methods available for developing the ConOps, and how the ConOps should be maintained.

2.2   Objectives

In this chapter you will learn:

- The purpose of and how to use and manage a ConOps document.

- The applicable IEEE standards for ConOps document.

- The advantages of using a ConOps document.

- The essential elements of a ConOps document.

- When should/can a ConOps document be written.

- Who should/can write a ConOps document.

- How to develop a ConOps document.

- The various roles of a ConOps document.

- How the identification, justification, and prioritization of changes can benefit project planning, budgeting, and scheduling.

- About user classes and how are they determined.

- About operational scenarios and how are they used.

- The different methods available to describe operational scenarios.

- The different operational modes of a software system.

- The recommended organization of a ConOps document.

- How the ConOps document should be controlled and maintained.

2.3 ConOps Purposes, Roles, Content, and Format

A ConOps document provides a mechanism for users to describe, in nontechnical terms, their view and expectation of the system and its required features and functionality. A complex system can have several different types and levels of users, all of whom have different perceptions and perspectives concerning the operation of the system. For example, one class of user may operate the system, while another class may be responsible for the systems administration or maintenance.

The IEEE ConOps standard states that "The ConOps approach provides an analysis activity and a document that bridges the gap between the users' needs and visions, and the developers' technical specifications." The software project manager should know and understand the application and benefits of using a ConOps document as part of the acquisition and/or development process and as a tool in aiding communication with the user.

A fundamental precept of ConOps development is *concept analysis. Concept analysis* is defined as the process of analyzing the problem domain and operational environment for the purpose of specifying the characteristics of a proposed system from the user's perspective. The goal of the concept analysis is to ensure that the system as a whole meets the user's individual functional requirements along with the overall system operational and functional requirements. Clarifying and resolving vague and conflicting user needs/requirements should be a significant component of the concept analysis process.

The software project manager and the ConOps development team should understand that concept analysis and the resulting ConOps document entail an iterative process that involves users, acquirers, and developers. The ConOps document provides the frameworks for subsequent system development activities including the analysis, design, implementation, and validation of the software system to be developed. The ConOps provides input for the software requirements specification, the user manual, and the verification and validation activity, as described in Chapters 3, 4, and 5, respectively.

2.3.1 Roles

The facilitation of communications between all of the involved personnel is one of the most important roles of a ConOps document. The personnel can include operational users, administrative users, acquirers, system and software engineers, and project managers. Each of these groups will usually view the system from different perspectives. By bridging gaps between groups of personnel, the ConOps can serve as the hub of project communications. Because the ConOps is usually a less technical document than the SRS, the system users can use it to communicate with project development personnel more readily and directly. By facilitating this, the ConOps will, in fact, aid in developing the SRS both by capturing information and by establishing a pattern of communication between the acquiring and developing organizations.

Other important roles that the ConOps can and should fulfill in a development effort are:

- Initiate the formal contractual relationship of the acquiring and developing activities.

- Initiate the risk management processes of the program.

- Initiate the verification and validation (V&V) activities of the program.

By starting these important program activities early, within a context of subject matter and expressive forms that both the acquiring and developing groups can understand, the ConOps can set the pattern by which the remainder of the program is managed.

2.3.2   Content

The software project manager should know and understand the essential elements of a ConOps document. An IEEE-compliant ConOps must include the following elements:

- A description of the existing operational condition, including any relevant existing systems (computer-based or not),

- A description of the needs that motivate modifying an existing system or developing a new system,

- The modes of operation for the proposed system,

- The classes of users and their characteristics,

- Desired features of the proposed system and their priorities,

- Operational scenarios for each operational mode and class of user,

- An analysis of the impacts of the proposed system, and

- A description of any recognized limitations of the proposed system.

The meaning and goals for developing each of these content items is discussed in Section 2.3.3 of this chapter. For all of there elements, keep in mind the management objectives that must be met as the ConOps is developed. These are discussed in Section 2.4.3.1.

2.3.3   ConOps Format

The format of the ConOps recommended by IEEE Standard 1362 is as follows:

1. Introduction to the ConOps document and to the desired system.

2. List of all external documents referenced.

3. Description of the current system or situation, including scope and objectives of the current system, operational policies and constraints, modes of operation, classes of users, and the support environment for the current system. If there is no existing system, describe the reasons that motivate development of a new system.

4. Nature of proposed changes and/or new features, including the justification for those changes and/or features.

5. Description of the proposed system, including scope and objectives for the proposed system, operational policies and constraints, modes of operation, classes of users, and the support environment for the proposed system.

6. Operational scenarios describing how the proposed system is to perform in its environment, relating system capabilities and functions to modes of operations, classes of users, and interactions with external systems.

7. Operational and organizational impacts on the users, acquirers, developers, and the support and maintenance agencies, during system development and after system installation.

8. Alternatives and trade-offs considered but not included in the new or modified system; analysis of benefits, limitations, advantages, and disadvantages of the new or modified system.

9. Notes, acronyms and abbreviations, appendices, and glossary of terms.

The use of this organizational format for a ConOps document provides a logical flow of information beginning with a description of the current system, passing through considerations of needed changes and the rationale for such changes, and leading to a description of the new or modified system. This will guide the reader through a description of the system, including both the current and desired conditions, in a simple and intuitive manner.

Of these areas, the most variable in format, because it depends on the backgrounds and communication styles of the personnel involved, is usually the description of the *operational scenarios*. Several alternative formats are available for the description of the scenarios:

- *Text narrative:* Written in natural language;

- *Sequential descriptions:* A step-by-step description of a scenario;

- *Pictorial methods:* Diagrams, such as data flows, structure charts, IDEF, UML, and state descriptions;

- *Prototypes:* Storyboards or software models, most commonly involving the user interface, if there is one;

- *Use cases:* Uses collections of scenarios.

Which of these techniques, or combination of them, will best serve to describe a scenario is a function of several factors:

- The personnel working on developing the ConOps. This includes both users and developers.

- The nature of the product being developed and the scenarios themselves. For example, does it even have a user interface?

- The tools and technologies available to the project.

The choice of format or formats for the ultimate documentation of scenarios will largely determine the method by which they are developed. As a result, unless both the using and developing groups have prior experience in this area, the choice of format should be made carefully and in due time. Premature commitment (that is, before it is necessary) to an inappropriate format will result in a delayed or incomplete ConOps. In extreme cases it may result in the termination of the ConOps effort, which would be a waste of effort in the near term, would set a bad example for the balance of the program, would damage team morale, and would increase the risk that the SRS will be incomplete. Likewise, excessive delay in selecting a format by which to document the scenarios will waste effort in the near term, delay the completion of the ConOps, and damage team morale.

Finally, note that two of the topics included in the ConOps standard format, *organizational and operational impacts* and *alternatives and trade-offs*, may be regarded by the acquirer as containing business-sensitive information. For example, the trade-offs section might reveal business strategy or tactics. If this is the case and the acquirer does not share the necessary information with the developer, irrespective of any nondisclosure statements agreed to by the developer, then the ConOps will be incomplete. In this case risk mitigation strategies should be put in place. Usually these will take the form of increased involvement by the acquirer in project and document reviews because the developer will not have a complete information base from which to conduct trade-offs later in the program.

2.4   Developing the ConOps

The key issues in developing a ConOps are (1) who develops the ConOps, (2) when the ConOps is written, and (3) how the ConOps is developed and documented.

The details of the relationship between the using and the developing organizations will determine the precise manner in which issues are addressed. The decisions will be guided, however, by fairly stable and universal concepts. The next three sections discuss each of these issues in turn.

2.4.1   Who Develops the ConOps

2.4.1.1   The Players and Their Roles

Who is available and appropriate to contribute to authoring the ConOps depends on the structure and formality of the acquiring and developing organizations and their precise relationship. For example, if the project is developing a product for use within the same legal entity as will develop it, then there is no acquirer but there is a user and, perhaps, a management oversight function external to both the user and the developer. If the product is, instead, being procured from another legal entity, then there should be an acquirer who serves as the contractual (but not usually technical) interface to the developing organization. These two options are usually described as a "make" or "buy."

In the case of a "make" decision, the organization should develop some document that authorizes the initiation of the project. This is commonly known as a project authorization request (PAR) or just a project authorization (PA). In the case of a "buy" decision, the acquiring organization should develop a request for proposal (RFP) or invitation to tender (ITT) document that is then sent to external contractors who develop proposals from this information.

It is critical for the software project manager, along with the management personnel of the acquiring organization, to appreciate precisely who the "players" are and what their roles are in the project.

The ConOps can be written by the immediate user(s), the oversight or management functions within the customer organization, the buying or acquiring group of the customer, the developer, or by a third party working under contract to one of them. However, the best arrangement is usually an interdisciplinary team consisting of user representative(s), customer management or oversight representative(s), and acquisition representative(s) and developer representative(s), supplemented by third parties when necessary. If the ConOps is to be part of a RFP package to be sent to multiple candidate developing organizations, then a third party who is not part of the competition should be utilized in place of the developer.

The project manager must realize that development of a successful ConOps requires a great deal of user involvement because the user best understands the problem domain, although usually from the perspective of the user interface. The ConOps must always reflect the users' perspectives and be written in language that can be understood and approved by the user.

The following sections give specifics on some of the typical groups that can provide individuals to serve as primary authors for ConOps documents. The primary author is the individual who leads and manages the ConOps development team process and takes responsibility for the generation of the actual document. The ConOps team should always include users and developers. In this regard, note that users often have to perform their regular job assignments while assisting or supporting the development team. If the users' routine workload is not reduced, it is unlikely that they will be available to support the development of the ConOps, to review specifications, to experiment with prototypes, or to attend training. This can only be corrected if the program manager obtains the support of the acquiring and using organizations.

2.4.1.2   The User/Customer as Primary Author

The user or an organization representing the user can be the primary author of the ConOps. Users or their representatives generally understand the nature and complexities of their business. This is not always the case for the developer. The users are in a unique position to describe the problems with their existing system and may have opinions about proposed solutions. However, the users may not always understand the current state of technology and some of the inherent difficulties associated with developing an automated solution or the costs of doing so. Conversely, they may know too much about the technology and may prematurely restrict the solution space allowed by the ConOps.

In addition, the user might not understand the software development life cycle and may have difficulties writing and controlling a ConOps document. Finally, if the developers are not involved then an opportunity to initiate communications is lost. If the organizations have worked together before, this is not as important as it would be if they have not.

2.4.1.3   The Acquiring Group as Primary Author

The acquiring or oversight groups can provide the individual(s) who describe the desired system to be purchased. An acquirer can use the ConOps as a communications bridge between the user's requirements and the developer's proposed system. The acquirer may include the ConOps as part of a RFP/PA package. The feasibility of this is highly dependent on the background of the acquiring or oversight groups because it requires that the staff within these groups know both the problem domain and the methodology of developing a ConOps document. The advantage of this choice is that conflicts of interest should be reduced for both the consumer and producer roles.

2.4.1.4   The Developer as Primary Author

The developing organization can provide the primary ConOps author. This often has advantages over selecting the primary author from the user or acquirer groups. The developer probably has more technical expertise that can be applied to describe the nature of the problem and solution.

Although the ConOps should be viewed from the user's perspective, the developer probably has more experience with the methods commonly used to describe the existing system as well as the proposed automated system. This assumes that the developer has had prior experience in problem domains similar to those of the user, and also requires the developer to divorce itself from its role as the ultimate implementer of the intended system. In this case the developer must remember that the ConOps must be written from the user's perspective in a manner that can be understood by the user and/or their representatives.

2.4.1.5   A Third Party as Primary Author

Use of a third party as primary ConOps author can be extremely advantageous, especially if the individuals have extensive experience with the problem domain as well as with writing similar documents. The third party should be impartial. Their goal is to represent the user while documenting the user's functional requirements. This combines the best features of the other approaches, assuming that the effort is conducted by a team of users and developers, with the third party serving as team leader, scribe, and author

2.4.2   When to Write the ConOps

The ConOps may be written before or after the determination to make or buy. Ideally, it would be written before this important decision because many of the topics covered by the ConOps will help determine whether or not to actually initiate the project and can also serve as inputs to the organization's make/buy decision process. In some cases the make/buy decision is obvious (e.g., the acquirer has no internal development capability).

As a general rule the earlier the ConOps is written the better, for all the reasons listed. However, every project has varying process needs and the ConOps can be written during any phase of a project's life cycle. The management team of the acquirer or the developing organization should identify at what point a ConOps would prove most beneficial to project planning and development and ensure that it is available at that stage of the project's development cycle. Typical points in the project life cycle when a ConOps can be written include during the make/buy decision, as a part of a RFP package, as a first task in a new project, or as one of the first tasks in the planning for system or acceptance testing.

2.4.2.1   As Part of a Feasibility Study

The ConOps document can be written prior to developing the system and, therefore, be used as a support mechanism to determine the feasibility of developing a software system. The process of developing a ConOps document, together with the document itself, can be very useful when deciding whether or not to develop a system. The ConOps can assist in determining the scope and the feasibility of a development effort. The ConOps describes the proposed system from the user's perspective and provides developers with a set of user requirements on which to base an analysis of the project's technical feasibility. Initial cost and schedule estimates, both for initial development as well as for subsequent operation and maintenance, can be developed from this information.

The cost and schedule estimates derived from the ConOps information can then be used to determine the feasibility of the project and its expected impact, financial and otherwise, on the customer's organization. The expertise needed to perform this business case analysis may lie outside of the software engineering domain. In addition, performance of this analysis may well require access to data to which the developer is denied access by the acquirer. If this happens, the software managers should satisfy themselves to the maximum extent possible that the appropriate individuals and groups within the customer's organization have performed such an analysis and have a realistic expectation of the product and its impact on their operation.

2.4.2.2 As Part of a Request for Proposal

The ConOps can also be developed prior to issuing a request for proposal and included in the RFP/PA package. Supplying a ConOps with the RFP/PA can be beneficial to both the customer and prospective vendors. The customer/user has an opportunity to consider the existing situation and to describe the proposed system along with their requirements. Prospective vendors can use the ConOps to prepare the quotation. This will ensure that the proposals will start from a common base of requirements.

2.4.2.3 As the First Task of a Project

A ConOps can be written as the first task of the development life cycle in cases where one has not already been written. In this case, the document can help bridge communications between users and the software requirements engineer. Understanding the user's operational environment and perspectives aids in preparing the software system specification and software requirements specification as described earlier. It is also an excellent opportunity to establish an effective communication pattern within the project.

2.4.2.4 As the First Task in System Test Planning

Because the ConOps describes how the system will be used and maintained, it is an excellent source of information for system test planning. The SRS will be the source of the test cases for the formal acceptance test, but the ConOps will describe the way in which the product will be used.

This information will assist in planning the personnel, equipment, facilities, and data needed to conduct operationally representative system testing. Because ideally the ConOps is created prior to the SRS, it will provide an early view of this information and will assist in identifying any of these items that have long lead times (such as test facilities) or severe impacts (such as requiring critical operational personnel) to ongoing customer operations.

2.4.2.5 At Any Time

A ConOps can be written any time one is determined to be beneficial to the project. If during some phase of the project life cycle, developers realize that the user's needs and expectations are not as well understood as was originally thought, then serious consideration should be given to developing a ConOps. Likewise, if the customer's operational needs change during development of the product, serious consideration should be give to developing a ConOps.

2.4.3   How the ConOps Is Developed and Documented

Two fundamental issues are associated with developing and documenting a ConOps. First, there is the process for managing the overall effort of ConOps development. The next section gives general guidance for this. Second, an approach for documenting the operational scenarios must be selected. Several of these are discussed after the description of the general process of managing the ConOps development process is given.

Finally, several concepts, although not as technically demanding as the development of operational scenarios, warrant discussion beyond that presented in the general ConOps management guide. These are discussed in Section 2.4.3.3.

2.4.3.1   General Process for Managing the ConOps Development

The process described below is intended as a guideline. If the process conflicts with what seems to be most appropriate for a specific situation, the guideline should be modified to fit the situation. For instance, there may be no current system or the new system may be a modification of an existing one. The topics emphasized in the ConOps document may be different for each situation. The object of the process, independent of the situation, should be to determine the user's requirements.

1. Determine the goals, objectives, roles, and team members for the ConOps process. The specifics of these will normally be determined by the situation that motivates development of the ConOps document. The management of the customer organization or its designated representative should be involved in approving goals and objectives, at the very least.

2. Tailor the recommended ConOps document format and obtain agreement on an outline for the ConOps document. This is important so that everyone understands the agreed-on format and content areas. The responsible user and development manager should review and approve this format prior to the start of work by the team.

In the following steps the team should work under normal oversight by management. A weekly or biweekly 1-hour review or equivalent written status should suffice.

3. Describe the overall objectives and shortcomings of the current system. Also, determine and document the overall objectives for the new or modified system. If there is no current system, describe the situation that motivates development of a new one.

4. If there is an existing system, describe that system's scope and boundaries, and identify any external systems and the interfaces to them. Also, establish and describe in general terms the scope and boundaries for the new or modified system, and identify the major external systems and interfaces to it.

5. Describe any operational policies and constraints that apply to the current system or situation and any changes to those policies and constraints for the new one.

6. Describe the features of the current system or situation. This includes the system's operational characteristics, operational environment and processes, modes of operations, user classes, and the operational support and maintenance environments.

7. State the operational policies and constraints that will apply to the new or modified system.

8. Determine the operational characteristics of the proposed system; that is, describe the characteristics the proposed system must possess to meet the user's needs and expectations.

9. Select an appropriate method for developing and documenting the scenarios. This often requires that several methods be tried on a small sampling of representative scenarios. The user and the developer must agree on the choice and report it to management before initiating full-scale scenario development. This can be done in parallel with many of the preceding steps.

10. Document operational scenarios for the new or modified system. Scenarios are specified by recording, in a step-by-step manner, the sequences of actions and interactions between a user and the system. This and the next step are often the most technically challenging and time consuming.

11. Validate the operational scenarios to ensure that they describe the desired product. Do this by walking through each scenario with representatives from all classes and groups of users, taking care to cover all modes of operation.

12. Obtain consensus for priorities for each operational scenario and feature of the proposed system. Group the scenarios and the operational features into categories as either essential, desirable, or optional categories. Within each category, prioritize the features. Verify that the scenarios create no conflicts or impossible situations. Describe all scenarios and features that were considered but not included in the proposed system.

13. Analyze and describe the operational and organizational impacts the proposed system will have on users, acquirer(s), developers, and the support/maintenance agencies. Also, include significant impacts on these groups that might occur during the development process. If any of the above represent risks to the project, ensure that they are so noted and included in the project risk management process.

14. Describe the benefits, limitations, advantages, and disadvantages of the proposed system compared to the present system or situation.

2.4.3.2 Operational Scenarios

What Are Operational Scenarios?

The advantage of complete and detailed operational scenarios is that they assemble the operational requirements together in such a manner as to provide a comprehensive picture of the proposed system from the user's perspective. Ideally, the development of the operational scenarios will be complete when the developer can understand the system's behavior in relationship to the user's operational requirements. As a practical matter the development of scenarios is limited by the available time and budget. The goal of the ConOps development team is therefore to strike the appropriate balance between completeness (as defined above), the available time and budget, and the risk of incompleteness to the subsequent development activities.

A scenario is defined as a step-by-step description of a series of events that occur in the course of system operation. These events may occur concurrently or sequentially. An operational scenario is a detailed description of how the proposed system should operate from the user's perspective. The following approach should be used to develop and document operational scenarios:

- Develop a set of scenarios that, to the extent possible, covers all modes of operations, all classes of external events, all classes of users, and all specific operations and processes of the proposed system

- Walk through each scenario with the appropriate users and record information concerning the desired, normal operating states as well as any unusual conditions that are relevant to the operation of the proposed system.

- During the walkthrough, establish new scenarios to cover abnormal operations such as exception handling, stress load handling, and handling of incomplete and incorrect data.

- Establish new scenarios whenever a branch in the thread of operation is encountered. Typically, walking though the initial scenario set will uncover additional scenarios. Different users may also have different views of some scenarios. If these variations are significant, include them as separate scenarios.

- Repeatedly develop scenarios until all operations, and all significant variations of those operations, are covered. Determine any needs for concurrency and exclusion between scenarios. That is, in multiprocessing systems, are any scenarios mutually exclusive by design or necessity?

For each operational scenario, develop an associated test scenario to be used in validating the operational aspects of the delivered system in the user environment. Establish a traceability matrix between operational scenarios and test scenarios. Each scenario should include events, actions, stimuli, the information being processed, and any interactions.

Methods for Documenting Operational Scenarios

The software project manager should understand the different methods of elaborating operational scenarios and be able to assist the ConOps team in selecting the methods that are most appropriate for the project.

The choice of technique will depend on the type of scenario being described. Some processes may be relatively simple and only require a sentence or two to describe what is going on in the scenario. However, with complex systems that may be more complicated, a pictorial representation may be more appropriate. In cases where the user interface and software program navigation are extremely important to the user, a paper storyboard or software prototype may be the best solution to describe operational scenarios. The following sections provide an overview of some of the methods available. The reader is referred to the references for in-depth discussions.

Although the software project manager does not have to be an expert on all of scenario representation techniques, he or she should know and understand how to read and understand the methods selected. The project manager should also consider the detail in which diagrams need to be developed compared to the project's degree of complexity along with project risk, budget, and schedule constraints.

All the methods for developing and documenting operational scenarios have some common features, namely:

- Unique identification number to aid in future tracking,

- Name of the operational scenario (should be descriptive),

- User classes or groups involved in the operational scenario, and

- List of events, the possible stimuli and responses for the given mode of operation.

The methods will differ primarily in how the response of the system, both primary (inputs and outputs) and secondary (internal state and data), is represented.

Narrative Representation

Initially it is usually easier for a team of users and developers to work with operational scenarios in narrative form. A format for capturing the information is shown in Figure 2.1. If the scenarios are not complex this may be all that is required. However, scenarios often become more complex, with multiple systems and users interacting together. When this occurs other methods are often used, often in combination with the narrative format.

Pictorial Representation

Pictorial representations are more easily used by the ConOps team when describing the system's operations and often are necessary as scenarios become complex. If properly done and explained, a pictorial style can likewise be easy for the customer to read and review for

1	Add Customer
	Players: Customer, User
	Stimuli: A customer wishes to purchase an item. The customer is the source of new data.
	Event: A new customer needs to be added to the software system.
	User: Searches to see if the customer already exists in the system by any of the following parameters: Last Name, First Name Telephone Number
	User: Adds customer record containing the following information: Last Name, First Name, Middle Initial Address Telephone Number

Figure 2.1: Narrative Operational Scenario

completeness and accuracy. Investments of time and effort in team building, training, and selection of the method will pay dividends at this point. Various representation methods are available to depict operational scenarios pictorially.

The pictorial style of representation chosen should be appropriate for the type of operational scenario that is being described. In selecting a pictorial format, the team must be careful not to slip into development of the SRS: The technique should be chosen for its capability to represent the operational needs of the user and should capture the critical aspects of the system. Formal methods, such as IDEFX and UML can also be used.

Using Prototypes to Explore and Document Operational Scenarios

Operational scenarios can be described by prototyping the proposed system. This can take the form of either paper storyboards or computer models. This approach is especially fruitful for systems that have significant user interface and human/machine interaction. To support an accurate description of the operational scenarios the prototype should represent the following for each user class and mode of operation:

- Menus, buttons, function keys;

- Screen formats;

- Screen navigation sequences;

- Response times;

- Help messages;

- Layout and content of reports;

- Frequency of use for each user feature; and

- Identification of the class or group of users of the screen(s).

A rich variety of tools are available to build such prototypes. Vendors have developed specialized capabilities to assist with prototyping. However, in many cases simple presentation and spreadsheet tools will suffice. In any case, keep in mind that the prototype alone does not complete the scenario development process. The implications of the scenario must be captured and analyzed. The ConOps team must always remember that it is developing the scenarios as part of the complete ConOps development process outlined earlier. Finally, the software manager and the ConOps team must ensure that all parties understand that any prototypes are not the final system: The software must go still through its development cycle.

2.4.3.3   Users, Modes, Changes, and Their Impacts

In addition to the development of the operational scenarios, several other demanding and critical activities have been identified with the ConOps development process:

- Identifying the classes of users and their tasks;

- Identifying the system's modes of operation;

- Identifying, prioritizing, and justifying changes or additions to the system; and

- Analyzing impacts of the system to the using organization, including their support and maintenance activities.

The first two of these activities should occur before the development of the scenarios, whereas the latter two occur after.

Classes of Users and Their Tasks

The ConOps document should describe all user classes according to their job functions and tasks, their responsibilities, and their skill level. The software project manager should know and understand what user classes are and how they are to be defined in the ConOps. If the actual users or acquirers author the ConOps, they should describe the various classes of users.

If the developing organization writes the ConOps, it should budget adequate effort and schedule toward understanding and documenting the different user classes. Complete and thorough documentation of user classes can provide valuable insight during the requirements specification and design phases. Design decisions and implementation strategies may be based on an understanding of the needs and requirements of the different user classes.

User Class	Experience Level
USER CLASS A—PERFORMS JOBS 1, 2, 3	ENTRY ROUTINE EXPERT
USER CLASS B—PERFORMS JOBS 4, 5	ENTRY ROUTINE EXPERT
USER CLASS C—PERFORMS JOB 6	ENTRY ROUTINE EXPERT

Table 2.1: Typical User Classes Performing Jobs at Different Experience Levels

On most systems, the user classes can be categorized using two attributes: (1) the job functions the users perform and (2) the users' skill levels (entry, routine, or expert) or their supervision level.

A given user's interactions should be considered operational if they occur while he is performing normal job functions. Thus many users will be concerned with the content of the screens and their navigation. However, another user's job functions may be of an administrative nature where they are responsible for managing user access to the system and maintaining the system-level configuration. Administrative users are usually concerned with controlling system resources, access, security, and availability.

Within a given user job classification, the users may still be further categorized by the level of experience or authority they posses. While most operational users are primarily concerned with the functionality of the system, their ability to perform certain functions may be limited by their experience, educational background, and authority. Table 2.1 illustrates such a breakdown. For example, users in Class A may perform jobs 1, 2, and/or 3. Their experience level may vary from job to job and from user to user within Class A. During the ConOps development process, the diversity of experience levels associated with each job function will often dictate, for example, how much online help is provided for the different functions available in the system. Likewise, the complexity and flexibility of the different aspects (or views) of the ultimate user interface will often be determined by the experience level of the individuals accessing various parts of the system.

Some organizations maintain position descriptions that may be of assistance in identifying the classes of users involved with the project and its product. In all cases the ConOps development team must remember why the user classes are being created: to assist in the development and analysis of the ConOps document and the resulting system.

Modes of Operation

Modes of operation represent the various states under which the system is expected to operate. Both the ConOps development team and the software project manager should be aware of and understand the required modes of operation of the system. For example, a system may be required to operate in regular, degraded, and emergency modes. Alternate modes may include maintenance, backup, training, or use of off-site facilities. For each identified mode, a description of the system's required operational processes, procedures, and capabilities must be described in the ConOps. Which, if any, of the modes are partially or totally mutually exclusive should also be identified.

Identification, Justification, and Prioritization of Changes and Features

An important part of the ConOps document is the identification of shortcomings of the current system or situation that motivate the development of a new system or the modification to an existing one. If there is an existing system, changes must be justified by describing deficiencies or limitations to the existing system. In some cases, the changes will improve the efficiency of the system by reducing the time required to perform tasks. In others, changing business conditions will require that new functions be added to the system. If a new system is being considered, a justification for the features of a new system should be included.

Changes and features should be described by their primary and secondary objectives. The following list provides examples:

- *Functional:* A function is being added or changed.

- *Interface:* The human/machine interface is being improved or changed.

- *Personnel:* The change allows for a reduction or increase in skill level required to perform a job function.

- *Modal:* An operational mode is being added or deleted.

- *Security:* The change is intended to enhance security.

- *Support:* The change is intended to improve the maintainability of the system.

- *Reliability:* The change is intended to improve the reliability of the system.

- *Compliance:* The change is intended to support environmental, safety, or other regulatory objectives.

Each changed and new feature must also be prioritized using the classifications of essential features, desirable features, and optional features. Essential features must be provided by the new or modified system. Failure to provide these features will result in a failed project. The project manager should pay careful attention to the essential features described in this section and ensure that the necessary life cycle processes, tools, and resources are in place to trace these essential features through the software development phases.

Any features that are desirable but not absolutely necessary for project success should be identified. Desirable features should be prioritized as a distinct group. A rationale for their priority should be provided. Optional features are those that might be provided by the new or modified system but are not required for project success. Optional features should be prioritized and a rationale provided for future reference.

The project manager can use these priorities and classifications to select alternatives if the project is headed toward budget or schedule cuts or overruns. For instance, if the project funding were cut, the project manager could use the list of optional features to offset the impending budgetary constraints. Another example is the situation in which difficulties in the development of the system cause a schedule or cost overrun. Removal of optional features could bring the delivery schedule back in line with the current project progress. In some cases it may even prove (with the concurrence of the acquirer) necessary to eliminate desirable or necessary features that have low priorities.

In this context, it is important for the program manager to be aware of the impacts of desirable and optional features on the product design, cost, and schedule. At the time of ConOps development, these impacts may not always be obvious but they will become clearer as the SRS and the design document are generated. For example, it is possible for a single, optional feature to impact the entire architecture of a product, thereby seriously impacting risk and cost. The program manager must be on guard against this scenario.

When discussing changes, it is important to document changes that were considered but not included as part of the list of new features or required changes. This will provide a record to those who might want to know if a particular change was considered and perhaps why it was not included. Perhaps a change was considered that proved to be costly to implement and the budget did not provide enough funding.

Impact Analysis

During the impact analysis process, the current situation is reviewed and the effects of the proposed changes are identified and evaluated. This analysis must be documented so that all stakeholders (users, customers, operators, and maintainers) can have an opportunity to see how the new system will impact their particular areas.

Impacts can occur during development, installation and cutover, and operation of the system. Impacts generally require resources (time and personnel) and are often caused by a change in operational procedures. For example, during development users must expect to expend resources reviewing documentation, attending demonstrations, commenting on proposed changes, and training on the new system. During the installation and cutover to a new system, users must work with both systems until the original system is removed from service. Also during this time, the developers will conduct acceptance tests, fix defects, and prepare the system for final production release. The operation of the new system may be different from the previous one, thus requiring the users to learn different procedures and work with different interfaces.

The software engineering project manager should ensure that an adequate impact analysis has been performed by the authors of the ConOps. This will increase the probability of a successful project because the necessary resources will be allocated to the project tasks and will not be diverted in response to unanticipated impacts. As a practical matter, the diligent project manager can reduce the likelihood of this happening. Problems of this type can never be fully eliminated.

2.5   Maintaining the ConOps

A ConOps should be considered a "living" document that can and should be updated throughout the life cycle of the product. The ConOps should be a configuration item (CI) and be bound to all of the configuration management standards, policies, and procedures of the organization. After the ConOps has been approved and a baseline established, any and all changes must follow the formal change control process in place for all deliverable CIs.

The software project manager should ensure that the ConOps document is identified as a CI and ensure that it is included in the configuration management processes. The project manager should ensure that the members of the Change Control Board (CCB) assigned responsibility for the ConOps have appropriate backgrounds and experience to support decisions involving the ConOps and its relationship to the other project documents.

It especially important for the requirements trace between the ConOps document, the system/software requirements specification, and the acceptance/regression test scenarios to be maintained. The project manager should ensure that adequate personnel are available to perform the necessary activities of managing the ConOps document and its impact on the project, consistent with all other project documents. For more details on the software configuration management (SCM) processes, CIs, and CCBs, the reader should consult Chapter 9.

2.6   Summary

The concept of operations document provides a mechanism through which users/customers can present their views of their requirements in a format that is comprehensible to both themselves and the developers. The ConOps is a "living" and "flexible" document that can be written by teams composed of users, acquirers, developers, or a third party at any time during the development life cycle, ideally working as a team. In all cases, the maximum benefits will be obtained when the ConOps document is written with significant involvement of the user at the beginning of a project.

The ConOps can help improve the developer's understanding of the user's needs. Communication among all involved parties can be improved with the use of a ConOps document. As a result, the ConOps helps to reduce development costs and schedule length. The ConOps bridges the gap between the developer and the user. Without such a mechanism, the technical specialists are deprived of guidance on the desired features, user interfaces, and decision logic and are forced to rely on their own sense of what is required.

The configuration of the ConOps document should be managed with the same processes as are applied to any other configuration item. These activities must be applied when corrections, changes, or deviations are made. Maintaining the ConOps and the traceability of dependent work products will not guarantee a successful software project; however, it can increase the probability the system developed will satisfy the user's needs.

One of the most important benefits of the ConOps is that it gives the users a sense of ownership in the product and the processes used to develop it. With traceability from the ConOps to the delivered system, the project can proceed with higher confidence that the product being built will be what is needed by the users.

Applicable Standards

IEEE Std 830-1998. *IEEE Recommended Practice for Software Requirements Specifications*. IEEE, New York.

IEEE Std 1362-1998. *IEEE Guide for Information Technology—System Definition—Concept of Operation Document*. IEEE, New York.

IEEE Std 12207.0-1996. *IEEE/EIA Standard. Industry Implementation of International Standard ISO/IEC 12207:1995 Standard for Information Technology—Software Life Cycle Processes*. IEEE, New York.

IEEE Std 12207.1 1997. *IEEE/EIA Standard: Industry Implementation of International Standard ISO/IEC 12207:1995 Standard for Information Technology—Software Life Cycle Processes—Life Cycle Data*. IEEE, New York.

IEEE Std 12207.2-1997. *IEEE/EIA Standard: Industry Implementation of International Standard ISO/IEC 12207:1995 Standard for Information Technology—Software Life Cycle Processes—Implementation Considerations*. IEEE, New York.

Additional References

[Constantine 1996] Constantine, L. L. (1996). "Essential Modeling: Use Cases for User Interfaces." Presentation at the Software Development Conference, San Francisco, 1996.

[Fairley & Thayer 1997] Fairley, R. E. and Thayer, R. H. (1997). "The Concept of Operations: The Bridge from Operational Requirements to Technical Specifications." in M. Dorfman and R. H. Thayer [eds.] *Software Engineering*, IEEE Computer Society Press, Los Alamitos, CA, pp. 73–83, 1997.

[Goguen & Linde 1993] Goguen, J. A. and Linde, C. (1993). "Techniques for Requirements Elicitation." *Proceedings of the International Symposium on Requirements Engineering*. Reprinted in R. H. Thayer and M. Dorfman [eds.], *Software Requirements*

Engineering. IEEE Computer Society Press, Los Alamitos, CA, pp. 110–121, 1997.

[Gordon & Bielman 1995]   Gordon, V. S. and Bielman, J. M. (1995). "Rapid Prototyping: Lessons Learned." *IEEE Software*, January, pp. 85–95.

[Jacobson et al. 1992]   Jacobson, I., Christerson, M., Jonsson, P., and Overgaard, G. (1992). *Object-Oriented Software Engineering: A Use Case Driven Approach.* Addison Wesley, Reading, MA.

[Schneider & Winters 1998] Schneider, G. and Winters, J. P. (1998). *Applying Use Cases: A Practical Guide.* Addison-Wesley, Reading, MA.

[Yourdon 1989]   Yourdon, E. (1989). *Modern Structured Analysis.* Yourdon Press, Englewood Cliffs, NJ.

Chapter 3

Software Requirements Specification

3.1   Introduction

Requirements are the foundation for any development project. If explicitly documented, they describe the product that is to be developed and delivered to customers and serve to guide the evolution of the project. If not explicitly documented, they will nonetheless implicitly determine or influence a major portion of the project's content, effort, and success. A software requirements specification (SRS) permanently documents, in a technical form usable to the development staff, statements of what features and properties are essential for the software product to possess, as well as those that are desirable or optional. The SRS and the statement of work (SOW) are two of the most critical documents for any development project. The SRS serves as a contract between the customer and developer stating exactly what is to be delivered to the customer. The SOW describes what activities will be performed during the life of the development contract.

Because the SRS has a central role in both the development of the product and the relationship with the customer, the software project manager must appreciate the importance of requirements, the processes used to develop those requirements, and the tasks required to generate an SRS from which a software system can be build that meets the customer's needs. In addition, the form (that is, how the requirements are represented and organized) and the level of detail of the requirements must be suitable for their subsequent use by the project staff as they perform the activities of the project's life cycle. Thus for very small, short-term, focused efforts the requirements will often be documented in a very concise and perhaps informal format, whereas larger (in terms of either product or development team sizes) or life-critical projects will need more voluminous or formal documents. In all cases, the IEEE standards can be used as a reference point, assisting the development team—and in particular the chief engineer, process architect, and project manager—in determining the form in which the requirements should be captured.

Correctly identifying and documenting requirements is critical. Without good requirements, expressed in a form that is appropriate to the project's life cycle and development methods, the cost and schedule estimate will be wrong and effort (cost) and time (schedule) will be expended building a product that does not match the customer's needs. This dissipation of critical resources often, in turn, results in decreased quality, as the program staff struggles to recover from the wasted cost and lost schedule caused by incomplete or incorrect requirements. A lack of good requirements results in many types of errors that are propagated from the requirements into the developmental stage of the software product. The longer an error in requirements goes undetected, the greater its impact on the project's cost, schedule, and, indirectly, quality.

Depending on the nature of the relationship between the customer and the developer, the SRS may be produced prior to the initiation of the development effort or as one of the first activities of that effort. The SRS may be developed by the customer, by the developer, or by a third party. Requirements can be developed in various ways from a variety of sources, including customer interviews, concept of operations documents, prototyping, and technical analyses (see Chapter 2 for a description of the concept of operations document). Likewise, requirements can be documented in several formats, including text, equations, tables, and diagrams.

No matter how they are created and how they are documented, the requirements must be evaluated to ensure that they are complete, correct, and consistent. The SRS forms the basis for this evaluation, and also establishes the baseline for all later phases of development.

Because the SRS is developed early in the project and does not directly produce executable code, the tendency to "rush" its development is often observed. The SRS is often seen as not relevant to writing the code, either by the customer or by some elements of the development staff. To convince the customer of the importance of this effort, the project manager should ensure customer involvement and visibility during the requirements development and documentation process. To ensure that the development staff believe in and support the requirement development effort, the project manager should ensure that the development personnel assigned to the project during the early phases have the appropriate backgrounds and skill sets. Attempts are often made to "staff up" the project early, which often results in the application of inappropriate staff to requirements tasks.

The SRS should provide several benefits. It:

- Establishes the basis for agreement between the acquirers and the suppliers on what the software product is to do.

- Bounds the project effort, thereby reducing cost and schedule risk.

- Reduces the development effort by supporting disciplined reviews of the requirements, identifying any missing, incorrect, ambiguous, or excessive requirements.

- Forms the basis of any user manuals.

- Is the foundation of all V&V activities performed during design, implementation, and test.

- In particular, SRS is the basis of the acceptance test procedures.

Thus, the contents and scope of the SRS should be directed toward achieving these benefits in a manner appropriate to the project. This helps determine the scope and content of the document and effort expended to develop and manage it.

IEEE Standard 830-1998, *IEEE Recommended Practice for Software Requirements Specifications*, describes the structure and content of an SRS document. An IEEE-compliant SRS organizes the requirements into an acceptable structure as prescribed by the standard and is consistent with other related IEEE standards and practices. IEEE Standard 1233-1998, *IEEE Guide for Developing System Requirements Specifications*, describes some important technical considerations involved in developing requirements.

This chapter describes these IEEE standards, together with some of the major methods and issues that arise in developing and documenting requirements. It is intended as an introduction for the software project manager in those topics. It provides an overview of the relevant IEEE standards and also provides a description of some of the major methods available for developing and documenting requirements. It also discusses the major management issues that can arise when developing and using software requirements.

Of necessity, this chapter cannot provide an encyclopedic recitation of all issues that can arise in these activities, nor can it describe all the methods, tools, and techniques currently available for use in developing and documenting requirements in all possible development models. For more detailed discussion of requirements elicitation, analysis, and documentation methods, the reader should consult the books and other publications listed in the references at the end of this chapter.

3.2 Objectives

In this chapter you will learn:

- The purposes and uses of software requirement specifications in a software engineering project.

- How an effective SRS will positively impact the project's ability to meet user needs, with an acceptable schedule and budget.

- The major issues that arise in managing requirements and their development.

- A sampling of the categories of processes used to develop software requirements specifications.

- Some of the techniques used to discover requirements.

- The common techniques available to perform requirements analysis.

- The role of interfaces in software requirements development and documentation.

- Some important technical methods used to document requirements.

- The styles and approaches used to write an SRS.

- The difference between an SRS written in natural language, semiformal, and formal notation.

- The required organization and content of an IEEE-compliant SRS.

3.3   Purposes of Software Requirements

3.3.1   The Importance of Requirements

The software requirements are the foundation of every software development program, irrespective of the software life cycle model. They describe, in a technical form, the functions, performance, and properties that the product is to possess. The requirements are the primary source of information that will be used to develop the design of the product, the executable code, and the procedures that will be used to verify that the product meets those requirements. As a result, errors in the requirements can have a pervasive negative impact on the cost and schedule of the program. At the same time, the scope, form, and content of the SRS will vary depending on the software life cycle model, the business and technical objectives of the project, and the organization, and the size and nature of the software product.

Table 3.1, which is typical of the results gathered over three decades of experience in developing large commercial, industrial, and military software projects, shows that requirements errors detected in the requirements phase cost very little to correct compared to those that are discovered in any of the later phases. Thus, fixing a problem in requirements during the integration or acceptance test phases costs between 20 and 50 times more than fixing the same problem during the requirements phase. Likewise, fixing a similar problem found after delivery can cost 40 times what it would have had it been found during design.

Phase	Relative Cost
Requirements	0.1–0.2
Design	0.5
Coding	1
Unit test	2
Acceptance test	5
Maintenance	20

Table 3.1: Relative Cost of Correcting Requirements Errors [Davis 1990]

This cost phenomenon is a natural consequence of the fact that effort is being continuously expended as the project progresses through its development phases. For example, the requirement development activity typically represents something in the range of 5 percent of the total cost of a project. This means that the other 95 percent of the program costs are expended implementing the system specified in the requirements. This represents a *leverage ratio* of 95:5, or 19:1. In other words, each dollar of effort expended on requirements impacts 19 dollars during development. Additionally, if a problem is found during acceptance testing that was induced during the requirements phase, then the design, coding, and unit test and integration processes must all, to some degree, be repeated. Such rework costs can include not only the immediate cost of making the change but also that of verifying that no other functions are impacted. The combined effect of the direct leverage ratio of 19:1 and the additional need for rework and reverification easily explains the range of ratios of 25:1 to 50:1 cited earlier.

The software project manager, realizing the potential cost of incomplete or incorrect requirements, should ensure that the project puts in place the practices needed to reduce the likelihood of such errors being introduced into the requirements. Understanding the types and nature of requirements, the manners in which they can be developed and documented, and the categories of requirements errors is the first step in eliminating them. Table 3.2 lists the percentage of each type of error that is most often found in requirements. Notice that simple errors of fact represent almost half of the errors introduced, followed closely by omissions. The table shows that 70 percent of errors in requirements are either missing or incorrect.

Type	Percentage (%)
Incorrect fact	40
Omission	31
Inconsistency	13
Ambiguity	5
Misplaced	2

Table 3.2: Types of Errors Found in Requirements [Davis 1990]

The software project manager should take proactive steps to cause such errors to be removed from the requirements. This is best done by ensuring that practices and procedures are in place that will increase the probability of finding requirement errors early. Inspection has been shown to discover 65 percent of errors found in all phases of software development. Table 3.3 shows the percentages of errors found by the different techniques.

Method of Detection	Percentage Errors Found (%)
Inspection	65
Unit testing	10
Evaluation	10
Integration	5
Other	10

Table 3.3: Methods of Error Detection [Davis 1990]

3.3.2 Definition, Purposes, and Roles of Requirements

3.3.2.1 Requirements

A *requirement* is a statement that has been constructed to describe a necessary functional capability, performance parameter, or other property of the intended product (or item). Here are some simplified examples of requirement statements:

> The system must be capable of supporting up to 100 simultaneous users, each performing the randomized mix of operational tasks documented in Appendix A, with an average response time of less than 1 second, and a maximum response time of less than 5 seconds.

> Error alerts must be displayed in the center of the dialog window, in 14-point bold Arial font, using the color red.

> The system must be capable of storing the transactions generated during 100 consecutive days of average operation.

> The communications interfaces must comply with the seven-tier ISO architecture.

> The error in the computation of the gyro rate must contribute less than 0.1 microradian per hour to the total gyro error rate when the system is operating under the specified environmental conditions.

IEEE Standard 830-1998 requires that requirements must possess a number of properties, individually and collectively. Each individual requirement must possess these five important properties:

1. *Necessary.* Is it needed?

2. *Unambiguous.* Can it be interpreted in only one way?

3. *Testable.* Can it be tested?

4. *Traceable.* Can it be traced from phase to phase?

5. *Measurable.* Can it be measured?

The reader should review the above examples and determine if they do or do not satisfy the five properties listed here.

Each of these properties of an individual requirement can only be verified by explicitly and specifically answering the corresponding question; vagueness and recourse to generalities are usually danger signs. Typically, it is progressively more difficult to answer the questions as the list is traversed from top to bottom. Thus, the question of *necessity* is answered with an explanation of why it is necessary. This is usually a direct consequence of the requirements development process. Whether or not a requirement is ambiguous or not is usually determined by performing a review of the requirements.

The question of testability is usually more difficult to answer, because doing so requires that a test concept be developed. This concept must be sufficiently detailed so that it can be verified that it will indeed be possible to test the requirement. Verification of the test feasibility should include an identification of any data and facilities needed. Measurability may be simple to verify if the question is one of presence or not of a feature. Usually verifying that a requirement is measurable requires that it be considered in light of what will occur during the design, implementation and the testing phases. Thus, testability is usually a subordinate but more detailed element of measurability. Finally, the question of how to trace a requirement from one phase of development can often be the most difficult of all, because it is rarely the case that a requirement is implemented in a single component of a design. Therefore, it becomes necessary to maintain tables tracing the implementation of the requirement across multiple components of the system, through multiple phases of the project.

The process of determining whether or not an individual requirement statement satisfies the five properties, while detailed and time consuming, will result in better, clearer statements of individual requirements. In addition, it often happens that, as one question (such as traceability) is considered, the realization is made that the initial answers to an earlier question (such as measurability) were incomplete.

Larger projects and organizations that are more sophisticated currently use systematic requirements analysis techniques and tools during the production of their requirements documents. Some of these methods provide systematic and automated capabilities that verify that the individual requirements possess the desired five properties individually and, further, that they collectively possess the four properties discussed in the next section. Depending on the methods and tools applied to this task, the order of difficulty will vary. For example, evaluating the traceability of requirements is often greatly simplified.

3.3.2.2 Requirements Specifications

A *requirements specification* is the formal documentation of all requirements statements for an item. In addition to the five properties that an individual requirement must satisfy, the IEEE standard specifies that the SRS must possess the following global properties:

- *Ranked for importance and stability.* Can the requirements be ordered?

- *Modifiable.* Can the individual requirements be easily modified without excessive impact to other requirement?

- *Complete.* Are any requirements missing?

- *Consistent.* Are any of the requirements mutually exclusive?

As with the early five properties of individual requirements, the difficulty of verifying that a document possesses these four properties increases as the list is traversed from top to bottom.

3.3.2.3   Primary and Derived Requirements

Primary requirements are explicitly stated as being necessary for the system to meet contractual obligations. *Derived requirements* are those properties not explicitly specified that the system absolutely must possess if one or more of the primary requirements are to be satisfied. Derived requirements are often identified during the requirements analysis process. Great care must be taken not to confuse derived requirements with design decisions.

3.3.3   The Need for Requirements

The two most common problem scenarios that occur in software development are as follows:

1. At the end of the development effort, the customer rejects the system because it does not meet their needs.

2. The cost and schedule of the project grows increasingly larger as a result of the requirements being improperly identified and documented.

Although it is not necessarily the case that all problems that occur in development projects are caused by requirements problems, these are usually the most significant and common sources of such problems. For example, even if the requirements were perfectly well understood, errors in the cost and schedule methodology or technical problems with the implementation can cause serious problems of the type listed above. In practice, this happens much less often and with less impact than do the requirements-driven scenarios, although there have been some spectacular failures driven by technology or estimation problems.

The high relative cost of correcting problems in requirements late in a project, as illustrated by Table 3.1, together with the technical and managerial complexity of the requirements development process are the fundamental reasons for requirements being the most common source of problems in programs.

Problems with requirements are rarely due solely to the technology available to develop and deliver them. It is much more common for the requirement to simply have been omitted or misstated due to the complexity and subtlety of the effort along with the sheer magnitude of the task. Developing requirements is a complex and subtle process because information from a variety of sources must be integrated to obtain a complete picture of the system requirements. As a result, the single most important activity of the requirements engineering process is the systematic discovery and documentation of the system requirements.

3.3.4   Roles of Requirements

When managing and developing the product requirements it is useful to remember what the requirements are to be used for. First and foremost, the SRS is the embodiment of what the product is to do and the environment in which it is to do it. Together with the SOW, it is the most critical document for the customer and the developer. Second, it is the management control point for much of the remaining effort of the project. Third, it is the formal, controlled starting point for the design of the product. Fourth, it is the basis for the creation of the product's acceptance test plan and user guides.

The reader should also realize what roles an SRS should not be expected to fulfill. First, it is not a design document. It is a *design-to* document. Excessive detail in an SRS can only serve to needlessly constrain the design and raise costs, not to mention the organizational friction it can create. Second, it is not a scheduling or planning document and should not contain information more properly allocated to the SOW, software project management plan (SPMP), software life cycle management plan (SLCMP), software configuration management plan (SCMP), or software quality assurance plan (SQAP) documents.

3.4   Categories of Requirements

System and software requirements fall into several categories:

- Functions;

- Performance;

- External interfaces;

- Design constraints; and

- Quality attributes.

Sometimes the software requirements are categorized into *functional* and *nonfunctional* (performance, external interfaces, design constraints, and quality attributes). Another less used categorization is *functional* and *design constraints*. The following subsections provide an explanation and examples of each of these categories of requirements.

3.4.1   Functional Requirements

A *functional requirement* specifies a particular function that the system or system component must perform. Examples of functional requirements are shown in Table 3.4.

In addition to a statement of the function to be performed, the requirement should also specify these items:

- All assumptions that should be made about or checks made for the validity of the function's inputs;

> The system shall calculate sales tax for all taxable inventory items sold.
>
> The system shall provide a method to allow the system user to change the sales tax percentages based on local rates.
>
> The system shall be capable of producing a monthly sales report.

Table 3.4: Functional Requirements

- Any sequencing within the function that is externally relevant;

- Responses to abnormal conditions including all internally or externally generated errors;

- Timing or priority requirements;

- Exclusion rules between functions;

- Assumptions that should be made about the internal state of the system;

- Any sequencing of inputs with outputs needed for the function to operate; and

- Any formulas for conversions or internal calculations.

Functional requirements normally make up the majority of the requirements and usually make up almost all of the initial requirements obtained via interviews and group sessions. As the SRS is being written, the functional requirements should be cross-referenced based on:

- The source of the functions;

- The data shared by the functions;

- The interaction of the functions with external interfaces; and

- The utilization of computing resources by the functions.

The IEEE standard refers to most functional requirements as *specific requirements* and assigns them to Section 3 of the SRS format. Specific requirements are discussed in the section of this chapter that describes the SRS development process.

3.4.2 Performance Requirements

A *performance requirement* specifies a performance characteristic that a system or system component must possess. Examples of performance requirements are shown in Table 3.5. Performance requirements often critically impact the design by implicitly excluding some design solutions that would satisfy the functional requirements. The classical example of this is sorting, where the specification of the time that can be spent sorting a record set of a given size will, for a given computer, determine what algorithms are admissible.

> The system shall calculate total sales tax for a given quarter within 5 minutes.
>
> The system shall retrieve a sales order in less than 1 minute from 100,000 records.
>
> The application must support concurrent access by 100 Windows 95/WindowsNT workstations.

Table 3.5: Performance Requirements

3.4.3 External Interface Requirements

An *external interface requirement* specifies a hardware, software, or database element with which a system or system component must interface. It may also specify formats, timing, or other factors. Examples of external interface requirements are given in Table 3.6.

> The accounts receivable system must provide updated information to the monthly financial status system as described in the "finance system description," 4th Revision.
>
> The engine control system must correctly process commands received from the flight control system, conforming to paragraphs 1 through 8 of Interface Control Document B2-10A4, Revision C.

Table 3.6: External Interface Requirements

It is unusual for an interface requirement to be totally self-contained in the SRS. As in the two examples given in Table 3.6, other documents describing the external systems and their interfaces are usually referenced. Replication of information should be avoided because this creates a maintenance problem. However, if the information needed for the current SRS does not exist, then it should be created as an appendix to the SRS and referenced internally. This can happen when the new system must interface with an older system developed under less rigorous management conditions.

In addition, any references to external documents should explicitly reference the precise version number of the document. If the SRS is itself not legally mutually binding (and it often is not), then the subject documents should be referenced in some plan or other document that mutually binds the developer and the customer. This protects both parties. If this is not done, the stability of the project is in serious jeopardy of being subjected to requirements *thrashing* (also called *churning*). Finally, the developing organization's master copy of the interface control document (ICD) or IRS should be controlled using the project's software configuration management practices.

Interface requirements typically fall into one of several major categories:

- *System interfaces*—Describe how the application interacts with, for example, other applications on a system, as distinct from an application. This is normally documented in an ICD or a system interface requirements (SIR) document.

- *User interfaces*—Specify the logical characteristics of the interface between the software product and the user. That is, the interface requirements should specify what data should be displayed to the user, what data are required from the user, and how the user interface is to be controlled by the user.

- *Hardware interfaces*—Relevant when the application being developed must directly respond to or control hardware components. If the software system must interface with devices, the type of support and protocols required should be stated. If necessary, an ICD should be developed or referenced.

- *Software interfaces*—Allow interaction with other software products, such as data management systems, operating systems, or mathematical packages.

- *Communications interfaces*—Specify the intended system's interaction with communications facilities such as local-area networks. If the communications requirements include the type of network that the system must operate in (TCP/IP, Microsoft Windows NT®, and Novell®) that information should be included in the SRS.

- *Memory constraints*—Describe applicable characteristics and limits on volatile and nonvolatile memory, especially if these are used to communicate with other processes in a system.

- *Operations*—Specify how the system enters into and interacts under both the normal and abnormal operations stipulated by the user. The modes of operation in the user's organization, including both interactive and noninteractive modes, any batch data processing support functions, as well as any requirements that describe system backup, recovery, and upgrade functions should be described.

- *Site adaptation requirements*—Describe the system installation and how a site must be modified to accommodate the new system.

3.4.4 Design Constraints

A *design constraint* is a requirement that limits the range of design solutions of a software system or software system component. Constraints, by their nature, are extremely difficult—if not impossible—to trade off or otherwise compromise. They must be satisfied. This property of constraints is the primary distinction between constraints and all other requirements. Many design constraints will directly impact the planning for the software project, requiring additional cost and effort to satisfy the functional, performance, and other classes of requirements. Examples of design constraints are given in Table 3.7.

The IEEE standard lists the following areas that should be considered when determining what constraints may be relevant to the product being developed:

- *Regulatory policies*—May include international, federal, state, and/or local laws and statues. The project manager should be aware of the various policy constraints because they will impact the project's schedule and budget and must be considered

The system must be written in C++ OR OTHER approved object-oriented language—unmeasureable).

Menus are required for the system user interface.

When averaged over any 10-second period, the application may utilize no more than 50 percent of the available computing power.

Table 3.7: Design Constraints

when planning the project. The process by which regulatory approval is obtained must be understood and planned for.

- *Hardware limitations*—Can be categorized as being technological or economical. Technological limitations are determined by the current state of the art in technology and include things such as processing speeds, signal timing requirements, storage capacities, communications speed, and availability.

- *Interfaces to other applications*—May impose constraints on the design of the new system. For example, certain operations of the new system may be prohibited when an external system is in a particular state. Care should be exercised to distinguish constraints from other interface requirements, as previously mentioned.

- *Parallel operations*—May be a required to concurrently (that is, in parallel) produce or receive data to or from different sources. Such timing constraints must be clearly described.

- *Audit functions*—Specify data or transaction recording criteria that must be satisfied by the software system. For example, if a user views or changes data, the software system may be required to record the actions of the system for later review.

- *Control functions*—Could be remote control of the administrative capabilities of the system, control of other external software, and control of internal processes.

- *Higher order language requirements*—May require that the product be written in a specific higher order language.

- *Signal handshake protocols*—As commonly used in hardware and communications control software, especially when specific timing constraints are specified, may be severe enough that they become a constraint. If not presented in an ICD then it should be included explicitly in the SRS.

- *Criticality of the application*—Determined by the potential loss/harm to human life or a potentially large financial loss. Many biomedical, aviation, military, or financial software systems fall into this category. The class and type of criticality should be well understood (see Chapter 5 on verification and validation).

- *Safety and security considerations*—If the former are extensive it may be appropriate for the project to develop a software safety plan according to IEEE Standard 1228-1994, *IEEE Standard for Software Safety Plans*. The need for such a plan should be established as early as possible. Security requirements are usually associated with authentication (identification), authorization (permission), and encryption (protection of data).

3.4.5 Quality Attributes

A *quality attribute* specifies a property that the software product must possess if it is to achieve a desired level of quality. Typical quality attributes, together with some examples, are listed in Table 3.8.

Attribute	Description
Reliability	Probability that the software will perform its logical operation in the specified environment without failure
Survivability	Probability that the software will continue to perform or support critical functions when a portion of the system is inoperable
Maintainability	The average effort required to locate and correct a software failure or to make a modification of specified scope
User friendliness	The degree of ease of use of learning a software system
Security	The probability that the software system can be made secure for a predetermined amount of time
Portability	The types of platforms on which the system must operate

Table 3.8: Examples of Quality Attributes

Specifying quality attributes that can be "designed to" and measured at completion of the project is an extremely difficult task and is often beyond the current state of the practice. More commonly, many of these quality attributes are defined when the early system engineering tasks are most active and then subsequently allocated to requirements.

3.4.6   Items to Exclude from the SRS

The project staff and customer must distinguish between what the delivered product and the development team are to do. The SRS should only address the product requirements. Project requirements address the contractual understanding between the customer and the developer and should be located in the SOW or some other project document.

    The following items should not be included in the SRS:

- Project cost;

- Delivery schedules;

- Reporting procedures;

- Software development methods;

- Quality assurance procedures;

- Configuration management procedures;

- Verification and validation procedures;

- Acceptance procedures; and

- Installation procedures.

These project requirements belong in the project management plan and/or the statement of work. Details of the creation, content, organization, and management of the project management plan are described Chapter 13.

3.5   Requirements Development Process

3.5.1   Identifying the Customer and User

The methods used to develop the requirements will vary depending on the nature of the product and the parties performing the requirement development activities. Thus, if the product is comprised solely of software, the requirements will often be derived from interviews with users, whereas if the software is embedded into a composite hardware/software product with indirect ties (if any) to a user interface, the requirements will come from more indirect sources, such as system requirements allocated through a systems engineering process.

    The requirements of composite hardware/software systems are usually best developed by a systems engineering team comprised of specialists representing the organization's systems, hardware, and software engineering groups. In this way, an effective system architecture can be designed. Further, the software representatives on the system team can then assist in the development of the software requirements by serving as the liaison between the software group, the consumer of the SRS, and the systems designers, the source of those requirements. Thus, the system engineering function becomes the customer for the software product.

Chapter 1, Software Systems Engineering, describes the relationship between systems and software requirements in the development of composite hardware/software systems.

For systems comprised of software installed on conventional computers, the roles of the systems engineer and the software requirements engineer are usually merged, with the customer of the software product being the actual user of the system. Much of the literature of software requirements is written from the viewpoint of such systems. This section will follow that model, with the implied understanding that the terms *customer* and *user* may in fact refer to an internal systems customer of the software for a composite hardware/software system.

3.5.2   Overview of Requirements Development

Developing an SRS can be broken down into a sequence of core activities. These are presented here as being performed sequentially, although some degree of iteration always occurs:

1. Discover and document the initial, or raw, requirements. The concept of operations (ConOps) document should be developed at this point. Other sources of requirements should be identified and their requirements documented as well.

2. Verify that initial requirements are valid, revising them as required.

3. Analyze the revised, initial requirements.

4. Develop and document the final technical specifications based on the analysis of the initial requirements. This step produces the draft SRS.

5. Verify that the technical requirements as stated in the SRS are valid, revising the SRS as required.

6. Release the final requirements specifications.

In the above description, the term *initial* requirements has been used to emphasis the importance of the requirements analysis process, which is performed using the initial (or raw) requirements as its primary source and produces the technical (or final) requirements specifications as its primary product. Thus, derived requirements are usually identified during the analysis process. IEEE Standard 1233-1998, *IEEE Guide for Developing System Requirements Specifications*, uses the term *raw* instead of *initial*.

The following sections detail each of the above activities.

3.5.3 Discover and Document the Initial Requirements

The process of discovering the initial requirements is sometimes referred to as requirements elicitation because in many cases the requirements are literally elicited from the user. However, not all requirements discovery techniques explicitly match this model. Numerous techniques are available for use when eliciting requirements. Most programs, depending on the skills of the requirements engineering staff and the nature of the product and contract, will use a combination of these techniques to develop the initial requirements.

All techniques share one property: The skills of the individuals performing the activity will significantly influence its success.

The techniques most commonly used to discover requirements include these:

- *Introspection.* Viewing the system as if the requirements engineers were the end users and asking this question: "If I were using the system, I would want . . . ."

- *Individual interviews.* Querying users and other elements of the customer to determine what capabilities the system should provide.

- *Observation.* Observing users as they perform existing procedures and processes that are related to the desired, new capabilities.

- *Group sessions.* Conducting collaborative, joint meetings of customer and developer personnel.

- *Extraction.* Reviewing technical documents, such as statements of need, functional and performance objectives, systems specifications interface standards, hardware design documents, and ConOps documents, and extracting the relevant information.

Each of these techniques has advantages as well as disadvantages in any particular context. While performing any of the above techniques, a variety of auxiliary methods can be utilized, including prototyping. Thus, a prototype can be used while conducting group sessions or can facilitate individual interviews. The chapter on the ConOps document discusses the use of prototyping in the development of that document.

3.5.3.1 Introspection

Introspection would seem attractive and may indeed be necessary if users are not accessible to the requirements engineers. However, for introspection to be successful, the requirements engineers must have knowledge of the application domain and processes much as end users would, together with a good imagination. Thus, if a law enforcement application is being developed, the requirements development staff must have experience in this domain. The same can be said for medical applications or any other specialized domain.

3.5.3.2 Individual Interviews

Interviewing is usually a better technique than introspection. The requirements engineer has the opportunity to directly ask the user what they want—the requirements engineer asks questions and the user responds. The success of this approach depends on the interviewer's ability to "ask the right questions" and the respondent's ability to provide answers to the questions that reveal the true nature of the requirements.

The risk exists that the requirements will grow in an uncontrolled manner during the interviews. If not managed properly this unexpected (and perhaps unnecessary) growth can threaten to exceed the cost and schedule limits of the project. For this reason the ongoing results of the interview process should be reviewed periodically by project and customer management.

Such unplanned and unbudgeted requirements growth can be a symptom of so-called *creeping elegance* or it may be an expression of legitimate needs that have heretofore not been recognized. Either situation, and sometimes both, can occur with any of the requirements capture techniques. One of the toughest challenges in managing the requirements development process is judging when to draw the line on such growth and when to inform the customer of the growth.

3.5.3.3 Observation

Observation of users performing existing tasks and processes or operating existing systems that are related to the new, desired system, if feasible, can clarify the context within which the system will be operated. Clearly understanding this context can be critical, especially if the new system must interface or interoperate with existing systems, processes, and methods of work. In theory, this information can be obtained during an interview, but it is as difficult for the users to explicitly explain every detail of an environment as it is for the requirements engineer to imagine them. Seeing it first hand, in concrete reality, is always better. Thus even if new requirements are not directly discovered during the observations, the requirements engineer can gain needed insight into the operational environment.

Customers may welcome or resist observation sessions. They may appreciate the fact that the developer has taken an interest in their operational realities or they may view it as a disruption of ongoing business. They might also believe that the developer should already have this understanding of their business before the award of contract, so the matter of conducting observations should be approached delicately.

3.5.3.4 Group Sessions

In group sessions, the requirements are developed collaboratively by representatives of the customer's organization. A representative of the developing organization, usually the lead requirements engineer or the software engineering project manager, facilitates the sessions. Numerous variations of this method exist, depending primarily on the application domain and the skills of the facilitator. The role of the *facilitator* is principally to maintain the forward progress of the group, without prematurely terminating discussions. The members of the group, in turn, must be selected carefully; both with regard to the knowledge of the operational environment as it exists now and as it is desired to be, as well as their personalities.

Several advantages accrue when using collaborative meetings to develop requirements. First, if meetings are properly organized and conducted, they can identify many requirements very rapidly. Second, the developers will be exposed to multiple views on any given requirement in a single session, which saves time that would otherwise be spent documenting individual interviews and then correlating them. Finally, conflicts between different views of requirements can be used to expose issues in the requirements, as well to assist the customer in achieving internal consensus. Joint application development (JAD) provides a formal method of conducting group sessions.

3.5.3.5 Extraction

Extraction is most relevant when parts of the requirements are already documented. Depending on the nature of the product, a considerable number of documents might need to be reviewed in order to determine if any relevant information is contained in them. In other cases, there will be few documents.

In most projects, the background documentation should be reviewed prior to undertaking any interviews, observations, group sessions, or introspection. If it has been developed, the ConOps document, which is described in Chapter 2, will contain many requirements. ICDs and system specifications should be reviewed as well, as should any applicable standards or policies.

3.5.3.6 Documenting the Initial Requirements

As the initial requirements are identified, they can be documented in a variety of ways, as described in later sections of this chapter. Because the initial requirements are to be first reviewed and approved by the customer, in the next activity they should be documented in a textual or graphical form that can be readily understood by the customer with minimal change to their representation—this is one of the major benefits of using the ConOps document. That is, the requirements should be expressed in the form closest to that in which they were obtained. This is intended to avoid wasted effort and to make it as easy as possible for the customer to review the initial requirements.

Changes in representation, while perhaps technically advisable, can impose a needless burden on the customer. On the other hand, it is desirable for requirements to be expressed in a common form, if for no other reason than to simplify the task of verifying the completeness of the requirements. These competing objectives can result in conflict. During the later stages of the SRS development process, more technical, specialized representations can and should be used, to support the technical analysis of the requirements needed to produce the draft of the complete SRS. Section 3.6 describes some of the available requirement representation methods.

Separate and distinct from the question of representation is the question of the organization of the SRS. The best choice is to follow the format specified in the IEEE standard. In addition to the advantage of being a format specifically designed for use with requirements, use of the standard format will familiarize the project staff (both developer and customer) with the standard format and will also simplify the process of ultimately creating the draft of the full requirements. The format specified in the IEEE standard is described in a later section of this chapter.

3.5.4   Verify the Initial Requirements

The initial requirements, as captured from the variety of sources listed above and documented in the format of the IEEE standard, can now be verified, both individually and collectively.

At the most fundamental level, the initial requirements must be reviewed by the customer to ensure that the requirements engineers correctly understood and captured what was said or written. Further, once the initial requirements are assembled in one place, the user may observe contradictions and omissions, or outright errors. In particular, the completeness of the initial requirements should be assessed at this point. Gaps in the requirements must either be filled in at this point or, if appropriate, during the analysis phase. If the gaps are matters of fundamental information, then they should be addressed now by repeating the techniques list above, as needed. If the gaps are matters of elaboration, then they should be filled in during the analysis.

Following the verification process, the initial requirements document should be revised.

3.5.5   Analyze the Initial Requirements

The analysis of the revised initial requirements marks the beginning of the technical effort of the requirements management process. The initial requirements should be evaluated using the five criteria for individual requirements and the four criteria of the full requirements set described earlier. Portions of this evaluation, especially the question of completeness, will require customer involvement, whereas the requirements development engineers working alone can perform much of the evaluation. One of the most difficult and subtle criteria to assess is consistency. Although some inconsistencies are obvious, the less obvious implications of the requirements must be clearly understood in order to fully assess their consistency. In addition, some of the requirements will be elaborated on, in some cases producing derived requirements. As the analysis process progresses, designers should watch for the following classes of problems:

- *Increases in scope.* While these can occur much earlier in the requirements development process, they can also occur during the analysis of the initial requirements because this is often the first time the full implications of the requirements are appreciated.

- *Suppression of inconsistencies and conflicts.* One of the primary objectives of the analysis is the discovery of inconsistencies and conflicts between the initial requirements. Yet news of such inconsistencies is often not welcome, because it often means that one of the requirements (and its "owner" in the customer community) must be compromised. Thus, there is a natural hesitancy to report such conflicts. The project manager must ensure that such conflicts are reported to the customer promptly. The analysis will often reveal alternatives to one or more of the initial requirements that will resolve the conflict.

Finally, depending on the form of the initial requirements, some degree of translation may be required to complete the analysis process. For example, if the initial requirements were captured using use cases and scenarios, then they must be translated into technical functions and operations.

3.5.6   Develop and Document the Draft SRS

Based on the analysis of the initial requirements the full, draft requirements document should now be completed using the selected format, based on that given in IEEE Standard 830-1998.

1. Introduction

    1.1 Purpose

    1.2 Scope

    1.3 Definitions, Acronyms, and Abbreviations

    1.4 References

    1.5 Overview

2. Overall Description

    2.1 Product Perspective

    2.2 Product Functions

    2.3 User Characteristics

    2.4 Constraints

    2.5 Assumptions and Dependencies

3. Specific Requirements (see Section 3.5.7 below)

    Appendixes

    Index

Care should be taken when creating Section 2 of the SRS because it is intended to be precisely what its name says, an overall description. Thus, Section 2 would identify the fact that certain types of functions are needed or that certain constraints or interfaces exist. It is left to Section 3 to describe the necessary specifics and details of such functions, constraints, or interfaces.

3.5.7   Verify the Specific Requirements

Section 3 of the IEEE Standard format, Specific Requirements, is the technical heart of the document. The standard, especially its Appendix A, provides guidelines and templates for how this section can be structured for several types of systems. The templates include the following:

A.1 Section 3 partitioned by the system operational mode, with the performance of the system specified in one subsection.

A.2 An alternative modal partitioning, in which the performance of each mode is embedded in the specification for that mode.

A.3 Section 3 partitioned according to the classes of users, with the functions performed by each user class embedded in that user class description. See Chapter 2 for an in-depth discussion of user classes.

A.4 Section 3 partitioned by object, with the functions associated with each object specified in that objects section.

A.5 Section 3 partitioned by system-level features, where the requirements for any given function may be distributed across several features.

A.6 Section 3 partitioned by stimulus, where the functions performed in response to each stimulus are specified.

A.7 Section 3 partitioned in a function hierarchy, where the functions are specified in terms of their action on information flows, the processing performed by the components of the flow, and the data passing through the flows.

A.8 A hybrid partitioning of Section 3 using user classes, functions, and features.

Other organizations of Section 3 are possible. The form ultimately selected should be appropriate to the organizational experience, the application and its environment, the language selected in which to express the requirements, and the method of organization chosen. The options available for expressing and organizing requirements are described in later sections of this chapter.

Irrespective of which template is adopted, the following principles should be applied to the creation and documentation of specific requirements:

- They should, of course, conform to the nine principles of a good SRS, listed previously.

- They should be uniquely identifiable to facilitate traceability.

- Specific requirements should be traced to any relevant parent documents.

- They should be structured or otherwise organized, as described earlier under the Functional Requirements section of this chapter, so that the document is readable.

- The Overall Description and Specific Requirements sections should be written in a consistent manner so that the reader can readily relate the general information contained in the former section with the specifics contained in the latter section.

- Conversely, the reader should be able to readily understand the context of a specific requirement by finding the corresponding information in the Overall Description section.

3.5.7.1 Validate the Draft SRS

Peer review can be used to identify errors in the software requirements specifications. During these reviews, it is often advantageous to include selected user representatives who are extremely familiar with the requirements of the system. Because of the high potential cost of peer reviews and the impact on the schedule, peer review may be conducted only for the most critical part of the system, especially in draft form. A series of reviews can be held for separate parts of the document with tailored review teams.

With completed draft SRS in hand, a software specification review (SSR) should be performed. For more details of software review processes, see Chapter 11. The key objectives of the requirements review of the draft SRS are:

1. Verify that the full SRS satisfies the nine key requirements of necessity, unambiguity, testability, measurability, traceability, completeness, consistency, ranked for importance and stability, and modifiability.

2. Perform a preliminary validation that the project, as represented by the requirement embodied in the SRS, can still be completed within the allocated cost and schedule. If the program utilizes an independent verification and validation approach, this issue, together with others, will be evaluated later when the final version of the SRS is reviewed.

3. Examine any and all external dependencies and constraints that the product must satisfy to ensure that:

   - They are necessary. Unnecessary dependencies, technical or otherwise, will needlessly constrain the development of the new product and will negatively impact cost and schedule.

- That the documentation for any external dependencies (system or interface) is current.

- That any expected changes to those external items are identified and their impact to the requirements and the contract are understood.

4. Ensure that the software design and test teams understand the requirements.

A SSR is often required by contract. If this review is held, care should be taken with the method of representation used. It must strike a balance between technical accuracy and the technical background of the customer. It might be more appropriate, for example, to have the customer review a ConOps document, instead of or in addition to, the SRS.

The action items of the review(s) should be documented and tracked to closure, using the project's management and change control processes.

3.5.7.2   Revise and Release the SRS

Based on the results of the reviews of the draft SRS, it should be revised using the project's configuration management processes and released to that system for distribution to the customer and the development team, as appropriate to the project's contract.

3.6   Expressing Requirements

A variety of methods can be used to express requirements. Most SRS documents use two or more methods because a single mode of expression is rarely capable of describing all types of requirements effectively. However, few SRS documents should require the use of more than three representations. Natural language is typically used to some extent. If multiple representations are used, the rationale should be well understood and guidelines created for when each representation method should be used.

The general categories of representation methods most commonly used to create SRS documents are (1) natural language, (2) semiformal notation, and (3) formal notation. This list is not encyclopedic. For a more complete listing and description of the representation methods available, together with more detailed examples, the reader is referred to the work of Peters and Pedrycz [Peters & Pedrycz 1999].

The choice of methods used to document the requirements of a product usually depends on these aspects:

1. Background and skills of the requirements engineers;

2. Nature, size, and complexity of the product;

3. Type of project and system being developed;

4. Safety and security requirements; and

5. Any customer stipulations.

Thus, products with serious security or safety requirements are often specified formally. These methods have the advantage that the specification can be executable, as described below.

3.6.1 Natural Language

Natural language can be used to write an SRS. Software requirements written using natural language usually consist of a list of statements describing the functionality that the system must provide, together with any constraints it must satisfy and will include references to any external interfaces with which the product must comply. Earlier examples of this chapter used natural language. Unfortunately, natural language can be ambiguous and can leave the SRS open to multiple interpretations.

An ambiguous SRS can lead to projects where the requirements are not clearly defined and therefore not delivered to the customer. Whenever possible, the best method to use is the one that produces an unambiguous interpretation such as semiformal or formal notation. However, an SRS expressed in natural language is better than no SRS at all.

3.6.2 Semiformal Notation

Numerous semiformal specification techniques are available, for example, graphical methods to document user and system requirements. Semiformal diagramming techniques can be used to functionally model the system or to create behavioral models of the system's states. For example, entity relationship diagrams are used most often to depict database requirements, whereas data flow diagrams are more suited for process-related requirements. Choosing the appropriate diagramming technique when documenting requirements will improve the understanding of the requirements by both the user and the developer. Table 3.9 lists the various diagramming techniques along with the type of requirements they are typically used to express.

3.6.3 Formal Notation

Several formal notation techniques and languages are available for use in an SRS. Formal notations are usually mathematical in nature and can provide a basis for rigorous requirements validation and verification methods. This is one of their great advantages. For example, Z (pronounced "zed") is a formal language that can be used write software specifications using mathematical notations. Z uses discrete mathematics and set notation to state requirements. Formal state machine representations are also frequently used.

Because some degree of mathematical expertise is required to use formal techniques, the software project manager, the chief designer, and the software process architect should together first determine whether formal specifications are appropriate for the project. If formal methods are appropriate, then the project manager should ensure that the requirements

Diagramming Technique	Used for
Entity relationship diagrams	Database-related requirements
Data flow diagrams	Process-related requirements
Data dictionary	Data-related requirements
Decision tree/table	Logical requirements
State charts/transition diagrams	State-related and timing requirements
Interactive state transition diagrams	Graphical user interface requirements
Petri nets	Concurrency and timing relationships
IDEF0 integrated definition	Comprehensive modeling language
IDEF$_{object}$	Conceptual, object-oriented modeling language

Table 3.9: Table of Semiformal Diagramming Techniques

engineer has adequate experience working with formal methods and can write a formal specification. In addition, the design engineering staff must also be able to read the specification so they can design and build a product meeting the requirements laid out by the formal methods.

The use of formal methods should not be dismissed solely because of their historical reputation for being mathematically difficult and hence hard to read and understand. The difficulty of reading some formal notations is often compounded significantly by the manner in which the expressions are formatted. Indeed, formal expressions used in many examples are extremely visually dense and difficult for anyone to read. Parnas [Parnas 2000] has argued compellingly that formal notations can be easily read by most engineers if the expressions are broken into smaller, mathematically equivalent fragments and then presented in tables. This improves both the readability and the maintainability of the SRS.

In addition to the suggestions of Parnas, other variations of the classical formal methods include these:

- *Executable specifications.* Various toolsets are commercially available that support this. Various formal representations are supported in this way, including state transition diagrams, extensions of IDEF0, VDM, and Z. For example, VDM++ is similar to C++ in its syntax. Typical leverage ratios of 10–50 have been experienced with these tools. That is, 1 line of formal specification ultimately results in between 10 and 50 lines of product code [Horl & Aichernig 2000]. In addition, executable specification methods usually support the design of test suites early in the project.

- *So-called "lightweight" formal methods.* In these methods, mathematical notation is used to express the requirements, with little effort expended on formal proofs. These methods are an attempt to provide the benefits of precise notation without imposing the steep initial costs historically associated with formal methods [Glinz 2000].

Classically, formal notation and languages have been used to specify systems that are extremely critical and involve the potential loss of life. Many experts have historically recommended that the entire system not be specified using formal notation because it has been viewed as difficult, costly, and time consuming. However, as discussed above, innovations in this area should increase the range of application of formal methods.

In the areas that require high integrity and quality assurance, formal notation can provide methods for proving the correctness of a specification, thus ensuring system integrity and quality. Note also that formal specifications and proofs do not guarantee that the specification is correct. Obviously, this is because human errors in assumptions, preconditions, postconditions, and proof of correctness are always possible. However, the use of formal methods makes it easier to identify such errors than is the case with natural language.

The project manager should also appreciate that an organization's first experience with formal methods for documenting user requirements will require additional training, management oversight, and risk mitigation. This is true for the first application of any technical innovation.

3.6.4   Combinations

Software systems are complex by nature and do not necessarily lend themselves to only one technique for their specification or implementation. Thus, it may be necessary to analyze and document user requirements using a combination of techniques. For instance, a software system may require a database, communications components, and a critical control section. The database requirements could be documented using an entity relationship diagram, and the communications requirements could be documented using a state transition diagram. It may be appropriate to document the critical control section using formal notations. The goal is to use the most appropriate methods available to document the user requirements such that the qualities of a good SRS are achieved.

The project manager does not have to be an expert on each and every representation method. The project manager's responsibility is to monitor the progress and status of the requirements development process to ensure that the results are in compliance with the project's quality, budget, and schedule goals. The project manager should also ensure that the particular documenting technique and approach is suitable for the size and complexity of the software system to be developed.

3.7   Managing the SRS: Product and Processes

Managing the SRS as a product, as well as the process by which it is developed and maintained, has two primary goals:

1. Control the requirements so a baseline can be established for software engineering and management use. This baseline is used to determine the number of changes made to the approved requirements. This helps isolate the root cause of a large portion of the most significant changes to a project's cost and schedule, both before and after they occur.

2. Ensure that software plans, products, and activities are kept consistent with the software system's allocated requirements.

The first step in achieving these goals is to ensure that the project follows a written policy. The policy typically should specify that the requirements shall be documented and that they are to be reviewed by the chief designer, software project manager, and other relevant parties. In addition, the policy should specify that the software plans (project management plan, configuration management plan, verification and validation plan), work products, and activities requiring change are documented and kept consistent with the allocated requirements. If the parent organization does not have such a policy on record, then the project should adopt one. The software engineering management plan is a good place in which to state such a policy.

Managing an activity implies that adequate funding and resources have been provided to perform it. Individuals with experience in the application domain and in software engineering should be assigned to develop and manage the requirements. Any tools or other resources needed to support these should be made available. Finally, the staff of any supporting functions, such as configuration management, quality assurance, and validation, should have the background and training needed to perform any special activities needed in support of the requirements management process.

Throughout this chapter the risks and impacts associated with requirements development and management have been discussed. Table 3.10 summarizes those considerations.

3.8 Summary

The software requirements specification represents the users' requirements written from the developers' perspective. They are considered the foundation for any software-intensive project. Software requirements are a critical element of the software development process and can provide a path to success or failure. Errors in requirements that are found early in the development phase cost significantly less than those found in the maintenance phase. Different methods are available to discover and analyze the users' requirements.

The several different categories of requirements include functional, performance, external interfaces, design constraints, and quality attributes. Of these categories, quality attributes that are both measurable and deliverable (that is, they are truly properties of the delivered item rather than the process that produced the item) are often the most difficult to specify.

Requirements can be written using natural language, semiformal notation (graphical representations), or formal notation (mathematical representations). Approaches to writing the document can be structured (process method), object oriented (object method), or formal. The method chosen should be appropriate for the type of requirement being specified, the project, and the development team. The choice of methods should be the joint decision of the requirements engineers, the chief software designer, the project process architect, and

Any additional or changed requirements, independent of their size, will impact planned resources. However, if they correct errors they cannot be ignored.

The project delivery schedule is almost invariably the area most severely impacted by changes to the requirements.

The effect of such rework is magnified because implementation staff must be diverted from other work.

The resulting magnified schedule pressure will impact quality.

Requirements that are unclear, ambiguous, or missing will most likely lead to changes to requirements or rework of the design and implementation.

Clear, professional communication with the customer is critical when issues are identified with the requirements. Bad news is never welcome but muddled bad news is damning.

Developing and writing good requirements demands intelligence, experience, and dedication. The selection of proper staff is critical.

Developing and writing requirements is often viewed as a professional diversion by developers. This reduces the talent pool available and sometimes impacts their motivation if assigned to the task.

The negotiation of proposals to implement change requirements cost time and money. Effort is required for writing, reviewing, approving, and implementing changes. The most senior technical and managerial staff will be diverted from their other duties.

The farther along the project is in its life cycle, the more it will cost to implement a change. The SRS should be under configuration management when the software requirements specification review is held.

Staffing the project prior to finalizing the requirements can be fatal.

Software requirements that are not stable by the time of the detailed design review generally result in a project that is in serious trouble.

The requirements should be complete but not excessive. Excessive detail in requirements constrains the design and often results in rework to both the requirements and the design.

The sources and importance of all requirements should be clearly understood. Otherwise, trade-offs are impossible.

Table 3.10: Considerations for Managing the SRS

the software engineering project manager. These methods can be used in combination with the goal of fully and clearly describing the requirements.

Of necessity, this chapter could do little more than provide an outline of the methods and tools available to a project. It has attempted to inform the software project manager of the major activities that must be completed along with some of the issues that can arise in the course of developing the requirements for a software product. Ultimately, the individuals fulfilling the roles of chief requirements engineer, chief software designer, software process architect, and software project manager must determine the approach that the project will use to develop and document those requirements.

Requirements analysis accounts for between 4 and 10 percent of the total cost of a software project, while largely determining how the remaining 80 to 90 percent of the funding is expended. Proper use of the IEEE standards, together with the selection of appropriate and sound requirements development and documentation methods, will provide a mechanism for controlling the requirements analysis and development process.

Applicable Standards

IEEE Std 830-1998. *IEEE Recommended Practice for Software Requirements Specifications*. IEEE, New York.

IEEE Std 982.1-1988. *IEEE Standard Dictionary of Measures to Produce Reliable Software*. IEEE, New York.

IEEE Std 1058-1998. *IEEE Standard for Project Management Plans*. IEEE, New York.

IEEE Std 1228-1994. *IEEE Standard for Software Safety Plans*. IEEE, New York.

IEEE Std 1233-1998. *Guide for Developing System Requirements Specifications*. IEEE, New York.

IEEE Std 1320.1-1998. *IEEE Standard for Functional Modeling Language—Syntax and Semantics for IDEF0*. IEEE, New York.

IEEE Std 1320.2-1998. *IEEE Standard for Conceptual Modeling Language Syntax and Semantics for IDEF1X97 (IDEFobject)*. IEEE, New York.

Additional References

[Boehm 1981]   Boehm, B. W. (1981). *Software Engineering Economics*. Prentice Hall, Englewood Cliffs, NJ.

[Coad & Yourdon 1991]   Coad, P., and Yourdon, E. (1991). *An Introduction to OOA-Object Oriented Analysis*. Yourdon Press, Englewood Cliffs, NJ.

[Davis 1990]   Davis, A. (1990). *Software Requirements Analysis and Specification*. Prentice Hall, Englewood Cliffs, NJ.

[Davis 1993]   Davis, A. (1993). *Software Requirements Revision Objects, Functions, and States*. Prentice Hall, Englewood Cliffs, NJ.

[Davis 1998]   Davis, A. (1998). "A Comparison of Techniques for the Specification of External System Behavior." *Communications of the ACM*, vol. 31, no. 9, September.

[DeMarco 1979]   DeMarco, T. (1979). *Structured Analysis and System Specification*. Prentice Hall, Englewood Cliffs, NJ.

[Gane & Sarson 1978]   Gane, C., and Sarson, T. (1978). *Structured Systems Analysis: Tools and Techniques*. Prentice Hall, Englewood Cliffs, NJ.

[Glinz 2000]   Glinz, M. (2000). "A Lightweight Approach to Consistency of Scenarios and Class Models." *Proc. IEEE 4th Int'l. Conf. Requirements Engineering*. IEEE Computer Society, Los Alamitos, CA.

[Horl & Aichernig 2000]   Horl, J., and Aichernig, B. (2000). "Requirements Validation of a Voice Communications System Used in Air Traffic Control." *Proc. IEEE 4th Int'l. Conf. Requirements Engineering*. IEEE Computer Society, Los Alamitos, CA.

[NCSC 1988]   National Computer Security Center. (1988). *Glossary of Computer Security Terms*, Fort George G. Meade, MD.

[Parnas 2000]   Parnas, D.L. (2000). "Requirements Documentation: Why a Formal Basis Is Essential." Keynote address to IEEE 4th Int'l. Conf. Requirements Engineering, Schaumburg, IL, July 2000.

[Peters & Pedrycz 1999]   Peters, J.F., and Pedrycz, W. (1999). *Software Engineering: An Engineering Approach*. John Wiley & Sons, New York.

[Svoboda 1997]   Svoboda, C. P. (1997). "Structured Analysis." *Software Requirements Engineering*, 2nd ed., R. H. Thayer and M. Dorfman, eds. IEEE Computer Society Press, Los Alamitos, CA, pp. 255–274.

[Thayer & Dorfman 1997]   Thayer, R. H., and Dorfman M., eds. (1997). *Software Requirements Engineering*, 2nd ed. IEEE Computer Society Press, Los Alamitos, CA.

[Thayer & McGettrick 1993]   Thayer, R. H., and McGettrick, A. D., eds. (1993). *Software Engineering: A European Perspective*. IEEE Computer Society Press, Los Alamitos, CA.

[Wheeler et al. 1997]   Wheeler, D. A., Brykczynski, B., and Meeson, Jr., R. N. (1997). *Software Inspection: An Industry Best Practice*. IEEE Computer Society, Los Alamitos, CA.

[Wordsworth 1992]   Wordsworth, J. B. (1992). *Software Development with Z, A Practical Approach to Formal Methods in Software Engineering*. Addison-Wesley, Menlo Park, CA.

Chapter 4

Software User Documentation

4.1 Introduction

Whenever the release of a new system or technology is scheduled, the need immediately arises for initial training in use of the new system and for technical support to aid in its continued usage. User documentation is intended to support both the initial training phase and ongoing use of systems. The need for quality user documentation has increased to match the increased internal and external complexity of systems. The forms and the media used to deliver the documentation are likewise evolving. As software systems continue to implement more business and social functions this trend will continue, with the attendant needs for documentation constantly changing and evolving. Users must learn how to use these new software systems, both individually and in combinations. As a result, they must be provided with concise, coherent, complete documents that allow them to rapidly begin to use such new systems and to readily find the information needed to continue to operate and maintain those systems.

The objective of software user documentation is to transmit to users the knowledge required to use a software system and to maintain the configuration and health of that system. To achieve this, user documentation must be clear, easy to understand, and relevant to the users, yet at the same time retain its technical accuracy. The ultimate challenge is to make the software useful to the user by merging the perspectives of the user with the operation of the technical product.

The *IEEE Standard for Software User Documentation*, IEEE Standard 1063-1987, provides guidance for developing effective user documentation. This standard lists the minimum requirements for the structure and information content of software user documentation. This standard applies to traditional documentation that helps guide the user to install, operate, or use a software system of any size. Adherence to IEEE Standard 1063-1987 does not preclude the use of additional requirements or standards.

4.2 Objectives

In this chapter you will learn:

- What software user documentation is.

- The different forms of user documentation.

- The importance of software user documentation.

- The role of software configuration management in software user documentation.

- The role of software quality assurance in software user documentation.

- How to determine what software user documentation is needed.

- How to determine the audience for software user documentation.

- The ways in which software user documentation is used.

- The elements of a software user document.

- The contents of a software user document.

- How to manage the document development process.

4.3   Uses and Forms of User Documentation

4.3.1   Purposes of Software User Documentation

IEEE Standard 1063-1987, *IEEE Standard for Software User Documentation*, defines a software user document as a body of material that provides information to users. That is the definition we use here. Throughout this chapter, the terms *software user documentation*, *user documentation*, and *documentation* are used interchangeably.

Historically, the two forms of user documentation for software systems have been (1) online (or internal) user documentation that is a part of the software system itself and (2) offline documentation (or external) that is not. To access online documentation, the system itself has to be in use by the user. Online documentation typically consists of online instructions, help screens, and help dialogs. Offline documentation typically consists of reference manuals, training materials, and user guides. Offline documentation is not restricted to noncomputer media; it simply is not integrated with the operational system.

Documentation is increasingly being delivered and accessed using digital and online means. In some cases such means are little more than substitutes for paper. For example, documents may be created, organized, and formatted using conventional word and document processing tools and then delivered as a CD set, or installed at a Web site for downloading, printing, or passive viewing. This does not affect the fundamental structure and content of the documents. In other cases, entirely new capabilities are provided to users for accessing and organizing the information in the documents, essentially treating the portions of the documents as data or objects in a database.

Because the software system of interest does not have to be running to use external user documentation, the range of media available is, at any given time, broader than that of online systems. External documentation comes in many formats: videotape, DVDs, CDs, computer-based, audio, and paper. The two broad categories of external user documentation are reference and tutorial. Many users will need both types, but with different emphasis. For example, maintenance staff may have need both types, with reference documents being their primary resource but tutorial materials being used to introduce new maintainers to the system. Likewise, marketing personnel would usually be introduced to the system by means of tutorial materials and would use these documents in their own work, having need for only occasional recourse to the reference material when specific, technical answers are needed to respond to the questions of clients.

4.3.2 The Importance of Good Documentation

As stated earlier, software systems and their technology are constantly changing and evolving. New and revised software systems are proliferating at an accelerating rate. Many of these systems are very sophisticated, possessing unique features and interactions, both internal and external to themselves. If customers are to obtain the full value of their investment in such systems, they must be provided with simple, effective user documentation. Software user documentation makes the difference between whether or not a system is accepted and used effectively. Effective user documentation makes software systems more useful by making them more usable.

Despite its importance, the creation of user documentation is often neglected—or not even done at all. Organizations that do attempt to develop good user documentation often find that the documentation, just like the software that it is attempting to describe, must be reworked as the software and its features evolve during development. Worse, in many cases user documentation is an afterthought and done at the last minute, often without adequate communication between the software developers and those creating the documentation. Some firms, citing proprietary or intellectual property concerns, actively resist revealing information on the internal operation of their products even if it would make their products more comprehensible and predictable to their users.

As a result of all of these issues inadequate and incorrect software user documentation is a common and widely acknowledged problem in the industry.

4.3.3 Scope of the Documentation Task

Determining what must be done to create useful, quality, software user documentation for a software product requires a careful examination of what types of documents are needed and who they are intended to help. A number of other questions related to the processes used for production and management of the effort and its products must be considered as well. In this way the effort can be carefully planned, executed, and managed.

First, we must answer the key questions of what types of user documentation are needed, why, and when? The latter two factors are often interrelated, as the reason for creation of an item of user documentation often determines when it is needed. This consideration, along with the development processes used by the product developer, will usually

Document Type	Why Needed	When Needed
Installation instructions	To assist in distribution of system	Before acceptance test
Release notes	To assist in distribution of system	After acceptance test
User/reference manuals	To provide help with use of system	After system test
User training materials	To provide help with use of system	Before installation
Maintenance manuals	To help maintain system	At FCA/PCA

Table 4.1: Example Types of User Documents

determine when a particular document is produced. Thus, installation instructions will usually be needed before the release of a set of maintenance manuals.

Typical examples of the types of user documents needed are given in Table 4.1. The order of events presented in this table assumes that a conventional full-scale development life cycle model is being used by the project. If other models are used (see Chapter 6) then the events in the When Needed column should be adjusted to be consistent with the sequence of events in the project life cycle model. Even for the model used in the example it is advantageous to prepare drafts of some of the documents earlier than Table 4.1 indicates. For example, it is often recommended that the draft user's manual be completed before the requirements review occurs. If a concept of operations (ConOps) document is produced, such a draft document can be produced more readily (see Chapter 2). The ConOps document, if produced, is often of significant value in planning the documentation effort. In addition, for smaller projects primarily focused on human/machine interaction and low algorithmic content, the user's manual may be the sole requirements document produced. Likewise, a single design description document may suffice for purposes of maintenance. Similarly, the installation instructions may be included in the design notes.

Once the types, objectives, and events/dates of the necessary documents have been initially established, the target audience for each item of user documentation must be determined. In reality, the two processes tend to be iterative, because the act of determining the target audience for each document will often show that some other document has been omitted. Nonexclusive categories of target audiences are given in Table 4.2.

Once the documents to be developed have been identified together with their target audiences, the actual production of the materials can be considered. You should consider these typical factors, including any existing processes within the organization:

- The use of style guides or document templates;

- The need for any special tools, such as document design, layout, production, and graphics tools;

Target Groups	Types of Documents
Novice users	Training materials, user guides, help screens
Intermediate users	Training materials, user guides, reference manuals
Data entry clerks	User guides, help screens
Information services staff	Installation instructions
Internal testers	Installation instructions, user guides
Alpha and beta testers	Installation instructions, user guides, help screens
Software engineers	Maintenance manuals
Requirements engineers	User guides

Table 4.2: Example Target Groups

- The types of distribution media needed, such as print, CDs, DVDs, and Web pages; and

- The approaches to be used for each type of documentation and target audience for performing configuration control, especially maintaining consistency between the software product itself and its documentation, and quality assurance, which normally should be performed by or consistent with the projects SQA mechanisms.

Much software is now intended for international distribution and use. The same software system or variations thereof may be used in multiple countries. In some cases the system may not be physically operating within a given country, but will be available internationally through computing networks. This means that some user documents must be translated.

At the most fundamental level, the translation of technical information can be a challenge; indeed, some languages may not even have words that correspond to certain technical words or concepts. At a higher level of sophistication, the online documentation of systems may be required to support multiple languages concurrently. This poses additional complexities for both the user interface and the online documentation. Finally, much of the work of document translation is not performed by the developing organization itself; it is instead performed by subcontractors who specialize in that type of translating. As a result the project quality assurance approach must include verification of the accuracy of the translated documents. This should take into account not only language differences, but also cultural differences that can impact comprehension of the documents.

4.4   Developing Software User Documents

Having defined the necessary types of documentation and the audience, the project can now determine how the documents will be structured, the level of detail, the sources of the information needed to create the documents, and the presentation style. Based on the results of this analysis, the processes and schedule can be established for the development of the documents. The key requirements are each discussed in the following sections.

4.4.1   Determine Required User Documents

To identify the user documents that are required, the software system and its expected users must be identified and defined. This can be done by identifying the software, its user interfaces, and all of the tasks the user is expected to perform with the software. In addition, the overall goals of the developing and using organization must be considered, along with the project's developmental processes.

Overall, the following factors must be considered when determining what documents are required and how they are organized:

- The nature of the product, its intended usage, the environment in which it will be used, and the complexity of the system as seen from an external viewpoint; that is, how complex it is to operate, install, and maintain;

- The level of sophistication of the expected users, installers, and maintainers;

- The internal size and complexity of the product, together with the technologies used to build and maintain it;

- The developmental process used to build the software product, which usually determines when the information is available and, for some documents, what is needed;

- The total cost and schedule of the program;

- Any contractual or regulatory requirements; and

- The user organizations' future plans for using, maintaining, and enhancing the product.

A key step is to identify the audiences. Software user documentation must be keyed to the needs of the user. Each intended audience of users has to be identified. The different levels of computer experience and the different ways in which users interact with software systems have to be considered when designing software user documentation. Identifying and defining the user audience is discussed below.

After the software system and audience have been identified, the next step is to determine the appropriate document set for each audience. A *document set* is defined as a document or group of documents that offers its audience the information needed to use or operate a software product. Each document of the set may be one or more volumes depending on the amount of information to be presented. It is often useful to categorize the documents at this time according to their usage modes (that is, how they will be used). Explicitly assigning primary and secondary usage modes to each document is often of material assistance in determining what information should be included in the document and how it should be structured and delivered.

Identifying the users determines *who* will use the documents (and helps set the expectation for their needs and capabilities), and identifying the usage modes determines *how* they will use the documents.

Thus, the document set must be designed to meet the needs of the users. The presentation style and level of detail should be tailored for the intended audience and the method of delivery: offline or online, external or internal, and with what delivery tools. When a document set must be prepared for audiences with widely differing needs, the documentation writer should use one of the following approaches:

1. Separate materials according to the needs of specific audiences. The needs of specific audiences should be covered in the introduction to help users pick out the sections of interest; or

2. Separate documents or document sets for each specific audience.

4.4.2 Determine the Audience

Software user documentation is designed to help users use software systems. It is extremely important to know the audience of users before any documents are written. A *user* is defined as a person who uses software to perform some task.

Users can form different audiences based on their level of computer experience and their informational needs. Each intended audience is identified and the documentation is planned and written to meet the needs of that particular audience. The identified audience dictates the way the document is structured, the level of detail, and the presentation style.

To get a better understanding of the audience, the documentation writer needs to consider the following areas:

*   *Education*—What is the educational level of the audience? What is their reading level?

*   *Attitude*—What is the attitude of the audience? Do they have a fear of computers? Are they resistant to change?

*   *Level of computer sophistication*—Brockmann [Brockmann 1990] identified five levels of computer sophistication: parrot, novice, intermediate, expert, and intermittent. The characteristics of the five levels are depicted in Table 4.3.

*   *Familiarity with the application.*

Computer Sophistication Level	Characteristics
Parrot	Little or no computer experience Deals with small chunks of information Low level of confidence Conscious performers Do not question or synthesize direction
Novice	Some computer experience Begins to understand isolated concepts Uses concrete examples Relies on system defaults Function or component oriented
Intermediate	Novice user with a few months of computer experience Begins to link isolated concepts Task-oriented Uses defaults and options

Expert	Evolves from intermediate user over a
	   period of months
	Understands relationships between
	   isolated concepts
	High level of confidence
	Understands abstract language
	Automatic performer
	Goal-oriented

Intermittent	May be a parrot, novice, intermediate, or
	   expert user on other systems
	Works infrequently with this software system
	Relies heavily on system menus,
	   messages, and commands

Table 4.3: Levels of Computer Sophistication [Brockmann 1990]

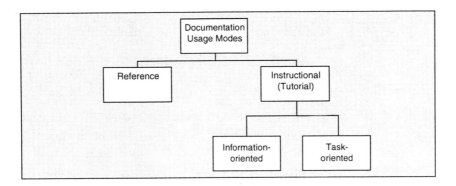

Figure 4.1: Documentation Usage Modes

4.4.3   Determine Usage Modes

In general, software users need documentation to learn about the software (instructional or tutorial mode) or to look up information about the software (reference mode). Instructional mode documents may be either information or task oriented. In addition, the usage mode should be described according to what delivery tools will be used to deliver the information to the user. Figure 4.1 depicts the different documentation usage modes.

4.4.3.1   Instructional Usage Mode

Documents intended for use in the instructional mode provide users with the information needed to understand the software system so that they can use or maintain it. The information is presented in a step-by-step manner, including examples that serve to reinforce the concepts and operations presented. Accurately determining the audience is especially important to documents that will be used for instructional purposes. Instructional mode documents can be either information or task oriented.

Information-oriented documents provide the reader with information needed to understand the system and its functions. This (background) information orients the user and helps her to use the software properly. Here are some examples of information-oriented instructional documents:

- Overviews;

- Theory of operation manuals; and

- Tutorials.

Task-oriented documents show the reader how to complete tasks or how achieve goals. They describe procedures needed to perform specific tasks or goals. Consider these examples of task-oriented instructional documents:

- Diagnostic procedures manuals;

- Operations manuals; and

- Software installation manuals.

4.4.3.2 Reference Usage Mode

Documents intended for use in the reference mode are designed to allow the user to rapidly locate information about the system. Reference documents should be organized to facilitate random access to the information. Reference documentation is more detailed and more technical than instructional documentation. Examples of reference mode documents include the following:

- Command manuals;

- Error message manuals;

- Program calls manuals;

- Quick reference guides;

- Software tool manuals; and

- Utilities manuals.

4.5 Structure and Content of a Software User Document

The structure and content needed for user documents is summarized in this section. Mandatory information is to be included in all documents, unless the information is not applicable. A software document has 12 basic components. Table 4.4 lists the requirements for each specific component of a software user document if adherence to the IEEE Standard 1063-1987 is desired. Components are listed as mandatory or optional. Additional information may be added as needed.

4.6 Producing Software User Documents

The process and tasks of producing or developing user documents should be approached and managed like those of any other developmental item. The key process steps, assuming a conventional development model, are as follows:

1. The requirements for the documentation set should be established.

2. The document set should be designed, allocating the requirements to the various documents.

Component	Single-Volume Document		Multivolume Document	
	8 Pages or less	More than 8 Pages	First Volume	Other Volume
Title page	Mandatory	Mandatory	Mandatory	Mandatory
Restrictions	Mandatory	Mandatory	Mandatory	Mandatory
Warranties	Reference[a]	Reference	Reference	Reference
Table of contents	Optional	Mandatory	Mandatory	Mandatory
List of illustrations	Optional	Optional	Optional	Optional
Introduction				
Audience description	Reference	Mandatory	Mandatory	Reference
Applicability	Mandatory	Mandatory	Mandatory	Mandatory
Purpose	Reference	Mandatory	Mandatory	Reference
Document usage	Reference	Mandatory	Mandatory	Reference
Related documents	Reference	Reference	Reference[b]	Reference
Conventions	Mandatory	Mandatory	Mandatory	Reference
Problem reporting	Reference	Mandatory	Mandatory	Reference
Body of document				
Instructional mode	c	c	c	c
Reference mode	c	c	c	c
Error conditions	Reference	Reference	Reference	Reference
Appendixes	Optional	Optional	Optional	Optional
Bibliography	Mandatory	Mandatory	Mandatory[d]	Mandatory[d]
Glossary	Mandatory	Mandatory	Mandatory[d]	Mandatory[d]
Index	e	e	Mandatory[d]	Mandatory[d]

[a]Reference: Include the section or a reference to where the information can be found within the document set.

[b]Address the relationship to other volumes.

[c]Every document has a body; each document set should address the instructional and reference needs of the intended audience.

[d]Mandatory in at least one volume in the document set, with references to information in the other volumes.

[e]An index is optional for documents under 40 pages and mandatory for documents of 40 or more pages.

Table 4.4: Software User Document Components [IEEE Standard 1063-1987]

3. The individual documents should be designed (outlined). The design should be re-viewed and approved when satisfactory.

4. The effort, schedule, and data/information needed to complete each document should be estimated using the outlines.

5. Any support from organizations outside of the document development group should be clearly identified and coordinated with those external organizations. The document development schedule should represent this external dependency.

6. A draft version of each document should be created. This should be reviewed and, when satisfactory, approved. Any necessary changes for creating the documents should be made to the schedule. The documents should be managed using the project's SCM procedures.

7. A final version of each document should be created, reviewed, and, when satisfactory, approved.

8. The documents should be tested using pilot or trial usage.

9. Individuals responsible for developing the documents and with providing the necessary information should be identified.

The scope of the documents will determine the amount of effort required to complete these steps. As with any development effort, the management oversight and effort should be appropriate to the criticality and magnitude of the task.

Because the above process creates both a draft and a final version, it is implicitly iterative. More explicitly, however, the above process outline mirrors the waterfall development flow. In most programs the document development process should follow the development model used to produce the software itself. Thus, if the software system is being delivered in increments of greater capability, then the user documents must be released in similar increments. The chapter on software life cycle models (Chapter 6) describes the development models currently in use in the industry.

In the case of online documentation systems or features, the document development task is often entangled with that of developing the user interface. In that case it is recommended that the structural requirements of any dialogs needed for the online elements of the documentation effort be included in the requirements review of the user interface. To ensure that the outlines/designs for the documents (that is, those documentation components that will be delivered online) are developed within a known delivery framework, they should be developed after the top-level design of the user interface is completed. If this is not feasible for scheduling reasons, then the document outlines should at the very least be reexamined after the user interface is designed.

To develop a coherent, consistent set of user documents, the project should adopt a style guide. This will also assist the project in implementing the requirements of the IEEE standards described in earlier sections of this chapter. The style guide should be managed and used in the same manner as are software design and coding guidelines or standards.

4.6.1   Determining Requirements for the Document Set

In Section 4.4 of this chapter the types and classes of documents were discussed, along with how to determine which documents are needed to support a software system. If required the table should reference any documents, such as the ConOps, systems and software requirements, or statement of work, that are needed to develop the subject documents. Using these data the document set should be designed, clearly identifying which documents satisfy which requirements. Usually, several documents will contribute to the satisfaction of any single requirement.

In the case of online documentation and help systems, third-party software systems often provide the necessary functionality to the user interface of the system. If the project has elected to use such a system to deliver part or all of the documentation, this should be considered in the design of the document set and the allocation of requirements to the individual documentation components. The developing organization must clearly understand the data and testing required by such online documentation tools prior to committing to a cost and schedule estimate.

Likewise, if parts of the software system itself are composed of off-the-shelf components, the role those components play in the operation and maintenance of the system must be carefully examined to see if the documentation effort is affected. In the case of many such components, specific information in the user documentation is not normally needed, with the possible exception of the maintenance manuals. A typical example is the configuration of commercial databases. Care should be taken at this step and later during reviews to ensure that no unnecessary or copyrighted information is included in the individual documents. Where such information is needed, the reader should be referred to the user documentation of the third-party component.

If the system includes third-party software that was developed under subcontract for the project, the information needs of the final systems documents should be reflected in the subcontract.

For each document a table should be created listing the items described in Table 4.4. Next, using the structure presented in that table an outline of each document should be created. A page budget should be estimated for each document, describing the size of the document. For training materials the number of slides and the number of hours of training should be estimated. The table, annotated with estimates, should be managed consistent with the project's configuration management practices. The intent of this table is to form the outline requirements for the development of the document. It will also form the basis of the cost and schedule estimates for the document.

Each table should be reviewed, following the procedures described in the SPMP, SLCMP, SCMP, SQAP, or any other applicable plan being used by the project. The objective of the review should be to determine the adequacy of the table as a basis for the later development of the document. The review of the document outline should include appropriate participation from the following functions:

- Document development;

- Software development;

- Quality assurance;

- Requirements engineering;

- Real or surrogate users; and

- Marketing or customer relations.

Subsequent to the review, the table should be updated. If extensive revisions are required, the table should be rereviewed. Finally, the structure and coverage of the entire document set should be reexamined for consistency and adequacy by doing a review of all outline tables. This review should carefully examine the question of when the supporting information needed to create the document will be available. This review should include representation from the functions listed above, together with project management.

4.6.2   Estimating and Scheduling Document Development

Using the outline described above, as supplemented by the page/slide budget, the total labor required to draft and finalize each document should be estimated. The labor needed to develop documents, like any other software item, can be estimated in various ways. Model-based methods usually estimate the total cost of producing the document set for an entire program. Based on the page or presentation time/slide count of the materials an estimate can be produced for each document. However, this method is most accurate if historical actual costs are available for producing individual documents.

Cost Input	Typical Minimum	Typical Maximum
Pages of documentation	1 hour/page	5 hours/page
Number of slides	0.1 hour/page	1 hour/page
Hour of training	20 hours of development/ hour training	80 hours of development/ hour training

Table 4.5: Range of Productivity in Document Development

Table 4.5 gives the range of productivity seen in several organizations for the effort of creating the documents—draft and final versions—assuming the necessary information is available to the document writers. Each organization should use historical costs to calibrate its own document development productivity.

In each of the three rows of Table 4.5, the minimum rate typically occurs when the authors are familiar with the material (or the information is readily available) and the material is of low technical content. The maximum rate typically occurs when the authors are not familiar with the subject matter and it is complex. Neither rate includes the costs of providing the authors with source data, nor does it include the costs of conducting the reviews of the documents. These should be estimated separately.

Because many documents exceed 100 pages, and many training courses last days, it is clear that considerable labor expenditures are required to produce useful documents and training materials.

The skill grade of the individuals needed to develop the various portions of the document must be considered when determining the costs of developing the documentation. Thus, sections requiring detailed technical knowledge will command different skills than those needed to develop informative graphics or produce a usable index.

The skill set needed for each section should be identified and used to produce the labor estimate, both for developing a cost estimate, as well as for supporting the detailed scheduling of the effort. This estimate should include any supporting effort that must be supplied by other groups in order to complete the development of the document. The typical example is technical support from the development or requirements groups.

The labor estimates derived above, together with the requirements for other supporting information and the availability of staff, should be used to schedule the development of the document, consistent with the procedures described in the SPMP. Based on the size of the document and effort required to develop it, the scheduling of the development task should be broken down into discrete activities. The chapters or sections of the document often provide a natural framework for this decomposition but care should be taken not to schedule tasks in excess of 100 hours without providing intermediate visibility. Dependencies between the chapters and sections, along with any dependencies on other documents, should be carefully considered.

Finally, as with any cost and schedule estimation effort, care and good judgment are necessary: Too low an estimate will produce either a cost or schedule overrun or sparse, poor-quality documents. Too high an estimate will result in inefficient behavior or excessive, verbose documentation. See Chapter 12 for a further discussion of these risks.

4.6.3 Managing the Document Development Effort

Once the document development activities have been scheduled, they should be managed using the same methods used to manage the development of other software items. As the document is developed the components should be managed, following the SPMP and SCMP, as would any other software item. Depending on the size of the document, individual chapter or section reviews should be held as each is completed. The attendees of the review should be as described in Section 4.6.1. Metrics, such as readiness for a review, or successful completion of a review, can be used to gain visibility into the document development effort.

As the document nears completion in draft form, a comprehensive review of the entire document should be performed. The complete, integrated document should be examined. The software quality assurance function should ensure that it can be reconstructed from its various sources and that those sources are under CM control, following the program policies and procedures.

4.6.4 Trial and Pilot Usage

Like most other software items, the final proof of the usability of a document or training materials occurs when the document or materials are in actual use. Prior to use by a customer, it is highly advisable that the documents be subjected to either trial or pilot use. Trial use typically consists of a user attempting to perform the tasks described in a document (such as a user's manual or guide) on an individual basis, providing an evaluation of the item on trial.

Pilot usage typically consists of a more structured activity, involving multiple users. It is often applied to training courses but is not restricted to that application. In some cases the pilot or trial usage may require the multiple document items be available.

Prior to pilot or trial usage, evaluation instruments should be prepared so that meaningful, consistent data can be obtained. In addition to prepared questions the user should be given the opportunity to comment in an ad hoc, written manner. For each pilot or trial usage, user feedback should be collected, analyzed, and archived. These data are the equivalent of system or customer acceptance data for the software system itself and should be viewed with the same importance. Serious deficiencies should be corrected prior to general release of the document(s) to the customers, consistent with the change control processes of the project.

Finally, if the software system is needed to conduct the trial or pilot usage of the document, then the version of the document used in the trial must be consistent with the version of the software system. The final release of the documents should be concurrent with that of the software system they support.

4.7 Summary

User documentation, together with a systems user interface, is one of the most highly visible aspects of a software system. High-quality, functional documentation can materially improve the utility and reputation of a software system. Likewise, poor or nonfunctional documentation can negatively impact the reputation of the system and its maker.

With the growth of the international market for software systems the importance of user documentation has done nothing but increase, along with the complexity of the documentation development task. Likewise, the use of third-party software items in the system must be recognized and included in the document development process.

The IEEE standards provide a framework for developing quality documents in response to the need for high-quality, functional documentation. The project should adopt a style guide for use in developing a document set with a consistent look and feel. This will materially assist the user navigating within and between the documents.

The development of user documents should be managed like any other development method, applying the practices described in the project's SPMP, SCMP, SQAP, and SLCMP. The document set should be designed together with the individual documents. The effort must be broken into discrete, manageable activities, and the results of each activity appropriately reviewed. Finally, the documents should be tested by means of pilot or trial usage.

Applicable Standards

IEEE Std 610.12-1990. *IEEE Standard Glossary of Software Engineering Terminology.* IEEE, New York.

IEEE Std 730-1998. *IEEE Standard for Software Quality Assurance Plans.* IEEE, New York.

IEEE Std 828-1998. *IEEE Standard for Software Configuration Management Plans.* IEEE, New York.

IEEE Std 1063-1987. *IEEE Standard for Software User Documentation.* IEEE, New York.

Additional References

[Barker 1998]   Barker, T. T. (1998). *Writing Software Documentation: A Task-Oriented Approach.* Allyn and Bacon, Boston.

[Brockmann 1990]   Brockmann, R. J. (1990). *Writing Better Computer Documentation: From Paper to Hypertext.* John Wiley & Sons, New York.

[Crown 1992]   Crown, J. (1992). *Effective Computer User Documentation.* Van Nostrand Reinhold, New York.

[Dorfman & Thayer 1997] Dorfman, M., and Thayer, R. H., eds. (1997). *Software Engineering.* IEEE Computer Society Press, Los Alamitos, CA.

[Katzin 1985]   Katzin, E. (1985). *How to Write a Really Good User's Manual.* Van Nostrand Reinhold, New York.

[Simpson & Casey 1988] Simpson, H., and Casey, S. M. (1988). *Developing Effective User Documentation: A Human Factors Approach.* McGraw-Hill, New York.

Chapter 5

Software Verification and Validation

5.1   Introduction

Society is increasingly dependent on systems in which software plays a significant role. Health care, financial, transportation, and military systems all rely on software to perform or support their functions. In many such systems, inappropriate operation of the software has the potential to create catastrophic conditions that can result in economic loss, human suffering, and even death.

In the course of developing the final, executable software and associated databases, software development projects produce a variety of complex, intermediate products. These include specification and design documents, the source code for the software, and test plans and results. Because these items play a significant role in the development of the final, executable software, they, together with the final software, should be evaluated in order to control or eliminate the risk of the negative consequences listed above.

Such evaluations often apply the dual concepts and methods of validation and verification. In everyday usage, the two words are virtual synonyms, but in the technical and contractual world they are not. In those domains validation and verification are defined as follows:

- *Verification:* The determination by objective, repeatable methods that an item satisfies its stated requirements.

- *Validation:* The determination by objective, repeatable methods that an item can be used for a specific purpose.

Verification is typically performed first, producing data products that can then be evaluated by a validation process. However, this is not axiomatic. The objectives and circumstances of any particular effort will determine what should be done operationally.

A third concept, which is applied purely in the contractual and programmatic domains, is that of accreditation:

- *Accreditation:* The official acceptance of a validated item by an authority for use within its span of control.

Because accreditation is not a technical activity and is not discussed in the IEEE standards it is not discussed in detail in the later sections of this chapter but is mentioned where applicable. When selecting and planning the verification and validation activities for a specific project it is important always to keep in mind the ultimate objectives of those activities. Accreditation often encompasses those objectives.

The concepts of verification and validation (V&V) as traditionally applied and as embodied in IEEE Standard 1012-1998, *IEEE Standard for Software Verification and Validation*, were developed for projects whose products would be used in life- or mission-critical systems or situations. Although the general concepts are not specific to software items, the discussion in the standard is restricted to such items.

Over time V&V has proven to be a powerful tool with multiple benefits when properly applied to development projects. Verification and validation can:

- Ensure that desired properties (features, quality, etc.) are planned for and ultimately built into the system.

- Reduce the volatility of requirements.

- Reveal errors earlier in the software life cycle, giving designers time to develop a comprehensive solution rather than last minute "fixes."

- Provide specific, structured, and objective data to management for use in decision making at key points in the project life cycle.

- Reduce the total costs of ownership over the products' life cycle, especially during operation and maintenance.

Achieving these benefits is neither guaranteed nor free. As with any other activity, V&V efforts can miscarry. They can fail to achieve their fundamental technical objectives. They can take on a life of their own under the stewardship of "true believers," demoralizing the staff trying to build the product. This should not happen.

In addition, incremental costs are associated with V&V activities, including not only the direct cost of staffing the V&V effort but also the impact to the rest of the software project. The direct and indirect costs of performing a vigorous V&V program can represent between 5 and 40 percent of the total project budget, depending on the nature and size of the application [Boehm 1981, Marciniak 1994, Neal et al. 1997]. These costs and the associated schedules must be included in the applicable cost and schedule estimates of the project and then managed as the program goes forward.

In other words, like any activity, the V&V effort must be properly planned, documented, and managed so that the benefits are obtained and the problems avoided. The key instruments for achieving this are the software verification and validation plan (SVVP), a systematic ongoing management effort, and competent staff.

To clarify the definitions given above, as well as to motivate the discussion, three major examples are discussed next, following which the concepts and content of the IEEE standard are described and discussed. Last, the form and content of the SVVP are described, together with suggestions for planning the V&V effort.

5.2 Objectives

In this chapter you will learn:

- The basic processes of software verification and validation (V&V)

- The applicable IEEE standards for the software V&V plan

- The difference between quality assurance and V&V

- The definition and use of integrity and independence levels in V&V activities

- What is necessary to manage a V&V effort

- How V&V processes relate to the software life cycle the uses of the five software V&V analyses: interface, risk, hazard, criticality, and traceability

- How to scope a software V&V effort

- The test planning, design, and implementation efforts needed to implement a V&V effort

- The reporting activities required by a V&V effort

- What documentation is required to perform a V&V effort

5.3 Verification and Validation Concepts and Examples

5.3.1 Basic Concepts

Verification and validation is a disciplined managerial and technical activity that helps ensure that delivered software will operate as specified in the software requirements and as needed by the user. This is accomplished through a proactive process of analysis, review, and test. These activities are conducted in parallel with development activities to objectively ensure that the software meets its goals of correctness, quality, performance, schedule compliance, and usability.

In software development, *verification* is the method used to ensure that the product of any activity (the item) or phase complies with the requirements of that activity or phase for correctness, completeness, consistency, and accuracy and that it will support the next activity or phase. In other words, the item implements the software requirements and the plan correctly.

Validation, on the other hand, ensures that the product is in agreement with its intended use—that the software performs according to system (as distinct from software) requirements. In other words, validation ensure that the software fulfills the users' needs, that it is the correct software product. For this reason the major validation activities occur late in the project life cycle, usually beginning with integration and test and continuing through to the end of the project.

5.3.2   A Safety-Critical System

To illustrate the general concepts of V&V, along with their relationship to quality assurance functions, consider the following example in which software plays no role.

Suppose that a new type of electronic equipment is to be installed in a particular model of commercial airliner. Before this can happen many tests of the new equipment must be performed, one of the primary of which is an evaluation of the electromagnetic emissions of the new equipment. The concern, of course, is that such emissions might interfere with the safe operation of other aircraft systems. The equipment under discussion might be off-the-shelf or designed specifically for the particular aircraft. The entire process of verification, validation, and accreditation for this item would be as follows.

- Test the electronic equipment for electrical emissions using a documented process in an approved test facility. This testing may be conducted by the parties performing the verification or by developer of the electronic equipment. In either case, a quality assurance function will have oversight responsibility to ensure that the testing is conducted in accordance with the documented process. Other tests will be conducted to provide data for other areas of concern, as required by the aircraft design authority (typically the original manufacturer). Usually, because the test processes are standardized by the industry, the equipment will only be tested once and the results applied to all aircraft.

- Evaluate the results of the tests to determine if the electronic equipment complies with the requirements of the specific aircraft for electrical emissions, along with any other areas of evaluation. This evaluation is typically done by a panel of avionics experts acting on behalf of the aircraft design authority, and it constitutes the verification activity.

  In the course of performing the evaluation, other sources of data can be used. For example, the verification effort could review the design, or a verification report produced during the design activity, to evaluate how the emissions would change over conditions of varying temperature. The V&V procedures of the aircraft design authority would determine if this step is necessary or allowed. In any case, the verification activity will conclude with the production of a report describing and evaluating all results, including any noncompliance issues. This process would likewise be monitored by a quality assurance organization, typically that of the aircraft design authority. Again, the objective of the quality assurance oversight is to ensure that documented evaluation procedures are followed.

- Review the verification report and validate whether or not the new equipment can be safely installed in the specific aircraft. This review is conducted by the aircraft authority. If the results of this validation are positive the aircraft authority will submit their recommendation to the appropriate air safety authority,[1] requesting approval to operate the aircraft with the new electronic equipment installed. Once again, this activity will be monitored for conformance to procedure by a quality assurance function, potentially that of the air safety authority.

- The appropriate air safety authority reviews the request and, if it accepts the recommendation of the aircraft authority that the aircraft will be safe to operate with the new electronic equipment installed, issues a certificate of airworthiness for this specific aircraft configuration. This accreditation completes the process.

This example demonstrates the classical features of V&V when applied to testing life-critical equipment:

- The activities are carefully partitioned between separate, independent entities.

- The designers and implementers of the equipment play little role in the process. Their involvement is limited to the testing and even that is optional and of a support nature.

- The quality assurance functions monitor the process to ensure that it is being conducted according to procedures. QA does not make technical judgments.

- Earlier in the design process the developers may well have used an informal V&V technique such as analysis or test to verify that subsystem specifications complied with the system specification, or that the design of the equipment complied with its specifications. These efforts may have produced other data that could be included in the final, formal V&V evaluation.

The processes used to verify and validate nuclear power plants, ordinance, and medical equipment are generally similar. Quite often such equipment contains software, but this is often transparent to the V&V processes since they are performed at the system level. However, sometimes software makes up the entire system. The following examples illustrate this.

5.3.3   A Safety-Critical Software Application

Suppose that a space launch facility desires to issue a contract for the development of a software application that will be used as a fragment scattering predictor. This predictor will be used to determine how fragments of a rocket will be dispersed in the event that the range safety officer commands the self-destruction of the rocket. The objective is to support the range safety officer in determining the best time to issue the self-destruct command in the

---

[1]By international agreement this is the civil aviation authority of the country in which the manufacturer resides. In the United States this is the Federal Aviation Administration. In the United Kingdom, it is the Civil Aviation Authority.

event the launch attempt miscarries. A hazard analysis shows that incorrect operation of this application could result in serious injury or loss. Examination of records from previous launch attempts at this and other facilities shows that the likelihood of this is not negligible.

Based on the determination that the hazard exists and is real, the management of the facility decides to issue two contracts. The first contract issued is for the development of the software requirements specification (SRS). The second contract is for the verification and validation of the SRS once it has been produced by the first contract. Either or both of the V&V evaluations could be performed by external organizations working under contract to the launch facility management or by groups selected from within the launch facility itself. These internal groups might or might not be part of the group that developed the SRS. Because of the criticality of this application, it is to be expected that the evaluations should be conducted with the greatest possible degree of technical and managerial independence. As a result, management decides to use two separate contractors, one to develop the SRS and the second to perform independent V&V evaluations.

Both of these contracts must complete successfully prior to soliciting bids for the development of the software. The intent is to include the SRS as part of the final bidder package.

The base technical information supplied to the first contractor might include the following:

1. The likely range of properties of the rockets the facility will launch, such as the physical dimensions of the rockets, their mass, fuel consumption rates, engine thrust curves, their controllability, and the location of the self-destruction charges.

2. The type, quality, and expected range of meteorological data at various altitudes that will be available at the time of launch.

3. The operational data available to range safety officers when they are likely to make a self-destruct decision. In particular, the accuracy of the data describing the location and direction of motion of the rocket.

4. A description of the modes of usage of the system, including the preexisting computer system on which the application will execute. This kind of information could be found in, for example, an operational concept document.

These data will be used by the first contractor in developing the SRS. Before the SRS is released for bids to software development organizations the second contractor will evaluate it using V&V techniques. Verification in this case would consist of an independent analysis of the SRS, the objective of which is to show that it is consistent with the base technical information. Validation would consist of another analysis of the SRS, the objective being to show that if a system is built according to the SRS it can be safely used at the launch facility. The hazard and risk analyzes performed earlier would be used to determine the scope of the V&V efforts.

The distinction between verification and validation, in this case, is that the *verification* of the SRS is restricted to comparing the SRS to the base technical data used to create it, whereas the *validation* of the SRS can consider more information. Of course, there is no point in performing the validation if the verification is not first successful. At the same time, the verification of the SRS might be successful, but the validation might not be. This implies that the base information used to derive the SRS was not complete. The remedy, most likely, would be to supplement this information and regenerate the SRS.

The role of the quality assurance function during these V&V efforts would be to monitor them to ensure that the procedures documented and referenced in the appropriate V&V plans are followed. The form and content of such plans are discussed in subsequent sections of this chapter.

When both the validation and verification activities have been completed—and have produced positive conclusions—the management of the launch facility can review the reports and, if they are acceptable, release the SRS to the procurement function. This is the accreditation step for this item.

Later in the development process the design, source code, or the final executable can be examined using applicable V&V processes. For example, consider the test process. *Verification* techniques can be used to evaluate if test plan coverage is complete, consistent, and traceable to requirements. *Validation* techniques can be used to determine if results obtained from performing the tests described in the test plan are consistent with its planned use at the launch facility. Again, either of these evaluations could be performed by the development group itself, by another group from within the developing organization, or by an independent group from outside the developing organization.

Likewise, during the design phase, the design can be evaluated to verify that it complies with the SRS precisely. Another evaluation of the design could validate that it is suitable to hand over to the implementation team.

Which of the many products of the specification, design, and implementation processes are examined using such V&V processes, as well as how the evaluations are structured organizationally, is a judgment that must be made based on the level of integrity desired.

5.3.4   A Business-Critical Software Application

As a final example, suppose that a company is developing a business-to-business (B2B) Web site. In addition to the features offered by the site, its reliability and security are critical. The users must be confident that their business data will not be exposed to unauthorized parties. They must also be confident that the data will not be lost and that the Web site will be available to their suppliers and to themselves. These properties, together with a list of applicable Web protocols and the desired functions, are described in the SRS of the application. Management has decided that a key selling point of the new B2B Web site will be its reliability and security capabilities.

While the SRS can, in general, be evaluated for correctness, completeness, and consistency, it can also be specifically evaluated to verify that the Web protocols and functions together do not create a conflict with the stated reliability and security requirements. Subsequently, the degree to which the specified maintenance procedures support the stated reliability and security requirements can be evaluated in a further verification step, while their suitability can be later validated using operational scenarios. Because of the importance given to these efforts, a specific V&V plan tailored to these objectives is developed and approved by management.

Later, the design itself can be evaluated to verify that it does indeed implement the stated security requirements and that it does not contain any features or protocol capabilities that are not contained in the SRS. Likewise, in a validation step, the design can be evaluated against the operational scenarios and also evaluated for suitability for implementation.

Depending on the technical capabilities of the organizations and the degree of independence desired by management, each of these evaluations can be performed by internal or external groups. The degree of product integrity desired plays a critical role in making that decision.

5.3.5   Relationship of Validation and Verification to Developmental Processes

As the examples show, many activities that might be viewed as V&V steps can occur when performing normal development activities. For example, in the IEEE standard on software requirements specifications the major properties that any SRS should possess are described. It is reasonable to assume that in the course of developing the SRS the authors will from time to time review their work product in an effort to verify that it does indeed possess those properties. It is also reasonable to assume that they would want to validate that the SRS describes a system that meets the intended need.

Evaluations of this type should be viewed primarily as an element of the organization's developmental processes and procedures. Their objective is to ensure that the work in progress is being done correctly and is producing, as far as the development team can tell, the right item. The question is this: Are they also V&V activities, even if secondarily?

The answer is yes, but the V&V is of a particular type. In later sections of this chapter, the various types of V&V activities are discussed, together with their relationship to the integrity level that is desired.

If this type of activity constituted the entire V&V effort, it would be reasonable not to generate a SVVP, but to instead describe the activities in the software life cycle model plan (SLCMPP). Even if this is the case, IEEE Standard 1012-1998, the *IEEE Standard for Software Verification and Validation* should be used as a guide to properly structure the relevant sections of the SLCMP. However, if the application is judged to be of sufficient criticality, the standard stipulates that more formal V&V activities be performed in addition to those intrinsic to the organization's developmental processes.

5.3.6 Relationship of Validation and Verification to Quality Assurance

In the previous examples, we stated that the function of quality assurance is to ensure that the organization performing the work does so in accordance with the documented methods and procedures of the project. This is completely consistent with IEEE Standard 730-1998, the *IEEE Standard for Software Quality Assurance Plans* described elsewhere in this book. Historically, however, there has been some confusion. Ted Lewis [Lewis 1992] compared 32 generic V&V activities, noting that more than two-thirds were not included in typical software quality assurance (SQA) activities. This is because V&V and SQA have different perspectives.

SQA is an internal methodology that deals primarily with adherence to standards and the flow of products from the developer to the customer. SQA does not evaluate the software itself for adherence to technical specifications, including those for safety, security, and quality, nor for functional and performance requirements. V&V activities fulfill that role.

V&V efforts focus on the technical attributes of the products of a project and its developmental processes. V&V provides the detailed engineering assessments needed to evaluate how well an item meets its technical specifications and its intended use. If organized properly V&V and SQA actually complement each other with little overlap, providing a comprehensive assurance program for software development efforts.

5.4 Defining the Objectives

The three examples and the subsequent discussion illustrate some considerations that must be evaluated when planning and performing V&V activities using IEEE Standard 1012-1998:

- *The selected integrity level.* The standard defines four levels of software integrity, which describe the criticality of the software, ranging from high integrity to low integrity.

- *The minimum V&V tasks recommended for the selected integrity level.* The standard also includes a table of optional V&V tasks that allows the user to tailor the V&V effort to address specific project needs and application characteristics.

- *The necessary intensity and rigor needed to perform the various V&V tasks.* The intensity and rigor applied to the V&V tasks will vary with the integrity level. The scope of the analysis across both normal and abnormal operating conditions determines the intensity, while rigor refers to the degree to which formal techniques and recording procedures are used, as well as the degree of technical and managerial independence required.

- *The detailed criteria for the V&V tasks.* The criteria to be applied when specifying V&V tasks, including minimum criteria for correctness, consistency, completeness, accuracy, readability, and testability are described in the standard, including a list of the required inputs and outputs for each task.

- *V&V tasks for systems.* If system-level issues are relevant, non-software-specific V&V tasks must be performed. Such system-level V&V tasks include hazard analysis, risk analysis, migration assessment, and retirement assessment. Specific systems issues are contained in the individual V&V task criteria.

- *The role of V&V in projects.* The possible relationships and interactions between V&V activities and the other tasks of development projects are outlined.

- *The structure and content of verification and validation plans.* The format of V&V plans is described.

By addressing these issues, the standard both structures and simplifies the task of selecting and documenting the V&V activities needed for a particular item and project. The IEEE standard contains specific guidance on each of these topics and is discussed next.

5.4.1   Determining the Scope of the Effort

To meaningfully apply the standard and create an appropriate V&V plan, we must first determine the scope of the effort. The factors that fundamentally determine the scope and the technical activities needed to complete the effort are as follows:

- *The nature of the product, what hazards might it create and how it is being built.* What is the operational environment? What hazards can be introduced by the application? What technology is being used to build the product and what risks are reduced or magnified by that technology?

- *The desired integrity level of the software and development processes.* What is the consequence of each specific noncompliance situation? What is the likelihood of such noncompliance?

- *The organizational context.* Who will perform the various tasks? What will be their relationship to the other parties involved with the project?

- *The programmatic context.* What are the project's objectives? What is the intended use of the evaluations? Who is planning the effort and when? What are the cost and schedule limitations?

Each of these topics should be kept in mind as the following sections are read because they discuss the criticality of the application and what that means to the project and product.

5.4.2 The Product and Its Criticality

The intended use of any given software product can vary considerably and, as a result, so can the implications and consequences of its incorrect operation. The IEEE standard under ST 1012 mandates that the SVVP specify a method of classifying the software integrity levels relevant to each deliverable product a project is producing. The criticality of the application and its functions is the fundamental concept on which integrity classification approaches are founded.

Due to the complexity of software systems, it is impossible to completely analyze each and every element of a software product or project. The logical permutations rapidly become seemingly infinite. Therefore, when planning the V&V effort, those areas or subjects of high risk and complexity that have the potential to cause significant loss must be identified. This is not to say that other areas should be ignored, but rather that the level of resource commitment should be greatest for the critical areas. That criticality is reflected in the integrity levels and in the effort applied to achieving that integrity.

Criticality analysis is the process used to identify, evaluate and categorize subjects and areas within the software product. Specifically, it is:

> A structured evaluation of the software characteristics (e.g., safety, security, complexity, performance) for severity of impact of system failure, system degradation, or failure to meet software requirements or system objectives. [IEEE Standard 1012 1998]

In other words, if the system fails outright, degrades, or does not achieve some software requirements or system objectives, what is the impact to safety, security, or performance? Complexity must be included in the evaluation but it is usually a root cause of problems, not a victim. Marciniak [Marciniak 1994] describes a method that uses system-level block or control flow diagrams. The steps are as follows:

1. Develop a block diagram or control-flow diagram of the system and its software. Each block or control-flow box represents a system or software module.

2. Trace each critical function or quality requirement through the block or control-flow diagram.

3. Classify all traced software modules as critical to either the proper execution of critical software functions or the quality requirements.

4. Focus additional analysis on these traced software modules.

5. Repeat the criticality analysis for each life cycle phase to determine if the implementation has changed the criticality of some items or processes.

Notice that in this scheme it is assumed that the original, specified functions and quality requirements have themselves already been ranked for criticality. This ranking may have been developed early in the acquisition phases of the project or it may be the result of other analyses performed at a systems level. Most commonly the criticality of a function is determined by a hazard or risk analysis. In addition, the criticality of each step and intermediate product arising during the development of the end item can be evaluated.

Hence, to complete the discussion of criticality, it is necessary to describe the dual concepts of hazard and risk analyses.

5.4.2.1 Hazard Analysis

Formally and at the systems level:

> A hazard is a source of potential harm or a situation with a potential for harm in terms of human injury, damage to health, property, or the environment, or some combination of these. [IEC 60300-3-9, 1995]

The IEEE standard, however, defines hazards more broadly to include economic loss, failure of mission, or adverse social impact. In the following discussion, hazards that fall within the IEC definition will be referred to as physical hazards.

The first step in performing a hazard analysis is to determine if any of the listed conditions exist. For many software applications, there are no physically hazardous conditions. In the example discussed previously, the initial evaluation is that no physical hazard is possible, but economic loss is. That is, while there is no way the application can cause physical harm to people or property, incorrect operation could negatively impact the finances of its users or owners.

A hazard analysis should be performed early in the project life cycle. For example, if incorrect operation of the product can have serious consequences, and the acquirer recognizes this, the analysis should be performed during the concept phase in order to establish the software integrity levels. This will help plan the acquirer's V&V effort.

The analysis should be repeated periodically during the remainder of the software life cycle. The initial analysis identifies potential system hazards, including possible combinations of independent, dependent, and simultaneous hazardous events or failures, and then categorizes those according to severity and probability of occurrence. The hazard analysis should then identify general strategies for eliminating or controlling each hazard.

Some of the techniques that can be applied to performing a hazard analysis include [Marciniak 1994]:

- Reviews and inspections;

- Checklists;

- Analysis of the effects of deviations on normal parameters;

- Fault-tree analysis (a logic diagram that assigns probabilities to credible event sequences, both mechanical and human, tracing hazardous events back to their sources); and

- Event-tree analysis (the tracing of a primary event forward to identify its consequences).

Some of these methods are best applied in group sessions where the potential hazards and failure modes can be explored, whereas others are best performed by focused, technical analysis. Examples of such analysis are the last two items, fault-tree and event-tree analysis, which are highly developed disciplines that have been used in areas such as nuclear reactor design since the 1960s [Barlow et al 1975, Birnbaum et al 1961].

5.4.2.2   Risk Analysis

Risks can be defined as potentially negative events whose consequences and likelihood of occurrence have been evaluated. The major category of risks would be the hazards that have been evaluated thus far. Risks discovered while performing a hazard analysis can usually be viewed as being intrinsic to the system, its application, its environment, and its planned usage. Thus in the B2B Web site example, given the fact that large amounts of customer funds are involved (the application), use of an infrastructure with marginal security attributes (the Internet, the environment) might be judged to constitute a hazard.

Other sources of risk, however, are not intrinsic. Such risks can be called extrinsic or coincidental (and often arise from the nature of software and software development). Here are some classical coincidental risks:

- *Unnecessary complexity.* The design may be more complex than is intrinsically required. This increases the likelihood that one of the intrinsic hazards will in fact materialize. Unnecessary complexity is an important special case of quality problems.

- *Low quality.* If the system is not built to a high standard of workmanship, it will not behave as expected. This can generate many new, unexpected hazards.

- *Requirements growth.* Introduction of requirements late in the development cycle can create unplanned interactions in the system, introducing new hazards.

- *Software tool and method problems.* Problems with tools and methods can range from hard-to-detect bugs in a compiler/linker to design methods that are ill suited to the application domain, resulting in needless complexity.

- *Unexpected interface behaviors.* While such behaviors could be considered an intrinsic risk (because such interfaces are part of the software's environment), the reality is often that risks of this type only surface during integration of the software. Examples of such interface problems include hardware-software interfaces, interfaces to operating systems, and interfaces to other applications.

The root causes of these risks are many and include the following:

- *Schedule and cost pressures.* Under such pressures product quality can and often does erode.

- *Lack of technical capacity.* Without appropriate staff and physical resources (including software tools, methods, and robust prototype hardware), all of the above problems can and will happen.

- *Lack of planning and management.*

- *The high rate of change in the underlying computer technology.*

However, when planning the V&V effort it is critical to remember that V&V, by itself, does not manage these root causes. That is the function of software project management, as described in Chapter 14 on risk management. V&V, SQA, and the ongoing developmental processes of the organization form a network of monitoring functions whose purpose is to determine if the risks have in fact eventuated. If they have, they are then quantified. Each of those functions has a different focus, as discussed earlier. V&V should focus its efforts on those risks that will impact the attainment of the required software integrity.

Once all the risks, both intrinsic and coincidental, have been identified, each should be evaluated and ranked. The ranking is performed by evaluating the risk using the following questions:

- What can go wrong?

- How and when is it likely to go wrong?

- What will occur when it goes wrong?

- Will it be detectable?

- What is the probability of loss if it occurs?

- If the losses are only economic, how much will be lost?

- What might be the losses if the worst case happened?

- What are the options for preventing it from occurring?

- Will the alternatives produce other risks?

The project can then implement a plan of action that targets each identified risk. Some of these will be encompassed by the evaluations described in the V&V plan, whereas others will be handed off to the risk management process.

The team performing the hazard and risk analyses should always remember their primary objective: identifying the critical functions and properties of the software so that integrity levels can be established. Those integrity levels will determine the remainder of the V&V planning process.

5.4.3 Integrity Levels

Having completed the hazard, risk, and criticality analyses, the integrity levels of the software can be determined. These levels will, in turn, be used to select what level and type of V&V activities are appropriate. Typically, projects that control life-sustaining processes or that would cause catastrophic results on failure, such as a flight control system or transaction processing for a major banking system, require greater and more intense V&V efforts than products whose failure will simply cause inconvenience, such as a stand-alone tool developed for personal use.

Integrity levels can vary within a project. However, if a series of evaluations is being performed, each supplying supporting data to the next, then the levels of integrity can only decrease as the sequence of evaluations is performed. Likewise, although integrity levels may also be adjusted during the software life cycle it may be necessary to revisit some evaluations previously performed in order to satisfy increased integrity levels of either those evaluations themselves or any others that use their products.

The IEEE standard specifies a four-level integrity scheme but other integrity schemes are acceptable as long as they are clearly defined. The levels correspond to degree of criticality, with 4 being the highest criticality level and 1 the lowest.

The integrity levels that a project could use to evaluate each specified function or software attribute are defined by the standard as follows:

- *High (Level 4):* Function or attribute affects critical performance of the system.

- *Major (Level 3):* Function or attribute affects important system performance.

- *Moderate (Level 2):* Function or attribute affects system performance, but workaround strategies can be implemented to compensate for loss of performance.

- *Low (Level 1):* Function or attribute has a noticeable effect on system performance, but merely creates inconvenience to the user if the function does not perform in accordance with requirements.

These definitions can be broadly paraphrased as follows:

- *High (Level 4):* If the function does not work correctly, the system is useless or even dangerous.

- *Major (Level 3):* Lack of the function is a serious operational impact. It may comprise the product in use but does not render it dangerous or utterly useless.

- *Moderate (Level 2):* Lack of the function is an operational impact but the system can be made to work by using a workaround.

- *Low (Level 1):* Lack of the function is an operational impact but the effect is minor and no explicit workaround is necessary.

Consequence	Probability			
	Reasonable	Probable	Occasional	Infrequent
Catastrophic	Level 4	Level 4	Level 3 or 4	Level 3
Critical	Level 4	Level 3 or 4	Level 3	Level 1 or 2
Marginal	Level 3	Level 2 or 3	Level 1 or 2	Level 1
Negligible	Level 2	Level 1 or 2	Level 1	Level 1

Table 5.1: Integrity Levels

However, the exact meaning of the standard's definitions for a particular project or product can only be understood when the term *critical* has been rigorously and specifically defined during the criticality analysis. Key elements of any criticality analysis are the assessments of the impact or consequence of event and the likelihood that the event will in fact occur. The hazard and risk analyses performed earlier provide the basis for the criticality analysis.

Table 5.1 shows an example of which integrity levels are appropriate according to the perceived consequences and probability of failure. Overlaps are intentional to allow for slightly differing interpretations of acceptable risk.

The actual integrity levels used on a project should be established using the involvement of the software acquirer, the developer, and any regulatory agencies responsible for approval of the end items.

5.4.4   The Organizational Context: Independence

Verification and validation techniques can be used by anyone to evaluate the items produced during software projects. The selection of personnel or organization(s) to plan and perform the various V&V tasks of the project depends on the nature of the software project-primarily the desired level of integrity. The allocation of responsibility for the various tasks can range anywhere from actual developers who unit test their own code to specialized organizations that have completely independent facilities which duplicate the development organization's software/hardware test environment.

5.4.4.1   Independence Discriminators

The key discriminators used to describe and determine the allocation of tasks are managerial, technical, and financial independence. The key issue in all cases is the degree of independence from the organization actually developing the software and the impact such independence has on the integrity of the software. Ultimately, the parties who are acquiring the software must be comfortable with the allocation of responsibilities. They are paying for the development and will bear the responsibility for dealing with any hazards or risks.

- *Managerial independence.* The V&V group is managed completely separately from the development organization and reports directly to the acquirer of the software/system. The V&V group has the authority to make decisions regarding all V&V work, including which items to analyze and test, which tools to use, and which problems to act on. The V&V organization provides information to both the developer group and the acquirer in parallel. Only the acquirer can change the conduct of the V&V effort.

- *Technical independence.* Persons outside the development group analyze the project and come up with their own unique evaluation of how to approach V&V, utilizing their own tools, methods, and resources. In some ways they act as surrogates for the users of the system. If cost or other considerations require that the V&V group use similar tools or environments, the V&V group should evaluate the tools/environment to ensure that those items provide the visibility necessary to detect anomalies.

- *Financial independence.* The budgets for the V&V activities are separate and distinct from those of development and all other program activities. Authority for creating or changing the budget rests outside of the development organization.

Having described the key parameters used to describe the organization of the V&V activities within a program, the typical assignments of responsibilities can now be discussed.

5.4.4.2 Types and Degrees of Independence

Differing degrees of independence may be associated with an independent V&V (IV&V) effort depending on the criticality of the final product. Level 4 products must adhere to the strictest forms of independence, whereas products with integrity levels of 1 or below (that is, none) need not be as rigorous. The four types of IV&V are *classical*, *modified*, *internal*, and *embedded*. Table 5.2, drawn from Annex C[2] of the IEEE standard illustrates the degree of independence typically provided by the four types in each of the three organizational discriminators.

	Independence Parameters		
Types of Independence	*Management*	*Technical*	*Financial*
Classical	I	I	I
Modified	I	I–Q	I
Internal	I–Q	I–Q	I–Q
Embedded	M–I	M–I	M–I

Key: I, rigorous independence; I–Q, independence with qualifications; and M–I, minimal independence.

Table 5.2: Types of Validation and Verification

[2]Annex C is considered "informative" in the nomenclature of the IEEE standards. This means that it is provided for the information of users. Compliance is not mandatory.

Classical IV&V is generally required for Level 4 software projects (i.e., loss of life, loss of mission, significant social or financial loss). Classical IV&V applies the highest degree of independence in all three areas. However, as in all other forms of V&V, the IV&V group (or contractor) should still maintain a good working relationship with developers of the software, providing them with findings rapidly so they can be encompassed in the ongoing development activities.

Modified IV&V is appropriate for Level 3 software projects (i.e., an important mission and purpose). Modified IV&V differs only in management. Development and V&V are separate organizations but both report to the same organizational parent who has been assigned responsibility for the software or system. However, budgets and technical staff are separately allocated within the overall organization.

Internal IV&V is used when the V&V group is part of the development organization but is still a distinct, recognizable entity. This is appropriate when risks are low and the benefits of preexisting staff knowledge outweigh objectivity, there are no formal independence requirements, and product integrity requirements are moderate or low. Managerial independence is compromised when V&V personnel and development staff work under the same organizational environment. Technical independence is compromised because both staffs may use similar tools and environments and work with similar assumptions.

Finally, financial independence is compromised because problems in development can cause resources to be diverted from the V&V activities.

Embedded V&V uses personnel from the development organization to perform the V&V activities. V&V personnel and product developers work side by side in inspections, walk-throughs, and reviews. This can compromise the technical independence of the effort. In this model, the V&V activities are not independent assessments; instead, they contribute to the assessments produced in the course of normal development. Similarly, the V&V budget is controlled by the development group.

Selecting which of the four types of IV&V to utilize is typically clear-cut in the case of products requiring Level 4 integrity; the classical model is almost always the best choice. For Level 3, either the classical or modified type of V&V is usually selected, based on evaluation of the risks involved. For Level 2, the choices are most commonly modified or internal. For products with Level 1 integrity requirements (or none), the decision is usually made to use the embedded model.

The ultimate test of any allocation of independence across the managerial, technical, and financial domains is that the entity which must bear the risk of not achieving the desired integrity level must be satisfied with the arrangement. This is often, but not always, the acquirer.

5.5   Validation and Verification Tasks Mapped to the Software Life Cycle

Software development projects are composed of tasks that the software life cycle plan groups into an interrelated series of defined activities. The activities of the V&V plan should parallel life cycle processes whose products and attributes they evaluate. Some V&V processes may, as a result, contain tasks and activities that are similar or identical to those performed by other groups or organizations. For example, the requirements engineering group will, as a matter of good practice, evaluate the SRS for completeness, consistency, and correctness. In addition, an independent evaluation of these attributes (if they are judged to contribute to achieving the desired integrity level) can be performed.

These two efforts should not be redundant, because the independent evaluators will not enter into the evaluation with the same assumptions as the developers of the document. In addition, they will bring their own experiences and expertise to bear on the matter. Thus V&V provides additional impetus for the software project and product to deliver what they should: software that conforms to system requirements and will satisfy the users needs.

To be in compliance with IEEE Standard 1012-1998, the V&V effort must parallel the processes of the software development effort, including those of acquisition, supply, and management. Processes or products judged (by the managerial authority of the V&V effort) not relevant can be excluded, provided this is noted in the SVVP. From the standpoint of the V&V effort, no process is concluded until its development products are verified and validated according to the defined tasks in the SVVP. The following sections list, by life cycle process and management task, the V&V activities required to achieve the different integrity levels.

5.5.1   Management

The goal of all V&V activities is to ensure that the software being produced possesses the required integrity. This is best accomplished by creating a positive management relationship with the development group, focused objectively on achieving the required integrity. The primary V&V management responsibilities involve planning, review, and control.

In this and subsequent sections, the integrity levels that apply to each task are shown in parentheses at the end of the item. The V&V management tasks include these:

- Software SVVP generation and maintenance (all);

- Change assessment (all);

- Management review of V&V activities (all, excluding acquisition and supply processes for Level 1 products);

- Planning, monitoring, and controlling the V&V effort (all);

- Management and technical review support (4, 3); and

- Interface with organizational and supporting processes (4, 3).

5.5.2 Acquisition

In one form or another all software projects begin with an acquisition process, which is usually initiated when an organization realizes it has a need for a new software system, product, or service. Depending on the organizational structure and processes, some form of statement of need is developed. Next, some form of *make-buy decision* is made. That is, the organization decides that it has the capabilities to develop the system internally (the *make* decision) or it decides that it is better to procure it externally (the *buy* decision). The make-buy decision is one component of the *acquisition strategy*, which would also include a decision on the criticality and how to approach the V&V processes.

As another part of the acquisition strategy the acquirer may issue several requests for information (RFIs). This is often done to determine what options exist for answering the needs statement before actually developing the request for proposal (RFP) package.

As the strategy is finalized, one or more RFPs, bid requests, or invitations to tender (ITT) are prepared and distributed to interested suppliers, including any potential V&V suppliers. The acquisition process continues through to negotiation of the contracts with the selected suppliers.

V&V tasks in support of the acquisition process include the following:

- Scope the V&V effort (4, 3, 2).

- Plan the interface between the V&V effort and supplier (4, 3, 2).

- Review system requirements (all).

5.5.3 Supply

The supply process is dual to, or the mirror image of, the acquisition process. That is, just as the buyer or acquirer must perform an acquisition process, the supplier must respond following some supply process. A V&V supply process is normally initiated when a candidate supplier decides to respond to an RFP. Thus the supply process focuses on determining if the RPF, requirements, and other information provided by the acquirer are consistent and, in the opinion of the supplier, will satisfy the needs of the user. This process is referred to as *contract verification*. At the same time the potential developer should be planning for the necessary interactions with the acquirer and any specified agents, including any IV&V contractors. Likewise, any potential IV&V contractors should begin the same planning process.

In summary, these are the tasks of the V&V supply process:

- Plan the interface between the V&V effort and supplier (4, 3, 2).

- Contract verification (4).

5.5.4 Development

Six activities are encompassed in the V&V development process, corresponding to the five described in the classical waterfall model of software development, plus one additional process: (1) concept V&V, (2) requirements V&V, (3) design V&V, (4) implementation V&V, (5) test V&V, and (6) installation and checkout V&V. Tasks associated with each of these activities are listed below.

If the project is using a life cycle model that renders these processes irrelevant or inappropriate, then the V&V processes should be modified so as to provide the required confidence in the product integrity.

5.5.4.1 Concept V&V

The concept V&V process is performed during the system architecture and trade-off phase. It evaluates the user requirements, assesses the risks intrinsic to proposed solutions, and evaluates the criticality of software items described in each alternative architecture or requirements set.

These tasks are part of concept V&V:

- Concept documentation evaluation (4, 3, 2);

- Evaluation of operational procedures (all);

- Criticality analysis(4, 3, 2);

- Hardware/software/user requirements allocation analysis (4);

- Traceability analysis[3] (4, 3, 2);

- Hazards analysis (4, 3);

- Risk analysis (4, 3); and

- SVVP generation or updating (all).

Notice that because the criticality, hazard, and risk analyses must be performed before the integrity levels can be established the standard makes the tacit assumption that a preliminary assessment will be performed to sufficient depth to determine the integrity level at a product level.

5.5.4.2 Requirements V&V

The functional, performance, and quality properties of the software product are defined and documented during the requirements phase. The main product of the requirements phase is the SRS.

---

[3]The objectives of traceability analysis can be found in Chapter 3, Software Requirements Specification.

The objective of the V&V activity during the requirements phase is to ensure that each item in the SRS is specified sufficiently to achieve the desired integrity level. V&V also checks that the SRS is traceable back to user needs and the system concept as defined in the concept documentation; that it is organized in such a way that it can be traced forward into the design, code, and test documentation; and that it is compatible with the hardware and software operational environment.

The V&V tasks performed during the requirements phase are as follows:

- Traceability analysis (4, 3, 2);

- Software requirements evaluation (4, 3, 2, 1);

- Interface analysis (4, 3, 2);

- Criticality analysis update (4, 3, 2);

- System V&V test plan generation and verification (4, 3, 2, 1);

- Acceptance V&V test plan generation and verification (4, 3, 2);

- Configuration management assessment (4,3);

- Hazard analysis update (4,2); and

- Risk analysis (4,2).

5.5.4.3 Design V&V

The V&V design process provides assurance that all the requirements from the SRS are represented in the design, that the design will satisfy the requirements, and that the design is testable and will lead to testable code. The design phase is an opportune time at which to catch as many remaining errors as possible before coding begins, while corrections are still relatively inexpensive. Hence V&V can make a real contribution to the cost and schedule objectives of the program at this time.

The general goals of V&V during the design phase are to determine if:

- Requirements are traceable through all design levels;

- There are no omissions or additions;

- The design is appropriate to the system objectives and the desired product quality attributes;

- All hardware, operator, and software interfaces are clearly described;

- The design conforms with all applicable standards, practices, and conventions;

- The design will satisfy the requirements when fully integrated;

- The design is understandable to those who write the source code and later maintain the product;

- Sufficient information has been supplied in the design to plan, design, and execute unit and integration tests; and

- All design configuration documentation is completed and delivered, especially when mixed media are used (e.g., graphic charts, text specifications).

As V&V tasks are repeated through each design level, the V&V methods or techniques used may change. The scope of the V&V effort will be determined by the complexity of the design.

The following V&V activities occur during the design phase:

- Traceability analysis (4, 3, 2);

- Software design evaluation (all);

- Interface analysis (4, 3, 2);

- Criticality analysis update (4, 3, 2);

- Component V&V test plan generation and verification (4, 3, 2);

- Component V&V test design generation and verification (4, 3, 2);

- Integration V&V test design generation and verification (all);

- System V&V test design generation and verification (all);

- Acceptance V&V test design generation and verification (4, 3, 2);

- Hazard analysis update (4, 3); and

- Risk analysis update (4, 3).

Note that the design evaluation is an example of a technical evaluation of the (design) product, as distinct from an evaluation of the adherence to policies and procedures, such as SQA would produce.

5.5.4.4 Implementation V&V

During the implementation phase, software requirements are translated into artifacts that together represent the end item software. V&V activities for this phase determine the adherence of code to the design specifications and standards with, as always, the objective being the assurance that the product achieves the stipulated integrity levels.

Other activities during the implementation phase include the generation of test cases and test procedures for component, integration, and system and acceptance test levels. At this time actual component level testing is performed.

The V&V tasks performed during the implementation phase are as follows:

- Traceability analysis update (4, 3, 2);

- Source code and source code documentation evaluation (all);

- Interface analysis update (4, 3, 2);

- Criticality analysis update (4, 3, 2);

- Component V&V test case and test procedure generation and verification (4, 3, 2);

- Integration V&V test case and test procedure generation and verification (all);

- System V&V test case and test procedure generation and verification (all);

- Acceptance test case generation and verification (4, 3, 2);

- Component V&V test execution and verification (4, 3, 2);

- Hazard analysis update (4, 3); and

- Risk analysis update (4, 3).

5.5.4.5 Test V&V

Execution of integration, system, and acceptance tests ensures that system and software requirements have been satisfied and that the required integrity levels have been achieved. For integrity Levels 3 and 4, the IV&V group must generate and control its own test processes, including test case plans, designs, cases, procedures, and execution. For integrity Levels 1 and 2, it is sufficient for V&V to verify test efforts by the development team. However, even for Levels 1 and 2 it is advantageous for the acceptance and systems tests to be conducted by an organization with some level of independence.

These V&V tasks are performed during the test phase:

- Traceability analysis update (4, 3, 2);

- Acceptance V&V test procedure generation and verification (4, 3, 2);

- Acceptance V&V test execution and verification (4, 3, 2);

- Integration V&V test execution and verification (all);

- System V&V test execution and verification (all);

- Hazard analysis update (all); and

- Risk analysis update (all).

Note that some of the activities associated with testing (such as the initial creation and verification of the acceptance test procedures) occur much earlier than the actual performance of the testing. Hence, the V&V activities performed in support of testing are in fact distributed throughout the software life cycle.

5.5.4.6   Installation and Checkout V&V

During the installation and checkout of the software products at the user's facility, V&V techniques are used to verify and validate the software performance when installed in the user's environment, as well as verifying and validating that any installation instructions and procedures are correct.

The V&V tasks performed during the installation and checkout phase are as follows:

- Installation configuration audit (4, 3);

- Installation checkout (4, 3);

- Hazard analysis update (4, 3);

- Risk analysis update (4, 3); and

- V&V final report generation (4, 3, 2).

5.5.5   Operation

After the system has started operation and is in use, V&V techniques can be used to assess the impact of any changes that might impact the integrity level of the system or might introduce a new hazard or risk. This includes monitoring and evaluating the operating environment for any changes that might occur after installation. V&V techniques can also be used to monitor and analyze operating procedures and usage patterns to determine if any new hazards or risks have arisen or if the impact or likelihood of any preexisting risks and hazards have materially changed.

These V&V tasks are performed during the operations phase:

- Evaluation of new constraints (4, 3, 2);

- Proposed change assessment (4, 3, 2);

- Operating procedures evaluation (4, 3);

- Hazard analysis update (4, 3); and

- Risk analysis update (4, 3).

For products having an integrity Level of 2 it would be reasonable to include the operations activities with those of maintenance. Proposed changes to the product itself are evaluated as part of the maintenance phase, discussed below. Indeed, a change to the operational environment of the product could increase a hazard materially, thereby requiring a maintenance action to reduce the risk to an acceptable level. The maintenance activity itself would then be the subject of other V&V activities.

It is not uncommon for a separate, multiyear contract to be issued to cover the operations and maintenance phases.

5.5.6   Maintenance

While a product is in service the need for changes is often identified. As discussed before, changes to the operational environment may mandate a change. More commonly, changes are required to add new features or to correct latent defects in the software. Maintenance actions are essentially smaller scale versions of the initial development, with the added constraint of dealing with the sheer volume of existing code. This can serve to both lower and raise risk. Finally, maintenance actions would include migrating the product to a new environment and complete removal from service.

The V&V tasks performed during the maintenance phase are as follows:

- SVVP revision (all);

- Proposed change assessment (4, 3, 2);

- Anomaly evaluation (4, 3, 2);

- Criticality analysis (4, 3, 2);

- Migration assessment (4, 3);

- Retirement assessment (4, 3);

- Hazard analysis update (4, 3);

- Risk analysis (4, 3); and

- As required by the change, iteration of specified tasks from other phases (all).

5.6   Creating the SVVP

Having discussed how the integrity levels for a software product can be established, how the verification and validation effort can be organized consistent with those levels, and what activities are recommended to achieve those levels, the task remains of creating a plan that can be used to guide and manage the V&V activity.

5.6.1   SVVP Outline

The IEEE standard provides an example outline, the headings of which are shown below.

1. Purpose

2. Referenced Documents

3. Definitions

4. V&V Overview

4.1 Organization

4.2 Master schedule

4.3 Software integrity level scheme

4.4 Resources summary

4.5 Responsibilities

4.6 Tools, techniques, and methods

5. V&V Processes

5.1 V&V tasks

5.2 Methods and procedures

5.3 Inputs

5.4 Outputs

5.5 Schedule

5.6 Resources

5.7 Risks and assumptions

5.8 Roles and responsibilities

6. V&V Reporting Requirements

6.1 Task reports

6.2 Activity summary reports, including:

    a. Description of the V&V tasks

    b. Summary of the results of those tasks

    c. Summary of any anomalies discovered and their resolution

    d. Assessment of software quality/integrity

    e. Identification and assessment of technical and managerial risks relevant to the software quality/integrity

    f. Recommendations

6.3 Anomaly report, including:

    a. A description and the location of the anomaly in either documents or code

    b. An assessment of the impact of the anomaly, especially to the product integrity

    c. The cause of the anomaly and a description of how it occurred

    d. An assessment of the criticality of the anomaly

    e. Recommendations for closure of the immediate anomaly as well as for avoidance of similar occurrences in the future

6.4 V&V final report, including:

    a. Summary of all V&V activities across all project life cycle phases

    b. Summary of the result of the V&V tasks

    c. Summary of anomalies and their resolutions

    d. Assessment of overall software quality/integrity

    e. Description of lessons learned and best practices observed

    f. Recommendations

  6.5 Optional reports

5.6.2 Developing the Software Verification and Validation Plan

While the first draft of the SVVP may be incomplete in some areas it should be as thorough, comprehensive, and specific as current information allows. The functional baseline of the SVVP should be established prior to the requirements phase, if not earlier as part of the acquistion strategy. Changes and additions are typically made at the end of life cycle phases or processes. However, they can be made at any appropriate time, subject to approval of the managerial authority.

In developing the SVVP, the following items should be taken into consideration:

- The project's objectives, product applications, and integrity needs;

- The projects overall approach to risk management, including any characterization of anticipated problems;

- V&V staffing requirements and strategies;

- Selection of testing techniques and metrics;

- Size and complexity of software items being delivered, along with the operational environment;

- Software development environment, including the test environment;

- Software capability of the developer;

- Relationships between V&V, development, and acquirer organizations;

- How to handle uncertainties as the project and plan evolve;

- Required approvals;

- Configuration control of the SVVP; and

- Any special project requirements.

5.6.3   Estimating the V&V Effort

The primary factors that determine the magnitude of the effort required to perform the V&V activities for a project are (1) the desired integrity level of the products; (2) the nature of the products, including their novelty; and (3) the size of the products.

The costs of a V&V program can be broadly viewed as immediate and consequential. The immediate costs are those expended directly in performing the V&V effort, while the consequential costs are those expended in support of or responding to the V&V effort. Typically, the group or groups performing the V&V activities incur the immediate costs, while other project personnel incur the consequential costs. This distinction should be clearly understood by all organizational elements so that adequate budgets for each element can be estimated and established.

General approaches that can be applied to the costing and scheduling of software projects are described in Chapter 13. This section gives some specific considerations that should be applied in estimating the magnitude of the V&V costs. In addition, it describes some special considerations that should be applied toward scheduling the effort.

5.6.3.1   Scheduling and Costing V&V Activities

By their nature, V&V activities occur in tandem with, or on completion of, other project activities. Thus in earlier sections of this chapter, V&V activities were classified according to which phase of the development life cycle was producing the activity or item that was the object of the V&V activity. As a result, the beginning of each V&V activity specified in the SVVP, in accordance with the desire software integrity level, will be determined by either the start of the activity being evaluated, or the completion of development of the item that is to be evaluated.

Likewise, the end of each V&V activity, or the completion of some intermediate product of that activity, is determined by what other events or activities in the total project schedule require the products of the activity.

In the case of the first category of V&V activity, a level of effort (LOE) task[4] can be initiated shortly before the time the activity being evaluated begins. The time between initiation of the evaluation task and the activity being evaluated should be used to perform any necessary final planning. The LOE task can then be supplemented with discrete tasks such as attending and evaluating special reviews, or creating an evaluation of the ongoing task. These tasks should then be entered into the project schedule and the immediate and consequential costs included in the project cost estimates.

For V&V activities that are intended to evaluate some specific item, the effort should be broken into the following discrete tasks, each of whose immediate and consequential costs should be individually estimated:

- *Final planning of the evaluation.*

---

[4]See Chapter 12, on software costing and scheduling, for more on the categories of tasks and the earned value system that can be used to manage them.

- *Performing the evaluation.* This would include any costs needed to interface with other elements of the project staff.

- *Documenting the evaluation.* This should be entirely an immediate cost.

- *Review of the evaluation.* This would consist of both immediate and consequential effort.

- *Finalize and release the evaluation.* This should consist entirely of immediate costs, with the possible exception of any extraordinary software configuration management (SCM) costs. Typically, the SCM costs would be minor and encompassed in an appropriate LOE task performed by the SCM group.

- *Distribution of the evaluation.* This can be minor or major. If many physical copies must be distributed to a number of geographically distributed locations, the copying, freight, and clerical costs can be considerable. This is, however, increasingly the exception.

The granularity of the budgets created using these estimates should be consistent with those of other project activities. In addition, the budgets for the immediate and consequential costs of performing the V&V activities should be assigned to work packages following the organization's general approach to accountability. For example, the budget needed to perform the immediate V&V activities would typically be assigned to work packages for which the V&V group is responsible, while the budgeted consequential costs would be assigned to work packages for which the supporting organization is responsible. This need not violate financial independence if the proper financial controls are in place, in particular, if the supporting work packages are distinct from those of other activities performed by the groups supporting the V&V effort.

When estimating the cost and schedule of these activities, the intended use of the evaluations must be constantly borne in mind. For example, if a design evaluation is needed to make a decision to begin implementing a design, then the evaluation should be completed prior to the design review. In that way all the information needed to make the decision is available simultaneously. Likewise, if the objective of an evaluation of the product code is to determine if it is excessively complex, then preliminary versions should be made available early in the implementation process, with a final evaluation produced before integration has been completed to any significant extent.

Thus scheduling the V&V activities is a trade-off between the time the items become available for evaluation, the time required to perform an evaluation of the required depth and rigor, and the needs of management for timely information. Depending on the desired level of software integrity, the importance of the earliest possible release date of the product, and the willingness of management or the customer to accept the risk of rework, rational compromises can be reached. This is, however, an area that demonstrates the importance of independence for products requiring high levels of integrity.

Finally, the combined immediate and consequential costs of the V&V activity, by phase, should be cross-checked using either a local database of project experiences or with a parametric model, such as COCOMO II (discussed in Chapter 12). If possible, both should be used. These cross-checks can be performed in two ways: (1) as an absolute amount or (2) as a percentage of the total project budget.

As an example, suppose that 1.4 million of lines of code are being developed for an air traffic control system. The 21 attributes of the COCOMO II model have been defined by the project estimation team and approved by management. According to this model the total cost of the project should be $120 million and the distribution of effort, by phase, that will be required to perform the V&V effort is shown in Table 5.3. Note two striking things about this table. First, a substantial increase is seen in the absolute amount of effort expended (both immediate and consequential) during the later two phases of implementation and integration and test. Second, note the considerable increase in the percentage required for the integration and test phase to perform the V&V activities. These are generic percentages and should not be used unless verified using the organization's own historical data.

	Requirements	Design	Implementation	Integration and Test
Percentage of total effort of phase	8%	8%	9%	28%
Average total staffing	2.4	4.8	11	27
Person-months of total effort	31	76	275	475

Table 5.3: Distribution of the V&V Effort by Phase

However, the rapid increase in the absolute V&V effort seen in the last two phases is caused by the following:

- There are more categories of items to evaluate in the latter two phases. Examination of the task lists in the SVVP plan outline confirms this.

- For each category there are many more items as well. Thus, although there was only one SRS or design document there will be many, many modules, test plans, test designs, and test procedures and cases to evaluate.

- During the latter two phases, the V&V effort must develop and perform the actual acceptance and systems tests.

This last item also explains the rapid increase in the percentage of the total effort of the integration and test phase that must be expended by the V&V activity, irrespective of who does the work.

5.6.3.2   Selecting V&V Staff

The reader should note that higher levels of V&V introduce additional layers of activity and management to the project, increasing documentation requirements and communication between the groups involved. The project manager should make sure the V&V staff is knowledgeable and experienced and has a good track record of giving accurate and timely information to the development group. This will help avoid incidents caused by, for example, the creation of invalid or inaccurate anomaly reports. The V&V processes should also focus on the critical areas of the development project to maximize its effectiveness.

Most V&V efforts require three categories of individuals:

- *Technical analysts.* These individuals will perform the analysis and evaluation tasks specified in the SVVP. This includes the criticality, hazard, risk, traceability, and interface analyses, as well as the evaluations of the design, code, and test artifacts. As result, they must be both technically skilled and experienced.

- *Test designers.* These individuals will design the acceptance and systems tests for projects with sufficiently high integrity requirements. They must be able to translate the requirements and operational scenario documents into test plans, designs, cases, and procedures. They must be familiar with the intent and design of the application and facile with the test environment.

- *Test executors.* These individuals will perform the formal tests specified by the test designers. They must be familiar with the test environment and facilities. To be able to produce meaningful anomaly reports, they must also be familiar with the intent of the application.

Depending on the technical complexity of the application, its intended environment, the implementation methodology, and the test environment, filling these positions can be extremely challenging. Many of the skills needed to perform V&V tasks can also be used in development. The tasks and functions of V&V are often not valued in organizations either corporately or, more often, individually. Such positions are often seen as technical dead-ends. As a result engineers will often hesitate or refuse to accept an assignment involving V&V activities, preferring instead to seek assignments in development.

One solution to this problem is to require that engineers, as part of their career growth toward senior technical positions, spend a fixed period of time working on V&V tasks. An example would be a senior or lead designer position. Clearly, an individual who aspires to hold such a position would learn many useful lessons while working on V&V tasks. Bluntly put, it would allow them to learn from other people's mistakes. Conversely, not every engineer aspires to or can be a lead designer, so such a requirement would not be perceived negatively by the majority of the staff members, nor would it impact them.

5.7 Summary

Software verification and validation provides a mechanism for ensuring that software achieves its most critical operational objectives. The methods of V&V can be used in a variety of organizational structures, depending on the degree of criticality of the application. At the same time, V&V can be used to monitor and provide in-process feedback to the development group. The activities of V&V produce information for management's use in determining whether the project can progress to the next development phase and, ultimately, if the product is acceptable or not.

Software V&V processes help define the required levels of quality and performance, such as specification conformance, quality compliance, and system performance. It characterizes anticipated problems, and using analysis and testing techniques, strives to detect system and software problems effectively.

The intensity, span, and depth of the software V&V effort should be adjusted according to the criticality of the items being developed. Software V&V is most effective when initiated early in the software project life cycle and continues in parallel throughout that life cycle, even including the operation and maintenance phases for some applications.

The software V&V effort can represent a significant portion of the cost of development of critical systems. As a result, the effort must be carefully planned and managed. The costs, scheduling, and staffing needs of the software V&V effort must be included in the planning of the project. The IEEE standard specifies a framework for doing this, including the format and content of the software verification and validation plan.

Applicable Standards

IEC 60300-3 9 (1995). *Dependability Management-Part 3: Application Guide—Section 9: Risk Analysis of Technological Systems*, International Electrotechnology Commission.

IEEE Std 610.12-1990. *IEEE Standard Glossary of Software Engineering Terminology.* IEEE, New York.

IEEE Std 730-1998. *IEEE Standard for Software Quality Assurance Plans.* IEEE, New York.

IEEE Std 828-1998. *IEEE Standard for Software Configuration Management Plans.* IEEE, New York.

IEEE Std 829-1998. *IEEE Standard for Software Test Documentation.* IEEE, New York.

IEEE Std 1012-1998. *IEEE Standard for Software Verification and Validation.* IEEE, New York.

IEEE Std 1028-1997. *IEEE Standard for Software Reviews.* IEEE, New York.

IEEE Std 1061-1998. *IEEE Standard for Software Quality Metrics Methodology*. IEEE, New York.

IEEE Std 1074-1997. *IEEE Standard for Developing Software Life Cycle Processes*. IEEE, New York.

Additional References

[Barlow et al 1975]   Barlow, R. E., Fussell, J. B., and Singpurwalla, N. D. (1975). *Reliability and Fault Tree Analysis*. Society for Industrial and Applied Mathematics Press, Philadelphia, PA.

[Birnbaum et al 1961]   Birnbaum, Z. W., Esary, J. D., and Saunders, S. C. (1961). "Multicomponent Systems and Structures, and Their Reliability." *Technometrics*, vol. 12, no. 2, pp. 55–77.

[Boehm 1981]   Boehm, B. (1981). *Software Engineering Economics*. Prentice Hall, Upper Saddle River, NJ.

[Deutch 1982]   Deutch, M. S. (1982). *Software Verification and Validation— Realistic Project Approaches*. Prentice Hall, Upper Saddle River, NJ.

[Dorfman & Thayer 1997]   Dorfman, M., and Thayer, R. H., eds. (1997). *Software Engineering*. IEEE Computer Society Press, Los Alamitos, CA.

[Eastbrook & Callahan 1996]   Easterbrook, S., and Callahan, J. (1996). *Independent Validation of Specifications: A Coordination Headache*, Technical Report NASA-IVV-96-013. NASA, Washington, DC.

[Howden 1987]   Howden, W. E. (1987). *Functional Program Testing and Analysis*. McGraw-Hill, New York.

[Lewis 1992]   Lewis, R. O. (1992). *Independent Verification and Validation—A Life Cycle Engineering Process for Quality Software*. John Wiley and Sons, New York.

[Lyu 1996]   Lyu, M. R. (1996). *Software Reliability Engineering*. McGraw-Hill, New York.

[Marciniak 1994]   Marciniak, J. J., ed. (1994). *Encyclopedia of Software Engineering*. John Wiley and Sons, New York.

[McDermid 1991]   McDermid, J. A., ed. (1991). *Software Engineer's Reference Book*. Butterworth-Heinemann, Oxford, UK.

[Neal et al. 1997]   Neal, R. D., et al. (1997). *A Case Study of IV&V Cost Ef-fectiveness*, Technical Report NASA-IVV-97-007. NASA, Washington, DC.

[Wallace et al. 1996]   Wallace, D. R., Ippolito, L. M., and Cuthill, B. C. (1996). *Reference Information for the Software Verification and Vali-dation Process*, NIST Special Publication 500-234. National Institute of Standards and Technology, Washington, DC.

[Whitten 1995]   Whitten, N. (1995). *Managing Software Development Projects*, 2nd ed. John Wiley and Sons, New York.

Chapter 6

Software Maintenance

6.1 Introduction

Experience has shown that changes are always required after a software product is delivered to the customer. Software maintenance is the activity of making changes to the software product and its supporting documentation. Repeated studies have shown that more than 60 percent of the costs associated with a software product are expended after the product is delivered, during the maintenance phase. In addition, because the product is already delivered and is being used by numerous users, any issues that arise during the maintenance activity can impact the customer severely and will be highly visible. Repeated serious mistakes during maintenance can negatively impact the reputation of the developing organization. Therefore, software maintenance is one of the most critical activities a software development organization can undertake.

The motive or immediate need for making a given change to a delivered product may be (1) to correct latent defects in the product itself, (2) to adapt the product to external changes, or (3) to improve the product's functionality. Independent of the motive, a given change may be more or less critical. Likewise, it may be more or less difficult to implement. In addition, maintenance changes must be applied to an existing design so the range of implementation options is often restricted. Finally, assignment to a maintenance activity is usually not perceived as positively as is assignment to a new product development project. The reality, however, is that maintenance can be a more technically challenging task.

Thus the management and performance of maintenance on a software product is financially important to both the customer and the developer, can impact the reputation of the developer, and is technically and managerially complex. The *IEEE Standard for Software Maintenance,* IEEE Standard 1219-1998, provides guidance for managing and executing software maintenance activities. This standard can be applied to any software product and is not restricted by size, complexity, criticality, or application. IEEE Standard 1219-1998 does not presume the use of any particular development model (waterfall, spiral, etc.).

6.2 Objectives

In this chapter you will learn:

- Why software maintenance is important.

- Different types of software maintenance.

- How to manage software maintenance.

- How to plan for software maintenance.

- Role of software quality assurance in software maintenance.

- Role of software configuration management in software maintenance.

- What metrics are useful in software maintenance.

- How to use metrics to manage software maintenance.

- How to use documentation in software maintenance.

- The seven phases of software maintenance.

- The process model for software maintenance.

6.3   Software Maintenance

6.3.1   Scope of Software Maintenance

Keeping their software systems operational is critical to the effective operation of modern organizations. The *IEEE Standard for Software Maintenance* defines software maintenance as the modification of a software product after delivery to correct faults, to improve performance or other attributes, or to adapt the product to a changed environment. This definition is used throughout this chapter. This definition encompasses not only changes to software code but also to supporting configuration data (such as tuning parameters) and documentation, including user manuals. It includes changes to these items made by both the developer and the user. However, because this book is intended to help the software engineering project manager, this chapter focuses on changes made by the developing organization. However, many of the principles and procedures described herein will be applicable to the other domains as well.

6.3.1.1   Types of Software Maintenance

Software maintenance is generally classified into three categories, according to what caused or motivated the change: (1) adaptive, (2) corrective, and (3) perfective changes. The nature of a change, as well as the process of making the change, can be described as being either adaptive, corrective, or perfective maintenance (Figure 6.1).

A change is *adaptive* if it permits the software system to continue to operate as its operating environment evolves. Classic examples are adapting to an updated operating system, changed or new hardware, software tools, and data format changes. Adaptive maintenance

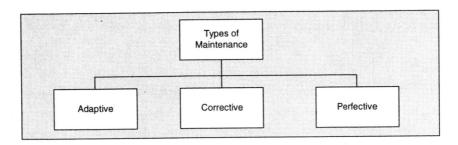

Figure 6.1: Types of Software Maintenance

has historically accounted for about 20 percent of all software maintenance efforts. As more software products are built utilizing commercial components, this percentage is likely to increase as those components and the underlying frameworks evolve and the market-place matures. In addition, as more products are being built using external networking and computing facilities as part of the end user service, the likelihood of adaptive changes can only increase. It should normally be possible to plan for adaptive maintenance in advance, with the obvious exception of a component, tool vendor, or infrastructure provider suddenly going out of business or announcing a radical change in their commercial strategy.

A change is *corrective* if it is intended to correct problems or faults. Corrective mainte- nance is usually reactive in nature. That is, a customer discovers a latent defect and notifies the system developer, who must then take action to correct it. Corrective actions are usually classified according to how immediate, or critical, the need is. The immediacy is usually classified as being either emergency or scheduled. *Emergency* changes are those needed to keep a system operational in the near term. The problem has to be corrected immedi- ately. If the customer can "work around" the problem for some reasonable period of time, then the change is classified as being *scheduled*. Typically a group of scheduled corrective changes, together with appropriate adaptive and perfective changes, are implemented into a new, scheduled release of the product. Corrective maintenance has historically accounted for about 20 percent of all software maintenance efforts.

Finally, a change is *perfective* if it is being made to improve performance or to meet new user requirements. Perfective maintenance has historically accounted for about 60 percent of all software maintenance efforts. Like adaptive changes, perfective changes can usually be scheduled in advance. However, as customers increasingly rely on computer-based systems to implement their business processes, the likelihood of perfective changes being requested on an emergency basis will only increase.

The above classifications and attributes, carefully applied, should be used in planning and managing software maintenance activities. Emergency corrective maintenance should get higher immediate priority than a perfective maintenance request. One of the classi-cal management challenges of software maintenance is responding to emergency changes without unduly disrupting the ongoing scheduled efforts. Emergency changes can place un-planned demands on the organization, thereby impacting the scheduled efforts. In addition the product itself will be modified by the emergency changes. This "moving of the earth" under the feet of the technical staff can have significant technical impacts on the product design, which, in turn, can result in reworking of the scheduled changes.

Adequate visibility into the classification and attributes of changes is therefore critical to the orderly management of software maintenance. The problem reporting and change tracking systems, as described in Chapter 9, Software Configuration Management, must provide the necessary facilities, methods, policies, and procedures to support the software maintenance needs of the organization. Although specialized plans, directives, and reports will typically be required to manage the maintenance effort, the fundamental facilities and data should come from the organization's configuration management (CM), quality assurance, scheduling, and cost control systems that are used to manage other development efforts. As with any other rule, exceptions can occur, but the case should be clear when they do.

6.3.1.2 Difficulty of Software Maintenance

As mentioned before, software maintenance is usually, explicitly or not, the largest single element of developing, owning, and operating a software system. It is also one of the most difficult. This is often not recognized, according to Boehm [Boehm 1976] and others. This commonly occurs for three reasons. First, maintenance efforts are not usually associated with new business opportunities and the attendant technical and managerial crises that draw the attention of management. Second, because maintenance efforts often have their own revenue stream, there is a tacit acceptance of "business as usual," provided the organization is not losing too much money on the activity. In many commercial software businesses the revenue from new feature releases is a major source of revenue. Finally, many engineers prefer to start with a "clean sheet of paper" when implementing a change. This is not unique to software engineers.

In many ways software maintenance is more difficult technically and managerially than is new development. For example, when implementing a specific change the development team must be careful not to disrupt all of the other features and capabilities of the released system. This can seriously constrain the range of implementation options and can make the task of designing and implementing such a change more difficult than would be a brand new design. Avoiding unintended consequences (that is, the introduction of secondary defects) often requires a global knowledge of the product. In addition, testing such changes can be very challenging, because full regression testing is almost never possible due to schedule and cost constraints. Yet the change must be adequately verified or else secondary defects, introduced during the maintenance action, will be inflicted on the customers. Finally, even if a new feature release represents an entirely new development, it will still have many backward compatibility requirements, which are typically intended to protect the users' investment in data and training.

An additional layer of complexity is added by the fact that all three categories of maintenance—corrective, adaptive, and perfective—are usually going on concurrently. The coordination and control of the design, implementation, test, and CM processes in this situation can be a daunting task, even with good control systems in place.

Thus software maintenance and its management are intrinsically complex, subject to many constraints, and often of high interest and visibility to customers.

6.3.2 Software Maintenance Management

Software maintenance management consists of the activities and tasks required to guide the implementation of changes, from initiation through delivery, to a released product. It uses all of the functions described in Chapter 13 of this book on software engineering project management. However, software maintenance management uses the functions of planning and control even more intensely than do the other modes of software engineering project management.

Proper planning of software maintenance requires that all issues relevant to the effort be identified, any necessary data gathered and analyzed, and courses of actions selected. Because multiple activities are typically going on concurrently, planning can become much more complex than is the case for a new development. Indeed, a new development may be embedded in the maintenance activity, making the management of the maintenance problem a superset of that of development.

Once maintenance is initiated, the control of the effort will have a similarly increased complexity. Multiple work groups will be working against common or different product CM baselines, making potentially conflicting or complementary changes. Distinct budgets, with different funding sources, may be involved in the different efforts. These must be kept financially distinct, yet circumstances often require that as much synergy as possible be achieved. Schedules may have similar issues, for both the planning and control activities.

Although the other management functions are important, most of the issues critical to good software maintenance management can be best discussed within the context of either planning or control. Therefore this chapter focuses on these two functions.

6.3.3 Planning Software Maintenance

Software maintenance planning consists of five activities: (1) determine the software maintenance effort, (2) determine required software maintenance process, (3) quantify the software maintenance effort (cost and schedule), (4) anticipate software maintenance requirements, and (5) develop a software maintenance plan. IEEE Standard 1219-1998, Appendix C, gives a recommended format for this plan.

6.3.3.1 Determining the Effort

The software maintenance actions that are necessary in the immediate future should be identified, documented, and categorized. Their impacts and needs should be assessed in sufficient detail to allow the software engineering project manager (PM) to get a clear picture of what resources and processes are needed to perform the maintenance actions. The first issue is to identify all maintenance actions that are required or are expected to be required in the immediate future.

The first source of changes that must be examined is the organizational problem or change tracking system. Next, customer support, marketing, and development staff should be interviewed to determine what other changes are needed or desired. Each candidate change should then be documented on a preliminary basis and reviewed to determine its schedule criticality and resource and technical requirements. A preliminary picture of the maintenance effort can then be formed and reviewed by the sources of the candidate changes, upper management, and, if appropriate, the customer. Several iterations of this analysis will typically be required.

Once the analysis has been accepted any changes not already documented in an existing problem tracking system should be so documented. If the organization does not have such a system, then one should be created. See Chapter 9, on software configuration management (SCM), for the requirements of such a system. Ideally, the organization will adopt such a system for broader use, along with other features of modern CM but if not then the maintenance activity should create its own. We will see in subsequent sections that controlling the maintenance process will be extremely difficult, if not impossible, without a robust SCM system.

6.3.3.2   Determine the Required Process

Having determined the near-term requirements of the maintenance effort (what is to be done), the question of the process (how to do it) should be addressed. The project will usually have an existing maintenance process, even if it is not recognized as such. In particular, the process used to introduce changes to the system during the later stages of system test will have many of the same attributes and requirements as maintenance. One can argue that, in fact, maintenance begins during product integration. Hence, even if it is not recognized, every project has an implicit process by which the products are maintained. If there is also an explicit maintenance process, then so much the better, because there are now two processes to review and compare.

Ideally this information is contained in the project life cycle model process plan. If it (or some similar document) does not exist, or if maintenance has been omitted, then observations of and interviews with employees will be the primary source of information. Additionally, if the project has a software architect (in title or in fact), then that person should be extensively utilized in the determination of the maintenance process requirements.

The review of the existing processes should focus on their suitability for maintenance. This chapter describes the major phases of maintenance, but note that IEEE Standard 1219-1998 provides a more complete description of them. It should be consulted and used as a template while reviewing any existing processes. These major phases form the architecture in which the specific technical processes are performed.

Typically, the technical processes used by the organization are targeted on new development. The same is true for much of the literature of software processes. In reviewing processes, the reader should keep these thoughts in mind:

- Maintenance changes are being applied to an existing design that was probably created by someone other than the maintainer. How will the maintainer obtain the necessary visibility into the design? What documents are available? How well do they support maintenance?

- How well suited to the maintenance processes are the existing review and analysis procedures? For example, the literature on code reviews is written almost exclusively from the viewpoint of reviewing new code. Thus most code review processes are concerned with the code as a whole, rather than the focusing on the impacts (desirable and undesirable) of changes to existing code.

- How appropriate are the test selection and execution processes to the maintenance effort? During full development a particular software item will be stressed by tests that are intended to find defects in that item. It will also be concurrently stressed unintentionally by tests intended to find defects in other items. During full development both circumstances will occur, whereas during maintenance of an item it is usually impractical to repeat all tests, developmental and otherwise, that occurred during the initial, full-scale development process.

- Are any new tools or facilities needed to perform the maintenance effort? For example, the maintenance effort may be of sufficient intensity to require separate computing facilities.

- As each process is reviewed it should be assessed for its suitability for various classes of maintenance changes. The change classes should be based on the scope of the change, what the change impacts, and how the change will be implemented. It is often the case that existing processes will work well for some classes of changes but not for others.

Any process deficiencies should be documented and ranked as to their criticality and how they can be pragmatically and economically remedied. Care should be taken to ensure that the project is able to meet its short-term needs. At the same time, critical process deficiencies should be addressed as rapidly as possible. The maintenance process derived from this activity will be included in the software maintenance plan of the project.

A common deficiency in such "inherited" processes is the lack of a requirements traceability mechanism. A requirements trace consists of the derivation and documenting of the sources of requirements and their subsequent refinement and allocation to elements of the design. This information is usually represented in the form of a requirements trace matrix. The rows of this matrix represent the requirements, and the columns represent the design components that implement the requirements. This allows the developer and maintainer to identify and document the source (upward) and allocation/flowdown path (downward) of requirements during the development and maintenance processes. In particular, it will allow the maintainers to identify the breath and depth of the impact of a required software system change. If a requirements trace matrix was not produced during the software development phase, a localized trace matrix should be developed around the system change required by the maintenance effort. This approach will reduce the likelihood of the so-called "domino effect" in which one software change triggers a cascade of numerous unexpected or unneeded secondary changes.

6.3.3.3   Quantify the Effort

The budget and schedule required to perform the maintenance can now be estimated quantitatively. The cost, staffing, and schedule requirements of each of the candidate changes identified earlier should be evaluated using the maintenance process derived in the previous section. The changes should be ranked according to their risk, difficulty, criticality of need, any special resources requirements, and the areas (both physically and logically) of the product that are impacted. This ranking may have to be repeated several times because new insights into the key product and market issues might occur when working through the process. Particular attention should be directed toward any changes whose solution will require specialized knowledge and background because these will be the most difficult to schedule.

6.3.3.4   Anticipate Requirements

To plan future maintenance efforts, it is necessary to anticipate what volume and types of changes are likely in the future. The dates at which the currently documented problems were first identified should be examined and any trends determined. This will provide a generic projection of the rate at which additional changes will arise in the near future. To obtain an accurate picture, it may be necessary to remove extraordinary changes from the baseline data before performing the trend analysis. The budget, schedule, and resource requirements of these extrapolated changes should be based on the averages, adjusted for any inflation or deflation, from the previous quantification effort. Finally, the time frame (planning horizon) of this projection should be consistent with the organization's other planning cycles.

6.3.3.5   Develop the Plan

Appendix C of IEEE Standard 1219-1998 provides a guideline for a software maintenance plan (SMP). The general format for the plan is:

Section 1: *Introduction.* The items to be maintained and the scope of the maintenance effort should be described.

Section 2: *References.*

Section 3: *Definitions.*

Section 4: *Software maintenance overview.* The organizational structure of the maintenance effort and how it relates to other activities should be described. The categorization and prioritization schemes used should be described, along with the approach to estimating effort required and schedules for the maintenance activities. The resources required to perform the maintenance activity should be described, along with the responsibility and authority necessary to carry out the efforts.

Section 5: *Tools, techniques, and methods.* The major phases to be followed while performing the maintenance effort should be described, along with any tools and techniques needed to perform and manage the effort. This section is discussed in detail later in this chapter.

Section 6: *Software maintenance reporting requirements.* The collection, analysis, and distribution of information needed to manage the effort should be described.

Section 7: *Software maintenance control requirements.* How the maintenance effort will be controlled should be described, including how anomalies and deviations from the plan or procedures are to be reported and resolved, how the effort and its work products will be configured, protected, and stored, and what standards, practices, and conventions will be applied to the effort.

Section 8: *Software maintenance documentation requirements.* The procedures to be followed to document the maintenance effort should be described.

6.3.4 Implementing Software Maintenance

Using the known and anticipated changes and the methods and procedures described in the SMP, the detailed planning and execution of the software maintenance activity can begin. Based on the categories and associated attributes of change requests, the available resources, and the plan, the detailed effort can be planned and scheduled. The factors that should be considered when doing this are:

- The priority of the changes;

- The cost and schedule requirements of the changes;

- The personnel requirements for the changes, especially any individuals with special knowledge or skills;

- The physical facilities needed to implement and test the changes;

- The areas of the product to which the changes will be applied;

- The regression test requirements of the changes;

- Any documentation or support equipment and software changes needed to support the changes; and

- Any special release requirements.

The factors should be evaluated both separately and in combinations. When all of these factors are considered, natural groups of changes will usually become obvious. Thus, several changes to the same area of the product may be implemented and tested more efficiently if done together. Likewise, it may be more efficient for the overall effort to group one noncritical change with several critical changes as a single change package. This would be the case, for example, if all of the changes in the package needed the talents and knowledge of a single individual, who might be available for only a single, short period of time for the foreseeable future.

When the change packages have been identified, they should then be formally scheduled, following the change implementation process detailed in the SMP. Based on the historical data and management estimates, some labor reserve should be allocated to the implementation of as yet unknown high-priority, time-critical corrective or adaptive changes. The personnel used to establish this reserve must either come from the maintenance group or agreements must be made with other managers in the organization to make the necessary staff available.

The feasibility of this last arrangement is highly dependent on organizational structure, personal relations between the managers, and the business environment of the company as a whole. Realistically, it is usually best to form some part of the reserve within the organization assigned responsibility for maintenance. This can be done by assigning specific individuals other, longer term, low-priority maintenance tasks that can be interrupted (and hence delayed within an established schedule reserve) for some period of time while they are performing the high-priority, time-critical tasks. These long-term, low-priority tasks for which schedule reserves have been established are often referred to as *background tasks*.

The maintenance reserve capacity is embedded in the schedule of the background tasks, whereas the budget allocated for the high-priority, time-critical tasks is separately identified and managed. These arrangements should be reviewed on a regular basis (monthly is often best) to ensure that the schedules of the background tasks are not at risk, that the projected costs of those tasks are not exceeding the allocated budgets, that the personnel are not becoming demoralized by being moved on and off their background tasks, and that the budget reserved for the high-priority tasks is adequate.

6.3.5   Controlling Software Maintenance

The second major management function of software maintenance management is control. The scheduling and cost accounting systems used by the organization to manage other software engineering activities should be applied to the maintenance effort. Two other major control techniques available to manage maintenance are software quality assurance (SQA) and software configuration management (SCM). In addition, metrics and documentation are important to controlling and performing the software maintenance effort.

6.3.5.1 Role of SQA in Software Maintenance

Within the context of software maintenance the objective of the SQA function is to ensure that work is done according to the published SMP and that work is performed using the proscribed methods, processes, and procedures. If the maintenance activity is being performed under contract, then the SQA function must also ensure that the quality provisions of the contract are being observed as well. The maintenance manager should use the SQA function as his or her mechanism to ensure that maintenance activities are being performed in accordance with the plan. For more detail on the activities and functions of SQA, see Chapter 10.

6.3.5.2 Role of SCM in Software Maintenance

SCM is the most important single discipline used to control and guide the software maintenance activity. At the outset, a reliable, disciplined change control system is needed so that maintenance actions can be identified, approved, planned, implemented, tested, and released. During the process of making changes, a reliable, flexible, CM system is required so that the implementation of changes can occur in an orderly manner. As mentioned earlier, multiple change efforts of occur concurrently and act on the same software items. Without a disciplined, capable software library system, supported by a robust change control process, the result will be chaos. Finally, the SCM system is the only way that SQA can objectively determine that the items released are indeed the items tested and approved for release.

6.3.5.3 Use of Metrics in Software Maintenance

Performing and managing the software maintenance effort will be materially simplified if a suitable set of metrics is used. The two major categories of metrics are managerial and technical. *Managerial metrics* are usually graphically represented by a line showing the expected performance and a second line showing the actual performance. Commonly used managerial metrics presented in this way include the following:

- Labor expended versus labor planned,

- Actual design and implementation task starts versus planned task starts,

- Actual design and implementation task completions versus planned task completions,

- Tests completed versus tests scheduled,

- Effort expended for completed tasks versus effort planned, and

- Projected effort to be expended for remaining tasks (planned versus actual).

The data needed to produce these charts should come from the scheduling and cost accounting systems of the organization. These charts not only allow the manager to form a picture of the current organizational performance, they also allow the manager to revise the plans based on the latest performance data. Thus if 20 of a group of 100 similar maintenance tasks require 50 percent more effort than planned, then unless some action can be taken the remaining 80 tasks will, in all likelihood, require 50 percent more effort as well. The "effort expended for completed tasks" chart would show the problem with the 20 tasks that had been completed to date, while the "projected effort for remaining tasks" chart would show the anticipated problem with the remaining 80 tasks.

Technical metrics are used to monitor and control the technical performance and quality of the product. They must be appropriate to the original product. That is, it is illogical to apply a standard based on a lines-of-code-per-module metric, when the original product development applied no criteria of this type. With that caveat, commonly used technical metrics include these:

- Percentage of available computing power used;

- Percentage of available memory used, both volatile and nonvolatile;

- Percentage of communication bandwidth utilized;

- Lines of code per module;

- Module complexity;

- Error per 1,000 lines of code; and

- Software problem reports per 1,000 lines of code.

6.3.5.4   Using and Maintaining Documentation

Documentation includes all information about the software. Examples are requirements, design, code, tests, operations manual, user manual, change logs, engineering notebooks, and trade studies. Complete and accurate documentation is essential to the software maintenance effort. Creation and maintenance of such documentation is necessary if the software maintenance effort is to be successful over time.

Documentation should be clear, unambiguous, and complete. Documentation for modified software systems should be updated or created to reflect the new changes as the changes are made. Invariably, if documentation updates are deferred they are either never done or are done poorly. The project manager should allow and plan for more time in the schedule to maintain the documentation. The CM system should be used to manage the documentation. In particular, the change control system should be used to identify the necessary change to the documentation. The change control system should then be used to manage and monitor the changes to the documentation so identified. Thus software maintenance is both a user and a producer of documentation.

6.4 The Seven Phases of Software Maintenance

If the SMP is being developed following the outline given in IEEE Standard 1219-1998, then Section 5 of the SMP will be titled "Tools, Techniques, and Methods." This section, as briefly described earlier, lists the activities to be undertaken, the steps to be followed, and the methods and tools to be used in performing the software maintenance effort. The standard provides a detailed, informative example of how software maintenance can be performed and managed, using a basic process model to describe each phase of software maintenance. The model decomposes the software maintenance activity into seven phases. The model describes the input, process, output, and control mechanism for each of these seven phases.

Phase	Objectives
1. Problem identification	Identify, classify, and prioritize modification requests.
2. Analysis	Determine feasibility, alternative solution approaches, and scope of changes.
3. Design	Develop a design for approved modifications.
4. Implementation	Make the required changes to the software.
5. System test	Verify that modifications have been satisfied and no new faults have been introduced.
6. Acceptance test	Perform acceptance test on the modified software system to ensure customer satisfaction.
7. Delivery	Deliver the modified software system and updated documentation.

Table 6.1: Software Maintenance Phases

The seven phases are identified and briefly described in Table 6.1. Inspection of this table shows that many of the activities are similar to those performed during the test and integration activities of the initial product development. The environment in which they are performed, however, can be very different, which often imposes additional constraints and requirements on maintenance. In particular, as discussed earlier, different groups of maintenance changes may be simultaneously under way, thereby placing greater demands on the CM systems. Likewise, schedule and cost constraints may in some cases mitigate against performing the full system and acceptance tests that were performed during the initial development.

In the following sections each of the phases listed in Table 6.1 will be described, along with how it is most commonly similar to and different from the activities of initial development.

6.4.1   Problem Identification Phase

The problem identification phase begins when the software change request (SCR) or software modification request (SMR) is received. The information should be captured in a special form, which should be described in the SMP. Figure 6.2 presents an example SCR form.

Software Change Request (SCR)			
Change Identifier			_____SCR
SCR Type		Deficiency Requirements Change Enhancement	
Change Identification			
Originator Identification		Urgency	Baseline Identification
Name		Critical	Project Name	
Title		Very Important	SCI Name	
Organization		Important	Configuration	
Date		Inconvenient	Identifier	
(M/D/Y)		Interesting	Version Identifier	
Requested Change			
Description of Requested Change:		Need for Requested Change:	
Change Modification Validation			
Accepted for Validation		Rejected for Validation due to: Incomplete Invalid Duplicate	
Validation Signature		Validation Date (M/D/Y)	

Figure 6.2: Sample Change or Modification Request Form

Each SCR is then identified, classified, evaluated, and prioritized. Table 6.2 presents an outline of the activities of the problem identification phase. A SCR review board [SCRB or SMRB; called a configuration control board (CCB) in many organizations] should be established to perform and coordinate these activities. The SCRB should be organized consistent with the other change review boards utilized by the project's SCM change control system.

Likewise, any systems used to implement other forms of change requests (CRs) should be used to implement the forms. See Chapter 9, Software Configuration Management for the details of CRs and how they are processed.

Input:	• Change/modification request (SCR/SMR)
Process:	• Assign change number to SCR. • Classify SCR. • Accept or reject SCR. • Determine preliminary estimate. • Prioritize SCR. • Target SCR to specific release.
Control:	• Uniquely identify SCR. • Enter SCR and documented process outputs into depository.
Output:	• Valid, classified SCR. • Understanding of requirements. • SCR priority. • SCR verification data and audit trail. • Initial estimate to implement. • Initial schedule.
Measures:	• Correctness. • Maintainability.
Metrics:	• Number of omissions on SCR form. • Number of SCR submittals. • Number of duplicate SCRs. • Time expended for problem validation.

Table 6.2: Problem Identification Phase

The objectives of this phase are as follows:

- Ensure that the problem is appropriately documented on the SCR form.

- Capture the data required to validate and verify the solution.

- Ensure that the SCR is saved and will be available in the future.

- Ensure that the problem is real and its impact is understood.

- Develop a preliminary estimate of the effort needed to implement the SCR.

- Preliminarily target the modification to a specific software release.

- Obtain adequate visibility (metrics) in this phase so that it can be managed.

Many of the processes used to perform the steps of this phase are common to other CM activities of the project, although keep in mind that the details and intended outcomes may be different. One area in which differences often arise is in the validation of the SCR. During initial development it is usually very easy to verify that, for example, an integration problem is real since the system is "on the bench" so the tests can be rerun. During maintenance the SCR activity will often be initiated externally, so recreating the problem can be a greater challenge. Similarly, if the SCR is a high-priority corrective action, the time available to verify and validate the change may be limited, whereas during initial test and integration the final verification and validation (V&V) tests have yet to be performed.

6.4.2 Analysis Phase

The objective of the analysis phase is to determine the scope and feasibility of the documented modification request. The validated modification request, the other products of the prior phase, and the system and project documentation are studied and analyzed. Both a feasibility study and a detailed analysis are conducted and the results are reported. A risk analysis is performed as part of the analysis phase. Using the results of the analysis, the preliminary resource estimate is revised, and a decision is made on whether to proceed to the design phase. Table 6.3 presents an outline of the activities required during the analysis phase.

6.4.3 Design Phase

The primary objective of the design phase is the creation of a design for making modifications to the system. The outputs of the analysis, together with the existing documentation, software, and databases, are all used in developing the design. Table 6.4 outlines the activities to be performed during the design phase.

Specifics of the design process depend on the design representation and methodology used in the original development, as well as on the size of the modification, the size of the existing system, the development and test environments available, and the impacts to the user of introducing secondary defects by making the change.

Selection and creation of regression tests must be taken into account when developing the design for the modification. Some design options may take longer to implement but be easier to test than others. Finally, any required product characteristics should be considered when developing the design, so that decisions on how existing software modules will be changed are taken into consideration, for example, the product's reliability and future maintainability.

6.4.4 Implementation Phase

In the implementation phase, the designed changes are made to the identified software items. The results of the design phase, together with the current source code and docu-

Input:	• Project/system document.
	• Validated SCR.
	• Documented outputs of prior phase from repository.
Process:	• Feasibility analysis.
	• Detailed technical analysis.
	• Update documents as needed.
Control:	• Conduct technical review.
	• Verify test strategy.
	• Verify documentation is updated.
	• Identify safety and security issues.
Output:	• Feasibility report.
	• Detailed analysis report.
	• Updated requirements.
	• Preliminary software item modification list.
	• Implementation approach and plan.
	• Test strategy.
Measures:	• Flexibility.
	• Traceability.
	• Reusability.
	• Maintainability.
	• Comprehensibility
Metrics:	• Number of requirement changes.
	• Documentation error rates.
	• Effort by functional group.
	• Elapsed time to conduct analysis.
	• Error rates generated by priority and type.

Table 6.3: Analysis Phase

mentation, are the inputs to this phase. Table 6.5 presents an outline of the implementation phase.

During this phase the source code, test plans, design, and user documentation are modified, using the design created in the earlier phase. The new and changed code items should be inspected and reviewed and then unit tested using the updated unit test plans. The items are then integrated into the product and tested. These steps are performed largely using the methods and procedures used during the initial development phase. Any anomalies (typically either defects that were present in the initial documentation or those induced during the maintenance activities) detected while performing these activities should be documented and adjudicated following the procedures documented in the project's SCMP and SMP.

At the conclusion of the implementation phase, a test readiness review (TRR) is conducted that assembles and analyzes the objective evidence, usually data from the unit and

Input:	• Project/system documents. • Source code. • Databases. • Analysis phase outputs.
Process:	• Identify impacted software items. • Create design for modification. • Modify design documentation. • Identify and create new regression tests. • Identify user documentation. • Update needs. • Revise software item modification list.
Control:	• Software inspection or review to verify design. • Verify req. trace. • Verify req. design, and test document updates.
Output:	• Revised modification list. • Detail analysis. • Implementation plan. • Updated design baseline. • Test plans.
Measures:	• Flexibility. • Traceability. • Reusability. • Testability. • Maintainability. • Comprehensibility. • Reliability.
Metrics:	• Software complexity and design changes. • Effort by functional group. • Test plans and procedure changes. • Induced error rates generated by priority and type. • Number of lines of code added, deleted, modified, and tested. • Number of applications using modified software items.

Table 6.4: Design Phase

Input:	• Source code.
	• Product/system documents.
	• Results of design phase.
Process:	• Code and unit test.
	• Update documents.
	• Integration and preliminary integration testing.
	• Readiness review.
Control:	• Software code inspection/review.
	• Verify update of documentation.
	• CM control of software.
	• Traceability of design.
Output:	• Feasibility report.
	• Detailed analysis report.
	• Updated requirements.
	• Preliminary software item modification list.
	• Implementation approach and plan.
	• Test strategy.
Measures:	• Flexibility.
	• Traceability.
	• Maintainability.
	• Comprehensibility.
	• Reliability.
Metrics:	• Size of change (function points or source lines of code).
	• Induced error rates generated by priority and type.

Table 6.5: Implementation Phase

integration testing steps, demonstrating why the modified system is ready for the next phase, system test. The implementation team presents these data to an audience composed of the system test team (which performs the next phase of the maintenance activity), the maintenance manager, and other parties, as required. The system test team presents its test plans. In addition, any facility or resource requirements of the system testing activity should be raised and addressed. The results of the review are documented in a report. If the TRR is not successful, then the software items should be returned to the appropriate earlier stages of the maintenance activity. If it is successful then the modified system will undergo the next activity, system testing.

Because the largest portion of the maintenance budget and schedule is expended during the implementation phase. the majority of the risks and performance problems will become visible there. It is recommended that the implementation effort be monitored closely. Task completions, schedule progress reports, and cost data should be used to quantify the risk. The approach should be based on the cost and schedule control mechanism described in the

SEMP, augmented as required in the SMP.

6.4.5   System Test Phase

The objective of the system test phase is to ensure that the modification requirements have been met and to validate that no faults introduced during the maintenance activity remain. The products modified during the implementation phase are tested, following documented and reviewed system test plans. Table 6.6 describes the system test phase.

Input:	• Updated software documentation. • Test readiness review report. • Updated system.
Process:	• Functional testing. • Interface testing. • Regression testing. • Test readiness review.
Control:	• Configuration management control of Code Listings. • SCRs. • Test reports.
Output:	• Tested systems. • Test reports. • Test readiness review report.
Measures:	• Flexibility. • Traceability. • Verifiability. • Testability. • Interoperability. • Comprehensibility. • Reliability.
Metrics:	• Error rates generated by priority and type. • Generated. • Corrected.

Table 6.6: System Test Phase

System tests are ideally performed on the fully integrated system in an operationally representative configuration. If necessary, multiple configurations are tested. The system is tested functionally from input to output. Each configuration must be subjected to a variety of input streams. These input streams should include both expected, or typical, and unexpected, or atypical, situations. Testing with unexpected input streams is called stress testing. The amount of stress testing required for a given system will be determined by the reliability requirements of the system, the complexity of the system itself, and the complexity of the space from which inputs is drawn. Simulation may be used in cases where it is not possible to have the completely integrated system in the test facility. Depending on the contractual requirements the customer and end user may witness the system test.

System testing should be performed in accordance with the project's documented procedures. These procedures should be documented in the project's SLCMP, supplemented as required by the SMP. The objective of system testing is to validate that the product operates correctly in the given operational environment. The original development effort should have produced a battery of system tests that is used as the baseline. When performing maintenance changes, new tests will usually need to be added. This occurs in virtually all cases for these reasons:

- If the change is corrective, then the earlier system tests did not discover the defect being corrected. New tests are needed to ensure that the defect has been removed.

- If the change is perfective, the new features introduced will need to be tested. New tests are needed to ensure that the new features function as intended.

- If the change is adaptive, then new system tests will often be needed to ensure that the software continues to operate in the modified environment. In some cases, however, adaptive changes require no new tests but a new test environment may be required.

In the case of a corrective release, a subset of the full system test is often conducted. Selection of any subsets is a critical technical and management decision. It is usually based on the reason for the changes, the nature and scope of the changes, the nature and scope of the implementation, and the criticality of the system itself. Major maintenance releases are usually subjected to a full system test.

On completion of the system test phase, an acceptance test or TRR is conducted. The system test team presents the objective results of the planned system testing, while the acceptance test team presents their test plans. The primary goal of the TRR is to ensure that the system produced by the system testing effort is ready to be tested. In addition, any relevant facility and resource issues should be raised and addressed at the TRR. The attendees of the TRR should be the system test team, the acceptance test team, the maintenance manager, and other parties, as required. The results of the review are documented in a report. If the TRR is not successful, then the software items should be returned to the appropriate earlier stages of the maintenance activity. If it is successful, then the modified system will undergo the next activity, acceptance testing.

Depending on the nature of the product and the terms of any contract, the system test phase may not be required. This would typically be the case when the product consists of a single executable that performs its functions on a single, off-the-shelf computer. In that situation integration testing produces a final product so no separate system testing is required and the process can proceed directly to the acceptance test phase. This question should be examined carefully and the decision documented in the SMP. Systems usually suffer from too little testing, not too much.

6.4.6   Acceptance Test Phase

The objective of the acceptance test phase is to ensure that the modified system and all related documentation are satisfactory to the user and customer. The system produced by the system test phase, together with all relevant documentation and data, is used during the acceptance test phase. Table 6.7 describes the acceptance test phase.

Input:	• Updated software documentation. • Test readiness review report. • Updated system. • Acceptance test. • Plans, cases, and procedures.
Process:	• Functional acceptance testing. • Interoperability testing. • Regression testing. • Perform test readiness review.
Control:	• Configuration management control of Code Listings. • SCRs. • Test readiness.
Output:	• Tested systems. • Test reports.
Measures:	• Flexibility. • Traceability. • Verifiability. • Testability. • Interoperability. • Comprehensibility. • Reliability.
Metrics:	• Error rates generated by priority and type. • Generated. • Corrected.

Table 6.7: Acceptance Test Phase

Acceptance testing is similar to system testing in that testing should be performed on the fully integrated, modified system. The main difference between the two is that acceptance testing is used by the customer (or their internal surrogates) to formally accept the modified system and may be contractually required.

Simulation can be used in cases where it is not possible to have the completely integrated system in the test facility. The customer or the customer's representative will either conduct or witness acceptance testing. The facility and data requirements may be supplied or specified by the customer or may be approved by them.

The customer or an authorized representative or surrogate may elect to use test results from the system test or implementation phases to satisfy the needs of the acceptance test phase. This is done to avoid duplicative testing. The opportunities for this should be identified and agreed on prior to but not later than the acceptance TRR. The acceptance test report should document which results were taken from previous tests.

6.4.7 Delivery Phase

The objective of the delivery phase is to deliver the modified software and updated documentation to the customer. Delivery may entail replacing the exiting system with the new version, duplication of the configuration controlled master for delivery to remote users, or digital transmission. Table 6.8 describes the delivery phase.

Input:	• Tested/accepted system. • Acceptance test reports.
Process:	• Physical configuration audit (PCA). • Install. • Training.
Control:	• PCA. • Version description document (VDD).
Output:	• PCA report. • VDD.
Measures:	• Completeness. • Reliability.
Metrics:	• Documentation changes (i.e., VDDs, training manuals, operation guidelines).

Table 6.8: Delivery Phase

The installation procedures should be designed to ensure minimal impact to system users during and after the installation of new versions of the software system. The plan should address any time- and safety-critical factors, together with any restoration and recovery procedures. In addition, it should specify any archival or backup processes that should be performed prior to the installation of the new system, along with any postinstallation testing that should be performed to verify the installation. In the event the installation is not successful, the procedures should describe how the earlier, archived version of the system can be restored to service.

User training may be required when the modifications result in major interface, documentation, or functionality changes. Training can include formal (classroom) and informal methods such as one-on-one instruction, videos, and self-directed instruction manuals. These items should have been updated during the implementation phase.

The key process of the delivery phase is the conduct of the physical configuration audit (PCA), which verifies that the version delivered will be the precise version tested and intended. This important CM activity, together with the concept of the version description document (VDD), is described in Chapter 9.

6.5   Summary

This chapter described the importance of software maintenance both to the developer and to the customers and users of software-based systems. The technical and managerial complexity of the maintenance task was described, together with the tools available to manage these challenges. The *IEEE Standard for Software Maintenance*, which provides an excellent framework within which to plan and execute software maintenance efforts, has been described. In addition, practical advice on how to perform the tasks outlined in the standard has been provided. Finally, the relationship between the processes documented in the software maintenance plan and those described in the other software management plans has been described.

Applicable Standards

IEEE Std 610.12-1990. *IEEE Standard Glossary of Software Engineering Terminology.* IEEE, New York.

IEEE Std 1219-1998. *IEEE Standard for Software Maintenance.* IEEE, New York.

Additional References

[Arthur 1988]   Arthur, L. J. (1988). *Software Evolution—The Software Mainte-nance Challenge.* John Wiley and Sons, New York.

[Boehm 1976]   Boehm, B. (1976). "Software Engineering." *IEEE Trans. Computers*, Vol. C-25, No. 12, pp. 1226–1241, December.

[Dart et al. 1993]   Dart, S., Christie, A., and Brown, A. (1993). "A Case Study in Maintenance," Technical Report SEI-93-TR-8. Software Engineering Institute, Carnegie Mellon University, Pittsburgh, PA.

[FIPS 1984]   Federal Information Processing Standards. (1984). *Guideline on Software Maintenance*, FIPS 106. Information Technology Laboratory, NIST, Gaithersburg, MO.

[Landis et al. 1992] Landis, L., McGarry, F., Waligora, S. et al. (1992). "Recommended Approach to Software Development," Software Engineering Laboratory Series SEL-81-305. Software Engineering Laboratory, NASA, Goddard Space Flight Center (GSFC), Greenbelt, MD.

[Longstreet 1990]   Longstreet, D. H. (1990). *Software Maintenance and Computers*. IEEE Computer Society Press, Los Alamitos, CA.

[Liu 1976]   Liu, C. C. (1976). "A Look at Software Maintenance." *Datamation*. Vol. 22, pp. 51–55.

[McConnell 1998]   McConnell, S. (1998). *Software Project Survival Guide*. Microsoft Press, Redmond, WA.

[NBS 1985]   National Bureau of Standards. (1985). *Executive Guide to Software Maintenance*, NBS Special Publication 500-130. Author, Washington, DC.

[Parikh 1986]   Parikh, G. (1986). *Handbook of Software Maintenance*. John Wiley and Sons, New York.

[Parikh 1985]   Parikh, G. (1985). *Techniques of Software Maintenance*. John Wiley and Sons, New York.

[Pigoski 1997]   Pigoski, T. M. (1997). *Practical Software Maintenance: Best Practices for Managing Your Software Investment*. John Wiley & Sons, New York.

[Takang & Grubb 1997] Takang, A., and Grubb, P. (1997). *Software Maintenance Concepts and Practice*. International Thomson Computer Press, London.

Part II

Process Management and Control

Part II, Chapters 7–11, describes how a project's software life cycle processes are defined, established, managed, and controlled. As the profession has matured it has been observed, irrespective of the technical methods employed to specify, design, implement, and test software systems, that developing software in a dependable, predictable manner requires that certain underlying practices and processes must be put into place, performed, and managed. Thus, while the previous part of the book argued that the probabilities of success of a software development project are enhanced when the products are regarded from a systems-level viewpoint, this part adds to that the proposition that the probability of success is further enhanced when the technical processes used to develop the software are managed in an organized, documented way. In particular, it describes some of the supporting activities that have historically been shown, when implemented correctly, to be effective in supporting and controlling the technical effort. The reader must always remember that the purpose of these supporting and controlling activities is to assist the software project manager and the development team. They do not exist for their own sake, no matter how important they are within the context of a software development effort.

The following chapters describe the key activities needed to establish, manage, and maintain a project's life cycle processes. The reader will observe that while the chapters of Part II describe the technical activities (and resulting developmental documents) needed to establish a project's software systems engineering effort together with one management plan (namely the validation and verification plan), these five chapters describe three plans.

Chapter 7, *Software Life Cycle Process Management*, presents the concept of a software life cycle model. Just as experience has shown that treating a software product as an entity from a systems viewpoint, it has further taught us that the activities needed to develop the software must be decomposed into a series of steps and then planned and managed. The realization that the items being developed by a project have a natural life cycle and work flow is not unique to software. However, since software has no material realization, this fact is not as obvious as it would be for the design and fabrication of a piece of hardware. For the same reason the explicit description and management of the flow of items through the processes is even more critical. Thus, how each step of this workflow (classically specification, design, code, and test and integration) is to be performed and evaluated should be described so that both the engineering and management teams have a clear picture of how the work will be done. The chapter then presents an overview of the most important life cycle models currently in use in the industry. Finally, the chapter describes how to create a software life cycle model and processes and how to document them in a software life cycle management plan using the format described in IEEE Standard 1074-1997.

A significant development in recent years has been the increased recognition of the importance of *Software Process Improvement*, the subject of Chapter 8. This chapter was specially written for this book by Professor Robin Hunter, of the University of Strathclyde, Glasgow, Scotland, a recognized expert in this area. It discusses both the broad themes of process improvement and the various national and international efforts to develop frameworks within which an organization's software process improvement efforts can be structured, and ultimately within which their capability and maturity can be evaluated.

The industry has further observed that as software items, whether they be documents or code, flow through the steps of the life cycle model, it must be possible to retrieve their correct version or configuration. This important underlying and supporting activity of software configuration management (SCM) is described in Chapter 9. SCM provides critical measures of stability, visibility, and dependability to the software development environment and processes. It provides mechanisms for storing versions of a project's items appropriate to designated points in the life cycle. It provides mechanisms for controlling when and how changes to those versions are approved and applied. Thus it provides management and the other supporting processes with a reliable repository from which versions can be extracted for measurement, evaluation, and review. Above all else it should provide a stable, responsive framework upon which the development team can base their work. It should be the backbone or framework upon which all the other processes are based. After describing the concepts and methods most commonly used to achieve these objectives the chapter describes the form and content of the SCM plan, as described in IEEE Standard 828-1990.

Experience has also shown that as cost and schedule pressures are applied to programs it is possible that some key steps of the life cycle will not be performed with the level of intensity specified in the life cycle processes. In extreme cases steps of the life cycle may be skipped altogether. If this occurs and the management team (or the customer) is not aware of it then there is no opportunity to correct the situation. Further, in more formal contractual environments an independent determination must be made that the software life cycle model and processes conform to contractual requirements. The discipline of software quality assurance (SQA) as described in Chapter 10, has evolved to address these needs. SQA is most commonly used by management and the customer to insure that the development team does what they said they would do in the plans and procedures of the project. Hence SQA provides independent and objective visibility into the conduct of the activities of the life cycle. In particular, that it renders judgments on procedural and performance, not technical grounds. Judgments on technical grounds are reserved to the V&V activities described in Chapter 5. After describing these key activities and goals of SQA the chapter describes the creation, form, and content of an SQA Plan, as described in IEEE Standard 730-1998.

As design documents, plans, and code items pass through the key steps of their life cycle models, experience has also shown that they should be subjected to some form of review. Depending on the specifics of the item and the stage of its life cycle that has been or is just being completed this review may take various forms. Thus the design of an individual piece of code might be reviewed by the designer, the individual who specified it, and several other designers whose code will interact with it. Such 'peer' reviews in fact make up the bulk of the reviews in most programs, but there are several other types. Chapter 11, which is based on IEEE Standard 1028-1997, describes the various types of reviews that can be utilized in the conduct of a software development program, as well as how they should be planned and executed. Reviews provide a critical feedback mechanism to both the quality assurance and the life cycle process management activities of a program. They also provide project management with insight into the status of the project between major milestones.

Chapter 7

Software Life Cycle Process Management

7.1   Introduction

This chapter discusses two important concepts: first, the decomposition of the development of a product or other item through a series of interrelated processes, and, second, the processes that operate on the product and how they are selected, managed, and maintained.

We first introduce the broader context of IEEE/EIA Standard 12207-1996, *Software Life Cycle Processes*, and, once having established that framework, go on to discuss the selection and management of the life cycle processes for use within a single project following IEEE Standard 1074-1997, *IEEE Standard for Developing Software Life Cycle Processes*.

7.1.1   Overview of IEEE/EIA Standard 12207-1996

Because the focus of this book is specifically on software project management, the current chapter, like the other chapters of this book, does not treat the broader set of processes that occur before, during, and after the development of the product. To be specific, IEEE/EIA Standard 12207 identifies three classes of processes—primary, supporting, and institutional—that can be used to develop a software system.

In the viewpoint adopted by Standard 12207, a *process* is a set of interrelated activities and tasks, which, when taken together, transform some input into an output. Thus, activities are a broad category of actions or groups of actions needed to complete the process. Finally, tasks are the elemental actions needed to complete activities. For example, *implementation* (or *construction*) would be an activity under the process of development, whereas detailed design, design reviews, coding, test plan and procedure development, code reviews, and unit testing would all be considered tasks, which together make up the implementation.

Standard 12207 defines the primary processes in acquiring a software system to be as follows:

1. *Acquisition*, the overarching process by which the acquirer obtains the product;

2. *Supply*, the process by which the product is provided by the supplier to the acquirer;

3. *Development*, the process by which the product is designed, built, and tested by the developing organization;

4. *Operation*, the process followed by the operator in its day-to-day use of the product; and

5. *Maintenance*, the process used to maintain the product, including the application of changes both to the product as well as to its operating environment.

Note that the supplier is commonly thought of as being the developer. Although this is often the case, it need not be so. For example, the supplier may choose to subcontract the actual development to a third party, performing the balance of the activities needed to deliver the product themselves. The specifics of the relationship of these entities and the processes they perform will be largely dictated by the situation.

Having established a broader context, however, this chapter focuses on the development process for a single project. We will from time to time refer to these broader primary processes; together with some of the lower tier processes described below.

In addition to the primary processes Standard 12207 identifies a number of *supporting life cycle processes*, which would be applied to the activities performed in the primary processes (or even other supporting or institutional processes) as required. Other chapters of this book discuss specifics of these processes as applied to a single project. The supporting processes and chapter cross-references are as follows:

- *Documentation* consists of the activities used to record specific information generated by any other process; discussed in Chapter 4.

- *Configuration management* activities are used to capture and maintain for posterity information and products produced during the processes; discussed in Chapter 9.

- *Quality assurance* consists of the activities used to objectively ensure that the product and the associated processes conform to their documented requirements and plans; discussed in Chapter 10.

- *Verification* activities are used to verify the product; discussed in Chapter 5.

- *Validation* activities are used to validate the product; also discussed in Chapter 5.

- *Joint reviews* are used by two parties to evaluate the status and products of other activities; discussed in Chapter 11.

- *Audits* consist of the activities used to determine compliance of the project with requirements, plans, and contracts; discussed in Chapter 11.

- *Problem resolution* describes the activities to be carried out when analyzing and eliminating problems of any nature and source; discussed in Chapters 9 and 11.

It is clear that many of these supporting processes will play a critical role in the development process.

Finally, Standard 12207 describes a number of *organizational life cycle processes*, which form the local organizational context within which the project is being executed:

- *Management* describes the activities of the organization's management, including but not limited to project management, as they relate to the other life cycle processes. This is addressed in Chapters 1, 13, and 15.

- *Infrastructure* consists of the activities needed to set in places the other life cycles processes. This includes but is not limited to capital and expense items, as well as personnel. See Chapter 12 for how this relates to the resources needed to execute a project.

- *Improvement* is made up of the activities used to improve the performance of any other process. See Chapter 8.

- *Training* defines the activities needed to supply appropriately trained personnel to the project. See Chapter 13.

These organizational processes are commonly intended to be applied across multiple projects. In more mature organizations (as measured by some process maturity indicator such as those defined by the CMM, CMMI or SPICE models), in fact, the expectation is that the organization identifies and institutionalizes its processes for use by programs. Thus, more mature organizations have developed and institutionalized what is often referred to as an *organizational base process*, which is then tailored (following a disciplined and documented process) to meet the requirements and conditions of specific projects and programs. These considerations will impact the improvement process in particular.

Figure 7.1 shows a very top-level view of the *primary, supporting*, and *organizational life cycle processes* of IEEE/EIA Standard 12207-1997.

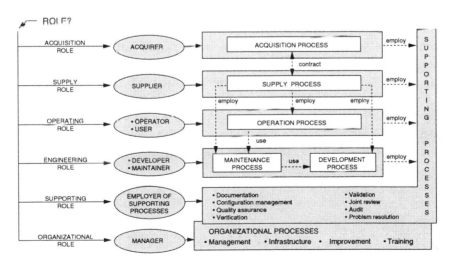

Figure 7.1: IEEE/EIA Standard 12207 Life Cycle Processes and Roles

7.1.2   Project Life Cycles

The developmental evolution of an item, whether it is software or hardware, is referred to as the item's *life cycle*. It is usually conceived as starting with the initial conception of the item and continuing through its removal from service. Figure 7.2 illustrates a simplified project life cycle with nine activities.

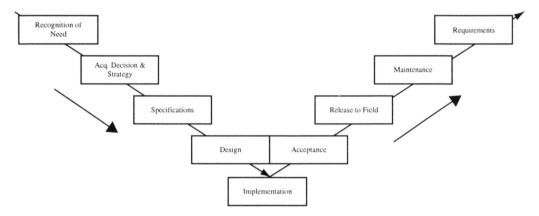

Figure 7.2: Simplified Project Life Cycle Model

Each of the tasks within a life cycle is accomplished by means of one or more processes. The combinations of all the relevant processes within the life cycle are called the software life cycle processes.

This chapter addresses the creation and management of software life cycle processes, but focuses on the technical activities required to develop the products, starting with specification and continuing on through acceptance testing. Thus, this chapter focuses on the primary process of development in the Standard 12207 model. In addition, this discussion should not be confused with the distinct but related topic of institutional software process improvement, as discussed in the previous section and in Chapter 8. Even if the processes in use in a given items life cycle were static (e.g., no improvement necessary or, alternatively, allowed), the processes, their relationships, and the flow of the product through the processes would still need to be defined and managed. That is, they must be:

- Planned,

- Organized,

- Staffed,

- Directed, and

- Controlled,

as would any other activity involving all but the smallest of groups performing the simplest of tasks.

If process improvement within the framework of a single project is desirable—and it usually is—then that activity should be managed consistent with, and as a part of, the entire life cycle and its component processes. Thus, this chapter discusses the introduction of changes into the software process, while another chapter of this book (Chapter 8) discusses software process improvement itself.

In a similar vein, this chapter treats metrics as tools to be used in monitoring the processes of the software life cycle and their relationships, while the chapter of that name (Chapter 15) discusses metrics in detail. Likewise, as noted earlier, the chapter on software process improvement describes that important topic in a broader organizational context. In turn, this chapter treats software life cycle process management as a subset of the larger and more general issues of software engineering project management, discussed elsewhere in this book.

Two primary dimensions are used to establish the software life cycle processes. The first is the selection of the global model of the software development life cycle. A *global process model*, usually referred to as a life cycle model, describes how the individual tasks or phases of a life cycle interrelate. The currently available models are discussed below. The second dimension is the selection of the individual processes by which the specific phases and their tasks are performed. The individual who is tasked to choose the (global) life cycle model and the processes to be used to perform the tasks within the model is referred to as the *process architect*.

The process architect may or may not be the software program manager, depending on the organizational, program, and contract structures in place. If the process architect is not the software program manager, then the manager must have a clear relationship to the architect and must understand the architect's work if the project is to succeed. Within the framework of the parent organization, the process architect may have access to institutional resources and processes that can tremendously simplify, and lower the risk associated with, the selection of methods and tools. However, it is not always the case that the project has access to such resources.

These factors, both organizational and technical, determine the major phases of software life cycle process management:

- Select the appropriate software life cycle model (SLCM) as a global network of processes needed to deliver and support the product(s), and the activities needed to complete those activities.

- Create the software life cycle (SLC) by identifying and defining the individual tasks.

- Establish the software life cycle process (SLCP), both organizationally and technically.

- Manage the SLCP throughout the product's identified life.

The key instrument for planning and documenting these activities is the SLCM plan, or SLCMP. IEEE Standard 1074-1997, *IEEE Standard for Developing Software Life Cycle*

Processes; IEEE/EIA Standard 12207.0-1996, *Software Life Cycle Processes*; and IEEE/EIA 12207.2-1997, *Software Life Cycle Processes—Implementation Considerations*, are the primary guides for creating this plan.

7.2   Objectives

In this chapter you will learn:

- Why the management of software life cycle processes is an important component of software engineering project management.

- How to define the content and scope of a software life cycle process management plan.

- What factors to consider when evaluating a software life cycle process management plan.

- How to determine the appropriate levels of software life cycle process management for specific types of software work products.

- What the most common life cycle models are.

- What activities must be incorporated into the life cycle processes.

- Who the process architect is and what role he or she fulfills in life cycle process management.

- Why software life cycle process management is more than just selecting a life cycle model.

7.3   Software Life Cycle Models and Processes

IEEE Standard 12207.0-1996 describes a software life cycle model as

a framework containing the processes, activities, and tasks involved in the development, operation, and maintenance of a software product, spanning the life of the system from the definition of its requirements to the termination of its use.

Applying this concept to the developmental processes, we find these basic features inherent in all models:

- They describe the major phases of development.

- They define the major processes and activities to be accomplished during each of those phases.

- They specify products of each of the phases and inputs at the beginning of the phases.

- They provide a framework onto which the necessary activities can be mapped.

The subsequent sections will describe these four primary life cycle models for development: (1) the waterfall model, (2) the incremental model, (3) the evolutionary model, and (4) the spiral model. In addition, three important modifiers to all four models will be discussed: prototyping, concurrency, and commercial components and reuse.

As will be seen, some of the models share multiple features and some may, indeed, be considered as special cases of others. Because the emphases between the processes and activities are different, however, they will all be treated separately to provide insight into the operation of the models.

7.3.1 The Waterfall Model

The *waterfall model* is the classical model of development for both hardware and software. This model is frequently called the *conventional model*. The project is expected to progress down the (primary) path through each of the phases (requirements, design, coding and unit test, integration, and maintenance) of development, with deliverables (software requirements specification, design documents, actual code and test cases, final product, product updates) at each stage (see Figure 7.3).

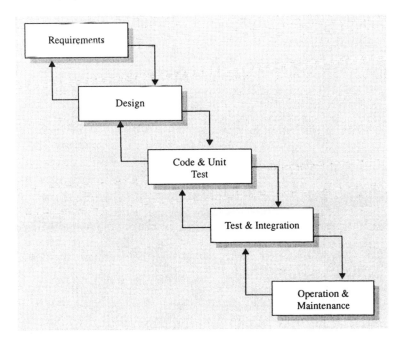

Figure 7.3: Waterfall Life Cycle Model

Work products (called *deliverables*) flow down the primary, stepwise path of normal development. The reverse flow represents iterative changes applied to a prior deliverable, the need for which has been only recognized in the next phase or even later. This is a natural consequence of the uncertainty associated with all development activity. Such changes are called *rework* and will require that not only some portion of the prior phase be repeated but the current one as well.

When considering this model and, indeed, any other, the process architect must evaluate the degree of uncertainty in the initial work product. This is usually the software requirements specification (SRS). Another issue is the historical proficiency the organization has demonstrated in performing each of the activities and tasks. Problems in either of these areas can result in excessive (that is, more than planned) backward flows and can significantly increase costs.

Although the waterfall model is reasonably "old," and newer techniques are available today, some advantages still accrue to users of this conventional model:

- The single requirements phase encourages specification of what the system is to do before deciding how the system will do it (i.e., specification before design).

- The single design phase encourages planning of the system structure before building the components (i.e., design before coding).

- The use of reviews at the end of each phase permits acquirer and user involvement.

- The model permits early imposition of baselines and configuration control.

- Each preceding step serves as an approved, documented baseline for the succeeding step.

Of course, there are also some disadvantages to the waterfall model:

- Customers must be able to express their requirements completely, correctly, and with clarity.

- Delays can occur in design, coding, and testing.

- Too much time can be spent on the production of little-used documentation.

- It is difficult to assess the true state of progress during the first two or three stages.

- Baselines and milestones place heavy emphasis on documentation in the early phases of a project.

- The developer must understand the application from the beginning.

- A large integration and test effort must occur near the end of the project.

- No demonstration of system capabilities can occur until the end of the project.

As a general rule, the waterfall model is best suited to situations in which the downward, progressive path dominates. That is, it is useful when the requirements are well understood and the process architect is confident that the developing organization is proficient (or can be trained to be proficient in time to support the project) in the processes needed to implement this model. However, the acquiring organization may insist on the use of the waterfall model simply because the flow is easy to understand and easily fits most contracting models.

The completion of one of the phases produces a concrete work product that can, if desired, be independently examined. Progress payments from the acquiring organization to the developing organization can be made contingent on completion of each phase. For both parties this means that the completion must be objectively verified.

7.3.2   The Incremental Model

The *incremental life cycle model* was one of the first variations to be derived from the waterfall model. The assumption behind the model is that the requirements can be segmented into an incremental series of products, each of which is developed somewhat independently (see Figure 7.4).

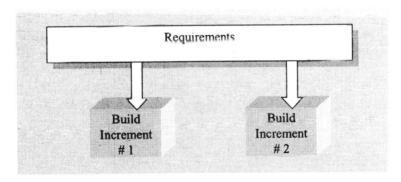

Figure 7.4: Incremental Life Cycle Model

Classically, this model is adopted when the requirements are all known at the start of development, when the product can be segmented into reasonably independent software deliverables, called *build increments*, and when it is desirable for some of those increments to be completed as soon as possible. An example of this would be a database system that must provide varying functions to multiple classes of users through distinct user interfaces. In such a case, it is advantageous to implement the complete database design, together with the functions and user interface of one high priority group of users, as one build increment, leaving subsequent builds to address the other classes of users.

Figure 7.5 illustrates how the waterfall model can be used to develop the incremental builds (sometimes called *blocks*) of the incremental development model. Even thought this figure suggests fully concurrent design and implementation, in fact the incremental model can be used to develop the increments with any desired degree of concurrency. Thus the design of the first increment can be completed and the lessons learned thereby transferred to the design of the second increment.

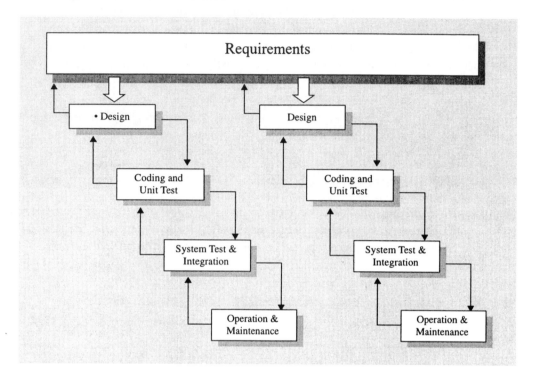

Figure 7.5: Incremental Waterfall Development Model

The increments are often called *builds* if they are not intended for delivery to the customer. If they are delivered they are treated as *released versions*. When writing the SLCMP, care should be taken to use terminology that is consistent with the customer's expectations, both informal and formal, as expressed in the contract and statement of work (SOW).

In addition to the benefits that arise from being a variation on the waterfall model, the incremental model has the following advantages:

- Less cost and time is required to make the first delivery.

- Less risk is incurred to develop the smaller systems represented by the increments.

- User requirement changes may decrease because of the quicker time to first release.

- Incremental funding is allowed; that is, only one or two increments might be funded when the program starts.

However, if the incremental model is inappropriate or is misused, it has the following disadvantages:

- Fielding of initial increments may destabilize later increments through unplanned levels of user change requests.

- If requirements are not as stable or complete as thought earlier, increments might be withdrawn from service, reworked, and rereleased.

- Managing the resulting cost, schedule, and configuration complexity may exceed the capabilities of the organization.

Considering the first and last points together, a potentially dangerous situation can arise if customer change requests are written against the early increments. If the customer considers these to be within the scope of the contract but the developer does not, a serious confrontation could occur. The only way to protect both parties from this is for the developer to have appropriate configuration management and cost accounting systems in place, along with a very clear *change clause* in the contract. In this way, if situations arise in which one or the other of the parties is not happy, there should be no question as to the facts.

Finally, if incremental funding is adopted, the customer should request option pricing on the unfunded increments. The developer should then require that those options have an expiration date (sometimes called the *last exercise date* or *date of last exercise*) so that they can manage the organization's resources and costs across multiple contracts.

7.3.3   The Evolutionary Model

The next logical step in life cycle model development is the *evolutionary model*, which explicitly extends the incremental model to the requirements phase. Figure 7.6 illustrates this, showing that the first build increment is used to refine the requirements for a second build increment. This refinement can come from multiple sources and paths.

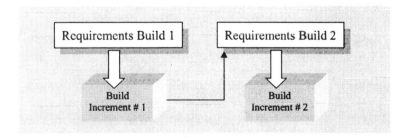

Figure 7.6: Evolutionary Life Cycle Model

First, if an early increment is released to users then they will provide feedback in the form of change requests that will assist in the development of requirements for the later increments. Second, the sheer act of developing a build increment will provide visibility into issues that were not recognized prior to actually starting work on that increment.

Within the evolutionary model the waterfall model can still be used to manage each evolutionary increment. Once the requirements are understood the phases of design, coding, and so on can be instituted as is done in the implementation of the waterfall model within the incremental development model.

Using the evolutionary model should not be an excuse to shortcut the requirements analysis phase. All of the requirements sources available should be evaluated commensurate with their importance and risk at the start of the project. Only in this way can the uncertainty in the requirements be identified and bounded. Only in this way can those requirements that are to be included in (at least) the first increment be identified. In addition, the contracting terms should reflect the development model. For example, the development and delivery of each increment could be negotiated as a separate contract, to include option pricing for labor rates and fees for the next increment, perhaps along with order-of-magnitude cost estimates.

Likewise, the cost accounting, scheduling, status tracking, and configuration management systems must be capable of supporting the model. Because the evolutionary increments are explicitly sequential the evolutionary model will usually be less challenging for these systems than is the incremental model. However, the reader should realize that some degree of concurrency is always present. Thus the systems must accommodate some level of concurrency, even if it is by exception.

The strengths and weaknesses of the evolutionary model are simular to those of the incremental model. More specifically, the advantages for the evolutionary model are as follows:

- The model can be used when the requirements cannot or will not be specified.

- The user can experiment with the system to improve the requirements.

- Greater user/acquirer involvement is required than in the waterfall method.

The disadvantages are:

- Use of the method is exploratory in nature and therefore constitutes a high-risk endeavor. Strong management is required.

- This method is used as an excuse for hacking or to avoid documenting the requirements or design, even if they are well understood.

- Users/acquirers do not understand the nature of the approach and can be disappointed when results are unsatisfactory.

7.3.4   The Spiral Model

The *spiral model* was developed by Dr. Barry Boehm [Boehm 1988] and represents the newest of the accepted process models. The spiral model is another life cycle in which the development effort is iterative. This means that as soon as one iteration of development is completed, another iteration of development commences.

This model focuses on the basic steps of problems solving whereby you identify the problem, identify alternatives, select the best alternative, follow the action steps, and conduct follow-up. Although the framework and global architecture of the spiral and iterative models are identical, the focus of the phases and their activities is different.

With the spiral model, the developer and client identify what the clent wants to accomplish, determine the alternative routes (analyzing the risks and payoffs), select the best alternative, develop the system, evaluate what has been completed, and start over. Hence, the spiral model expands the scope of the management task beyond that of the incremental model, which is founded on the assumption that the requirements are the primary and perhaps sole source of risk. In the spiral model the scope of the decisions and risk reduction is much broader. Figure 7.7 illustrates the spiral model.

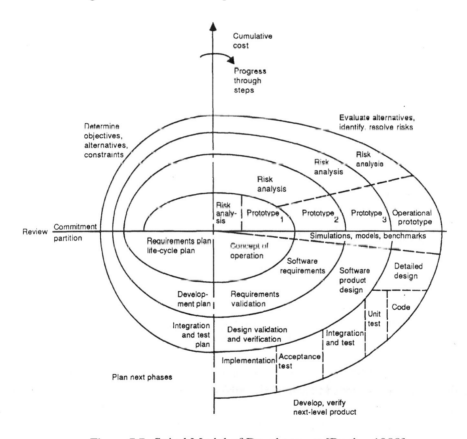

Figure 7.7: Spiral Model of Development [Boehm 1988]

Another feature of the spiral model is that, in fact, only one cycle of the process may actually develop software deliverables. The spiral model is good when dealing with very high risk development projects or dealing with a client who is not exactly sure of the requirements, including the need for a system or what type of system in the broadest sense. The spiral model depicted is from Boehm's original article [Boehm 1988]. Figure 7.7 displays one instance of the spiral model with emphasis on prototyping. Note that the spiral model does not require prototyping but is well suited to this process.

Like the evolutionary and prototyping models, the spiral model is compatible with the use of the waterfall model as an embedded process. The waterfall process of analysis, design, coding, implementation, and maintenance becomes one part of a trip around the spiral.

7.3.5   Applying Prototyping to Life Cycle Models

A natural next step in the progression of life cycle models is to explicitly plan on using one or more of the evolutionary increments as an explicit requirements exploration tool. Such increments are called prototypes, following the usage of that term in other areas of engineering. Prototypes, although they may be used by the customer in some limited way, are not viewed as fully functioning increments. Instead, they are used to explore the requirements that will be implemented later in fully functional deliverable, supportable increments.

In addition to their role in exploring requirements, prototypes can be used to determine technical, cost, or schedule feasibility for some part of or all of the project. Here are some examples of questions a prototype would assist in answering:

- Can a new development environment or tool set be used to meet a customer's cost or schedule constraints?

- Can an installed or available hardware and software infrastructure support a customer's new performance and capacity requirements?

- Can the product be built? That is, is it feasible?

Prototyping is particularly popular in systems with user interfaces and databases, sometimes known as *rapid application development* (RAD). However, the definition of what methods and tools constitute RAD and prototyping varies with time. Thus a few years ago the term was widely applied to efforts using the Visual Basic and Delphi development environments. Today these tools are used to build to build prototypes and the ultimate systems in a fairly seamless manner.

Prototyping typically begins with a statement of objectives for the prototype, along with the specific requirements needed to achieve the objectives of the prototype. This is followed by a design scaled to match the toolset used to build the prototype targeted toward those aspects of the software that will be visible to the client or that address a key technical risk. After the design, the developer builds the prototype. The prototype is then used in some form of evaluation. This often involves turning the prototype over to the customer so that the customer can experiment with the prototype and gain a better "look and feel" for the eventual system.

These experiments have the most obvious objective of exploring the customer's interface needs. However, the fact that the user can now interact with a prototype system will often help to crystalize their functional and performance needs as well. The client then provides feedback about the prototype to the developers, who, in turn, document what was learned and apply this knowledge to the actual requirements. These requirements are then elaborated and implemented using one of the other life cycle models.

Although prototyping has signficant advantages in many situations, it also has risks:

- Both the customer and the developer may not appreciate how much work must be done to turn a prototype into a fully functioning system. Because they see an elaborate and sophisticated user interface, customers might assume that the bulk of the work has been done.

- Because it appears to be so successful, the prototype may grow in an unplanned manner beyond what was intended or needed, consuming schedule, monetary, and human resources at the expense of the final, full version. In other words it becomes, contrary to the stated plan, a first incremental delivery.

- The team developing the prototype may not adequately communicate what they have learned to the team developing the full product. This is can happen, for example, if the prototyping team is part of a separate organizational function, such as marketing. In addition, the toolset used to develop the prototype might not be interoperable with the toolset that will be used on the full development effort.

- The prototype may not scale, either in terms of performance or capacity.

- The prototype may actually perform the functions it implements better than a fully functional deliverable ever can. This can happen because the prototype does not have to support the full functionality. In this case, customers might feel that they have lost something in going from the (cheap) prototype to the (expensive) full system. Explaining the situation can be very difficult.

All of these risks can be managed if they are identified and monitored by the team early in the project's life. All may happen to one degree or another. The point is that they must be recognized and worked.

7.3.6   Role of Concurrency in Life Cycle Models

As a program passes through the phases of its selected life cycle it enevitably occurs that some processes overlap others, whether planned or not. For example, the requirements of a program may be very well understood. As a result, for reasons of cost and schedule efficiency the classical waterfall model may be selected. This would seem to preclude concurrency. The reality can, however, be very different. For example, it is not an uncommon cirumstance for the detailed design for one subsystem to be completed before another. In that case, provided the interface between the two subsystems is stable, then proceeding with coding of the one subsystem may be a reasonable thing to do: The developers of the detailed design that is completed can often be most efficiently employed leading the coding team for that subsystem, rather than helping with the detailed design of the second subsystem. This will lead to concurrency (on a system level) of the detailed design and coding phases, which are usually thought of as being sequential.

The organization's management systems must be capable of supporting this situation. This includes the scheduling, cost control, status tracking, and configuration management systems, and the mechanisms by which technical reviews are conducted, as well as any design tools. In addition, the interface between the two subsystems must now be monitored more closely than would be the case if both subsystems were simultaneously in the same phase of development.

Note also that concurrency is implicit in the existence of backward flows (that is, changes that must be made to a document or other product that has already completed its development) in all of the life cycle models. As discussed before, this is inevitable. The issue is one of materiality, that is, how much?

Thus, two important issues surround the use of concurrency:

1. *Degree of concurrency.* The degree of concurrency can range from the incidental, with a few backflow change requests, to the aggressive, with one increment being designed while the prior one is being integrated. The requirements that these two situations place on the technical and managerial systems are very different.

2. *How concurrency is managed.* Irrespective of whether concurrency was or was not planned to the degree it is currently present in a program, what matters is what is done to manage it now. For the current project, what is done about concurrency once it arises is a different matter than why it became necessary or how well it was planned for. However, if the organization is to improve its performance over time, these questions should be dispassionately examined.

7.3.7   Role of Commercial Items and Reuse

To an increasing extent, modern software systems are being built using either commercial application frameworks, commercial components, or reuse of internally developed components and frameworks, and, of course, reuse of institutational practices and procedures. There are three sources of these trends:

1. Competitive pressures of time-to-market and cost;

2. Increasing complexity and standardization of delivery environments, such as the Internet; and

3. The emergence of *product line engineering*, in which the development and evolution of multiple, related software products are systematically planned and executed, reusing parts of the design and implementation across all members of the product line.

The implications of these trends to a project's life cycle processes can range from the trivial to the profound. For example, if a product is being built using a commercial application framework that is new to the development organization, then a prototype could be developed to both gain experience with the framework and to demonstrate its suitability for the application. If the framework were an internally developed one, then it still might be appropriate to develop a prototype to evaluate the suitability of the framework for the application under development. Because selecting a framework is such a fundamental design decision, this means that the prototyping must be performed early in the project life cycle, if at all possible prior to committing to the project's costs and schedule.

If internally developed or externally purchased components are to be incorporated into the new system, then the suitability of those components must be evaluated early in the project. Exactly when is determined by how extensive and fundamental the usage of the components is. For example, if a large part of the product involves user interactions, then the components implementing the graphical user interface should be carefully evaluated to ensure they support the required functionality. This could be done immediately following the development of a concept of operations document.

If a commercial component provides a small but critical portion of the product, then its suitability should be evaluated during or prior to the design phase, so that in the event it is found to be unsuitable, an alternative component can be procured or built.

As a general rule, if preexisting components or frameworks, regardless of the source, are being used in the development of a product, then those items should be evaluated. The evaluation process should be explicitly represented in the life cycle model. In some cases, such as the first examples, the evaluation process may profoundly influence the life cycle model selected, resulting, for example, in the selection of a spiral model instead of an incremental one.

In addition to such structural changes in a project's life cycle model, the use of preexisting components can profoundly influence the individual technical processes. For example, if reused components represent a significant portion of the product, then the relative percentage of the testing effort applied to unit testing will decrease, while the portion spent on integration will increase. Likewise, the design process will be effective because subprocesses must be established or modified to ensure that the design is consistent with any reused (or purchased) frameworks or components.

7.4 Selecting a Software Life Cycle Model

After evaluating the strengths and weaknesses of each model, the process architect must select the best life cycle model for the assigned project. This is an important and complex task, so it must be approached in a systematic, careful manner.

IEEE Standard 1074-1997 lists the steps to be followed to select a project's life cycle model:

1. Identify the SLCMs available to the development project. It may happen that some management systems and tools needed to support a particular SLCMs cannot realistically be made available soon enough to meet the project's schedule.

2. Identify those attributes of the desired end system and the development environment that will impact the choice of SLCM. For example, are the requirements firm? Is it certain that the tools will support the project needs? Is there a specific technical risk? Is the system a well-understood one or is it unprecedented?

3. Identify any constraints that might be imposed on the selection. These may be externally or internally imposed. Examples would be contractual requirements from the customer or shortages of key development skills. A specific example would be a customer-mandated program schedule, with specific milestones. A strategic decision to utilize a particular application framework or key component is another.

4. Evaluate the various SLCMs based on past experience and organizational capabilities. The evaluation should initially be based on the first three areas listed and then examined for realism using the experience and capabilities of the organization. The creation and maintenance of an organizational project database, together with a set of institutionalized policies and procedures will be of tremendous aid.

5. Finally, select the SLCM that will best satisfy the project attributes and constraints. As with any important decision, this process should be documented and reviewed.

Here is a list of some criteria that should be considered during the evaluation of life cycle models:

- The tolerance of the model to the risks that are likely to be encountered;

- The extent to which the development organization has access to end users;

- How well defined the known requirements are, that is, the extent to which there are unrecognized requirements;

- Importance of early (partial) functionality;

- The intrinsic complexity of both the problem and the likely candidates for solutions;

- The anticipated frequency and magnitude of requirement changes, as well as when during the schedule any changes are anticipated to arise; estimating this can be very difficult;

- The general maturity of the application, which is concerned with the requirements and when they will become known of the system under discussion but also the general maturity of similar systems concurrently under development in the marketplace, along with the underlying or interfacing systems;

- The availability and the priority of funding;

- The flexibility within the schedule and budget (That is, must funds be committed and spent during a given period? Can the delivery of increments be modified so as to optimize cost or minimize risk?);

- The criticality of meeting the schedule and budget, in both the short and long terms;

- The institutionalized software processes and tools of the developing organization and how well they fill the needs of the model; and

- Likewise, the match between the organization's managerial capability and systems and the needs of the model.

The software process architect should create a project specific list of criteria; this list is merely offered as a starting point. The software architect and the software engineering program manager should agree on this list.

While performing the evaluation, the process architect must always bear in mind the possibility that any given determination made in the evaluation process that is subjective may be wrong. The potential consequences of such errors—both immediate (how the risk first evidences itself) and ultimate (what is the final impact of the risk)—must be considered as part of the evaluation process. In some cases, these considerations may change the ultimate selection. In others, the risks should be encompassed in the risk management plan. An inappropriate software life cycle selection can lead to disaster.

In 1991, Alexander and Davis [Alexander & Davis 1991] published, "Criteria for the Selection of a Software Process Model." The article gives a detailed methodology by which the five steps of the IEEE process can be performed. They proposed 23 project- or application-specific criteria that describe profiles of projects suitable for each life cycle model in question. They proposed that the selection of a life cycle model could be accomplished by creating a profile for the current project and then matching this profile to one of the profiles of projects.

This method still applies to life cycle model selection today. The process architect must have a clear understanding of the current project so that a profile can be created and then matched to the list of predefined profiles. This methodology does not mechanistically produce a correct decision but it does establish a structure by which software process life cycles can be examined and evaluated. Its one weakness is that it is ill suited to organizations that do not have an applicable, documented library of profiles. Organizations that have institutionalized their policies and procedures, complete with comprehensive project histories, will be able to develop these profiles more easily than will others.

7.5   Creating the Life Cycle Processes

Having selected a software life cycle model, the process architect's next responsibility is to map the associated life cycle activities onto the software life cycle model.

Both IEEE Standard 1074-1997 and IEEE/EIA Standard 12207 define an activity as a constituent (component) element of a process. A task is defined as the smallest unit of work within an activity that is subject to management accountability, as discussed in Chapter 13, which covers cost and schedule estimation and control. That is, it is necessary to project completion dates and monitor their status. A task is thus a well-defined work assignment for one or more project members. Related tasks are usually grouped to form activities, usually referred to as *work packages*. The task of creating the life cycle processes is thus that of selecting and implementing the methods, tools, and capabilities needed to perform the tasks.

The steps to map the activities to the life cycle model include these:

1. Compare activities to the SLCM requirements and identify those activities that are not needed for the SLCM selected and project requirements.

2. Identify how many instances of each activity are appropriate.

3. Place the activities in time sequence and check information flows.

Each of these steps is detailed below.

7.5.1   Compare Activities to SLCM Requirements

Utilizing the annex of IEEE Standard 1074-1997, the process architect can generate a list of all activities necessary. This step is essentially a checklist to ensure that all activities have been considered and that appropriate activities have been allocated to the appropriate process in the SLC.

7.5.2   Determine the Frequency of Activities

To properly plan and implement the processes needed by the life cycle model, it is necessary to identify how often the activities are performed and what role they play in the product flow through the life cycle process. For example, if an activity is to performed multiple times by many individuals, then investments in special tools and training materials would be appropriate. Likewise, if the activity is used, or invoked, by several other activities, then the interfaces (or handoffs) between the activities needed to be designed to support such multiple uses. Viewed in this way each activity can be classified as an invoked activity, and as a single or a multiple-instance activity.

More formally, an *invoked activity* is one that is called or utilized in several other activities. The action may be performed in parallel with actions of the invoking activity. When the invoked activity is completed, the results are returned to the invoking one. Invoked activities are analogous to procedures or subroutines. Examples of invoked activities include "conduct review," "perform configuration control," and "implement module code." Multiple-instance invoked activities can be used by other activities such as "manage project" or "implement subsystem code."

A single-instance activity appears only once in the SLC and produces all of its outputs only after receiving all of the necessary inputs. An example of the single instance activity would be "perform system test" in the waterfall model. Of course, there are likely to be multiple instances of subactivities with the system test activity itself. In an iterative life cycle model, "perform system test" would itself be an invoked, multiple-instance activity.

The distinction can be significant: In the case of the iterative model, provision must be made to store final system test results for each version separately in a distinct partition of the SCM library, whereas in the waterfall model only one version of the final system test results will exist. This distinction could have important implications for the SCM library and even for the selection of the SCM toolset.

7.5.3 Sequence the Activities and Check Information Flows

During this step, all activities are placed in a general time line but they do not necessarily have actual dates. This process is required to determine sequencing between activities as well as to identify any dependencies. It is very similar to the process of sequencing the work packages of a scheduling network, as described in Chapter 13.

Using our SLC example, the activities are placed in time sequence. The next two phases, project initiation and concept development, are organized into lists below to illustrate the concept of what actions need to be planned. Activities can be listed by numeric value (following IEEE Standard 1074-1997) and moved across the page to signify the time periods; however, the simple grouping of activities by project phase serves to remind the process architect of the ordering of activities in time.

I. Project Initiation

    A. Identify candidate SLC models

    B. Select project model

    C. Map activities to SLC model

        1) Conduct feasibility studies

        2) Plan system transition

II. Concept Development

    A. Allocate project resources

    B. Establish project environment

    C. Plan project management

    D. Prioritize and integrate software requirements

    E. Select or develop algorithms

7.5.4 Writing the Software Life Cycle Management Plan

7.5.4.1 Relationship to Other Plans

The software life cycle management plan (SLCMP) is the primary mechanism used to define and manage the software development processes used to perform the developmental tasks needed to perform a project. However, other plans exist whose content can and should play a significant role in supporting the life cycle processes. These include the following:

- The software engineering management plan (SEMP);

- The software configuration management plan (SCMP);

- The software quality assurance plan (SQAP);

- The software verification and validation plan (SVVP); and

- The software metrics plan (SMP).

For any given product, project, and organization the substance of some of these plans may well be included in another. Thus one of the most early important decisions a project faces is how to partition the topics covered by these plans and, more importantly, how to identify and manage the interfaces between them, with the goals of minimizing overlap while ensuring consistency and coherency of the whole. Thus, Section 6 of the SEMP must contain an overview of the life cycle processes that is sufficiently detailed to make clear how the project's life cycle processes relate to, among other things, the project schedule. Likewise, the SLCMP must clearly describe how the configuration management system is used in and supports the development processes at specific points, without replicating the content of the SCMP needlessly. Conversely, the SCMP must identify the configuration control boards used by the processes described in the SLCMP without needlessly replicating information found in that document.

The allocation of coverage of these plans is a critical decision in the early phases of a program and must be made with discretion, based on the objective needs of the project and any contractual requirements. In the remainder of this discussion, we will assume that all of the other plans are being developed and each will contain only the subject matter described in relevant IEEE Standards.

7.5.4.2   Outline of the Plan

The IEEE Standards do not specify a particular format to the SLCMP. However, using the other plans as models, a template can be derived that consists of the following topics:

1. *Overview.*

    1.1. *Purpose, scope, and objectives.* Describe the purpose and objectives of the document, together with the project's processes.

    1.2. *Assumptions and constraints.* Describe any constraints or assumptions that impact or constrain the processes of the project; for example, any contractual process requirements.

    1.3. *Classes of deliverables.* Describe the classes or types of deliverables being produced by the project. The purpose is to motivate any distinct processes or subprocesses needed to develop the various classes.

1.4. *Schedule dependencies between deliverables.* Describe any logical schedule relationships between deliverables that impact the relationships between the development processes for different deliverables.

2. *References.* Present any references needed to understand or that impact the content of the plan.

3. *Definitions.* Define any specialized terms used within the document.

4. *Relationship to other plans.* Describe the relationship between this SLCMP and any other project plan. The interfaces between the impacted plans shall be delineated, as well as the precedence scheme to be used in adjudicating discrepancies between these plans.

5. *Global process description.* Describe the overall project approach to software development. This shall include:

   a. The deliverables of the project, including their classes;

   b. Any external data or processes impacting or initiating project software development processes;

   c. An identification and description of any external or internally procured software items that will be integrated or otherwise included as part of a project deliverable;

   d. An identification of the software processes used to qualify those procured items for delivery;

   e. A process flow network, showing how the individual processes interact to develop the project's deliverables;

   f. A description of the inputs and outputs of each process, sufficient to describe the relationships between the developmental processes; and

   g. A brief description of each process sufficient to understand the overall software development processes of the project.

6. *Specific process descriptions.* Describe each software development process in detail including any standards that the process or its inputs, outputs, or other data items must comply with. The description shall include:

   a. The inputs to the process;

   b. The outputs;

   c. The objective of the process, together with a detailed description of the process, including any intermediate products and subprocesses;

   d. Any metrics produced by the process or its subprocesses;

   e. Any training or tools needed to implement or maintain the process;

    f. Any critical organizational assets needed to implement or maintain the process; and

    g. Any process-specific risks.

7. *Management of the processes.* Describe the approach used to manage the processes. This shall include a description of:

    a. How critical organizational assets, tools, or other facilities needed to perform the processes will be obtained and maintained;

    b. Any training needed to implement the processes of the software life cycle;

    c. How process metrics will be used to manage the processes;

    d. The approach to monitoring and responding to process-specific risks;

    e. Any special methods used to manage the process individually and together; and

    f. An impact analysis of the process flow network, focusing on processes where a failure of the plan will produce negative impacts.

8. *Maintenance and management of the plan.* Describe the approach to be used in maintaining and managing the plan. This shall include any review and approvals needed to effect changes to the plan, including any customer approvals. Criteria to be used in identifying need for revision of the plan should be given.

7.6 Implementing and Managing the Software Life Cycle Process

After the process architect has verified that the appropriate activities have been mapped onto the selected model, the full life cycle is elaborated. Next, the organizational process assets are applied to the SLC activities. The result of this process is the established software life cycle process.

7.6.1 Using Existing Assets and Capabilities

The organizational process assets and capabilities are existing organizational items that are relevant to the creation and execution of the project's software life cycle processes. Within the framework of organizational and process maturity models, these are commonly referred to as *institutionalized processes*. Such assets and capabilities often include these:

- Policies,

- Standards,

- Procedures,

- Existing SLCPs,

- Metrics,

- Tools, and

- Methodologies.

Each software project is unique, so that while every attempt should be made to build on previous experience, the resulting processes must satisfy the unique requirements of the current project. The institutionalized organizational assets provide capabilities that should be objectively assessed and, as appropriate, incorporated into the SLC to create a final process satisfying the project's particular requirements. Incorporating appropriate preexisting capabilities and assets into the project life cycle can significantly reduce the risk of implementing the life cycle and its processes. At the same time, forcing the incorporation of an existing asset and capability into a project when it is not a good fit can induce serious problems into a project.

7.6.2   Managing the Software Life Cycle Process

This section discusses how to start up the processes of a project and how to monitor and maintain them. It does so from the standpoint of achieving the goals of a specific, immediate project. Therefore it is concerned with monitoring and making changes to processes for an active, ongoing project and should not be confused with the more institutional usage of process improvement discussed in another chapter in this book.

7.6.2.1   Establishing the Life Cycle Processes

Once the process architect has produced the SLC and in turn the SLC processes, the project management team, which should include the process architect, will embed the software life cycle into the logic flow of the program schedule. For example, the SLCM might show that multiple subsystems would be developed concurrently, whereas the full program schedule would include the expansion of each subsystem development. A program schedule will usually have additional data and structure beyond that of the software life cycle itself. However, they must be consistent, as discussed in the third step of the IEEE SLCM selection process presented earlier.

7.6.2.2   Monitoring the Life Cycle Processes

The conduct of the program must be monitored to ensure that the software is being developed effectively and as planned. The following data sources are available for the software program manager and process architect to aid in performing this task:

1. *Tracking of progress to the schedule.* This may reveal process deviations, unexpected scope growth, tool, or resource problems.

2. *Examination of trends in quality data.* This can be used to determine if the software implementation team is following the life cycle processes as intended.

3. *Examination of minutes and action items from design, code, and test plan reviews.* This can be used to determine if the processes are producing the expected results. That is, given that the processes are being followed, are they effective?

4. *Examination of change request and test anomalies report trends.* These will also provided insight into how effective the processes are, as well as determining if the loading on the configuration management system is within a supportable range.

5. *Utilization of critical resources.* This will sometimes detect hidden deviations from the plan.

6. *Talk to the project staff.* The project staff doing the work should be interviewed both formally and informally as to how the processes are working. Their insights, supported by the objective data described above, can be invaluable in detecting process problems or opportunities for improvement.

The above sources of information must be monitored on a regular basis but not so often as to be onerous. For example, schedules will be revised on a periodic basis for other good reasons: Life cycle process monitoring should impose no additional schedule evaluations. As a general rule, a particular life cycle process should be examined at 10 to 20 percent increments of its schedule progress. For example, the indicators for the design process could be examined when the design is 20, 40, and 60 percent complete for a moderate size product. The rationale for this is that with less than 20 percent of the work done the sample of indicator data will not be large enough, whereas beyond the 60 percent complete stage it is too late to change a design process unless something is catastrophically wrong.

Utilizing the above information, the software program manager and the process architect should determine if changes to the life cycle and its processes are required. This determination must be made with great care, because an inappropriate change to the life cycle processes can be disruptive to the program, impacting the technical work and employee morale. On the other hand, implementing an appropriate change, the need for which is recognized by the project staff, can be an extremely positive development.

7.6.2.3 Evaluating the Impact of Changes on the Life Cycle Processes

Once the process monitoring activities have indicated that a particular life cycle process is not performing as intended, the project manager and the process architect must evaluate the alternative courses of action, which include the following:

- *Do nothing.* The negative impacts of making a change may exceed the benefit.

- *Reinforce the process.* This would be the correct course of action if the process works, but the initial training was not adequate or the institutionalization was insufficiently reinforced.

- *Adjust the process.* If the indicators show that the process works but needs minor adjustment (for example, revision of a checklist or updating a peer review process), then it should be modified and the employee training updated.

- *Replace the process.* If the indicators show that the process is fundamentally flawed (for example, with only 10 percent of the system integrated, the toolset being used to monitor performance is consuming 90 percent of the processing resources), then it must be replaced.

- *Some hybrid of the above.*

The impacts of making such changes must be evaluated in multiple dimensions:

- *Rework required.* In some cases, a change will only impact the currently active process steps. In others, it may require that some earlier stages of the process be reworked. In either case, the full schedule and cost impacts of a change must be considered.

- *Resource requirements.* Making process changes may increase or decrease certain resource needs. This may include staff, hardware, and tools. The total costs resulting from making life cycle process changes must be considered, as well as any additional lead times required to obtain the resources.

- *Timing.* If a project is using the evolutionary or spiral life cycle models and the need for change is identified in an early cycle, it may be best to postpone the change until the next cycle. This would allow the change to be made in a more orderly manner.

- *Employee morale.* Making a change, especially a major one, can negatively impact employee morale. This is especially the case if the process being changed is a "sacred cow" to either the staff, to management, or to the profession. This consideration should never stop the project manager and process architect from doing the right thing, but it should be seriously considered when implementing the change. If done right and explained properly to the project staff, who may be the ones who first pointed out the problem, a change can be a real plus.

- *Benefit to the project and the customer.* In the final analysis, the reason for the life cycle processes is to deliver a product to the customer. As a result, this is the dominant consideration and the one that should form the context in which the other factors are evaluated.

7.6.2.4 Making the Change

Introducing a change to a process that is in progress must be done with great care. Depending on the timing of the change, some or all of the following will be required:

- *Discuss the situation with the customer on a preliminary basis.* This should be done with tact and discretion.

- *Announce the need for change to the project staff.* How this is done is critical. It must be done objectively and rationally. Blame is not the issue. Building the best product for the least cost is.

- *Plan the change.* This would include the date at which the process will change, the resources and training required, and any items that may need to be reworked. Any changes to the software planning documents, both process and schedule, must be made. Any necessary coordination with the customer must occur, per contractual and business requirements, as well as the dictates of simple courtesy. Any items whose configuration must be frozen must be identified. Any rework that is necessary must be planned. Areas where work can continue unchanged must be identified. The schedule for the change must include time and activities needed to obtain and implement any needed resources and training. Determine which of the process monitoring activities described above must be done on an increased basis or changed.

- *Implement the change.* Execute the plan for the change. Keep your eyes open and talk to the project staff.

7.7   Summary

The software life cycle and its processes describe the "machine" that builds the products of a software project. This chapter has described several of the standard life cycle models, as well as how concurrency, prototyping, and commercial items and reuse can play a role in each of them. It presented a process and guidelines by which the suitability of these models can be evaluated for their application to a particular software project. It then described how to elaborate on the processes within the life cycle model. Finally, it described how the life cycle processes should be instantiated for a project and how they should be maintained.

Applicable Standards

IEEE Std 1074-1997, *IEEE Standard for Developing Software Life Cycle Processes*, IEEE, New York.

IEEE Std 1465-1998, *Information Technology—Software Packages—Quality Requirements and Testing*, IEEE, New York.

IEEE Std 1420.1a-1996, *IEEE Supplement to Standard for Information Technology—Software Reuse—Data Model for Reuse Library Interoperability: Asset Certification Framework*, IEEE, New York.

IEEE/EIA Std 12207.0-1996, *Industry Implementation of International Standard ISO/IEC 12207:1995 Standard for Information Technology—Software Life Cycle Processes*, IEEE, New York.

IEEE/EIA Std 12207.1-1997, *Industry Implementation of International Standard ISO/IEC 12207:1995 Standard for Information Technology—Software Life Cycle Processes—Life Cycle Data*, IEEE, New York.

IEEE/EIA Std 12207.2-1997, *Industry Implementation of International Standard ISO/IEC 12207:1995 Standard for Information Technology—Software Life Cycle Processes—Implementation Considerations*, IEEE, New York.

Additional References

[Alexander & Davis 1991]   Alexander, L., and Davis, A. (1991). "Criteria for the Selection of a Software Process Model," *Proc. 15th IEEE Int'l Conf. Computer Software and Applications (COMPSAC '91)*. IEEE CS Press, Los Alamitos, CA, pp. 521–528.

[Boehm 1988]   Boehm, B. W. (1988). "A Spiral Model of Software Development and Enhancement." *Computer*, May, pp. 61–72.

[Clcland 1990]   Cleland, D. I. (1990). *Project Management: Strategic Design and Implementation.* Tab Books, Blue Ridge Summit, PA.

[Davis 1997]   Davis, A. M. (1997). "Software Life Cycle Models." *Software Engineering Project Management*, R. II. Thayer, ed. IEEE Computer Society, Los Alamitos, CA.

[Dorfman & Thayer 1997]   Dorfman, M., and Thayer, R. H., eds. (1997). *Software Engineering.* IEEE Computer Society Press, Los Alamitos, CA.

[Gomaa & Scott 1981]   Gomaa, H., and Scott, D. (1981). "Prototyping as a Tool in the Specification of User Requirements," *Proc. 5th IEEE Int'l. Conf. Software Engineering.* IEEE, New York, pp. 333–342.

[Humphrey 1989]   Humphrey, W. S. (1989). *Managing the Software Process.* Addison-Wesley, Reading, MA.

[King 1992]   King, D. (1992). *Project Management: A Guide to Successful Management of Computer Systems Projects.* Prentice Hall, Upper Saddle River, NJ.

[McConnell 1996]   McConnell, S. (1996). *Rapid Development.* Microsoft Press, Redmond, WA.

[Pressman 1992]   Pressman, R.S. (1992). *Software Engineering: A Practitioner's Approach*, 3rd ed. McGraw-Hill, New York.

[Royce 1971]   Royce, W.W. (1971). "Managing the Development of Large Software Systems: Concepts and Techniques," Western Electronic Show and Convention, Los Angeles, August 25–28, 1970, 1970 Wescon Technical Papers, vol. 14.

[Thayer 1997]   Thayer, R.H., ed. (1997). *Software Engineering Project Management.* IEEE Computer Society Press, Los Alamitos, CA.

[Thayer & McGettrick 1993] Thayer, R.H., and McGettrick, A.D., eds. (1993). *Software Engineering: A European Perspective.* IEEE Computer Society Press, Los Alamitos, CA.

[Yourdon 1989]   Yourdon, E. (1989). *Modern Structured Analysis.* Yourdon Press.

[Yourdon 1996]   Yourdon, E. (1996). *Rise & Resurrection of the American Programmer.* Prentice Hall, Upper Saddle River, NJ.

[Yourdon 1997]   Yourdon, E. (1997). *Death March: The Complete Software Developer's Guide to Surviving Mission Impossible Projects.* Prentice Hall, Upper Saddle River, NJ.

Chapter 8

Software Process Improvement

Robin B. Hunter, Ph.D.
University of Strathclyde
Glasgow, Scotland

8.1   Introduction

The process approach to the production of quality software on time and within budget is based on the following premise:

The quality of a software system is governed by the quality of the process used to develop and maintain it.

Thus improvement to the software process will lead to better quality software being produced in a timely manner and at a predictable cost. Process improvement requires process assessment, and process assessment is normally based on an assessment model, a number of which are in existence. One of the first such models to be produced, is known as the capability maturity model for software (SW-CMM), and was developed by the Software Engineering Institute (SEI) in Pittsburgh, Pennsylvania. This model has evolved from its original form in 1987 and has been the inspiration for other software process assessment and improvement models.

The generic process assessment standard ISO 9001 has also been used to assess software processes, particularly in the United Kingdom, though also in other parts of the world.

The SW-CMM has not been standardized at either the national or international level. However, to bring together the many approaches to software process assessment and improvement in existence, the SPICE (Software Process Improvement and Capability dEtermination) project was set up to assist in the production of an international standard for software process assessment, capability determination, and software process improvement. This resulted in the production of the emerging standard ISO/IEC TR 15504.

In this chapter the ideas of *software process assessment, capability determination*, and *software process improvement* are introduced. A number of the models used for software process assessment, capability determination, and software process improvement are described, along with related standards such as ISO/IEC 15504, ISO/IEC 12207, and the ISO 9000 series. The benefits of software process improvement, both qualitative and quantitative, are described, and the prospects for convergence between the various assessment and improvement methods are discussed.

8.2   Objectives

In this chapter you will learn:

- Why many experts believe that management of the software process is the key to developing quality software on time and within budget.

- The relative advantages of process and product approaches to achieving quality in software.

- How the development of the capability maturity model for software at the Software Engineering Institute was the foundation for software process improvement.

- The details of other assessment and improvement models inspired by the SW-CMM.

- The role that ISO 9000 can play in software process assessment and software process improvement.

- How the SPICE project is contributing to an international standard in capability determination and software process improvement.

- What qualitative and quantitative benefits can be derived from software process improvement.

- What current or emerging international standards are relevant to software process improvement.

- How many of the current approaches to software process improvement are converging.

8.3   Background

8.3.1   Software Quality

The production of quality software on time and within budget has largely eluded the world-wide software industry for several decades now. Consideration of software development and maintenance as an engineering discipline has helped to alleviate the situation and offers hope for the future. When the term *software engineering* was coined in 1969 [Naur & Randell 1969] it was hailed as identifying an approach to software production that would lead to an engineering type process for developing (and maintaining) software. Since then contributions in this direction have been made, including the following:

- The use of structured analysis and design,

- The introduction of the object-oriented approach to software development, and

- The application of software measurement.

While the benefits of the engineering approach have been real and significant, the software "crisis," as it has become known, has refused to go away. Software "disasters" continue to occur and according to Curtis [Curtis 1995] 25 percent of software projects still do not reach fruition, many projects are up to 40 percent over budget, and project schedules are only met about half of the time.

8.3.2   Process and Product Approaches

The emphasis on the engineering aspects of software development and maintenance can lead to an overemphasis on the use of *methods* and *tools* to produce software products, whereas it is now being realized that *process* and *people issues* also have to be addressed if quality products are to be produced.

The *process* approach to software development and maintenance attempts to model all significant aspects of software development and maintenance. The ultimate aim of this approach is to produce software in a controlled way that will be on time, within budget, and of appropriate quality. The process approach is not so much about using particular methods or tools but more about using a well-defined and controlled process, which may of course be supported by appropriate methods and tools.

According to Humphrey [Humphrey 1989] the software process is defined as "the set of tools, methods and practices we use to produce a software product." An alternative to focusing on the process in order to produce quality software is to focus on the product. This approach involves monitoring the product from the early stages of development through into industrial use. The product is tested with an emphasis on functional testing, including statistical testing, and measurement of various process outputs are used in order to spot anomalies.

Although the product approach would appear to give a more direct assessment of product quality (rather than inferring it from characteristics of the process) it is generally believed to be of less predictive value than the process approach to achieving software quality. In addition, as we shall see, the process approach has more to offer in terms of controlling the cost of a software project and ensuring adherence to schedule than the product approach.

8.3.3   Software Process Improvement

8.3.3.1   Software Process Assessment

At the heart of the process approach to software development and maintenance/evolution is the concept of *software process assessment*, which is concerned with assessing a software process against a process standard or framework. Standards are used in two ways, first as a reference model and second as a gauge of compliance. In the first case the standard is used internally by an organization to guide its process improvement efforts. In the second situation a standard is used in a normative manner to determine whether or not the organization is in compliance with the standard or not. Frameworks, on the other hand, normally incorporate a number of capability levels of increasing severity, with the framework serving as a road map for long-term improvement efforts. The SW-CMM, for example, has five levels of achievement, each based on increasing capability in key process areas.

8.3.3.2 Uses of Software Process Assessment

Software process assessment can be used for a number of purposes, the two principal ones being (1) *capability determination*, which is used by software procurers to determine the capability of potential contractors (software producers) and (2) *software process improvement*, which is used by software producers to improve their software processes in line with their business aims.

In addition, the results of process assessments are sometimes used to represent the state of the practice in software development and maintenance, though this should only be done with care, because the sample used for this purpose is rarely representative of the industry as a whole.

8.3.4   The Need for Software Process Improvement

The need for software process improvement follows from the premise first enunciated by Humphrey [Humphrey 1987]: "The quality of a software system is governed by the quality of the process used to develop and maintain it." From this statement, it follows that investment in the software process will be repaid in terms of increased quality in the software product developed and maintained by the process. Further benefits from process improvement follow from the increased quantitative and qualitative control over the process that can be achieved by high-quality processes.

According to Paulk, Weber, Curtis, and Chrissis [Paulk et al. 1995] the control, predictability, and effectiveness of software processes all increase as processes are improved. The ultimate test of whether software process improvement is a worthwhile endeavor rests on *return on investment* (ROI) arguments. ROI arguments compare the costs involved with process improvement with the financial benefits that ensue from improved processes. ROI arguments are considered later in Section 8.6.3.

8.4   Models for Software Process Improvement

During the last decade or so a large number of models for software process assessment and improvement have been developed. The best known of these is the SW-CMM, which first appeared in 1987 and is described in Section 8.4.1. Other models derived from the SW-CMM are described in Section 8.4.2, and Section 8.4.3 describes a complementary approach to software process assessment based on the application of ISO 9000 to the production and maintenance of software. Finally, Section 8.4.4 describes the activities of the

SPICE project in developing an international standard for capability determination and software process improvement.

8.4.1   The Capability Maturity Model for Software

By far the best known model for software process improvement, based on software process assessment, is the SW-CMM. In this section its development is traced and some experiences gained through its use are described.

The SW-CMM has a history going back about 15 years and has evolved from a relatively simple model to a more complex one capable of providing a rich characterization of the current state of a software process.

The first public version of SW-CMM, known then as the software process maturity framework, was developed in 1987. It was based on two sets of questionnaires, a maturity questionnaire and a technology questionnaire. The maturity questionnaire was concerned with the maturity of the software process (principally how well it was defined and managed), whereas the technology questionnaire was concerned with the extent to which advanced technology was used in the process. The result of a process assessment depended on the answers to the questions in both sets of questionnaires, and was two dimensional, with low-maturity, low-technology processes being represented on the bottom left of a two-dimensional grid and high-maturity, high-technology processes on the top right of the grid. It was also suggested that an organization might progress from the bottom left position of the grid to the top right position of the grid in a period of around 4 years, though this rate of progress would now be considered rather ambitious.

As far as the route that an organization might take to go from the bottom left to the top right of the grid was concerned, it was strongly suggested that priority should be given to getting the process to mature in the first instance, followed by increasing the level of technology to support the mature aspects of the process. At the time, this was seen as radical thinking in a context where many software producers were trying to "buy their way out of trouble" by investing in the latest technology.

8.4.1.1   Development of the SW-CMM

Later versions of the SW-CMM were one (rather than two) dimensional, the emphasis now being on *maturity* rather than use of advanced *technology*. However, the original two-dimensional framework is still reflected in the diagonal layout of the five capability levels defined in the SW-CMM, as shown in Figure 8.1.

The following description of the five levels of the SW-CMM appeared on the SEI Web pages (http://www.sei.cmu.edu):

1. *Initial.* The software process is characterized as ad hoc, and occasionally even chaotic. Few processes are defined, and success depends on individual effort and heroics.

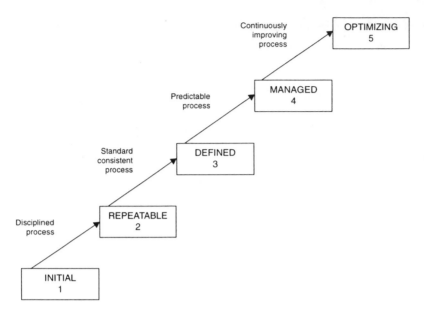

Figure 8.1: SW-CMM Maturity Levels

2. *Repeatable.* Basic project management processes are established to track cost, schedule, and functionality. The necessary process discipline is in place to repeat earlier successes on projects with similar applications.

3. *Defined.* The software process for both management and engineering activities is documented, standardized, and integrated into a standard software process for the organization. All projects use an approved, tailored version of the organization's standard software process for developing and maintaining software.

4. *Managed.* Detailed measures of the software process and product quality are collected. Both the software process and products are quantitatively understood and controlled.

5. *Optimizing.* Continuous process improvement is enabled by quantitative feedback from the process and from piloting innovative ideas and technologies.

Figure 8.2 shows the detailed structure of version 1.1 of the SW-CMM. All software processes are at level 1 at least, by default. In general, any process at level n $(1 \leq n \leq 4)$ is deemed to be at level $n + 1$ if certain *key process areas* satisfy their *goals* (defined by the model). For example, whether a Level 1 process is a Level 2 process depends on assessing whether the process is *disciplined*, which in turn depends on assessing whether the goals of the following key process areas have been satisfied:

• Requirements management,

- Software project planning,

- Software project tracking and oversight,

- Software subcontract management,

- Software quality assurance, and

- Software configuration management.

As an example, here is one of the goals of *requirements management*: Software plans, products, and activities are kept consistent with the system requirements allocated to software.

The key process areas corresponding to the various transitions between adjacent levels are given in Table 8.1. The key process areas are further refined into *key practices* capable of direct observation and measurement. The refinement is performed using five *common features*, namely: (1) commitment to perform, (2) ability to perform, (3) activities performed, (4) measurement and analysis, and (5) verification of implementation.

Level 1–Level 2: *disciplined process*	Requirements management Software project planning Software project tracking and oversight Software subcontract management Software quality assurance Software configuration management
Level 2–Level 3: *standard consistent process*	Organization process focus Organization process definition Training program Integrated software management Software product engineering Intergroup coordination Peer reviews
Level 3–Level 4: *predictable process*	Quantitative process management Software quality management
Level 4–Level 5: *continuously improving process*	Defect prevention Technology change management Process change management

Table 8.1: Key Process Areas

Each *common feature* (CF) applied to a *key process area* (KPA) produces one or more *key practices* (KPs). In a more mathematical notation this might be written

$$CF(KPA) \Rightarrow KPs$$

As an example,

Ability to perform (Software subcontract management)

produces

Periodic technical reviews and interchanges are held with the software subcontractor

as well as several other key practices.

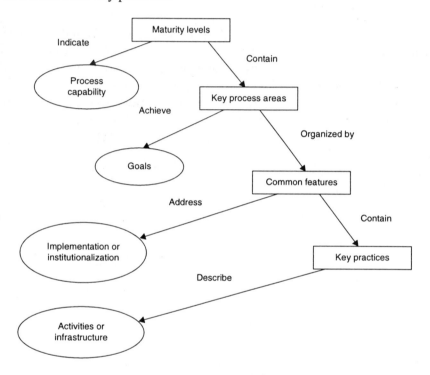

Figure 8.2: Structure of SW-CMM

8.4.1.2   Using the SW-CMM

Considerable experience has been gained, especially within the United States, in using the SW-CMM, and this experience has had considerable influence over the various revisions to the model, especially the creation of version 1.1. One of the best sources of advice on how to use the SW-CMM and what to expect from it remains Humphrey's original book [Humphrey 1989]. Assessments can be performed using internal or external resources. The SEI trains and licenses individuals and organizations to conduct assessments. Some larger organizations have chosen to have individuals trained by the SEI, whereas others contract with licensed contractors. The SEI Web site maintains a list of licensed assessors. Note that the SEI itself does not "certify" assessments. It only trains and licenses the individuals and the organizations who conduct the assessments.

8.4.1.3 Humphrey's Principles

In his book *Managing the Software Process*, Humphrey [Humphrey 1989] lists six basic principles of software process change:

1. Major changes to the software process must start at the top. Senior management leadership is required.

2. Ultimately everyone must be involved. Software engineering is a team effort.

3. Effective change requires a goal and a knowledge of the current process. To use a map, you must know where you are.

4. Change is continuous. Software process improvement involves continual learning and growth.

5. Software process changes will not be retained without conscious effort and periodic reinforcement.

6. Software process improvement requires investment. It takes time, skill, and money to improve the software process.

Each of these principles is expanded in the sections of Humphrey's book, which follow the statement of these principles.

8.4.1.4 Experience in Use

Many papers have been published describing successful (and occasionally less successful) use of the SW-CMM [Paulish & Carleton 1994, Grady 1996, Lowe & Cox 1996]. In particular, these authors point out the requirements for software process improvement and some of the benefits of SPI.

The principal requirements for successful software process improvement (SPI) would appear to be as follows:

- Engineers need to be convinced of the need for a standard process.

- Appropriate training is essential.

- A clearly defined improvement model is required.

- Fault and failure analysis is important.

The principle benefits identified were

- Increased ability to respond to change,

- Possible reduction of times spent on the investigation phase of a project, and

- Higher maturity levels, which lead to accelerated spread of proven best practices across an organization.

8.4.2   Other Models Inspired by the SW-CMM

The SW-CMM was the first *staged* model used for process assessment, where the term *staged* refers to the discrete levels inherent in the model. In due course other staged models appeared mainly for use in particular industries, in particular regions of the world, or for particular types of software. BOOTSTRAP [Kuvaja & Bicego 1994], which started off as an ESPRIT project, was designed particularly for use in Europe, whereas TRILLIUM [Coallier 1995], designed in Canada, was intended for use in the telecom industry.

In parallel with these developments, Humphrey developed two new models, clearly inspired by the SW-CMM but serving slightly different purposes, the personal software process (PSP), which, according to Humphrey [Humphrey 1995] was "a self-improvement process designed to help you control, manage, and improve the way you work" and the team software process (TSP), which was designed to perform a similar role for teams of software developers as the PSP performed for individuals. These models are briefly described in the sections that follow.

8.4.2.1   BOOTSTRAP

The BOOTSTRAP model [Kuvaja & Bicego 1994] was originally developed as a European ESPRIT project. BOOTSTRAP is clearly based on the SW-CMM, with additional features added, in order to adapt it to the European environment. These features included aspects of the ISO 9001 approach to process assessment (see Section 8.4.3) and of the European Space Agency's process model standard (PSS-05).

The phases of a BOOTSTRAP assessment are similar to those of a SW-CMM assessment: (1) preparation, (2) assessment, and (3) action plan derivation.

Since the end of the ESPRIT project, which originally developed it, the BOOTSTRAP model has been in the care of the BOOTSTRAP Institute, an independent body set up by the BOOTSTRAP partners. The model is under continual development and has now been brought in line with ISO/IEC 12207 (*Software Life Cycle Processes*) and ISO/IEC 15504 (see Section 8.4.4).

8.4.2.2   TRILLIUM

TRILLIUM [Coallier 1995] was developed around 1991 through a partnership among Bell Canada, Northern Telecom, and Bell Northern Research. It was clearly inspired by the SEI's SW-CMM and can be used as a customer-focused benchmark for one of two purposes: (1) assessment of a supplier's development process or (2) internal process improvement.

TRILLIUM (unlike the SW-CMM) has a clear product focus, where the product is defined to be the software that is delivered to the customer including, in the case of embedded software, the system of which the software is a part. TRILLIUM emphasizes *road maps* that lead from one level to another, as distinct from the *key process areas* emphasized in the SW-CMM.

8.4.2.3   PSP/TSP

Humphrey's major contributions since his development of the SW-CMM at the SEI have been (1) the personal software process (PSP) and (2) the team software process (TSP).

The PSP is described in Humphrey's 1995 book, *A Discipline for Software Engineering*. The purpose of the PSP is to improve the effectiveness of software engineers by encouraging them to plan, track, and measure their personal performance as part of the software process.

According to Humphrey, the basic steps taken by the PSP are as follows:

1. Identify those large-system software methods and practices that can be used by individuals.

2. Define the subset of these methods and practices that can be applied while developing small programs.

3. Structure these methods and practices so they can be gradually introduced.

4. Provide exercises suitable for practicing these methods in an educational setting.

The PSP has a framework similar to the SW-CMM. Clearly some of the key process areas of the SW-CMM such as software project planning, peer reviews, and defect prevention may reasonably be addressed by the PSP while others, such as software quality assurance and software subcontract management, may not.

Humphrey suggests that the ideas inherent in the PSP may be sufficient to build programs up to 10K lines of code (LOC), but not larger. For larger programs the TSP may be used to supplement the PSP.

The TSP [Humphrey 1999a] builds on PSP training and focuses on structured weekly team meetings including a 3-day meeting at the start of each new project and 2-day relaunch meetings at the start of each project milestone. The initial meeting for each project is used to (1) develop team working practices, (2) establish goals, (3) select roles, (4) define processes, and (5) make plans.

TSP provides forms, scripts, and standards that lead the PSP trained team through the process steps.

8.4.2.4   CMM Integration

The SW-CMM, originally just the CMM, has inspired other CMMs to be developed at the SEI including people CMM, systems engineering CMM, software acquisition CMM, and integrated product management CMM, each of which is used for a distinct, but complementary, purpose to the SW-CMM. Further information on each of the above CMMs can be obtained from the SEI Web site (http://www.sei.cmu.edu).

Around 1997 it was decided that the SW-CMM, currently in version 1.1, was due for major revision and a project was set up at the SEI to produce version 2 of the SW-CMM by around 1999. It was also envisioned that a further version of SW-CMM (2.1), a relatively minor revision of version 2, would appear about 2 years later. Extensive industrial consultation took place over the form of version 2 of SW-CMM, but version 2 was never released. Instead the SEI launched a new project to integrate three of the key CMMs that had been developed, namely, SW-CMM (CMM for software), SE-CMM (systems engineering CMM), and IPD-CMM (integrated product development CMM). The new project was titled *CMM integration* or *CMMI* and further information concerning it can be found at the CMMI Web site (http://www.sei.cmu.edu/cmm/cmms/cmms.integration.html).

The reasons for not proceeding with version 2 of the SW-CMM have been explained by Schaeffer [Schaeffer 1998]. According to Schaeffer, they resulted from acquisition reform within the Department of Defense (DoD) creating a significant paradigm shift from a "how to" mentality approach to an approach based on statements of objectives and performance-based requirements. This and the clear commonality between the SW-CMM, the SE-CMM, and the IPD-CMM in terms of configuration, quality, and requirements management, led to the abandonment of SW-CMM version 2 and the creation of the CMMI project.

8.4.3   ISO 9001 and TickIT

An approach toward software process quality that is quite distinct from the SW-CMM approach, and developed independently from it, is to use the ISO 9000 series of standards, a series of generic process standards that can be applied to a wide range of service and manufacturing industries. The current version of the ISO 9000 series, ISO 9000:2000, has a number of principal components:

- ISO 9000 Quality Management Systems—Fundamentals and Vocabulary,

- ISO 9001 Quality Management Systems—Requirements,

- ISO 9004 Quality Management Systems—Guidelines for Performance Improvements, and

- ISO DIS 19011: Guidelines on Quality and/or Environmental Management Systems Auditing.

8.4.3.1   Basic Ideas

The use of the ISO 9000 series (also known as BS 5750 and EN 29000) was basically a British initiative based on the original version of ISO 9000. The United Kingdom scheme, which was launched in 1989, was known as TickIT. (A *tick* is a check in the United States. Therefore, TickIT would be CheckIT in American!).

One of the issues involved in the use of TickIT was the extent to which software products and the processes used to develop and maintain them are similar to other manufactured products. Earlier studies commissioned by the U.K. government found that (1) it was appropriate to apply ISO 9000 to software [the Logica report [Logica 1988]] and (2) the anticipated costs and benefits of applying ISO 9000 to software suggested that it was cost effective to do so [the Price Waterhouse report [Price Waterhouse 1988]].

The part of the original ISO 9000 series considered most appropriate for application to software was ISO 9001 (equivalent to BS 5750 part 1, which preceded it, and EN 29001, the European version of the standard) and a guide to the application of ISO 9001 to software entitled *Guidelines for the Application of ISO 9001 to the Development Supply and Maintenance of Software* was produced. This guide is known as ISO 9000-3.

TickIT is supported by a guide subtitled *Making a Better Job of Software*, now in its fourth edition and recently updated to bring it into line with the 1997 revision of ISO 9000-3 and the 1995 edition of the standard ISO/IEC 12207 on software life cycle processes. The guide defines the scope of TickIT and describes the organization behind it. It provides guidance for software customers and software suppliers as well as for auditors. It also contains listings of other relevant standards and relevant reading as well as guidance to relevant standards information on the Web. Information concerning the guide is available at the TickIT Web site (http://www.tickit.org). Information concerning other support material for TickIT including a video, details of case studies, and a quarterly international journal entitled *TickIT International*, are also available at the Web site.

The TickIT scheme certifies software organizations for compliance with ISO 9001. The bulk of TickIT certifications have taken place in the United Kingdom. In June 1998, 70 percent of the 1,486 active certificates were held in the United Kingdom. However, at that time only half of the certificates being granted were in the United Kingdom, suggesting a gradual spread of TickIT toward other countries. Approximately 10 percent of certificates are held in North America (United States and Canada), and the European countries where TickIT has made the most impact are Ireland and Sweden. Elsewhere in the world TickIT has made the largest impact in India, Korea, and Japan. Overall, the number of TickIT certificates held has grown steadily during the last few years from just over 600 in 1994 to nearly 1,500 in 1998.

A list is maintained (accessible over the Internet) of bodies able to award TickIT certificates, all of which have been approved for the purpose by UKAS (United Kingdom Accreditation Service). UKAS lays down detailed criteria to which certification bodies should conform in the areas of impartiality, confidentiality, competence, maintenance of records, and appeal procedures.

Although TickIT has clearly had its greatest impact in the United Kingdom, there is no doubt that it has also had considerable influence worldwide.

8.4.3.2 Experience in Use

A number of studies have been made of ISO 9001 applied to software. One of these [Stelzer et al. 1998], entitled *Benefits and Prerequisites of ISO 9000 Based Software Quality Management*, presents a study of the experiences of 12 European software organizations who have sought ISO 9001 certification. In particular it summarizes the benefits of seeking such certification, and the prerequisites for seeking certification, as seen by the 12 organizations.

The *benefits* are much as would be expected under the circumstances:

- Improved project management,

- Improved productivity,

- Improved customer satisfaction,

- Improved product quality, and so on.

In 26 percent of cases a positive return on investment was also indicated.

The two top prerequisites, *management commitment and support* and *staff involvement*, were also fairly predictable. However, the next two prerequisites, *providing enhanced understanding* (acquiring and transferring knowledge of current practices) and *tailoring improvement initiatives* (adapting quality management practices to the specific strengths and weaknesses of different teams and departments) are perhaps less obvious.

In another paper entitled *How ISO 9001 Compares with the CMM* [Paulk 1995], the use of ISO 9001 for software is compared to the SW-CMM. The paper answers these two questions:

1. At what level in the SW-CMM would an ISO 9001-compliant organization be?

2. Can a SW-CMM level 2 (or 3) organization be considered compliant with ISO 9001?

The SW-CMM and ISO 9001/TickIT differ from each other in a number of ways. One difference is seen in their scopes. For example, certain aspects of ISO 9001 are not addressed at all by the SW-CMM. However a mapping can be made from the ISO 9001 requirements onto the key process areas at each level of the SW-CMM and from this a reasonable level of equivalence can be established. This mapping suggests that an organization that is ISO 9001 compliant for software would be at least equivalent to one gaining somewhere between Levels 2 and 3 of the SW-CMM. However, it is completely possible for a SW-CMM Level 1 organization to satisfy the requirements of ISO 9001 as a matter of practice because each assessment requires interpretation of data and interviews.

Another difference between the SW-CMM and TickIT in practice is in the frequency and cost of repeat (formal) assessments (called *surveillance audits* in ISO terminology). TickIT certificates last for 3 years, and brief unannounced surveillance visits take place two or three times per year during this period. The SEI does not specify a time period after which assessment results are invalid, although 2 years is a commonly accepted time period in the industry.

Finally, the cost of performing a CMM assessment for an organization of between 100 and 300 software engineers can be in the range of $100,000 to $300,000 when the total cost of the assessment is included [Christensen 2000]. These costs include the following:

- Employee training (needed to ensure that the employees use terminology in a manner consistent with the assessment team; this does not include training in the processes themselves),

- Payment to the assessment contractor, and

- Employee time during the assessment itself.

For smaller organizations the costs can be lower, although they would not typically decrease in a linear manner.

Internal assessments can, of course, be conducted on a much more economic basis and, as a practical matter, for many organizations this is all that is needed. Finally, always keep in mind that an ISO 9001 certification is binary (certification is either awarded or it is not), whereas the SW-CMM model is staged. As a result, SW-CMM assessments can be used to motivate and document continuous process improvement explicitly.

8.4.4 SPICE/ISO/IEC 15504

The plethora of models and standards for software process assessment and improvement led to an international initiative to create an international standard in the area. The project associated with this initiative is known as the *SPICE project*. Descriptions of the early work on SPICE and some of the work that led up to it can be found in Dorling and Simms [Dorling & Simms 1991] and El Emam et al. [El Emam et al. 1998].

8.4.4.1 Development of the Standard

As an international standardization project, SPICE is unique in two ways:

1. During its development, the standard is being subjected to extensive trials (or "pilot tested" in U.S. terminology) throughout the world (the SPICE trials).

2. It is using a fast-track route to standardization via a series of technical reports.

The SPICE trials have a number of objectives including these:

- To promote process improvement in general and the SPICE approach to process improvement in particular.

- To identify weaknesses in the early versions of the SPICE model and their associated documentation.

- To ensure the applicability of the emerging standard throughout the world and throughout a wide range of industries and product type.

The normal route to ISO/IEC standardization goes through the following stages:

- New work item,

- Working draft,

- Committee draft,

- Draft international standard, and, finally,

- International standard.

The technical report route, however, has different stages after the working draft stage: proposed draft technical report, then a draft technical report, and finally a technical report.

The technical report route is sometimes used by a standards working group when it is not sure that the degree of consensus required for an international standard is present. The set of documents produced by the working group is known as a *technical report type 2* or a *TR-2* and is expected to be replaced by a full international standard within 2 years of its publication. The standard being produced by the SPICE project is currently at the TR-2 stage and is known as ISO/IEC TR 15504:1998.

To manage the SPICE project, a regional structure was adopted and technical centers were set up for four (later five) regions of the world, initially, the United States; Canada and Latin America; Europe and Africa; and the Asia Pacific region. Later the Asia Pacific region was split into two parts: Northern Asia Pacific (mainly Japan and Korea) and Southern Asia Pacific (centered on Australia). More details about the development of the 15504 standard can be found in El Emam et al. [El Emam et al. 1998].

8.4.4.2 Comparison of ISO/IEC TR 15504 and SW-CMM

A number of significant differences exist between 15504 and the SW-CMM, the principal one being that 15504 is a *continuous model*, whereas the SW-CMM is a *staged model*. The difference between the two is that in 15504 (a continuous model) each of the 40 processes is assessed at each of the capability levels, whereas in the SW-CMM (a staged model) only the relevant key process areas are assessed at each level. Thus, while the 15504 *capability levels* measure process capability, the SW-CMM *maturity levels* are a measure of organization maturity. Paulk, Konrad, and Garcia [Paulk, Konrad, & Garcia 1995] discuss the differences in the two architectures in more detail.

Clearly the amount of data produced by a 15504 assessment will tend to be greater than for a SW-CMM assessment because, potentially, each process is assessed at each level in a 15504 assessment, whereas in a SW-CMM assessment only processes within the key process area are assessed at each level.

Another important difference between 15504 and the SW-CMM is that SPICE uses a four-valued logic for measurement, each process attribute having one of the values *fully*, *largely*, *partially*, or *not* present. In the SW-CMM, on the other hand a two-valued logic is used, each key process area being *fully* or *not* implemented, although some assessors will indicate partial implementation if a significant number of the practices of a KPA are implemented by the organization. Handling the results of a process assessment (whether based on 15504 or SW-CMM) is a nontrivial task and one that can certainly benefit from tool support [Hunter et al. 1997].

8.5 Capability Determination

Although the main theme of this chapter is software process improvement, another application of software process assessment should be borne in mind, namely, *capability determination*. In fact, the SW-CMM was originally developed for procurement purposes by the DoD and capability determination was the main aim of the model at this stage rather than process improvement. Part 8 of ISO/IEC TR 15504 defines process capability determination as

> A systematic assessment and analysis of selected software processes within an organization, carried out with the aim of identifying the strengths, weaknesses and risks associated with deploying the processes to meet a particular specified requirement.

Capability determination is normally carried out in connection with a procurement-related decision. A software procurer may be interested in assessing the risk of placing a contract with a particular software supplier, or a contractor may be interested in assessing its own capability before deciding whether to bid for a particular contract.

A software procurer may specify a target capability for potential contractors and may identify areas in which a contractor's capability falls short of the target capability as areas of risk for the proposed project. The process-oriented risks identified would then be considered as part of the overall risks involved in completing the project on time and within budget. In some cases the procurer may take into consideration the current capability of a potential contractor and its current process improvement plans in order to identify the risk in placing a contract with that contractor.

The topic of software acquisition has led to the production of the software acquisition CMM (SA-CMM) through collaboration between the DoD, federal agencies, and the SEI. Despite the existence and growing experience of the SW-CMM, the immaturity of the procurement process itself has, in many cases, limited the effectiveness of the procurement function. The SA-CMM [Kind & Ferguson 1997] has five levels similar to those of the SW-CMM ranging from Level 1 (competent people and heroics) to Level 4 (quantitative management) and Level 5 (continuous process improvement). The SA-CMM builds on the experiences and success of the SW-CMM and is applicable to large and small procurements, and for both large and small projects

In 1997, Volume 10, issue 3, of *Crosstalk, The Journal of Defense Software Engineering*, was devoted to software acquisition management, emphasizing that this is a live topic and not an issue that has been completely solved through the existence of the SW-CMM.

8.6 Software Process Improvement

Part 7 of ISO/IEC TR 15504 defines the eight steps of software process improvement as follows:

1. Examine an organization's needs.

2. Initiate process improvement.

3. Prepare and conduct process assessment.

4. Analyze results and prepare action plan.

5. Implement improvements.

6. Confirm improvements.

7. Sustain improvement gains.

8. Monitor performance.

Once all eight steps have been executed, the organization should start again at step 2 and so on.

The SPIRE Handbook [Sanders 1998] was produced by a European research project and provides sound advice for organizations involved in process improvement based on the preceding eight steps. The handbook aims to "help management and staff in small software development organizations to improve their businesses by systematic software process improvement," though this is not to say that much of the advice given is not equally applicable to large or medium-sized organizations.

Expanding on the eight steps, the handbook emphasizes these aspects of the process:

- To be effective, a process improvement initiative should be conducted as a project in its own right.

- An external "mentor" should be used where appropriate.

- Planning an assessment includes defining the purpose, scope, constraints, resources, and timescale for the formal process assessment.

- Prioritizing processes for improvement is a necessary, but not trivial, task.

- Experimenting with improvements on a pilot project may be useful.

- When the process improvement plan has been completed, it is necessary to check whether the anticipated benefits have been realized.

- Systematic data collection and analysis should be used to ensure that process improvements are sustained.

Under the heading of "Managing Process Improvement," the handbook describes how the eight steps might be executed for a typical software process improvement project.

Many cultural and interpersonal issues arise in the context of software process improvement [Jansen & Sanders 1998]. These include the following:

- The need for leadership and support from all levels of management;

- The effect of software process improvement on staff values, attitudes, and behavior;

- The need to motivate staff in order to ensure that process improvement goals are achieved;

- The need for effective communication and teamwork among those involved in process improvement; and

- Identification of the role of education and training for effective process improvement.

Not all software process improvement plans are successful; some may even have a totally negative effect. To maximize the chances of a successful outcome of a software process improvement project, it is important to plan well, allocate sufficient and appropriate resources, and build on the experiences described in the literature. As we will see in the next section, the benefits of a successful software process improvement project are significant and, in the right circumstances, even substantial.

8.6.1   Benefits of Software Process Improvement

The practice of SPI in the first instance was based on intuition and experience rather than on sound empirical evidence. However, now that a considerable amount of data concerning the effects of SPI have been collected, we can deduce many positive benefits that arise from using SPI. The benefits fall into two categories: qualitative benefits and quantitative benefits.

The following organizations systematically collect software, process assessment data from which the benefits of software process improvement can be deduced:

- SEI (http://www.sei.cmu.edu),

- European Software Institute, from process improvement experiments conducted under the European Systems and Software Initiative (http://www.esi.es), and

- The SPICE project from its trials activities (http://www.sqi.gu.edu.au/spice/).

8.6.2   Qualitative Benefits

Among others, the organization responsible for the space shuttle software (originally part of IBM Federal Systems but now owned by the Lockheed Martin Corporation) has reported that extremely favorable results were obtained through software process improvement. Billings et al. [Billings et al. 1994] describe experiences with SPI over many years. They also confirm, from their own experiences, the importance of many widely acknowledged prerequisites for producing good software such as attention to requirements, good customer relations, and collection of fault data.

An SEI report [Herbsleb & Goldenson 1996] follows up SEI assessments that were performed between 1 and 3 years after the original assessment. The survey performed supported the view that successful SPI led to the following:

- Increased product quality,

- Increased productivity,

- Increased staff morale,

- Increased customer satisfaction, and

- Increased ability to meet budget.

In addition 74 percent of those questioned agreed that the SW-CMM assessment was worth the money and effort expended on it.

The SEI study was also used to identify the prerequisites for successful SPI. These included (perhaps not surprisingly) having clear, well-understood goals and having minimal organizational politics.

Results of phases 1 and 2 of the SPICE trials have been published [SPICE 1996, SPICE 1998] and tend to show general support for the effectiveness of software process improvement and for testing of the various versions of the SPICE model involved and their associated documentation. Other SPICE studies [Simon et al. 1997] on the reliability of process assessments, based on inter-rater agreements, have produced generally positive results.

8.6.3 Quantitative Benefits

Quantitative benefits of SPI are more difficult to show. In this section we discuss how economic arguments can be made in favor of software process improvement. Readers will also find two articles by Watts Humphrey [Humphrey 1999b, Humphrey 2000] relevant to this issue.

The costs of SPI are not too hard to itemize and include the following:

- Costs of staff training,

- Costs of regular process assessments,

- Cost of staff responsible for the process,

- Costs of data collection for process monitoring, and

- Costs of assessments.

According to a SEI guideline, these costs should amount to between 3 and 5 percent of software development costs [Krasner 1994]. Clearly, the lower these costs are kept, the greater the opportunity there is for recouping them from the benefits of software process improvement.

The financial benefits of software process improvement initiatives are harder to measure and predict than the costs. Some of the benefits are more qualitative than quantitative and can only be estimated from appropriate indicators. For example, increased staff morale can be indicated by lower staff turnover, and the consequent savings measured in terms of lower staff training costs and avoidance of additional project costs following from lack of staff continuity. In a similar way, increased customer satisfaction can be inferred from increased repeat orders, and quantified in terms of the value of these orders.

Increased maturity of the process should lead to fewer faults appearing in the software due to human error and, hence, reduced rework. This is just one of the reasons why productivity should increase as the software process is improved. It is interesting to note that COCOMO II (http://sunset.usc.edu/COCOMOII/cocomo.html) includes a process maturity factor to evaluate the effort required to complete a software project. Applying this model to moderately sized efforts (100K LOC) produces an 8 percent decrease in predicted software development costs for a one-step increase in process maturity. Clark [Clark 2000] reports that a one-step increase in maturity results in a 15 to 21 percent decrease in total project cost.

We can see, therefore, that over a period of time it is possible, based on some reasonable assumptions, to measure the effects of software process improvement, and to estimate the return on investment over the period.

A number of detailed case studies on the return on investment from SPI have been conducted and are described by Krasner [Krasner 1994]. Among the organizations and activities involved are the Software Engineering Laboratory at the University of Maryland, the space shuttle program, and Hewlett Packard. The general conclusion drawn from the case studies is that ROI benefits of between 5 to 1 and 9 to 1 may be expected over a 2-year period.

Additional information on ROI can be found at the SEI Web site (http://www.sei.cmu.edu) and at the University of Southern California Web site (http://www.usc.edu). See also the doctoral dissertation of Clark [Clark 1997].

8.7 Existing and Emerging Standards

8.7.1 ISO/IEC 12207

ISO/IEC 12207, Software Life Cycle Processes—1995, describes the major component processes of a complete software life cycle and is based on earlier military standards. It does not assume any particular life cycle model, but it has been suggested that it suits the waterfall model particularly well. It has been adopted as an IEEE standard, IEEE/EIA 12207. This standard was expanded to include:

- IEEE/EIA 12207.0-1996, *Industry Implementation of International Standard ISO/IEC 12207:1995 Standard for Information Technology—Software Life Cycle Processes*, contains ISO/IEC 12207 in its original form and six additional annexes (E through J): basic concepts, compliance, life cycle process objectives, life cycle data objectives, relationships, and errata.

- IEEE/EIA 12207.1-1997, *Industry Implementation of International Standard ISO/IEC 12207:1995 Standard for Information Technology—Software Life Cycle Processes— Life Cycle Data*, provides additional guidance on recording life cycle data.

- IEEE/EIA 12207.2-1997, *Industry Implementation of International Standard ISO/IEC 12207:1995 Standard for Information Technology—Software Life Cycle Processes— Implementation Considerations*, provides additions, alternatives, and clarifications to the ISO/IEC 12207's life cycle processes as derived from U.S. practices.

ISO/IEC 12207 groups the activities that may be performed during the life cycle of a software into five primary processes, eight supporting processes, and four organizational processes.

- *Primary processes:* acquisition, supply, development, operation, and maintenance.

- *Supporting processes:* documentation, configuration management, quality assurance, verification, validation, joint review, audit, and problem resolution.

- *Organization processes:* management, infrastructure, improvement, and training.

Each process is further divided into a set of activities and each activity is divided into a set of tasks. As of 2000, ISO/IEC 12207 was undergoing revision.

8.7.2   ISO/IEC 15504

As already described in Section 8.4.4, the emerging standard ISO/IEC 15504 is currently at the technical report (TR) stage and is expected to become a full standard around mid-2002. The development of 15504 has been supported by the SPICE project and the standard is sometimes known (informally) as the SPICE standard or SPICE99. Standard 15504 has been developed in parallel with ISO/IEC 12207 and the current (TR) version is described in Section 8.4.4. Like 12207, 15504 defines the software process to consist of component processes.

According to 15504 these process are grouped into five categories: customer supplier, engineering, support, management, and organization. The categories are not dissimilar to those used in 12207. However, a strong case has been made that they should not just be similar to those of 12207 but they should be identical; and successive versions of what is now known as 15504 have brought the two sets of component processes more closely together.

As far as the current (TR) version of 15504 is concerned, it is possible to impose a higher level structure on the process categories to bring them close to the 12207 categories. Thus we can group the 15504 processes as follows:

- *Primary processes:* all processes in the customer supplier and engineering categories.

- *Supporting processes:* all processes in the support process category.

- *Organizational processes:* all processes in the management and organization process categories.

Further discussion about the convergence of ISO/IEC 12207 and ISO/IEC 15504 is given in the next section.

8.7.3 Convergence

The areas of software process assessment and software process improvement are clearly now ready for convergence and consolidation. Several issues need to be addressed:

- The fact that ISO/IEC 15504 is a continuous model, whereas the SW-CMM is a staged model;

- The fact that the process architectures of ISO/IEC 12207 and ISO/IEC 15504 are not the same; and

- The fact that ISO 9001 as applied to software is not compatible with any of the software process standards.

Fortunately, it appears that the desired convergence may well take place within the next few years. As far as the continuous versus staged model choice is concerned, it seems likely that the CMM integration project will define one or more mappings between the results of a CMMI mapping (which is staged) onto the format of the output from a SPICE assessment (which is continuous), thus making CMMI assessments 15504 compatible.

As far as the process architectures of ISO/IEC 12207 and ISO/IEC 15504 are concerned, their incompatibility is seen as a major issue within ISO/IEC JTC1/SC7, the parent committee of WG7, which is responsible for 12207, and WG10, which is responsible for 12207. As of 2000, WG7 and WG10 were planning a series of joint meetings to resolve the issues. One possible outcome of these meetings would be a new process architecture standard on which both 12207 and 15504 could build.

The remaining issue of compatibility between ISO 9000 is not so great now that ISO 9000:2000, which is more supportive of process improvement than previous versions of the ISO 9000 series, has been published. Although the standards world may at times seem to be slow moving, it is in fact constantly changing, always seeking consensus, consistency, and—where appropriate—change!

8.8 Summary

Software process improvement is a well-established and accepted method of controlling the software process in order to deliver high-quality software products on time and within budget. Software process improvement is normally dependent on a software process assessment model of which a number exist. The best known, and longest standing, such model is the SW-CMM, which is widely used for two purposes: (1) determining the capability of software contractors and (2) software process improvement. A number of alternative models of process assessment have been developed based on, or inspired by, the SW-CMM.

Although most methods of process assessment are software specific, the generic standard ISO 9001 is also used for software process assessment. In recent years an international standard, ISO/IEC 15504 (sometimes known as SPICE), has emerged based on virtually all of the existing software assessment methods, and many of these methods have become 15504 compliant. There are also indications of a general convergence in the area of software process assessment.

The benefits of software process assessment are now being realized and may now be quantified so that while software process improvement may have begun as an act of faith, it is now beginning to be possible to predict the benefits that can be obtained from it.

Applicable Standards

IEEE Std 610.12-1990. *IEEE Standard Glossary of Software Engineering Terminology.* IEEE, New York.

ISO 9000-3 (1991/7). *Quality Management and Quality Assurance Standards—Part 3: Guidelines for the Application of ISO 9001 to the Development, Supply and Maintenance of Software (also known as BS 5750, Part 13).* International Standards Organization, Geneva.

ISO 9000:2000. *Quality Management Systems.* International Standards Organization, Geneva.

ISO 9001 (1991). *Quality Systems—Model for Quality Assurance in Design, Development, Production, Installation and Servicing.* International Standards Organization, Geneva.

ISO/IEC 9126 (1995). *Information Technology—Software Quality Characteristics and Metrics,* ISO/IEC JTC1/SC7 WG 6. International Standards Organization, Geneva.

ISO/IEC 12207 (1995). *Information Technology—Software Life Cycle Processes,* ISO/IEC JTC1/SC7 WG 7. International Standards Organization, Geneva.

ISO/IEC TR 15504-9, 1–9 (1998). *Information Technology—Software Process Assessment— Parts 1–9,* ISO/IEC JTC1/SC7 WG 10. International Standards Organization, Geneva.

Additional References

[Billings et al. 1994]   Billings, C., Clifton, J., Kolkhorst, B., Lee, E., and Wingert, W. B. (1994). "Journey to a Mature Software Process." IBM Systems Journal, vol. 33, no. 1, pp. 46–61.

[Christensen 2000] Christensen, M. J. (2000). "The Cost of SW-CMM Call Backs." Private correspondence.

[Clark 1997] Clark, B. K. (1997). *The Effects of Software Process Maturity on Software Development Effort.* PhD dissertation, Computer Science Department, University of Southern California, August. Available at http://www.usc.edu/ bclark/research.

[Clark 2000] Clark, B. K. (2000). "Quantifying the Effects on Effort of Software Process Maturity." *IEEE Software*, vol. 17, no. 6, November/December, pp. 65–70.

[Coallier 1995] Coallier, F. (1995). "TRILLIUM: A Model for the Assessment of Telecom Product Development and Support Capability." *IEEE Software Process Newsletter*, vol. 3, pp. 3–8.

[Craigyle & Fletcher 1993] Craigmyle, M., and Fletcher, I. (1993). "Improving IT Effectiveness through Software Process Assessment." *Software Quality Journal*, vol. 2, pp. 257–264.

[Curtis 1995] Curtis, B. (1995). "Building a Cost Benefit Case for Software Process Improvement." Tutorial presented at 7th Software Engineering Process Group Conference, Boston.

[Dorling & Simms 1991] Dorling, A., and Simms, P. (1991). *ImproveIT Study Report*, U.K. Ministry of Defence.

[El Emam et al. 1998] El Emam, K., Drouin, J.-N., and Melo, W., eds. (1998). *SPICE: The Theory and Practice of Software Process Improvement and Capability Determination.* IEEE Computer Society Press, Los Alamitos, CA.

[Grady 1996] Grady, R. B. (1996). "Software Failure Analysis for High-Return Process Improvement Decisions." *Hewlett-Packard Journal*, vol. 47, no 3, pp. 15–24.

[Herbsleb & Goldenson 1996] Herbsleb, J., and Goldenson, D. (1996). "A Systematic Survey of CMM Experience and Results." *Proceedings International Conference on Software Engineering, ICSE-18.* IEEE Computer Society Press, Los Alamitos, CA, pp. 323–330.

[Humphrey 1987] Humphrey, W. S. (1987). "Software Process Program." Presented at SEI Affiliate Symposium, Pittsburgh, PA.

[Humphrey 1989]   Humphrey, W. S. (1989). *Managing the Software Process.*
                           Addison-Wesley, Reading, MA.

[Humphrey 1995]   Humphrey, W. S. (1995). *A Discipline for Software Engi-
                           neering.* Addison-Wesley, Reading, MA.

[Humphrey 1999a]   Humphrey, W. S. (1999a). *Introduction to the Team Soft-
                           ware Process.* Addison-Wesley-Longman, Reading, MA.

[Humphrey 1999b]   Humphrey, W. S. (1999b). "Making the Strategic Case for
                           Process Improvement." *SEI Interactive*, vol. 2, no. 4, De-
                           cember 1999. http://interactive.sei.cmu.edu/news@sei/-
                           columns/watts_nw/1999/December/watts-dec99.htm

[Humphrey 2000]   Humphrey, W. S. (2000). "Justifying a Process Im-
                           provement Proposal." *SEI Interactive*, vol. 3, no. 1,
                           March 2000. http://interactive.sei.cmu.edu/news@sei/-
                           columns/watts_nw/2000/March/watts-mar00.htm

[Hunter et al. 1997]   Hunter, R., Robinson, G., and Woodman, I. (1997). "Tool
                           Support for Software Process Assessment and Improve-
                           ment." *Software Process: Improvement and Practice*, vol.
                           3, pp. 213–223.

[Jansen & Sanders 1998]   Jansen, P., and Sanders, J. (1998). "Guidelines for Pro-
                           cess Improvement." *SPICE: The Theory and Practice of
                           Software Process Improvement and Capability Determi-
                           nation*, K. El Emam, J.-N. Drouin, and W. Melo, eds.
                           IEEE Computer Society Press, Los Alamitos, CA, pp.
                           171–192.

[Kind & Ferguson 1997]   Kind, P.A., and Ferguson, J. (1997). "The Software Ac-
                           quisition Capability Maturity Model." *Crosstalk*, vol. 10,
                           no. 3, pp. 13–17.

[Krasner 1994]   Krasner, H. (1994). "The Payoff for Software Process Im-
                           provement (SPI): What Is It and How to Get It." *IEEE
                           Software Process Newsletter*, no. 1, pp. 3–8.

[Kuvaja & Bicego 1994]   Kuvaja, P., and Bicego, A. (1994). "A European Assess-
                           ment Methodology." *Software Quality Journal*, vol. 3, pp.
                           117–127.

[Logica 1988]   Logica Consultancy Ltd. (1988). *Quality Management
                           Standards for Software.* Author, London.

[Lowe & Cox 1996] Lowe, D. E., and Cox, G. M. (1996). "Implementing the Capability Maturity Model for Software Development." *Hewlett-Packard Journal*, vol. 47, no. 3.

[Naur & Randell 1969] Naur, P., and Randell, B., eds. (1969). *Software Engineering: A Report on a Conference Sponsored by the NATO Science Committee*, NATO, Brussels.

[Paulish & Carleton 1994] Paulish, D. J. and Carleton, A. D. (1994). "Case Studies of Software Process Improvement Measurement." *IEEE Computer*. vol. 27, no. 9, pp. 50–57.

[Paulk 1995] Paulk, M. C. (1995). "How ISO 9001 Compares with the CMM." *IEEE Software*, vol. 12.

[Paulk, Konrad, & Garcia 1995] Paulk, M. C., Konrad, M. D., and Garcia, S. M. (1995). "CMM Versus SPICE Architectures." *IEEE Software Process Newsletter*, no. 3, pp. 7–11.

[Paulk et al. 1995] Paulk, M. C., Weber, C. V., Curtis, B., and Chrissis, M. B. (1995). *The Capability Maturity Model: Guidelines for Improving the Software Process.* Addison Wesley, Reading, MA.

[Price Waterhouse 1988] Price Waterhouse (1988). *Software Quality Standards: The Costs and Benefits.* Author, London.

[Sanders 1998] Sanders, M., ed., and the SPIRE Project Team. (1998). *The SPIRE Handbook.* Centre for Software Engineering, Dublin, Ireland.

[Schaeffer 1998] Schaeffer, M.D. (1998). "Capability Maturity Model Process Improvement." *Crosstalk*, May 1998, vol. 11, pp. 4–5.

[Simon et al. 1997] Simon, J.-M., El Emam, K., Rousseau, S., Jacquet, E., and Babey, F. (1997). "The Reliability of ISO/IEC PDTR 15504 Assessments." *Software Process: Improvement and Practice*, vol. 3, pp. 177–188.

[Stelzer et al. 1998] Stelzer, D., Reibnitz, M., and Mellis, W. (1998). "Benefits and Prerequisites of ISO 9000 Based Software Quality Management." *IEEE Software Process Newsletter*, no. 12, pp. 3–7.

[SPICE 1996] SPICE Project. (1996). *SPICE Trials Phase 1 Report.* The SPICE Project, http://www.sqi.gu.edu.au/spice.

[SPICE 1998]   SPICE Project (1998). *SPICE Trials Phase 2 Interim Report*. The SPICE Project, http://www.sqi.gu.edu.au/spice.

[Webb & Humphrey 1999]   Webb, D., and Humphrey, W. S. (1999). "Using the TSP on the TaskView Project." *Crosstalk*, February, pp. 3–10.

Chapter 9

Software Configuration Management

9.1   Introduction

Software configuration management (SWCM) is a formal software engineering discipline that provides methods and tools to identify and control software throughout its development and use. SWCM activities include the following:

- Identification and establishment of baselines;

- Review, approval/disapproval, control, tracking, and reporting of changes;

- Audits and reviews of evolving software products; and

- Interface and vendor control.

IEEE Standard 828-1998, *IEEE Standard for Software Configuration Management Plans*, provides guidance in planning SWCM activities and establishes the minimum required content of a software configuration management plan (SCMP). The SCMP serves as formal documentation of the SWCM activities to be performed on a given software development project. Use of this standard can aid software engineering project managers and other personnel who are planning and performing SWCM activities and preparing a SCMP.

9.2   Objectives

In this chapter you will learn:

- Why software configuration management can be the most important discipline supporting the software process life cycle.

- How to define the content and scope of a software configuration management plan.

- How to review a software configuration management plan.

- How to determine the appropriate level of configuration control for the different varieties of software work products.

- How to determine the appropriate level of configuration control for software work products at various points in their life cycles.

- What the most common software configuration items are.

- What baselines are and how they relate to software life cycle phases.

- What software libraries are and how are they used in software configuration management.

- Why software configuration management is more than just change control and what additional activities are included.

- What change control is, the common sources of change, and how changes are approved and implemented.

- How to establish and maintain a configuration control board.

- What configuration status accounting is and who performs it.

- What configuration audits and reviews are and why they are needed.

- The activities involved in interface and subcontractor/vendor control.

- What software configuration management resources are and how are they used.

9.3   Software Configuration Management

9.3.1   Need for SWCM

Change is a fundamental feature of all software development projects. Requirements often change during the life cycle of a software development project, as do the design and code as they are initially created and as they mature. In the extreme, uncontrolled and unmonitored changes to a software development project's configuration can lead to software that does not meet user requirements, schedule, or budget needs. Without appropriate configuration control, projects can and have failed.

Before a software product is released, it must be validated to prove that it is correct, consistent, and complete. This validation activity (often performed through testing) must be performed using a known entity. If the configuration tested or reviewed during one phase of development is different from the configuration delivered to the next phase, the effort can be completely negated. The objective of SWCM is to ensure that every component of a software development project's configuration is identified and proven reliable, traceable, and repeatable. SWCM helps to reduce such problems as reappearing faults, developed and tested features that mysteriously disappear, and fully tested programs that suddenly malfunction.

By coordinating the work of the many different personnel involved in a software development project, SWCM helps to prevent personnel overriding each other's updates and shared code updates without notification of all parties affected. In addition, SWCM helps to ensure that defect fixes occur across all released software versions. SWCM should form the backbone of a project's life cycle processes.

9.3.2 Historical Development of SWCM

The roots of SWCM can be traced back to the more general problem of configuration control for manufacturing industries, especially those that produced complex hardware. The classical examples lie in the automotive and aerospace industries, where hardware drawings, including bills of materials (both raw materials and purchased parts), test procedures, and assembly instructions, were and are used to guide the design, assembly, and test processes of manufactured items. It was therefore natural that the first requirements for SWCM emerged in the aerospace industry in the 1960s and 1970s, where both the customers and the industrial base were familiar with the general concepts of configuration identification and control from their work with hardware. During the same time period large management information systems were being developed and the need for configuration management during and after the development process was becoming apparent there as well.

During the 1980s, the realization was made that SWCM had some specialized requirements that went above and beyond those typically associated with hardware products:

- Many more engineers were involved in the development over a much longer period of time. Hence the CM system had to deal with change over a longer span of the product life cycle.

- The logical complexity of software resulted in much greater rates of change to the design and code than was the case for hardware. Requirement uncertainties added to this factor.

- More artifacts were typically produced, per engineering hour worked, in the development of software products, so more items exist whose configuration must be managed. As the software product progressed through its development more "baselines" had to be established for each artifact than was the case for hardware.

These factors combined to increase both the complexity of the relationships between the items under configuration management as well as the volume and rate of change to which they were subjected. As a result, while conceptually similar to the earlier configuration management systems used to support hardware developments, developers realized that systems for software configuration management had different requirements. This has resulted in both research into, and tool development for, software configuration management. Developments in this area continue as this is being written.

Since the late 1980s, the general level of interest in applying SWCM has increased dramatically due to the availability of more capable toolsets, simultaneous with the appearance of the Software Engineering Institute's capability maturity model (CMM). The CMM is a standard for measuring how well a company builds software and was originally aimed at the military contracting world, although commercial (largely industrial) usage now exceeds that in the Department of Defense (DoD) sector. The CMM consists of five levels numbered one to five with five being the highest level. To qualify as a level 2 provider, an organization must have a configuration management process. The DoD has mandated that all companies competing for the largest categories of contracts must be at level 3 or above.

9.3.3   Objectives of SWCM

The fundamental objective of SWCM is to maintain the integrity and traceability of the configuration of a software development product throughout its life cycle and to protect the software documents from uncontrolled changes. In addition, SWCM will allow the developers to recreate or modify a product from a controlled, managed baseline. In its simplest, most basic form, SWCM can be thought of as a formalized document-naming scheme that is used for managing a software development project's documents, including source code. SWCM can be further described as an integrated process for identifying, documenting, controlling, evaluating, tracking, and approving all changes made during the life cycle of a software development project.

As with any activity it must be recognized that distinctions exist between an organization's software configuration management group and the processes that support that group. Thus an organizational entity entitled SWCM is often the steward of the data being configuration managed, but it is not the owner. That role is usually assigned to the developer or to an internal or external customer. Likewise, the SWCM organization is not necessarily the decision maker determining what changes are applied to the data. It must, however, facilitate and support those changes so that they are done in an orderly, visible, repeatable manner.

The configuration of a software item refers to the *functional* and *physical characteristics* of the item as defined in technical documentation and as realized in a software item. The configuration of an item encompasses all of the characteristics of the software including its content, the content of documents that describe it, the different versions of software and documents generated as changes are made, data needed for software operation, and other essential elements that make the software what it is. The configuration needed to recreate a specific instance of the item is referred to as a *version, build,* or *release.* The process of applying changes to one version to create another in a dependable, visible manner is called *change control.* The group that reviews and approves (or does not approve) proposed changes is referred to as the Change Control Board (CCB). Elements of a software configuration may have different CCBs at different stages of their life cycle. The mechanism for storing and tracking the evolution of an item is referred to as a *library.* These concepts are discussed in later sections.

After a change is made, the change control function must be able to answer these questions:

- What? (What changes were made to what version?)

- Who? (Who made the changes?)

- When? (When were the changes made?)

- Why? (Why were the changes made?)

- Where? (Where were the changes made?)

Versions that support specific technical or contractual events are often referred to as *baselines*. The transition from one baseline to another is usually accomplished by one or more versions that represent some intermediate levels of change.

9.3.4   Initiating SWCM for a Project

Two stages are necessary for establishing configuration management for a project: planning and implementation. In the planning stage, the scope and objectives of the SWCM activity must be evaluated and agreed on by all interested parties. This usually includes the software project manager, the process architect, the project configuration manager, and any institutional configuration management functions. Depending on the nature and terms of the contract and organization, it may also include an external customer or a representative of the business arm of the organization, who will act as the internal customer. Based on the outcomes of the planning activity, the implementation stage will produce a software configuration management plan (SCMP) specific to the given project and its agreed-on life cycle process, contractual, and general business requirements. Some requests for proposals (RFPs) actually require that a draft SCMP be submitted as part of the proposal. In other cases, an outline SCMP is required.

The actual activity of SWCM begins when a software development project begins and ends only when the software is retired and taken out of operation. If components of the retired system have subsequently been reused in other products, the span of the SWCM activity will extend beyond the retirement of any particular software item. Development of the full SCMP can begin at this point with identification of potential software configuration items.

Because the proposal itself is a document and product, it should, if for no other reasons than legal, be placed under configuration management. If the developing organization maintains a separate document control system for this purpose then this should be used. If not, then the document should be placed into the SWCM system. Certainly, any prototypes used to develop the contract should be placed into an SWCM system, even if they must later be transferred to a project specific system.

9.3.5   Matching SWCM to the Life Cycle

A principal concern when planning and implementing SWCM is that the level of control be appropriate to the life cycle phase. Thus the initial version of a document would be controlled at a different level than a later version that was intended for release to a customer. The needs of the two situations are very different and the review process to which changes would be subjected would often be different.

The general concepts of SWCM would be the same in the two situations but the sensitivities are different. As a result, changes under these two conditions will often be reviewed by CCBs with different memberships. It may even be appropriate for the CCB authority over a specific item to be delegated to specific individuals in the early phases of development, with CCBs being created with different memberships as the product moves into the later phases.

9.3.6   External versus Internal SWCM

It is useful to distinguish between internal and external SWCM. Internal SWCM is usually performed during the development phases of a project. External SWCM is usually initiated during delivery and is subsequently active during the operation and maintenance phase.

Internal SWCM refers to SWCM performed during software development and prior to a software product's release outside of the developing organization. Subsequent to this release, the SWCM process is thought of as being an external one. External SWCM is usually designed to support a very low rate of change when compared to internal SWCM.

The relationship is, however, not one directional. Very often, an externally released version is later used as the starting point for new developments. If this is the case, great care must be taken to ensure that the externally released product can be recreated without being contaminated by the changes that are being introduced as part of the new, internal development. Modern SWCM toolsets support this, and the organization procedures must consider this important relationship.

9.4   Software Configuration Management Concepts and Mechanisms

Six core activities are needed to perform SWCM in modern development environments, although the level of effort required in each of them will be somewhat product and technology dependent. Figure 9.1 shows the six activities.

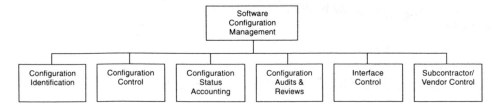

Figure 9.1: Software Configuration Management Activities

The mechanisms by which these each of these activities is performed and the degree of formality involved in their performance may differ by the type and size of the software product being developed. On a small, stand-alone project, SWCM may be a somewhat informal process with no need for interface or subcontractor/vendor control. On a large project, which is part of an integrated system, SWCM will be a highly formalized process with interface control being a major activity.

The six activities are discussed in Section 9.5. In these discussions the key concepts and mechanisms will be those of software configuration items (SWCIs), baselines, change requests, change control boards (CCBs), and libraries. In brief:

- The SWCIs are what is being configuration managed.

- The baselines identify groups of SWCIs that represent specific major developmental milestones or events.

- Change requests are the mechanism by which the need for a change is identified.

- CCBs are the mechanism by which the change requests are reviewed and approved or rejected and the implementation of the change tracked to completion.

- Libraries are the mechanism by which SWCIs and their change histories are stored for subsequent retrieval and reconstruction.

The definitions of these functions and mechanisms are now elaborated on and their roles expanded.

9.4.1 Software Configuration Items

The fundamental entity of *configuration identification* is the *software configuration item* (SWCI). A SWCI is a specific, documented collection of work products resulting from or used during the life cycle processes. A *work product* can be defined as any tangible item that results from a software development project function, activity, or task. Work products include management plans, test plans, requirements specifications, design documents, code, meeting minutes, memos, schedules, and budgets. A SWCI can be thought of as a work product or collection of related work products that is placed under SWCM and, thereafter, treated as a single entity.

A SWCI is, therefore, any part of the development or deliverable system that needs to be independently identified, stored, reviewed, used, changed, delivered, or maintained. The items placed under SWCM include not only the software products that are delivered to the customer, but also the items that are required to create these software products (such as documentation).

Items typically identified as SWCIs themselves or combined to form SWCIs include the following:

- Management plans (project, schedule, budget, quality assurance, testing, SCMP, etc.);

- Requirement and design documents;

- User and maintenance documentation and manuals;

- Test documentation, test drivers, and data;

- Support software (including compilers and operating systems);

- Data dictionaries and various cross-references;

- Source code, including that of any externally procured items, as available;

- Executable code, including any externally procured components;

- Link maps and other products of the build processes;

- Product release notes, such as the version description document;

- Databases used to build or operate the product;

- Interface control documents, if not separately maintained in a systems engineering CM system; and

- Any item used to support the development and operation of the product. Some of these items may be in executable form only.

Keep in mind that some SWCM systems store only text-readable documents. As a result binary information must be stored in some expanded (such as ASCII hex) format.

Finally, please note that many of the types of SWCIs listed above are not typically delivered to customers. In addition, the bulk of the change traffic that must be controlled typically occurs in the developmental items themselves; that is, in the requirements and design documents, in the source and executable code, and in the test documentation, test drivers, and associated data.

9.4.2 Baselines

A *baseline* is a set of one or more configuration items (CIs) whose content and status have been reviewed technically and accepted at some step in the product life cycle. On initial creation, SWCIs are reviewed in order to verify completeness and accuracy before they are accepted into the baseline. Prior to such review and acceptance, they may well be placed in a developmental library under a tailored change control scheme. This should be done so as to ensure that the item accepted into the baseline is indeed what was reviewed.

Once SWCIs have been reviewed and formalized into an initial baseline, that baseline serves as the starting point for the next developmental activities in the product life cycle. Eventually these activities will themselves result in the formation of yet another baseline. Changes can be made to the baselined SWCIs only through the software development project's established change control procedures.

The life cycle model (waterfall, spiral, incremental development, rapid prototyping, etc.) being implemented for the software development project determines the number and types of baselines. For each baseline, the following must be documented:

- The event that creates the baseline,

- SWCIs that are to be associated with the baseline and configuration control together,

- Changes that have been made to the baseline since its creation,

- Procedures used to establish and change the baseline and its component SWCIs,

- Authorities required to approve changes to the SWCIs in the baseline, and

- How changes will be identified and associated with the baseline and its component SWCIs.

In general, four generic baselines have been identified as common to most life cycle models. Each represents a reference point that serves as a starting point for further project development. In some cases customer reviews or payments are associated with these baselines. The four generic baselines are (1) *functional*, (2) *allocated*, (3) *developmental*, and (4) *product*.

The involvement of the customer in the approval of changes in any of these baselines is a matter that must be clarified in the contract. Some customers will not acknowledge a baseline formally unless they are involved in the change control process for that baseline. In any case, the baselines exist, whether contractually recognized or not.

The *functional baseline* describes what functions the system will perform and is the configuration established after the system requirements review (SRR) and systems design review (SDR). It is typically the initial baseline established on a software development project. The documents incorporated into the functional baseline specify all necessary functional characteristics of the SWCIs, system-level tests required to demonstrate achievement of those characteristics, any necessary interface characteristics, performance requirements, quality attributes, and any design constraints. They do not distinguish between which functions are performed by the software and which by the host hardware and its operating system.

The *allocated baseline* (sometimes called the software requirements baseline) documents what functions the software to be developed will perform and is the configuration established after the software specification review (SSR). The term *allocated* comes from the concept that requirements have been allocated from the system specification of the functional baseline. The documents incorporated into the allocated baseline specify all necessary functional and performance requirements allocated from higher level SWCIs, tests required to demonstrate achievement of those allocated requirements, any necessary interface requirements, and any design constraints.

The *developmental baseline* is a constantly evolving and cumulative baseline that occurs between the allocated and product baselines. This baseline is most appropriately identified as an internal baseline that describes the configuration at any stage of the design, coding, or testing activities. Items residing in the developmental configuration are baselined incrementally as they are reviewed and tested by the development team. The bulk of the effort expended by the project staff is expended working with this baseline. As a result, the developmental baseline is commonly regarded as an *internal* one. The other three baselines are correspondingly regarded as *external*.

The *product baseline* is the configuration established after the system-level validation and verification activities confirm that the deliverables meet the requirements enumerated in the SRS and the SDD. It must also be verified that the design documents reflect the final software configuration. The product baseline thus fully documents the final version of software. All external releases will then come from this baseline. This baseline is then used to support the released versions of the product. It is also the starting point for the development of any subsequent versions.

Table 9.1 summarizes the four generic baselines, and their associated activities, formal reviews, and SWCIs for a large product being developed under the waterfall life cycle model.

9.4.3 Change Requests

The mechanism for identifying the need to change a SWCI is the software change request (SCR) or the software trouble report (STR). The change request documents the need for the change to the item. It should indicate the reason for making the change (such as new requirement, detection of an anomaly by inspection or test), the item impacted (both the SWCI and the baseline in which it resides), the urgency of the change, the source of the change (internal or external), the individual requesting the change, and other relevant data. Change requests must be formal and must be maintained. This is most commonly done using some type of online system, commonly called a *problem tracking system*. The source and nature of the change sometimes means that the change is not necessarily a "problem" as the word is commonly interpreted.

Although SCRs do not themselves drive the change process (the underlying technical activity does that), SCRs are the objective evidence that the change is occurring and provide a measure of activity in the program and its life cycle processes. It is also important to make the distinction, at each phase of development, between the change request and the underlying process event that results in the change request. Thus, when an item is technically reviewed minutes and action items should be produced, documenting what needs to be done to the item.

Eventually, in accordance with the project's life cycle processes, one or more change requests must be written so that the item can be modified. Likewise, if testing of an item produces anomalies, the testing or test anomaly reports will document the fact that a change is necessary, with the one or more resulting change requests being written to modify the item. This situation may appear inefficient but it serves to decouple the mechanization of changes, SWCM, from the technical processes that drive change.

Baseline	Functional	Allocated	Developmental Configuration	Product
Associated activities	System requirements analysis	Software requirements analysis	Software preliminary design, Software detailed design, Coding and unit testing, Software integration and testing	Software performance testing
Associated formal reviews	System requirements review (SRR), System design review (SDR)	Software specification review (SSR)	Preliminary design review (PDR), Critical design review (CDR), Test readiness review (TRR)	Functional configuration audit (FCA), Physical configuration audit (PCA)
Associated SWCIs	System/segment specifications (SSS), Software develop ment plan (SDP), Software configuration management plan (SCMP), Software quality assurance plan (SQAP), Concept of operations (ConOps), Statement of work (SOW), Work breakdown structure (WBS), Preliminary software require- ments specifi- cation (PSRS), Preliminary interface requirements specification (PIRS)	Functional baseline plus approved changes, Software requirements specification (SRS), Interface requirements specification (IRS)	Allocated baseline plus approved changes, Software design description (SDD), Interface design description (IDD), Database design description (DBDD), Software test plan(s) (STP), Software test description(s) (STD), Software test report(s) (STR), Source code, Executable code, Support software (operating systems, compilers, case tools, CM tools, etc.)	Developmental configuration baseline plus approved changes, Software product specification (SPS), Software instal- lation plan (SIP), Version description document (VDD), Software user manual(s) (SUM), Software maintenance manual(s) (SMM)

Table 9.1: Baselines, Associated Activities, Reviews, and SWCIs [Thayer 1997]

9.4.4   Configuration Control Boards

One of the primary objectives of SWCM is the orderly, timely, and correct processing of changes to the SWCIs. The primary mechanism for this is the concept of the configuration control board (CCB). One of the first actions performed on a new SCR is the determination, based on the SWCI and the baseline, of the assignment of that item to the appropriate CCB. Depending on the baseline, the SWCI involved, and the life cycle processes currently active on the SWCI, the CCB may be an individual (such as a technical lead for a small subsystem) or it may be a committee composed of the program manager, the customer, and the software quality manager.

The activities of a CCB are the same in all cases, although the scale will be different depending on the considerations listed above. A CCB will evaluate the impact of the change not only from a technical point of view, but also from logistic, strategic, economic, and organizational points of view, as appropriate to the level of the baseline. A CCB will compare the desirability of a change versus its effect on the project budget and schedule. The goal of a CCB is to maintain a global perspective and assess the impact of the proposed change beyond the baseline in question.

For internal SWCM, the CCB may consist of just the project manager or the chief designer. On medium projects, the CCB may be composed of the project manager plus one or two other individuals. On large projects, the CCB should include members from project management, system engineering, program engineering, design, configuration management, quality assurance, testing and integration, support, and maintenance. Multiple levels of CCBs may exist depending on the degree of project complexity or the baseline involved.

For external SWCM, the CCB membership will usually include customer representatives. Sometimes customer membership is a contract requirement, most appropriately at the product level of baseline. CCBs with senior customer and contractor staff members are generally required on government projects, and they may be desirable on large software development projects in order to reduce the time to obtain required customer approval for certain types of changes.

The CCB(s) should be established at the start of a project in order to be available to evaluate any changes generated from early design reviews. Regular meetings of the CCB do not generally begin until later in the project, usually during the development stage. The frequency at which a given CCB meets will depend on the project schedule and the severity of the requested changes. The board's responsibilities continue into the maintenance phase.

As part of the SCMP, each CCB and its level of authority for approving proposed changes must be identified. When multiple CCBs are used, the SCMP must also specify how the proper level for a given change request is determined, including any variations during the various phases of the project life cycle.

Configuration control boards may approve, disapprove, or defer a change request. Disapproval means the CCB has concluded a requested change is not needed, is not feasible, or there is a better alternative. *Deferrals* mean the CCB requires additional information and may cause the software change request to be returned to the evaluation function for further analysis. The software change request originators is often invited to the CCB meeting where their request is reviewed in order to answer questions. Deferrals may also occur when the CCB is waiting for other known changes to be evaluated or implemented.

Configuration control boards do not merely decide whether a change request will be implemented. They also determine who should implement the requested change, its priority among all approved changes, and how and when the implementation should occur. Further, the CCB determines how implementation will be tested and verified. This may require rerunning tests specified in the test plan or developing additions to the test plan. Regression testing will usually be specified in order to ensure that errors have not been introduced by the change.

The CCB is responsible for designating the conditions under which an updated baseline will be released. These conditions can include CCB review of the final inspection and test results. The CCB must also determine the new version identifier to be assigned after implementation approval. The implementation requirements and directives designated by the CCB are often summarized on some type of software change directive form, which is given to personnel responsible for implementation, testing, and verification of the change.

The activities of a CCB require the investment of time and money. Implementing the following procedures can increase the effectiveness and efficiency of a CCB, especially when the board is concerned with the more mature versions and baselines:

- *Publish a written charter:* Avoids confusion by identifying CCB members, the scope of their activities and responsibilities, and the procedures to follow. Ideally the general charter should be in the SCMP.

- *Schedule regular meetings:* Reviewing a large number of software change requests that have accumulated over a long period of time is unproductive. The frequency of meetings can be increased as a project progresses in response to increases in the submission of change requests.

- *Limit meeting duration:* Short meetings are more productive than long meetings. The frequency of meetings can be increased in order to shorten their duration.

- *Prioritize changes:* The highest priority changes should be examined at the beginning of the meeting to ensure that adequate time is spent on their review.

- *Designate member alternates:* Alternate personnel should attend when regular members are unavailable, thereby ensuring the availability of a quorum and reducing the risk of wasted meetings.

- *Require mandatory meeting attendance:* Reduces the risk of wasted meetings because of the inability to obtain a quorum. Either regular members or their alternatives should be able to make a meeting if it is scheduled well in advance.

- *Publishing CCB meeting agendas:* Reduces meeting time because individuals have examined materials in depth prior to having to make a decision. CCB members should receive the agenda well in advance of the meeting to allow thorough review time.

- *Designate a CCB secretary:* Ensures that paperwork, including agendas, documentation to be reviewed, and minutes of previous meetings, is distributed in a timely manner. This helps to keep CCM members informed and allows them advance time to prepare for meetings.

- *Designate a CCB chair:* For external CCBs, the chair is usually a senior customer representative. Because configuration changes can be expensive to implement, it is only the customer that can authorize the expenditure of funds. For internal CCB the chair is usually the project manager or the technical lead. The chair should not only be responsible for running the meetings but for limiting extraneous discussion, thereby decreasing meeting time. The chair should have authority to resolve disputes and break deadlocks.

9.4.5   Libraries

Software libraries provide the storage mechanism need to implement the control and change history functions needed to implement SWCM so that the evolutionary history of the SWCI baselines can be tracked and any desired version recreated. Software libraries have historically been composed of hardcopy documentation and software on machine-readable media. Advances in information technology have encouraged the transition to maintaining all SWCI information on machine-readable media.

The number and kinds of software libraries required vary with each software project and are a function of the required levels of control for the project. Three generic kinds of software libraries are generally used: the dynamic or programmer's library, the static library, and the controlled/master library.

The *dynamic library* is primarily under the control of the project's software engineering staff. The engineers initially developing documents and code use it to hold newly created or modified SWCIs. In can be viewed as an in-box or holding area for new or changed items prior to their acceptance into the controlled/master library.

The *static library*, sometimes called the *software repository*, is used to archive baselines that have been released for general use. The master copies of items that have been formally released for operational use are maintained in this library. The static library can be viewed as the out-box of the system.

The controlled, or master, library is used for storing baselines and for controlling changes made to them. This is the primary library involved in the process of configuration control. Items are initially placed in the library only after being identified as SWCIs, baselined, named per documented procedures, and accepted by the responsible CCB. Access to items stored in the controlled library is restricted, most commonly to read-only format and the responsible CCB must authorize any changes made to items in this library.

The controlled/master library can be thought of as residing between the in-box of the dynamic library and the out-box of the static.

At a minimum a controlled software library should provide these features:

- Multiple control levels with associated access restrictions,

- Storage and retrieval of baselines,

- Sharing and transfer of baselines between control levels within the library,

- Storage and recovery of archived versions of baselines,

- Storage, updating, and retrieval of records, and

- Production of reports.

To conserve storage space, many controlled software libraries store archived versions using deltas. Only the differences between versions are stored, as opposed to each version being stored in its entirety. Libraries that use *forward deltas* store the oldest version in its entirety and later versions as deltas. Libraries that use *reverse deltas* store the most recent version in its entirety and previous versions as deltas.

The software libraries that will be used by the project must be identified in the planning stage, as well as how the SWCIs are to be physically placed under library control. Further, the format, location, documentation requirements, receiving and verification requirements, and access control procedures must be specified for each library. In addition, because the libraries of large, long-lived systems will grow to occupy considerable amounts of online storage, the SCMP must address how early versions and changes will be archived and retrieved. In addition, the SCMP must address how the project libraries will be backed up and how the project will implement disaster recovery.

9.5   Software Configuration Management Activities and Functions

Having defined the fundamental mechanisms of SWCM, we now turn to how the functions of SWCM are performed. Those functions, as described in Figure 9.1, are as follows:

- Configuration identification,

- Configuration control,

- Configuration status accounting,

- Configuration audits and reviews,

- Interface control, and

- Subcontractor/vendor control.

A key attribute of a SWCM system is that it must be a closed-loop system. That is, once an activity is initiated, there is feedback to the participants and activities always result in a documented, stable, visible state.

9.5.1 Configuration Identification

Configuration identification is the process of determining the software configuration items and related baselines that will be placed under SWCM change control.

Configuration identification consists of three interrelated activities: (1) identifying, (2) naming, and (3) acquiring SWCIs. Unique issues are associated with each of these activities. Because they must be performed early in the product's life cycle, they are often done with partial information and yet must be done with great care because they can have a significant influence over later phases of development.

9.5.1.1 Identifying SWCIs

Two interrelated tasks must be performed when identifying software configuration items: Select the SWCIs and group them into baselines (Figure 9.2). The selection of SWCIs for a specific baseline can have a profound effect on the success or failure of a software development project. A common problem in software development projects is to divide the product baseline into too many SWCIs. The control of each SWCI incurs costs in the form of documentation, review, development, and management effort. These costs must increase significantly when changes are applied at the product baseline, because the risks of an incorrectly implemented or applied change are much higher at this point in a product's life cycle. Ultimately, the number of SWCIs at the product baseline should be determined by how the product will be deployed and maintained in the field.

In the earlier developmental baseline SWCIs are typically identified at a level of granularity consistent with the product architecture and the development team structure. Thus they will usually vary in complexity, type, and size. Typically, a SWCI is established for each component of the software development project that can be designed, implemented, tested, and modified independently. The costs of operating the SWCM function will be lower in the developmental baseline so this fine-grain approach becomes feasible.

Figure 9.2: Identifying a Software Configuration Item (SWCI)

The ultimate goal of configuration identification is to identify the most significant and critical items that will require examination, evaluation, and control consistent with the purposes of the baseline in which the SWCI will reside. Selection of SWCIs typically involves a team composed of the customer/user and the software project's manager, team leader, development personnel, quality assurance personnel, test personnel, configuration management personnel, and maintenance personnel. The exact composition of the team is a function of the baseline into which the SWCIs will be inserted and the contract.

Because both too few and too many identified SWCIs can cause problems, project management generally determines and formalizes the criteria for identifying SWCIs. Examples of criteria that are commonly used include these:

- Sheer size and complexity of the item;

- The baseline into which the item will be inserted;

- The expected rate of change of the item in the intended baseline;

- The costs of making changes to the item in the intended baseline;

- Any intended reuse of the item;

- Identification of the item as being high risk for development;

- Identification of the item as safety critical;

- Identification of the item as performance critical;

- Dependency of the item on a toolset different from the other SWCIs;

- Role of the item in system or subsystem architecture;

- Ability of the item to be individually complied;

- Ability of the item to be installed by itself;

- Ability of the item to execute by itself;

- Ability of the item to perform a useful function by itself; and

- Evaluation that the item will be subject to substantial, individual, modification during maintenance.

Not all of these criteria are equally important for any given project or baseline within a project. Their importance will depend on business and contractual conditions, as well as the costs of operating the change control system and the baseline for which the SWCI is intended.

Finally, keep in mind that the relative importance of and related time spent managing the identified SWCIs change throughout the life cycle of a software development project.

When a software product is being designed, requirement documents are typically subject to high rates of change, whereas design documents will typically change only two or three times. When coding begins, however, design documents generally become the items subject to the highest rate of change.

During integration and testing, the code and its detailed design document are usually the SWCIs that are changed most often. Finally, when the software product is ready for release or has been released and is being maintained, the entire set of items will be subject to change.

9.5.1.2   Naming Software Configuration Items

The activities of naming and acquiring SWCIs are often done in tandem since the "naming" is often done by the entity "acquiring" the SWCI (Figure 9.3). Software libraries and their associated automated SWCM tools are generally the "namers" and "acquirers" in modern software development environment.

Figure 9.3: Naming and Acquiring Software Configuration Items Activities

The methods and conventions to be used for naming SWCIs must be described in the SCMP. Each SWCI that is baselined and subject to configuration control must be "named" by assigning it a unique identifier. Organizations often have established formats for creating identifiers. Some customers may have their own conventions for naming SWCIs. Much SWCM and library support software can be configured to automatically assign identifiers to SWCIs when they are baselined.

The identifier of a SWCI usually contains three distinct pieces of information: the name of the item, a configuration identifier, and a version identifier. The name is often a combination of the project or product name and the function of the SWCI. An example would be "ProjectA_SRS" for the SRS SWCI for ProjectA. The configuration identifier is typically a unique number and is usually used by the SWCM system for internal library management. The version identifier may be a number or letter that is incremented with each new version created. The assigned identifier may also include other fields that indicate the item's type. Examples of item type would be code, document, or data. Other fields can be used to specify the storage media (hardcopy, machine-readable, etc.) as applicable.

In selecting an identifier format, keep in mind that SWCIs exist in several different forms (source, object, executable) and categories. The categories of SWCIs that may need identifiers assigned include these:

- *Product SWCIs.* This is either the software product being developed or part of the end software product.

- *Purchased SWCIs.* This is software that is bought from and maintained by a vendor. It is usually explicitly incorporated into the software product. It includes both subcontracted and off-the-shelf items.

- *Customer-supplied software.* This is software that the customer provides to be incorporated into the product or to aid in its development.

- *Test software.* This is software used to test deliverable software. This category includes software used in both developer and formal acceptance testing. Examples would be test drivers, test stubs, and test data, as well as test capture and analysis software.

- *Product-support software.* This is software used to support development and maintenance of the software product being developed (compilers, assemblers, standards checking tools used to verify that code complies with requirements, etc.).

Notice that these categories need not be mutually exclusive. Thus, a customer could supply test data.

The SCMP must specify the naming and version conventions that will be used to uniquely identify each item to be controlled. The SCMP should also describe the activities of version marking, labeling of documentation of executable software, serialization and altered item marking for executable code, and identification of physical packaging.

9.5.1.3   Acquiring Software Configuration Items

Once a SWCI has been identified, baselined, and named, it must be stored in a controlled environment to prevent unapproved changes. This is the process of *acquiring SWCIs.* Software libraries in the form of databases and their associated database management systems have traditionally been the repositories used to store baselined SWCIs and their related documentation. Many organizations document the process of initially "acquiring" a SWCI by the same change control mechanisms and forms that are used to change an already acquired SWCI.

9.5.2   Configuration Control

Configuration control, sometimes erroneously referred to as "change control," involves creating a managerial review and approval process that prevents software developers from changing software autonomously. It involves the systematic request for, evaluation of, approval or disapproval of, and implementation of approved changes in the configuration of a SWCI after formal establishment of its baseline and configuration identification (Figure 9.4).

An orderly change control process ensures that appropriate consideration is given to the impact of each change. It ensures that only approved changes are implemented into any baselined SWCI and that all approved changes are implemented. Together with the schedule

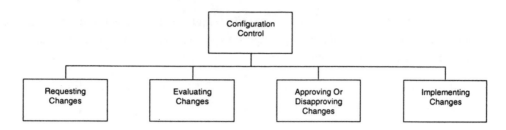

Figure 9.4: Configuration Control Activities

and cost control systems it provides visibility into the technical activity and progress of the project.

The change control policies an organization will follow for a given software project must be described in the SCMP. The SCMP must specify the records to be used for tracking and documenting a proposed change to each baseline, and the appropriate authority level for controlling changes must be identified for each SWCI (or class of SWCI) in each baseline.

Table 9.2 shows an example for a system composed of two major subsystems. In this example the first subsystem has three types of components that must be managed with different processes. For example, Component Type A.1 might be internally developed code unique to this project, Component Type A.2 might be externally supplied software, and Component Type A.3 might be code that is being reused across multiple projects. Notice that, in this example, only the subsystem architecture and the sources of the code were considered in creating the table. The details of the software design are not relevant and should not be included in the SCMP unless they are relevant to the processes.

9.5.2.1 Implementation of Change Control

The activities of change control are typically implemented and documented using a set of forms, which are usually available online. The information on the forms is used by the project engineering and software configuration management staff to perform the change processes of the product life cycle, as well as to create a permanent, objective record of the project's development. In addition, some contracts may impose specific needs that should be reflected in the forms. This occurs most naturally with changes to the functional or allocated baselines because these come directly from or directly impact the customer. It is less likely to be the case for the developmental baseline unless it is explicitly required by the contract. Safety-critical applications would be an example where this might well be the case. The need for such requirements should be examined and well understood.

As part of the SCMP the project must select and use forms that accurately reflect the selected change control processes. Irrespective of the name used by the institution for a particular form the functions are often similar. Thus the form used to request a change may be a *software change request* in one institution, and a *software change proposal* in another. One institution may use a *software problem report* to document a deficiency, while another will use a *software incident report*. Some institutions will combine the two forms into a

Baseline	Software Change Control Form to Be Used	Software Change Authority Required
Functional		

Allocated
  System
  Subsystem A
  Subsystem B		

Developmental/
Configuration
  System
  Subsystem A
  Component Type A.1
  Component Type A.2
  Component Type A.3
  Subsystem B
  Component Type B.1
  Component Type B.2		

Product System		

Table 9.2: Generic Baselines, Change Control Forms, and Authority

problem/change report. The critical issue is not the name but rather the relationship of the document or form to the project's life cycle and configuration management processes.

The different states a change request passes through during the configuration control process are discussed in the following sections and summarized in Figure 9.5.

Identification of a Change

This is the point of origin of the change control process. The identification of the need for a change will rarely come from within the SWCM activity itself, although administrative maintenance of the libraries may in some circumstances require that a change request be issued. Rather, the initial acquisition of an item, or the need to change an item already acquired, is triggered by some event outside of the SWCM system. Review action items or software test reports are the most common examples. These make up the bulk of the changes that will impact the developmental baseline. However, the functional and product baselines will often be the subjects of requirements changes and enhancements, which will in turn propagate to the SWCIs in the developmental baseline (Figure 9.6).

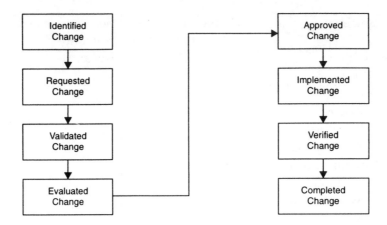

Figure 9.5: States of a Change Request

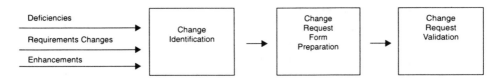

Figure 9.6: Requesting Change Activities

Requesting a Change

The next step in the configuration control process is the preparation of a software change request form. This is a formal document that the requester uses to describe the identified change. At a minimum, the information to be documented includes the name and version of the subject SWCI, the originator's name and organization, the date of the request, the requestor's view of the urgency of the change, the need for the change, and a description of the requested change. This may include references to other documents, such as a software test anomaly report. The project SCMP should document which of these fields must be completed prior to submission of the change request. Electronic forms are increasingly being used as direct interfaces to SWCM support tools.

Validating the Change Request

Each project must designate a mechanism to receive submitted software change requests and assign unique identifiers to them for tracking. This mechanism could be an automated system that associates individuals with SWCIs and baselines. This function could also be performed in small projects by an individual.

The submitted software change requests must then be validated for clarity, completeness, and correctness. The individual designated to perform this validation may be the software configuration manager, but can be any appropriate and specified project team member.

Change requests directed at different baselines, for example, of different SWCIs might be examined by different, designated individuals.

Change requests may arise due to misunderstandings by the person submitting the request or may duplicate existing requests. If the examination indicates the requested change is incomplete, invalid, or has already been evaluated, the request should be rejected and the reason for the rejection should be communicated to the person who submitted it. A record of the request and its disposition should be retained in all cases.

Evaluating the Change Request

Figure 9.7 shows the activities involved in evaluating a validated software change request.

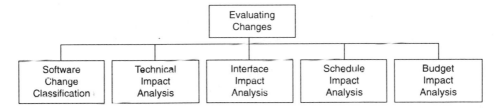

Figure 9.7: Activities Required for Evaluating a Software Change Request

The first step in the evaluation process is the classification of the newly validated change into one of several types. The purpose of any classification scheme is to assist in performing subsequent steps in the change control and configuration processes, as identified in the SCMP. Examples of classification schemes are as follows:

- *By urgency.* This is the evaluator's view of the urgency, not the originator's.

- *By nature of the change.* Usually classified as a deficiency, a new requirement, or another type recognized by the project SCMP.

- *By the nature of the item changed and the potential impacts.* For example, code or data from outside the project would typically be treated differently than would be project-developed items. SWCIs designated as safety critical would likewise be treated differently in subsequent activities.

- *By the type of analysis required.* The change might be classified by the type of analysis required, as well as retest, or other activities that will be required later in the change control or implementation processes.

- *By other classification schemes documented in the SCMP.*

Following the classification of the change, it must be subjected to some kind of technical analysis. It is very useful if the classification scheme used serves to focus attention on specific areas of concern during the analysis. Often a change will be classified in more than one dimension. That is, a change can independently have high priority and be a new requirement.

The SCMP must specify the analysis required to determine the impact of a proposed change as well as the procedures to be followed for reviewing the results of the analysis. Care must be taken to ensure that the analysis procedures are both specific enough to ensure a level of consistency and yet not too detailed. The intent and the scope of the analysis should be made clear but it is impossible to foresee every possible circumstance. In general, validated change requests should be evaluated according to their effects on deliverables and on project resources in multiple dimensions. The analysis procedures will often vary as a function of the SWCI type and the baseline in which it resides.

Each CCB must designate a mechanism, which is sometimes an individual and sometimes a committee, to evaluate software change requests that have passed validation. This evaluation committee may be composed of members of the configuration control board(s), SWCM staff, and/or project team members, depending on the type of SWCI and the baseline. In many cases, lower level CCBs evaluate change requests in their assigned area of responsibility. For example, a software CCB would evaluate a software change request and make its recommendation to a system-level CCB. The CCB's assigned responsibility is to evaluate the impact the requested software change will have on the project and to make implementation recommendations. Ideally, the evaluation committee should contain representatives from all areas that will be affected by the change to the affected items and baselines.

The length of the evaluation varies according to the category of the requested change, the SWCIs involved, and the baseline. The team may conclude that the requested change will lengthen the target delivery date, require additional resources, or extend the budget. It would be incorrect to presuppose that changes only have negative impacts. Changes can also have positive impacts such as shortening the duration of the project or improving the final product. A working knowledge of the project life cycle model and processes can be critical in assessing the impact of a change. At least some members of the evaluation team should have this knowledge.

The evaluation of changes should include impacts to the technical performance, interface, schedule, and budget of the program and conversely the impact of not making the change. Technical assessment should include consideration of not only how (in general terms) but when to best implement the change. Interface assessment should include a description of the impact of the change on other SWCIs. Schedule and budget assessment should account for not only the costs of implementing the change, but possibly changing other components to accommodate the change. All four of these areas interact and so the analysis must include trade-offs among the areas.

If required by contract or desired by the developing organization, a specific software change evaluation can be prepared to summarize the evaluation information and include the implementation recommendations of the evaluation committee. An alternative would be to reserve space on the change request form itself. If more space is needed (as would be the case for a major change), then the evaluation documents can be included by reference. In that case those documents themselves become SWCIs.

The questions, by impact area, that would typically be asked during evaluation are listed in Table 9.3. Remember that, depending on the phase of the product life cycle, the SWCI involved, and the baseline in which it resides, some of the questions are more relevant in a given situation than are others. For example, only a few of the questions are relevant in the case of a blatant defect in a single routine that is detected early in development, whereas virtually every question is relevant in the case of an enhancement request to a released item.

Adjudicating and Approving the Change

Figure 9.8 shows the activities involved in approving or disapproving software change requests.

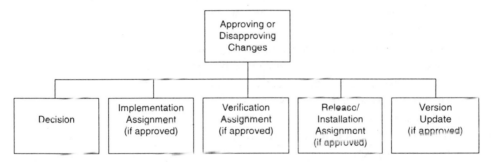

Figure 9.8: Approving or Disapproving Change Activities

Based on the results of the analysis the CCB will make one of these decisions:

- Direct the implementation of the change. In other words, the change is accepted.

- Suspend or defer the change.

- Reject the change.

In the last case, the originator of the change should be notified and all records of the change retained. Later events may prove that the decision to reject was in error, so the records must be retained against that event.

The second case, suspension or deferral, is an unusual event but does occur. It happens most often when changes to the functional or allocated baselines are involved, the analysis is completed but other decision processes outside of the control of the CCB are under way. A classic example is contractual negotiations. Suspended change requests should be highlighted in the SWCM reporting system, including how long the request has been in that state.

In the case of an accepted change, the implementation can proceed according to the selected implementation schedule. The modification should be performed consistent with the project's life cycle processes. The implementation schedule is almost always expressed in one of three forms:

Technical Impact
Operational – What effect will this change have on the final product? What is the impact of not making the change? **Quality/Reliability** – Will this change increase/decrease the quality/reliability of the final product? **Size** – How many new and/or changed lines of code will be required to implement this change? **Alternatives** – Are there any alternatives to making this change? If alternatives are available, is this change the best choice? **Resources** – What resources are required to make this change and are they available? **Test** – Does this change generate any special test requirements? **Benefits** – Are there any advantages to be derived from implementing the change such as improved performance? **Urgency** – How critical is this change? **Dependencies** – Does another change supersede or invalidate this one? Is this change dependent on another change or other changes?
Interface Impact
Complexity – Does this change affect other SWCIs or baselines? **Impact** – What is the nature of any impact to other SWCIs or baselines? **Communication** – If other SWCIs or baselines are affected, who has to be consulted, notified, or warned?
Schedule Impact
Length – How long will it take to implement this change? What are the planned and required dates of implementation and completion? **Timing** – When can this change be made? Should this change be made immediately or scheduled for subsequent implementation?
Budget Impact
Cost – What is the estimated cost of implementing this change? **Benefit** – Are there any cost savings to be gained from implementing this change? **Feasibility** – Can this change be implemented in a reasonably economical manner?

Table 9.3: Software Change Request Evaluation Questions

1. *As soon as possible.* The change is intended to fix a problem in an item in the developmental baseline. It must be fixed so other work can proceed.

2. *Implement by a specific date.* Other events inside or outside of the project make a date desirable.

3. *Implement into a specific version of an item.* It is desirable for technical or operational reasons to release a group of changes together.

This, together with an indication of the group or individuals who will modify the SWCI, makes up the *implementation assignment.* This will usually be obvious, because the SWCIs will usually have "owners," most often the original developers or individuals who are assigned groups of SWCIs for maintenance purposes. If it is not obvious, then software project management must be involved in this decision, either directly or indirectly, because the software project manager controls the resources of the project.

At the same time, the CCB should assign an individual or a group the task of verifying the change. This will often be obvious as well from the project life cycle processes and organizational structure. If it is not obvious then, again, software project management must be involved in the decision.

The last two steps, *release/installation assignment* and *version update*, are most critical when dealing with the product baseline, although they are relevant to the other baselines. The release/installation assignment step will identify what individuals and groups will be responsible for releasing or installing the altered SWCIs into their environment. This is most commonly the operational environment but it may be a test environment as well. Finally, the documentation of the new version (often called the *version description document*) must be updated, explaining what changes are included in the new version.

Implementing the Change

Figure 9.9 shows the activities involved in implementing approved software change requests.

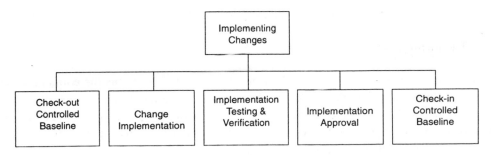

Figure 9.9: Implementing Changes

Project personnel use the instructions and authority given to them by the CCB to check out a copy of the baseline from the controlled library and implement the approved change to it. Rarely should a CCB give implementation specifics to the project's software engineering staff. General guidance is most appropriate.

The CCB will also have designated the personnel responsible and activities required for verifying that the change has been properly implemented. This often involves rerunning tests specified in a test plan, which itself may have been one of the SWCIs modified. Regression testing is usually performed to ensure that no errors have been introduced or unwanted side effects have occurred as a result of the change. This should be done as outlined in the project life cycle process description.

The type and number of verification approvals required would vary according to the item and the baseline in which it resides. Thus SWCIs in the product baseline that will subsequently be released will typically require integration and testing, along with software quality assurance. Some type of software implementation conclusion form can be used to document the implementation and verification activities and associated approvals.

The general activities and approvals used when implementing and verifying an approved change must be described in the SCMP. The proscribed activities must take into account coordinating multiple changes, reconfiguring SWCIs, and delivering new baselines. Additionally, the plan must specify activities for release planning and control. The details of the actual implementation and test methods, however, belong in the software life cycle process plan.

Once the CCB has concluded that the change has been correctly implemented and verified, the version identifier of the baseline can be updated. The final procedure to complete the change is to check the updated baseline into the controlled library. The minimum information to be recorded for the completion includes:

- The associated change request(s),

- The names and versions of the affected SWCIs,

- The verification date and responsible party,

- The release or installation date and responsible party, and

- The identifier of the new version.

Baselines must be checked in and out in a manner that maintains the correctness and integrity of the controlled library. The librarian of the controlled library must verify that an individual has authorization to check out a baseline before he or she releases a copy. For obvious reasons changes will be made to the copy, sometimes referred to as the *extracted version*, and not directly to the original.

Locking the baseline to updates until after the checked-out copy has been returned enforces synchronization control and prevents one change from overwriting another. Project personnel are still able to access the baseline, but are prevented from submitting conflicting updates. A change log should be maintained to keep track of all changes made to baselines.

The librarian must also be provided with proper authorization before a modified baseline can be checked into the controlled library. The existing baseline is then archived and replaced by the modified version and library documentation is updated accordingly.

Modern configuration management toolsets provide functions that simplify and automate much of the above processes, thus reducing the administrative burden. However, discipline and the knowledge needed to direct the system must be provided by the project engineering and configuration management staff.

9.5.3   Configuration Status Accounting

Change is the norm throughout the life cycle of an identified software item change. The prior sections discussed how an item, or collection of items, are identified and how changes are applied to them in a controlled manner using the projects' SWCM system. Because of the importance of configuration control to a project, the health of the SWCM system, along with the change histories of the items themselves must be examined on a regular basis. The process of examining the SWCM system and its contents, including their change histories, is called *status accounting*.

The minimum data set that should be used for accounting for the status of the SWCM system is [IEEE Standard 828-1998]:

- The initial approved version of an SCI.

- The status of all requested changes for the SCI.

- The implementation status of all approved changes for the SCI.

Additional information that is often useful in evaluating the status of an SWCM system and the project it supports include:

- Total number of change requests, aggregated by SCI, project, or on some other basis that is meaningful to the project. It is often useful to break these down into some major categories, such as documentation changes, code changes, and so on.

- Change request 'aging' reports, showing how long it takes to for a change request to move through the activities needed to review, approve, implement, and test, and final acceptance.

- Any change requests that are 'lingering' or 'floating' in the system longer than some pre-established period of time.

- Growth of storage over time. That is, how many gigabytes of disk the SWCM system is consuming.

- How many anomalies arise from the operation of the SWCM system itself, including the CCBs?

In planning the accounting activities of a project the following considerations should be addressed:

- What are the purposes of the accounting effort? Are there distinct project, product, and process focuses? Which reports are most relevant to development (the dynamic library)? Which are most relevant to released products?

- Who is the audience for each accounting report? Is it intended for use by the operator of the SWCM system? For quality assurance? For the project manager? For the customer?

- How often should each report be produced? Who should receive it? Should this change over time? What is the policy for retaining accounting records?

- Are the accounting activities consistent with the project life cycle model and development efforts?

9.5.4 Configuration Audits and Reviews

The general conduct of reviews and audits are discussed in Chapter 11, with the primary distinct between them being the degree of formality, with greater formality being usually associated with audits. Within the context of SWCM both mechanisms are most commonly used to verify that:

- The status of a specific SCI is in fact what it is assert to be,

- Or, some aspect of the operation of the SWCM system itself is as it should be.

Thus, when a new version of an item is released a build record (such as a link map) might be audited to ensure that the correct versions of the component SCIs were in fact included in the build. Or the change history database might be reviewed to verify that only the desired changes were included in the new release. Alternatively, it may be necessary to verify that the SWCM system itself has retained its integrity. Such an audit would look for change requests that remain in the system with no action being taken to disposition them, or for software items which appear or change miraculously with no or inappropriate procedural documentation. It might focus on the adequacy of the SWCM procedures themselves.

Chapter 11 discusses two important product audits of the configuration of released items that the SWCM system must support, the Functional Configuration Audit (FCA) and the Physical Configuration Audit (PCA). The Version Description Document (VDD) is a key product of the SWCM process, assembling a description of what is included in a released version, together with why (that is, what change requests are included, or what contractual requirement the version satisfies).

The scope of any review or audit should be carefully documented, together with its timetable, who will be involved with the activity, and who will receive the results of the review or audit. In particular, reviews and audits should encompass any relevant subcontracted items included in the product configuration. Failure to do is a common error.

9.5.5   Interface and Subcontractor/Vendor Control

Most modern software development efforts are not totally self-contained: The software must interface with hardware or other software, the development and released configuration of which will lie outside the immediate scope of the project SWCM system. Thus any of the following conditions can and do often occur:

- Hardware may be co-evolving as part of a larger systems effort.

- The products of the project must operate on a commercial computing platform, interfacing to the platforms' operating system.

- The product will be integrated or distributed with off the shelf components.

- The development of a component of the product is subcontracted to an external supplier (or vendor). The component must be integrated into the product prior to release, or must be distributed with the product.

In the first example, that of co-evolving hardware and software, the Software Configuration Management effort should be encompassed in a larger Systems Configuration Management. At the very least, there should be a systems-level CCB, which determines how changes are allocated to hardware, software, or both. These allocated changes will then become change requests for the separate hardware and software, with any changes to the interface between the two (such as the I/O subsystem) being documented and tracked in each system. Thus a change to interface of an I/O device should be documented as a requirement change to the software and the appropriate items in the SWCM system modified.

In the second and third examples, the specifics of the interface of the commercial items (which will usually evolve independent of any specific project's needs), including the version number of the commercial items, should be recorded and made part of the configuration record. As the commercial items evolve their changes must be tracked (usually by a development/systems engineer assigned to that task) and the appropriate changes applied to the configuration. The VDD must document what versions of the commercial items are supported as in the operating system example, or used, as in the example of off-the-shelf components.

The final example, that of a subcontracted item, requires that the SWCM system of the prime contractor flow change requests down to the subcontractor (or vendor) and have procedures to accept and include those changes into the SWCIs which reside in the SWCM system of the prime contractor. This requires that the library structure and procedures of the prime contractors SWCM system have distinct mechanisms in place to deal with this condition. In addition, it means that the subcontract must impose appropriate requirements on the vendor to support these mechanisms, along with any obligations the prime contractor has to their customer.

A common practice would be, for example, to allocate a portion of the dynamic library to act as the 'inbox' for an item produced by a vendor. The mechanisms of the SWCM system should impose acceptance criteria on this item similar to those used for internally developed items prior to passing the item onto the next level of the library. These criteria could include:

- Inspection of test and design information communicated by the supplier with the changed item.

- Execution of a battery of tests, performed by integrating the item with an earlier version of the ultimate product, or with a special test driver or environment.

- Acceptance of the change by the responsible technical parties.

Once the changed vendor item is accepted the changed version (together with changes to the relevant documentation) would then be included in the next steps of the development process and would be migrated to the appropriate library of the prime contractors SWCM system.

Finally, the prime contractor should review and audit the vendors SWCM system to insure that it is compliant with the needs stated in the subcontract. Typically, the prime contractors SWCM and SQA staff would support such audits and reviews.

9.6   Summary

SWCM has been identified as a software engineering "best practice" and key process area. SWCM should be a key part of every software project, but the scope of the implementation of configuration management on a given software development project will vary with the size of the project, the nature of the product, and the available resources.

The effort and resources expended in implementing SWCM are more than paid back by increases in the reliability and quality of software and visibility into the software development process. Because SWCM allows a program to quantify the time and cost impact of changes, it can significantly contribute to the success of a project by ensuring that it is delivered on time and within budget.

In addition to contributing to the success of a given software development project, the development history and metrics derived from SWCM activities can contribute to the success of future projects.

The role of the software project manager in SWCM can be substantial. On many small projects the software project manager will be wholly responsible for performing the SWCM activities, including writing the SCMP, maintaining the software library, enforcing access control, and performing configuration control.

On large projects, the SWCM activities are generally handled by a SWCM function staffed by a software configuration manager and staff independent of the project manager. Regardless of the size of the project, the project manager is usually a member—often the chairman—of the CCB. Knowing and understanding the procedures and activities involved in SWCM can aid a software project manager no matter what his or her role and responsibilities with regard to SWCM.

Applicable Standards

IEEE Std 610.12-1990. *IEEE Standard Glossary of Software Engineering Terminology.* IEEE, New York.

IEEE Std 730-1998. *IEEE Standard for Software Quality Assurance Plans.* IEEE, New York.

IEEE Std 828-1998. *IEEE Standard for Software Configuration Management Plans.* IEEE, New York.

Additional References

[Berlack 1992]   Berlack, H. R. (1992). *Software Configuration Management.* John Wiley and Sons, New York.

[Bersoff et al. 1980]   Bersoff, E. H., Henderson, V. D., and Siegel, S. G. (1980). *Software Configuration Management: An Investment in Product Integrity* Prentice Hall, Upper Saddle River, NJ.

[Blum 1992]   Blum, B. I. (1992). *Software Engineering: A Holistic View.* Oxford University Press, New York.

[Buckley 1993]   Buckley, F. J. (1993). *Implementing Configuration Management: Hardware, Software and Firmware.* IEEE Computer Society Press, Los Alamitos, CA.

[Dorfman & Thayer 1997]   Dorfman, M., and Thayer, R. H., eds. (1997). *Software Engineering.* IEEE Computer Society Press, Los Alamitos, CA.

[Humphrey 1989]   Humphrey, W. S. (1989). *Managing the Software Process.* Addison-Wesley, Reading, MA.

[Jalote 1991]   Jalote, P. (1991). *An Integrated Approach to Software Engineering.* Springer-Verlag, New York.

[Knutson & Bitz 1991]   Knutson, J., and Bitz, I. (1991). *Project Management: How to Plan and Manage Successful Projects.* American Management Association, New York.

[Marciniak 1994]   Marciniak, J. J., ed. (1994). *Encyclopedia of Software Engineering.* John Wiley and Sons, New York.

[Pressman 1997]   Pressman, R. S. (1997). *Software Engineering: A Practitioner's Approach*, 4th ed. McGraw-Hill, New York.

[Sommerville 1995]   Sommerville, I. (1995). *Software Engineering*, 5th ed. Addison-Wesley, Reading, MA.

[Thayer 1997]   Thayer, R. H., ed. (1997). *Software Engineering Project Management*, 2nd ed. IEEE Computer Society Press, Los Alamitos, CA.

[Thayer & McGettrick 1993] Thayer, R. H. and McGettrick, A. D., eds. (1993). *Software Engineering: A European Perspective.* IEEE Computer Society Press, Los Alamitos, CA.

[Whitten 1990]   Whitten, N. (1990). *Managing Software Development Projects: Formula for Success.* John Wiley and Sons, New York.

Chapter 10

Software Quality Assurance

10.1 Introduction

Software quality assurance (SQA) is the discipline, methods, and procedures used by an organization developing a software item to ensure that the item (1) is developed in accordance with the organization's documented plans and processes and (2) that these plans and procedures satisfy any specific quality provisions of the contract.

The SQA function provides the software engineering project manager, together with the customer and upper management as required, with an independent assessment of the conduct of the development activities. The general discipline and methods for performing the SQA function originated in the more general discipline of product assurance, which historically evolved in safety critical industries, such as health and aerospace.

IEEE Standard 730-1998, *IEEE Standard for Software Quality Assurance Plans*, provides guidance in planning SQA activities and establishes the minimum required content of a software quality assurance plan (SQAP). This standard applies to three groups:

1. The *user*, who may be another element of the same organization developing the software, has a need for the product. Further, the user needs the product to meet the requirements identified in the specification. The user thus cannot afford a "hands-off" attitude toward the developer and rely solely on a test to be executed at the end of the software development time period. If the product should fail, not only does the same need still exist, but a portion of the development time has also been lost. Therefore, the user needs to obtain a reasonable degree of confidence that the product is in the process of acquiring required attributes during software development.

2. The *developer* needs an established standard against which to plan and to be measured. It is unreasonable to expect a complete reorientation from project to project. Not only is it not cost effective, but, unless a stable framework exists on which to base changes, improvement cannot be made.

3. The *public* may be affected by the users' use of the product. These users include, for example, depositors at a bank or passengers using a reservation system. Users have expectations, including legal rights, which preclude haphazard development of software. At some later date, the user and the developer may be required to show that they acted in a reasonable and prudent professional manner to ensure that required software attributes were met.

Not every software project develops source code for a new product. The primary deliverables of some projects are feasibility studies or requirements. Others produce only the design of a product, while the objective of others is the modification of existing software products. The IEEE SQA standard is applicable to all types of software projects; applicability is not limited to projects that develop source code for new products, nor do project size or type of software product limit application of this standard. Small projects may require less formality in planning than large projects, but all components of the standard should be addressed by every software project.

The SQAP serves as formal documentation of the SQA activities to be performed on a given software development project. It is the guide that controls all software quality efforts. A well-developed and adhered-to SQAP provides the following benefits to a software project [Marciniak 1994]:

- Delivery of reliable, eminently usable, and maintainable products;

- Control of programming projects to reduce the risk of late delivery and cost overrun; and

- A general improvement in the quality of future software products.

As can be seen from the above, a solid quality program provides benefits not only to the customer or user of the product, but also to senior development management, who are interesting in maintaining control over projects and minimizing costs. The third item is important in order to attain consistent software reliability, reliability that is now taken for granted in other engineering activities.

10.2   Objectives

In this chapter you will learn:

- The processes of software quality assurance (SQA).

- Why projects need SQA.

- Who performs SQA.

- The roles of a SQA engineer.

- Who is responsible for SQA.

- The relationship between SQA and management.

- The costs of SQA.

- The risks incurred if the SQA effort is inadequate.

- The requirements of a SQA plan (SQAP).

- The difference between SQA and verification and validation (V&V).

- The difference between SQA and the software process improvement group (SEPG).

- What is necessary to manage a SQA effort.

- How SQA processes relate to the software project life cycle.

- The role of SQA in reviews and audits.

- Examples of tools, techniques, and methodologies used in performing SQA activities.

- The reporting responsibilities of SQA.

10.3   Software Quality Assurance

10.3.1   Definition of Software Quality Assurance

According to IEEE Standard 610.12-1990, *SQA* is:

(1) A planned and systematic pattern of all actions necessary to provide adequate confidence that an item or product conforms to established technical requirements.

(2) A set of activities designed to evaluate the process by which products are developed or manufactured.

Notice that the above definition does not state or imply that the SQA group is responsible for making quality products. That is the responsibility of the group making the software product. SQA is responsible for making sure that all SQA processes for a particular project are planned and implemented so that the project achieves its objectives. To do this the SQA group reviews and audits project processes and products and alerts management to any deviations. To be objective, the SQA function is performed by a group that, although part of the developing organization, must have some degree of independence from the group actually making the software product. The precise degree of independence depends on the organizational culture, the nature of the product, and contractual requirements.

The Software Engineering Institute's capability maturity model (CMM) is a standard for measuring how well a company builds software. SQA is a key process area (KPA) for level 2. The KPA lists four goals for SQA:

1. Software quality assurance activities are planned.

2. Adherence of software products and activities to the applicable standards, procedures, and requirements is verified objectively.

3. Affected groups and individuals are informed of software quality assurance activities and results.

4. Noncompliance issues that cannot be resolved within the software project are addressed by senior management.

Unless care is exercised, it is easy to confuse SQA with validation and verification (V&V). The goal of both activities is to monitor the project and product to ensure that the customer acquires a quality product. The two activities do, however, approach this goal from very different perspectives. SQA is an internally focused activity that deals primarily with adherence to standards and methods as the product flows through its life cycle processes from the developer to the customer. V&V, on the other hand, takes a more direct role. It analyzes and tests the work products of the development effort directly. Ultimately V&V evaluates the software itself for adherence to technical specifications. Thus V&V is an activity, separate from development, that is primarily concerned with the engineering and analytical aspects of the software products of the project's processes, whereas SQA is concerned with the conduct of the development group in performing those processes. Thus, V&V and SQA actually complement each other with some overlap, providing a comprehensive assurance program for software development projects.

10.3.2   Need for SQA

The driving forces behind SQA efforts have historically been customer satisfaction and improved visibility and control of project processes. A successful SQA program gives the software project manager assurance that the software processes designed to deliver a reliable, usable, and maintainable product are being adhered to. It provides an additional degree of control over the software project so that the product is delivered on time and within budget. This benefits the customer, who receives a product with improved fitness for use and within the estimated cost. The developer benefits through increased profitability and market share.

Conversely, the following risks and costs are related to a deficient software product due to the lack of effective SQA:

- *Developer risks:* loss of market share, claims and liability for nonperformance, and damage to image and reputation;

- *Acquirer risks:* damage to customer health and safety and late delivery of product;

- *Developer costs:* additional cost of fixing errors and additional cost of rework;

- *Acquirer costs:* cost of downtime and cost of lost productivity (poorly designed/implemented product).

10.3.3   The SQA Group and the Function

As stated previously, a quality product is not produced by the SQA function or group but rather by the organization and individuals actually performing the development effort. It

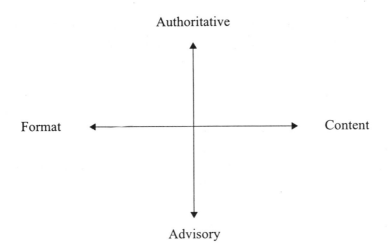

Figure 10.1: The Dimensions of Software Quality Assurance

is the SQA organization's job to ensure that the defined tasks required to make a quality product are actually performed so that the resulting product includes the quality attributes that will satisfy the customer.

This group can vary in size and content, from a single individual working part time to several departments dedicated to full-time quality assurance activities. Factors that determine the size and composition of the SQA group include the size of the project, assigned tasks or activities, the organizational structure, and the organizational culture. It is important that responsibilities be specifically assigned. By failing to assign responsibilities the slogan "quality is everybody's business" will become "quality is nobody's business."

A number of different SQA organizational models are in use within industry today. Figure 10.1 illustrates two fundamental dimensions of SQA: the authoritative-advisory dimension and the format-content dimension.

In some organizations, SQA is advisory only, that is, SQA personnel are available on a consultation basis but have no authority on software projects. In other organizations, SQA has authority over many aspects of a project. These might include chairing of the configuration control board; determining satisfactory completion of acceptance criteria for work products; ensuring compliance with standards, policies, and procedures; developing and conducting internal acceptance tests for software products; and overseeing the entire process of product release.

In other organizations, the format extreme of the format-content dimension defines the charter for SQA. In these organizations, SQA is concerned with policies, procedures, standards, and guidelines (in either an advisory or authoritative capacity) but makes no determination of the technical quality of a software product.

In yet other organizations, the content extreme defines SQA. In this case, SQA is primarily responsible for determining that a software product satisfies its functional, performance, design constraint, quality attribute, external interface, and other technical requirements—but SQA is not terribly concerned with adherence to standards and procedures. In these cases, SQA is in reality fulfilling the roles of validation, verification, and testing.

IEEE Standard 730-1998 supports the advisory-format model. However, regardless of the model used, an explicitly defined corporate policy should be in place that defines the authority and responsibility of SQA. SQA, as a functional group, should report to management through a path that is independent of software project management. An independent SQA organization can better provide management with the confidence that objective information on project processes and products is being reported. In the event that conflicts arise between SQA and the development groups that cannot be resolved at the project level, senior or corporate management is responsible for investigating and resolving the conflict.

10.3.4   Costs of SQA

Field studies of the industry over a 20-year period have reported software quality costs, expressed as a percentage of total development project costs, ranging from 3 to 20 percent [Beizer 1984]. These data must be interpreted with care, because some studies include only those funds expended by the SQA group to perform their efforts, while others include all costs associated with making a quality product. Thus, for example, some studies include in their estimates the total costs of conducting design or code inspections or walkthroughs, while others include only the effort of the SQA group to ensure that those activities are performed according to published procedures, policies, standards, and conventions. The later viewpoint is most appropriate when discussing the costs of the software quality *assurance* effort. These costs are largely expended directly within the SQA group and typically are a few percent of the total program cost. The return on this modest investment can be considerable, sometimes making the difference between delivering a product or not.

10.3.5   Relationship to Process Improvement

As a result of the impact of the capability maturity model of the Software Engineering Institute, many software development organizations have established software engineering process groups (SEPG). Such groups typically are charged with identifying, developing, refining, and disseminating software processes improvements within the organization across multiple projects. Although the ultimate objectives of the SEPG and SQA functions are the same—the timely delivery of quality products—the actual activities performed are different. A major difference is that SQA has direct responsibility for performing project tasks, while the SEPG, as a support function, does not. Thus the primary objective of the SEPG is to improve the software development processes of the organization as a whole, while that of SQA is to ensure that the immediate product is being built in accordance with published procedures, policies, standards, and conventions.

For example, the SEPG may propose to the software engineering project manager (SEPM) or process architect that a process change (developed in another venue) be introduced into a project. If the SEPM and process architect concur with the change technically and believe that making the change is logistically feasible, then SQA should be tasked with reviewing the proposed change for compliance with contractual requirements. This review may show that there is no impact on contractual requirements. Alternatively, it may show that customer consent, usually in the form of approval of a revision to the SPP or software life cycle model plan (SLCMP), is required to implement the change. In either case, once the concurrence of the necessary parties is obtained, a process transition plan must be developed and examined for risks to product quality. During the execution of the transition plan by the SEPM and process architect, SQA should monitor the affected processes to ensure that the plan is being followed and that product quality is not negatively impacted. SQA should provide additional, special reports to the SEPM, management, and the customer during this transition activity.

The foregoing example shows the distinction between the SEPG and SQA functions when implementing a process change. Earlier in that process, when identifying potential areas for process improvement, SQA personnel will often materially assist by identifying areas requiring improvement to the SEPG or process architect. At the very least, quality data collected and analyzed by SQA will play a rule in highlighting processes that would benefit from improvement. Based on firsthand observations, the SQA organization may directly identify improvement opportunities.

10.4   Software Quality Assurance Plan

IEEE Standard 730-1998 provides a format for the SQAP. To be compliant with the standard, the plan must contain or reference the following sections in the order listed:

1. Purpose

2. Reference documents

3. Management

4. Documentation

5. Standards, practices, conventions, and metrics

6. Reviews and audits

7. Testing

8. Problem reporting and corrective action

9. Tools, techniques, and methodologies

10. Code control

11. Media control

12. Supplier control

13. Records collection, maintenance, and retention

14. Training

15. Risk management.

Deviation from the above is permitted in two ways: (1) The order of the sections may be different as long as a cross-reference table is included at the end of the SQAP relating the actual plan structure to the above structure, and (2) sections may be deleted if not relevant to the project. Any sections not used must be listed in the plan stating "this section is not applicable to this plan" along with an explanation for the exclusion.

The first three sections of the SQAP relate to the plan itself: its purpose, other documents originating outside of the SQAP, and SQA management structure. Sections 4 through 15 document the tasks required to implement an effective quality assurance program for the intended project. The software engineering project manager should be involved in the creation and approval of the SQAP. In the case of smaller organizations the SEPM may be the author.

10.4.1   Purpose

This section explains why the SQAP exists. The following questions should be answered before writing this section:

- What is the intended use of the software covered by this SQAP?

- What is the scope of this SQAP?

- Why is this SQAP being written?

- Which software items are covered by this SQAP?

- Which portions of the software life cycle apply to each of the software items covered?

- Why were the documents that form the basis of this SQAP chosen?

- What, if any, are the deviations from those documents?

10.4.2   Reference Documents

By definition, reference documents are documents that originate outside the project such as military, industry-specific, or corporate quality assurance standards and guidelines. The SQAP should note any special conditions concerning any referenced documents and ensure that, in the case of changing documents, only the specific version of the document intended is referenced.

10.4.3 Management

The management section of the SQAP describes the organization, tasks, and responsibilities for project quality assurance.

The SQAP should detail the specific organizational structure for the particular project covered. This should include an explanation describing the nature and degree of relationships with all organizational elements responsible for software quality and development including the following:

- A description of each element that interacts with the SQA element;

- The organizational element that will delegate authority and delegated responsibilities of interacting elements;

- Reporting relationships among the interacting elements identifying dependence/independence; examples include the SCM organization, project management, management outside of the organization, and the SEPG;

- Identification of the organizational element with product release authority;

- Identification of the organizational element or elements that approve the SQAP; and

- Reporting lines for escalating conflicts and the method by which conflicts are to be resolved among the elements.

SQA responsibilities should be listed in the management section of the SQAP. This identifies who is responsible for which SQA tasks throughout the product life cycle, including the maintenance of the SQAP. Required signature authority for approvals and reviews should also be listed. For easier understanding, some type of matrix or table should be included that references the individual or organizational element responsible for each task described in the SQAP.

10.4.4 Documentation

IEEE Standard 730-1998 lists documents that need to be generated to help ensure delivery of a quality product. The following list gives those specified in the standard and which historically must be developed in order to produce critical software that complies with the standard. It is not an exhaustive list and does not imply that additional tasks or activities cannot be implemented where appropriate. For noncritical products, a subset of tasks can be chosen. The precise set of documents will ultimately depend on the activities and processes defined in the project's SLCMP.

The minimum documents required by the standard for a software project include these:

- Software requirements specification (SRS),

- Software design description (SDD),

- Software verification and validation plan (SVVP),

- Software verification and validation report (SVVR),

- User documentation, and

- Software configuration management plan (SCMP).

The SQA task then becomes to ensure that the development of these documents, together with the product source and object code, conforms to the project's processes as described in the SLCMP and other procedural documentation.

10.4.5   Standards, Practices, Conventions, and Metrics

The primary role of SQA is to ensure that the standards and procedures selected for the project are followed during the development process and that they are adequate to the task. This section of the SQAP should identify the internal (e.g., project or corporate) and/or external (e.g., military or industrial) standards, practices, conventions, and metrics to be employed during the conduct of the project, including those applied to third-party developers, vendors, and management. If required the project SLCMP should be referenced.

The scope of the standards, practices, conventions, and metrics should include the entire development effort and would typically include the following:

- *Requirements phase:* requirements stability and traceability;

- *Design phase:* external design (architectural or preliminary design) and internal structure and interfaces for each program module (detailed design);

- *Implementation phase:* end use hardware, programming language(s), module size, declaration statement conventions, naming and labeling conventions, component layout standards, use of structured coding techniques, and computer-aided software engineering (CASE) tools;

- *Testing phase:* all levels of testing including unit, integration, system, acceptance, and regression; test environment; and certification of test tools;

- *Maintenance phase:* collection and analysis of data and change request procedure.

In addition, some processes must be monitored for compliance with published procedures during all phases of development:

- Administration of software libraries;

- Operation of the change control system; and

- Operation of the metrics collection and analysis system.

Monitoring of these activities is performed in a variety of ways, including these:

- Attending general reviews and audits;

- Conducting specific SQA audits;

- Direct, ongoing, monitoring of development activities; and

- Direct inspection of work products.

10.4.6 Reviews and Audits

Reviews and audits are two of the primary tools of SQA. The SQAP should document the planned reviews and audits that will be conducted during the project's life cycle. These include the following tasks:

- Identify the specific technical and managerial reviews and audits to be held. Care should be taken not to duplicate information in the SEMP.

- Describe the SQA procedures to be used during the reviews and audits.

- Identify the parties performing the SQA functions of the review and their specific responsibilities.

- Describe review/audit report generation and follow-up including identification of specific responsibility for the preparation of reports on review/audit completion; the person(s) responsible for preparing the reports by position or job title; report format, report distribution list, and management responsibilities; description of follow-up actions to ensure implementation of recommendations; time interval between review/audit and follow-up to recommendations; and those responsible for performing follow-up.

The five types of reviews and audits typically required for a software project are described in detail in Chapter 8. The five types of reviews and audits are (1) management reviews, (2) technical reviews, (3) inspections, (4) walkthroughs, and (5) audit.

The role of SQA will differ depending on the nature and objective of the review activity. The following sections describe some of these roles.

10.4.6.1 Management Reviews

During management reviews SQA commonly plays one of two roles. First, as an observer of the proceedings. In this role the SQA representative will monitor the conduct of the review to ensure that it complies with published procedures and to detect any adverse trends in the program that may not otherwise be detected. Second, the SQA representative will be required to report on the project's quality status, as well as the status of the quality assurance program itself. Of particular interest will be any significant, adverse, trends in unresolved quality noncompliances.

10.4.6.2   Technical Reviews

During technical reviews the SQA representatives again function as observers, ensuring that the review is conducted in compliance with published procedures. They also review the technical material reported in order to detect adverse trends, and also report and comment on the technical quality metrics used by the project.

10.4.6.3   Inspections and Walkthroughs

Inspections and walkthroughs are intended to examine work products (items) in order to determine their compliance with requirements, including standards, practices, and conventions. The role of SQA in these activities is almost entirely that of an observer and, due to the large number of meetings involved, SQA personnel may only attend a sampling of the inspections and walkthroughs of a particular program. The SQA representatives attending either of these activities should not be excessively concerned with the degree to which an individual item being examined is compliant with the applicable standards, practices, and conventions but more importantly with how well the process of the inspection and walkthrough itself conforms to its own requirements. Serious noncompliances with published policies, standards, and procedures, or serious shortcomings in the policies, standards, and procedures themselves, that threaten the integrity of the project's products should be documented and immediately reported to the individuals responsible for the policies, standards, and procedures. Less critical noncompliances should be documented and reported through more routine mechanisms.

10.4.6.4   Audits

Audits differ from the four types of reviews discussed previously in that a third party examines a specific set of processes or products for a specific purpose. Audits can be planned or unplanned. They may be requested by the organization whose products or processes are being audited or they may be requested by another organization. In some audits, the SQA group is the auditing agency while in others it is an observer, much as in an inspection or walkthrough.

In some cases audits are conducted face to face with the responsible parties. For example, if a project's SLCMP states that each development subgroup will establish its own specific desktop procedures for developing unit test cases following guidelines documented in the SLCMP, then the SQA function could perform an audit of those procedures to ensure that the subgroups were indeed faithfully implementing the guidelines. This is best done by a personal meeting with the leader of the subgroup. In other cases, such as verifying that every code review conducted to date has faithfully completed the required review form, the audit could be performed by extracting files from the project's configuration management libraries.

10.4.7 Testing

The SQAP should clearly define the methods to be used to verify and validate that the test plans, test data, and test activities of those tests are developed and performed as planned. Here are some activities that may be required to ensure the quality of the testing process:

- Monitor test planning and testing activities to ensure that they follow established standards and design and test plan documentation.

- Ensure that testing guidelines exist and are being followed, including guidelines for test environments and test procedures.

- Ensure that integration and system testing are witnessed to verify that accurate test results are being logged, all discrepancies are reported, and appropriate test reports are completed and distributed.

- Monitor the corrective process to verify that changes arc incorporated into documentation and code, that changed code/modules arc retested, and that regression testing demonstrated that the changes did not impact other code.

- Verify that specific organizational elements are assigned to be responsible for test and test report functions.

- Ensure that all test tools and other test support hardware/software are certified according to established requirements.

10.4.8 Problem Reporting and Corrective Action

A failure of any software item, activity, or process to meet its requirements or standards is considered an anomaly, noncompliance, or nonconformance. The SQAP should describe what information would be provided to management about nonconformance issues, including the criticality of open problems and number of errors found per product. Level of criticality should be assigned according to the impact of not correcting the problem, the resources needed to correct the problem, and the impact to other baselined items if the problem is corrected.

10.4.9 Tools, Techniques, and Methodologies

This section of the SQAP should identify the tools, techniques, and methodologies needed to specifically support the project's quality assurance effort. This includes those already available, as well those to be specially developed for the project. SQA techniques are the technical and managerial procedures used in the evaluation and improvement of software quality. Tools assist in implementing the techniques.

The techniques and methodologies used to accomplish a task or activity should be well documented and should provide a description of the process to be used. Sample techniques used during the SQA effort include [Humphrey 1989, Marciniak 1994, Dorfman & Thayer 1997]:

- *Pareto analysis:* This graphical technique is used to show the distribution of an event across a class of entities; for example, the distribution of defects across a group of modules. This shows that a small number of modules are often responsible for a majority of defects. This helps to focus major failure analysis and improvement efforts of the vital few processes that are critical to the software project.

- *Trend data analysis:* Charting of actual against planned data points illustrates if quality is on target or not. The success of this technique is based on the source of expected data—usually historical—and its accuracy.

- *Failure analysis:* Identifies common failures, uses root cause analysis to determine the cause of failure, and then catalogs and disseminates this information so it can be used in software improvement efforts.

- *User feedback:* Used both for current and future software improvement. The most prevalent form used is *beta testing*, in which a preliminary software product is distributed to a select group of users in order to solicit their feedback. Other methods of user feedback include user interviews, comment cards, user group meetings, and customer assistance programs.

- *Fishbone diagrams:* These help developers focus on relevant issues for process cause and effect. For software development five main control points are established: staff, method, software development environment, measurement, and product definition. The fishbone diagram can be exploded iteratively to any degree of detail.

- *Direct measurements of software products:* These measurements consist of two types: goodness and structure. *Goodness* is the number of known defects in a released product. These defects can be tracked from release to release so as to monitor trends for potential future corrective action. *Structure* describes the complexity of software. Considerable evidence suggests that complexity is associated with quality—the lower the complexity of the code, the fewer the number of defects. Several commercial tools are available for measuring complexity in code, including McCabe's *graph-theoretic calculation*, Woodward's *knot calculations*, and Halstead's *software science*.

10.4.10   Code Control

Control of code is used to ensure the validity of completed code. The SCMP generally incorporates the mechanisms for code control. SQA should ensure that the policies and procedures for implementing and performing code control in the SCMP are followed properly. If the SCMP does not contain information on code control, then SQA should place that information in the SQAP. See Chapter 9 on software configuration management for more information on this topic.

SQA should verify that the products delivered to the customer can be exactly reconstructed from the specified source versions. SQA should also verify that any products tested or otherwise validated and verified can likewise be faithfully reconstructed from their sources. Evidence that the product performs as intended can include SQA reports, software test reports, corrective action records, and software product evaluation records.

10.4.11 Media Control

Typical storage media for software items includes DVD, CD-ROM, RAM, disks, tapes, and program listings. The SQAP should describe the media control methods and facilities that ensure the following:

- The items are stored and can be retrieved.

- Off-site storage and retrieval are provided for critical items and copies of baselined code.

- The items are accessible only to those who need access.

- The environment is controlled so that the physical media on which the items are stored do not degrade.

- A description is provided of how compliance with the above is ensured.

10.4.12 Supplier Control

Third-party software products, whether tools or code intended as part of the final delivered product, must meet all required standards of the project. SQA should verify that subcontractors have established procedures that meet or exceed contract requirements and that these procedures are being followed. This would include listing in the SQAP actions available to the purchaser if the supplier fails to be in conformance with its SQAP.

10.4.13 Records Collection, Maintenance, and Retention

Procedures for the collection, maintenance, and retention of records needed to perform the activities of the project should be included in the SCMP. If this is the case, then the SQA must conform to the SCMP. The objective of maintaining records of SQA activities is to provide contractual evidence that SQA processes were actually followed and to provide historical and/or reference data to be used for productivity, quality, and methodology studies.

In the event the SCMP does not describe the necessary procedures, the SQAP should specify the methods to be used for maintaining the records, including location, type of media, length of time, and protection.

10.4.14 Training

SQA activities require personnel trained in their implementation. A training matrix listing the skill requirements for each activity and the existing skills of personnel designated to perform those tasks is a helpful tool. Three primary groups are associated with software quality: members of the SQA organization, SQA management personnel, and development engineers. The SQAP should describe any training needs that must be satisfied in order to perform the SQA processes, techniques, and methodologies.

10.4.15 Risk Management

The general topic of risk management is described in detail in Chapter 14. In the event that the project implements a risk management process or program, the SQAP should describe any risks that are specific to the SQA effort, exactly how they will be monitored, and how their occurrence will be detected and what potential remedies are available, using the plan for the project-wide risk management program to provide the general approach. If the project does not implement a general risk management plan, then this section of the SQAP must also include a description of the general management approach to be applied in managing risks to product quality.

10.5 Summary

An effective SQA program can materially assist a software project to deliver a product that meets user requirements in terms of quality, schedule, and cost. IEEE Standard 730-1998 describes the contents of a software quality assurance plan geared toward the development and maintenance of critical software. Noncritical software development can benefit from following the standard or an appropriate subset of the standard. The SQAP documents how SQA is to be implemented and managed. It serves as a guide for the development organization from product concept through product implementation.

The manager responsible for the SQA effort should ensure that all mandatory requirements of the IEEE standard are included in the SQAP, that all contractual and company SQA standards are addressed, that any exceptions to the standard are justified and noted, and that SQA requirements listed in the SQAP are enforceable and measurable. Subsequently the manager must ensure that the plan is implemented and maintained.

An effective SQA program alone does not guarantee a quality product, but adherence to a standard such as IEEE Standard 730-1998, when implemented with the full backing of management and the development staff, greatly increases the probability that the resulting product will satisfy its user.

Applicable Standards

IEEE Std 610.12-1990. *IEEE Standard Glossary of Software Engineering Terminology.* New York: IEEE.

IEEE Std 730-1998. *IEEE Standard for Software Quality Assurance Plans.* New York: IEEE.

IEEE Std 828-1998. *IEEE Standard for Software Configuration Management Plans.* New York: IEEE.

IEEE Std 829-1998. *IEEE Standard for Software Test Documentation.* New York: IEEE.

IEEE Std 1012-1998. *IEEE Standard for Software Verification and Validation.* New York: IEEE.

IEEE Std 1028-1997. *IEEE Standard for Software Reviews.* New York: IEEE.

IEEE Std 1061-1998. *IEEE Standard for Software Quality Metrics Methodology.* New York: IEEE.

IEEE Std 1074-1997. *IEEE Standard for Developing Software Life Cycle Processes.* New York: IEEE.

Additional References

[Beizer 1984]   Beizer, B. (1984). *Software System Testing and Quality Assurance.* Van Nostrand Reinhold Company, New York.

[Dorfman & Thayer 1997]   Dorfman, M., and Thayer, R. H., eds. (1997). *Software Engineering.* IEEE Computer Society Press, Los Alamitos, CA.

[Frankovisch & Pan 1989]   Frankovisch, J., and Pan, D. (1989). *Software Quality Assurance.* University of Calgary, http://www.cpsc.ucalgary.ca/p̄and/seng/621/sqa-detail.html.

[Humphrey 1989]   Humphrey, W. S. (1989). *Managing the Software Process.* Addison-Wesley, Reading, MA.

[Lewis 1992]   Lewis, R. O. (1992). *Independent Verification and Validation—A Life Cycle Engineering Process for Quality Software.* John Wiley and Sons, New York.

[Lyu 1996]   Lyu, M. R. (1996). *Software Reliability Engineering.* McGraw-Hill, New York.

[Marciniak 1994]   Marciniak, J. J., ed. (1994). *Encyclopedia of Software Engineering.* John Wiley and Sons, New York.

[McDermid 1991]   McDermid, J. A., ed. (1991). *Software Engineer's Reference Book.* Butterworth-Heinemann, Oxford.

[Onoma & Yamaura 1995]   Onoma, A. K., and Yamaura, T. (1995). "Practical Steps Toward Quality Development." *IEEE Software,* September, pp. 68–77.

[Paulk et al. 1993]   Paulk, M. C., et al. (1993). *Key Practices of the Capability Maturity Model, Version 1.1,* Technical Report CMU/SEI-93-TR-025. Software Engineering Institute. Carnegie Mellon University, Pittsburgh, PA.

[Seah & Yap 1993]   Seah, K. L., and Yap, C. S. (1993). "Managing Software Quality Assurance." Presented at Pan Pacific Conference on Information, Taiwan.

[Smith 1997]   Smith, R. C. (1997). "Software Development Process Standards: Challenges for Process Assurance." *Proc. IEEE Int'l. Symp. Software Engineering Standards.* IEEE, New York.

[NASA 1989]   *Software Assurance Guidebook and Standard.* (1989). NASA-GB-A201,   http://satc.gsfc.nasa.gov/assure/-assuregb.html.

[SPAWARSYSCEN 1997]   *Software Quality Assurance (SQA) Process, Version 1.4.* (1997). Space and Naval Warfare Systems Center (SPAWARSYSCEN), San Diego, CA.

[Wallace & Ippolito 1994]   Wallace, D. R., and Ippolito, L. M. (1994). *A Framework for the Development and Assurance of High Integrity Software,* Special Publication 500-223. National Institute of Standards and Technology, Washington, DC.

[Wallace et al. 1992]   Wallace, D. R., Peng, W. W., and Ippolito, L. M. (1992) *Software Quality Assurance: Documentation and Reviews,* Report NISTIR 4909. National Institute of Standards and Technology, Washington, DC.

[Whitten 1995]   Whitten, N. (1995). *Managing Software Development Projects,* 2nd ed. John Wiley and Sons, New York.

[Williamson & Reading 1994] Williamson, A. G., and Reading, D. J. (1994). "Applying IEEE Quality Assurance Standards to Computer Based Laser Jet and Service Equipment." Presented at Conference on Software Quality Management II, Building Quality into Software. British Computer Society.

Chapter 11

Software Reviews

11.1 Introduction

Reviews serve multiple purposes in any development project:

- First and foremost, reviews provide visibility into the technical and programmatic state of the project.

- Second, they provide opportunities for project and nonproject personnel to discuss specific topics in an open, structured forum.

- Third, they provide intermediate milestones for the program, providing a sense of progress for the project long before any item has been developed to a deliverable state.

- Finally, reviews are an integral part of modern software development processes. They are used to assess the technical adequacy of an item or of some aspect of the project.

Reviews that focus on a program's overall status or that address a particular topic, such as the status of the software quality assurance effort, or some particular phase of development, such as coding or integration, allow the program personnel to assess the health of the activities and products of the program.

Adverse trends that can only be detected when data are collected either from multiple sources or from a single source over time are often highlighted when preparing for, or during, reviews. The early detection of adverse trends across multiple items will serve to reduce the "sunk costs" that must be written off when processes are revised and items returned to earlier phases of development.

Likewise, when dealing with individual technical artifacts such as requirements, designs, code, and user documents a review is one of the only ways, short of operating (e.g., testing) the item in some form, to detect defects and shortcomings in the item. Reviews are one of the verification and validation (V&V) methods used to detect defects (see Chapter 5).

By the time an item has been developed to the point at which it can be tested, considerable effort and time will have been expended, often by many more individuals than those directly involved in the development of the item. In other words, considerable sunk costs will have been invested before the item can be tested. Although the sunk costs are lower, the same is true for defects that remain undetected in one phase of the development process only to be discovered in the phase that immediately follows.

Reviews are not the only tool used to manage the program. The project's schedule, cost, quality, and technical metrics should be routinely collected and analyzed. Risks should be regularly evaluated. Regular staff meetings should be held, and regular technical and managerial assessments of the program should be developed and published. However, observations during the past three decades have indicated that many of the defects seen later in the development process could in fact have been detected by an appropriate review earlier in the development of the item. Hence, properly conducted reviews are cost-effective quality control mechanisms. Depending on the nature and objective of a review, it will generally occur according in one of the four following forms:

1. *Single reviews that occur on a particular date.* An example of a single-occurrence, time-driven review is often the systems requirements review (SRR). This is a function of the contract between the developing and the acquiring activity. Alternatively, but more rarely, the SRR may be an example of the next type of review.

2. *Single reviews that occur when a particular condition occurs.* Depending on the contract and the project's life cycle model, the SRR may be a single-occurrence, event-driven review.

3. *Multiple reviews that occur on a periodic basis.* Monthly or quarterly program reviews with senior management or the customer are examples of multiple-occurrence, time-driven reviews.

4. *Multiple reviews that occur when particular conditions occur.* Although they may be scheduled to occur at a particular target date, code reviews are examples of such multiple-occurrence, event-driven reviews.

When preparing for reviews, in particular, when determining the review scope, objectives, and audience, thought should be given to the benefits and the costs of the review. Needless, unproductive reviews, conducted by or with inappropriate persons, are a waste of effort. What is worse, such reviews will negatively impact the morale of the project staff. Needed, productive reviews, conducted with the appropriate presenters and audience, on the other hand, are well worth the effort. Such reviews will focus the program staff on the tasks at hand and will give the project a sense of direction.

This chapter is based on IEEE Standard 1028-1997, *IEEE Standard for Software Reviews*. It also contains guidance on preparing for, conducting, and using the results of software reviews that is not provided in the standard.

Section 11.3 provides and overview of software reviews and then the sections that follow describe the five different types of reviews covered by the standard: management review, technical review, walkthrough, inspection, and audit. The salient aspects of each review type, including review targets and scheduling, review participants, and guidelines for effective reviews, are discussed.

This chapter should aid software engineering project managers in their understanding and implementing of software reviews.

11.2   Objectives

In this chapter you will learn:

- Why reviews and audits are necessary.

- The five types of different reviews: management, technical, inspection, walkthrough and audit.

- The difference between a management review and a technical review.

- The difference between a walkthrough and an inspection.

- Who conducts and participates in reviews and audits.

- What key issues to look for in requirements and design documents during a technical review.

- What a peer review is.

- The software products that are subject to each review type.

- How long review meetings should last.

- The origin of software inspections.

- The key attributes of successful reviews.

- Some of the "red flags" that auditors look for.

11.3   Overview of Software Reviews

11.3.1   Scope of Software Reviews

IEEE Standard 610.12-1990 describes a *review* as "a process or meeting during which a work product, or set of work products, is presented to project personnel, managers, users, customers, or other interested parties for comment or approval." It describes an *audit* as "an independent examination of a work product or set of work products to assess compliance with specifications, standards, contractual agreements, or other criteria." Later sections of this chapter amplify these definitions.

The primary subject of this chapter, IEEE Standard 1028-1997, *IEEE Standard for Software Reviews*, describes the minimum requirements for "systematic" reviews, that is, reviews that:

- Require team participation,

- Have documented procedures for conducting the review, and

- Produce documented review results.

The standard further describes five specific types of reviews: (1) management review, (2) technical review, (3) walkthrough, (4) inspection, and (5) audit. It also explains the specific characteristics of each review type and how each review is carried out. The standard presents this in the following format:

- *Introduction.* Describes the objectives of the systematic review and provides an overview of the systematic review procedures.

- *Responsibilities.* Defines the roles and responsibilities needed for the systematic review.

- *Input.* Describes the requirements for input needed by the systematic review.

- *Entry criteria.* Describes the criteria to be met before the systematic review can begin, including authorization and the initiating event.

- *Procedures.* Details the procedures for the systematic review, including planning the review; an overview of procedures; preparation; examination, evaluation, and recording of results; and rework and follow-up.

- *Exit criteria.* Describes the criteria to be met before the systematic review can be considered complete.

- *Output.* Describes the minimum set of deliverables to be produced by the systematic review.

This chapter is not intended to duplicate the standard, but rather to supplement it with guidelines intended to assist in performing reviews and using them to maximum advantage. In particular, the reader should realize that the standard, partly for historical reasons and partly for reasons of simplicity, was written as if all projects followed the classical, full-scale development model, as described in this book in the chapter on life cycle processes (Chapter 7). In reality, many projects, most particularly smaller projects with rapid development objectives, will only implement a part of the reviews described in the standard. This occurs for two reasons, as discussed next.

First, smaller projects are subject to personnel limitations, wherein all too often there is only one or perhaps two individuals who are knowledgeable about a particular area of a design or of system use. This makes it difficult to perform desired reviews consistent with the standard. If this is the case and a particular review is judged to be necessary, then it may be useful to temporarily add staff with applicable experience to the project. This will, of course, incrementally add labor costs to the project. Such costs must be evaluated in light of the risks that will arise if the review is not held.

The alternative is to perform the review using only project staff, which may result in a less effective review or may impose additional schedule delays while the review is conducted. Again, these costs must be balanced against the risks that later activities in the project will be exposed to if the subject reviews are not conducted.

Second, these risks are best evaluated in the context of the project's development processes and the organization's prior experience with them. In particular, the project manager should always bear in mind these primary objectives of all reviews, especially product reviews:

- Improve the quality of the product being reviewed, in particular, the suitability of the product for use in the next stages of the project's processes or for delivery to a customer.

- Dissemination of information through the project. For example, a requirements review may provide useful information to the individuals planning the integration of the product.

- Identify systemic technical and managerial problems in the conduct of the project.

The cost of conducting a review must be evaluated and compared with the utility of achieving the goals listed above. Thus the utility of a review usually reduces to a question of avoiding risk to the project, either by identifying technical errors in the items being reviewed or by exposing systemic managerial or technical risks to the objectives of the project.

One difficulty is that the cost of a review is immediate and obvious, whereas the value of avoiding a risk is not as obvious; it is just a *potential* value. This tends to bias organizations against reviews. The historical experience of the software engineering community in avoiding such risks is discussed in the following sections, along with indications of how much of a project's total cost should be allocated to reviews. Within the context of an individual project or organization, these risks can best be evaluated using the organization's experience with its particular development processes.

11.3.2   Role of Management in Software Reviews

Although the standard lists products that can profitably be subjected to each type of review, it does not mandate the need for specific reviews or when software products should be reviewed. Each project must determine if and when reviews are to be conducted. The project's software project management plan (SPMP), software life cycle management plan (SLCMP), software quality assurance plan (SQAP), and software configuration management plan (SCMP) should describe the conditions and timing of the various project reviews. In addition, other IEEE standards, such as 1012-1998, 730-1998, and 1074-1997, which mandate the use of reviews, can be used for establishing the context for review use and disposition of review results.

For each of the five different types of reviews, the project manager must ensure that the planned reviews are performed as required by the project's process and contractual requirements. These responsibilities include the following:

1. Provide funding and facilities required to plan, define, execute, and manage the reviews, inspections, walkthroughs, or audits.

2. Ensure that the required personal receive any required training and orientation on the review, inspection, walkthrough, or audit procedures applicable to a given project.

3. Ensure that individuals with sufficient levels of expertise and knowledge of the software product and technologies are included in the review.

4. Ensure that planned reviews, inspections, walkthroughs, and audits are conducted.

5. Ensure that any recommendations, findings, and action items arising from reviews, inspections, walkthroughs, or audits are appropriately responded to.

Obviously, for any but the smallest programs, the software engineering project manager (SEPM) does not personally perform every activity in the above list and will often delegate some or all of their day-to-day execution. It then becomes the responsibility of the SEPM to ensure that these things are indeed done.

The five types of reviews covered by the standard can be grouped into two categories according to their participation:

1. Reviews with no restrictions on who can participate and have access to review material, or

2. Reviews with restrictions on who can participate and have access to materials.

In addition, some reviews are performed by groups operating independently of the project team. Financial audits are a classic example, and V&V activities for safety-critical programs are another.

Management and technical reviews fall into the first category. Participants include both project and functional managers along with nonmanagers associated with the product under review. No predetermined limit is set regarding the number of participants in a review, but those who do participate must be qualified to contribute to the review. Larger groups allow for more diversity of opinion but raise costs, are more difficult to manage, and, if large enough, serve to inhibit communication. The subjects of such reviews are not restricted in size or scope. Products, such as the software specification requirements, may contain hundreds or thousands of pages. Schedule, cost, or subcontractor reviews may encompass activities that cost thousands or millions of dollars, or hundreds or thousands of hours of effort.

In the case of reviews of significant scope or technical and managerial significance, it is strongly recommended that the reviewers be provided with the materials well in advance of the meeting. For example, if the review is intended to examine the high-level design document, system requirements specification (SRS), system test plan, or other major item, it should be provided to the review team well in advance so members of the team can absorb the materials and organize their comments. This may require that the item being reviewed be distributed some months in advance. In such circumstances is it also recommended that the review team provide their major comments well in advance of the meeting so that the developers can:

- Comprehend and integrate the comments.

- Develop meaningful responses to the comments.

- Discuss the situation with the designated points of contact of the review team.

In the event that major problems are found in the item under review it may be advisable to reschedule the review so that the problems can be corrected. This process should be documented in the statement of work or as a series of terms and conditions to the contract.

Walkthroughs and inspections fall into the second category. Specifically, individuals wielding management authority over participants are excluded. Such reviews are viewed as peer reviews in that all participants have similar (but not necessarily identical) job descriptions and authority within the organization. Inspection and walkthrough groups are also limited in the number of participants and quantity of material that can be reviewed. In some cases the maximum duration of these reviews is constrained, often to 1 or 2 hours.

The exclusion of management from these classes of reviews results from the fear that if management (either project or functional) is represented (1) the participants will behave differently, either constraining their comments or making inappropriate comments (sometimes called *showboating*), precisely because management is present; (2) any managers present will not review the product but rather will judge the people; or (3) all this will happen before the developer's peers have examined the item under review; in other words, the review by management is premature.

For some managers this constraint seems insulting and inappropriate. For others it is all too necessary. The standard decided to err on the side of caution. The issue fundamentally comes down to that of why would the SEPM, for example, wish to attend a design review of a 200-line code item? Legitimate reasons would include these:

- The SEPM wishes to verify that the team is conducting the reviews in accordance with the project policies and procedures. In that case the SEPM should task the software quality assurance (SQA) staff to attend a sampling of reviews and report on the degree of compliance exhibited in the reviews.

- The SEPM is concerned that a critical part of the system be adequately reviewed. In that case the SEPM should task the chief designer, software architect, or other senior designer to provide the necessary confidence, either by attending the reviews or, if that is not appropriate, conducting an independent technical review of the relevant items after the peer reviews have occurred.

- The SEPM is concerned with the technical adequacy of the project's developmental processes. In that case the SEPM should task the process architect, SQA group, or the organization's software engineering process group (SEPG) with analyzing the results of reviews and, as required, auditing reviews on a sample basis.

Finally, management has access to the item being reviewed, as well as the documentation of the meeting itself. So there really is no good reason for the SEPM to need to attend such a review.

Audits fall into the last category. The primary characteristic of an audit is that it is carried out by personnel who are independent of the development group that produced the product to be audited. Similar to inspections and walkthroughs, audits are limited in the number of participants. As with management and technical reviews, audit material is not limited in scope.

11.3.3   Need for Software Reviews

Software reviews help an organization deliver a quality product on time and within cost. Quality doesn't just happen; it requires an organized, planned, and disciplined effort. Software reviews are critical parts of that process. They help ensure that quality is built into the product by examining individual project and product documents early in the product's life cycle, while broader reviews of products and processes identify problems spanning multiple items as well as systemic, process-related problems.

Problems found early on are more easily corrected than problems found later in the product's life cycle. It is also substantially less expensive to correct defects earlier in the product life cycle than later. Accurate requirements and design documents lead to code that, when implemented, more accurately performs to the customer's expectations. Improved code requires fewer fixes, thus shortening the test/fix phase and hence reducing the time to market. Improved technical and managerial processes strengthen the project across the board.

Finally, the knowledge gained through reviews helps improve overall project performance. When properly and appropriately (as defined by the project's development processes) conducted, reviews help build an image of the product and a vision of the project in the minds of the project team.

Consider these specific reasons for implementing software reviews:

- Verify compliance with software development standards, regulations, and contractual requirements.

- Provide visibility and feedback to project management and the customer.

- Identify the risk factors in the project and the organization's project processes.

- Contribute to the professional growth of project team members by exposing them to the ideas and comments of their peers and by allowing them to see the "big picture" of the program.

- Determine if the development plan is being followed.

- Determine if the project is making satisfactory progress.

- Determine if the product is ready to continue to the next development phase.

In the case of large contractual efforts virtually all of these motives are valid. In the case of internal (that is, the immediate customer and the developer belong to the same entity) developments the emphasis is on the later objectives, most specifically the determination of the readiness of products for the next phase of development.

11.3.4 Cost of Software Reviews

The introduction of reviews into any software project is not without initial cost. As with most efforts designed to improve and control processes, an up-front cost is incurred for training plus the staff hours required for preparing for and conducting the reviews.

Not much hard data are available regarding software management reviews, technical reviews, walkthroughs, and audits. However, these activities are commonly conducted in other technical and business domains and are generally believed to be valuable to either the developer or the customer. On the other hand, inspections have been the subject of numerous field studies.

Johnson [Johnson 1998] described a project where one full person-year of effort of skilled technical staff was required to inspect 20,000 lines of code. That translates to a review rate of 1/10 of a labor hour per line of code, or 10 lines of code per hour of review labor. Bell Northern Research data from a 2,500-KLOC project required one skilled staff hour per defect found from inspections. In another study, Fagan showed that the overall average project cost for inspections equaled about 15 percent of total project costs [Wheeler et al. 1997].

These figures are believable if we remember that the bulk of the data are concerned with peer reviews of code. Suppose, for example, that a review is being conducted of a component that is part of a mission-critical or life-critical system. Such a review will typically be conducted on a software item comprised of 200 lines of code and will last for 1 hour. Usually five people participate in the review. Hence somewhere between 10 and 15 hours of effort will be expended preparing for and conducting the review. The COCOMO II model would predict that writing the 200 lines of code would require something in the range of 20 to 50 hours. Hence the peer review will represent something like 30 percent of the coding effort, which in turn is usually 25 percent of the total project cost. In this example, therefore, the code reviews alone will represent approximately 8 percent of the total project cost, roughly consistent with the result of Fagan. Although not trivial, this review expense is usually recovered in reduced costs in later phases, most notably in the integration of the product, where fixing defects that were not found in earlier steps of the development process can be very expensive.

Notice that in this example 200 lines of code required 10 to 15 hours of review effort, for a rate of 20 to 13 lines of code per hour of review effort, which is roughly the rate reported by Johnson [Johnson 1998]. Finally, the Bell Northern result of 1 staff hour per defect found in reviews would be consistent with the discovery of from 10 to 20 defects when the 200-line code item is reviewed, which is broadly consistent with studies of software defect rates. The reader should appreciate that the exact cost ratios and defect rates for a particular program can vary from those of the studies. Only by studying historical data from similar projects, which followed stable development practices, can the precise inferences be drawn.

The costs of conducting reviews are more than offset by the overall savings incurred by catching and correcting defects earlier in a product's life cycle. Fagan also showed that the 15 percent costs generated by inspections was recovered by total project savings of 25 to 35 percent due to rework not done later in the project [Wheeler et al. 1997], whereas Knight and Myers [Knight & Myers 1993] indicate that large projects which use reviews save between 50 and 80 percent over the life of the project. In 1988 Raytheon implemented a software inspection process. Historically, defect correction costs had been approximately 43 percent of the total cost of a project. By 1994 that cost had dropped to 5 percent [Gilb 1998].

As mentioned in the introduction to this chapter, much of the cost savings is the result of less effort spent downstream on rework, which can be very expensive. IBM, one of the first organizations to widely apply reviews and inspections, documented the number of staff hours for finding and fixing one defect from inspections, tests, and field use to be 1 hour, 20 hours, and 82 hours, respectively [Holland 1996]. The Bell Northern Research project cited above showed 1 hour, 2 to 4 hours, and 33 hours, respectively [Wheeler et al. 1997]. Studies of large military development projects have shown even greater savings during the later testing phases, in some cases as high as 100 to 1. Section 3.3 of this book discusses this same "leverage" effect when dealing with requirements errors.

Tempering the above discussion is the fact that many projects are much smaller than those from which the above statistics are drawn. This does not mean that small projects do not need to perform any reviews, but it does imply that the specific reviews conducted and how they are conducted may vary from the global guidance embodied in the standard. The best policy when introducing reviews into a project is to use the types and descriptions of reviews described in the standard as a starting point, evaluating each type of review in the light of the organization's development processes, the project management plan, and the project risks. Factors that should be considered include these:

- The sheer size of the project in terms of its schedule duration, cost, and technical description (e.g., lines of code);

- Any contractual or institutional requirements;

- The development processes, including methods and tools, being used by the project;

- The organizational development experiences, including both the technical and managerial aspects;

- The risks and penalties associated with the project, together with the extent to which reviews can help reduce them (see Chapter 14 on risk management);

- The value of a review in disseminating information to project staff; and

- The cost of conducting each review.

Thus, an internal project producing a non-life-critical application and having a schedule that lasts only 6 months may have only one management review during its entire history, with normal weekly reports (as described in Chapter 12 on cost and schedule estimation) providing the necessary visibility at other times.

Likewise, for a project producing only a few thousand of lines of code, the various (quality, management, configuration management) plans could all be reviewed in a single session. Indeed, the plans themselves could be consolidated. For such a project a single design review could likewise suffice, together with a small number of code reviews. In addition, the nature and size of the project may shift the focus of the review from the generic intent of the standard. Thus, for many smaller projects the design review will often focus on the database and user interface designs, together with how the product integrates into any necessary infrastructure (such as the World Wide Web). For other projects, the focus may well be on the internal memory organization and algorithms.

Finally, the time needed to perform the reviews must be included in the project schedule. For example, if each engineer is to attend two reviews per week that require 2 hours each to prepare for and attend, then the 4 hours must be made available in the schedule. This reduces the time available for the engineers to work on their other tasks.

11.3.5 Action Items

Although reviews serve other nonmaterial purposes (such as maintaining communications), the principal material product to come out of any review is the action items. Action items are used to identify areas of the project that need attention. They identify particular defects or anomalies in an item that need corrective action. They often provide the most direct, objective evidence that the project is or is not following the development processes documented in the SPMP, SLCMP, SQAP, and SCMP.

The process for retaining and managing action items should be consistent with the broader configuration management processes of the project. These should be described in the SLCMP and SCMP and, ideally, should require that the action items be treated as software items. In the case of technical reviews, walkthroughs, and inspections, this is particularly desirable. Proper configuration management of action items will materially assist and simplify the SCMP, SQA, and V&V efforts of the project. The overall management of the item being reviewed will be simplified if the action items are stored in the same system and are managed by the same mechanisms as are the subjects of the review themselves.

It is likewise recommended that forms be used to capture the action items for technical reviews, walkthroughs, and inspections. The use of such forms is particularly valuable in the conduct of the project's metric and process improvement efforts. Forms can be online or in hardcopy form. However, when selecting the media explicit thought should be given to what access and access controls are required to satisfy the developmental, quality, and contractual requirements of the project. If the online system is not adequately secure or convenient, a hardcopy action item list can be created during the review and signed by the participants at the end of the meeting. The action item information can then later be entered into an online system. The hardcopy can then be retained as objective proof of the review. If the online system is sufficiently secure and convenient to use during the review, then the hardcopy version can be eliminated.

11.4   Management and Technical Reviews

11.4.1   Management Reviews

A *management review* is a formal evaluation of a project-level plan or a project's progress relative to its plan. The management review monitors the status of schedules, evaluates the compliance of the project with its technical and procedural requirements, and determines the effectiveness of the approaches being used to achieve project goals. A management review has these objectives:

- Inform management of project status, directions being taken, technical agreements reached, and the overall status of the project.

- Resolve issues that could not be resolved during the technical reviews.

- Arrive at agreed-on mitigation strategies for near-term and long-term risks that could not be resolved during the technical reviews.

- Identify and resolve management-level issues and risks not raised during the technical reviews.

- Provide needed background to management or the customer to obtain the commitments and approvals required to complete the project.

Typical decisions that are made during or as a result of management reviews include the following:

- Corrective actions needed to keep the project in compliance with established organizational and project processes;

- Changes in allocation of resources for the project;

- Changes in project direction or scope; and

- Changes in schedule.

11.4.1.1   Objectives and Scheduling of Management Reviews

IEEE Standard 1028-1997 does not specify when or why management review should occur. Project management staff has the responsibility of identifying when the preplanned reviews are to occur and entering them into the project's planning documents. In a major software project, changes from one life cycle phase to another usually trigger management reviews.

Similarly, monthly or quarterly program reviews are often required by the organization's business practices or by the contract.

In the case of life cycle phase reviews, management often has the responsibility of certifying that the products from one life cycle phase are complete and sufficient to allow development to continue to the next phase. These reviews should be scheduled after the necessary documents and artifacts have been subjected to technical reviews. The results of those reviews should be presented, along with a technical assessment of their implications.

Finally, project plans and project reports should be subjected to a management review. The major project plans include these:

- Software project management plan (SPMP),

- Software configuration management plan (SCMP),

- Software quality assurance plan (SQAP), and

- Software verification and validation plan (SVVP).

In turn, these documents will identify the project's preplanned management reviews, as well as any foreseeable conditions that would trigger unplanned reviews.

When reviewing these plans, it is critical that they be consistent among themselves, with the contract, with the business practices of the organization, and with any legal and regulatory requirements.

Other types of plans subject to management review include, but are not limited to, risk management plans, software installation plans, contingency plans, and backup and recovery plans. The first two of these will often specify reviews of their subject matter.

Reports generated during a typical software project that are subject to management review include, but are not limited to, these:

- Technical review reports,

- Cost and schedule reports,

- Technical and quality metric reports,

- Verification and validation reports,

- Anomaly reports, and

- Audit reports.

Unexpected problems or serious concerns may also trigger management reviews.

11.4.1.2   Management Review Participants

Management reviews can be chaired or conducted either by the project managers or by individuals acting on their express direction. This includes persons with authority to make cost and schedule decisions. Other attendees of management reviews should be selected based on need and/or contractual obligations. Attendees should only be limited by their capacity to contribute purposefully to the review results and aid in the understanding and disposition of the subject of the review. Attendees include:

- Customer representatives,

- Senior management of the developing organization,

- Members of the configuration control board,

- Software quality assurance management or representatives,

- Senior development team members, and

- Verification and validation management or representatives.

Generally, the size of the review group depends on the size of the product being reviewed and will vary accordingly, from two persons upward. The products under review are not limited in size and, in some cases, are quite large, spanning several documents and thousands of pages. Therefore, it is not unusual for reviews of larger products to span several meetings. It is the responsibility of the review leader to ensure that the review process is managed according to IEEE Standard 1028-1997 irrespective of size.

In many organizations senior management will periodically review projects for good business reasons. Those reviews are not within the scope of the standard but, if desired, the concepts of the standard can be applied.

11.4.1.3   Responsibilities of the Participants

The primary responsibilities of the review team are as follows:

- First and foremost, assess the adequacy and completeness of any items being reviewed.

- Understand the material presented.

- Determine whether or not the status of the subject of the review corresponds to the planned status, recording any deviations for action.

- Assess the status of any relevant (to the object of the project) risks and identify any new risks.

- Determine if factors not originally considered in the planning phase are constraining the progress of the project.

- List any issues and recommendations to be addressed by upper management and others that can affect the project.

- Identify any actions to be taken following the review, assigning responsibilities and preliminary closure dates.

- Authorize any additional reviews and audits.

- Identify other issues that need to be addressed.

In order to meet the above responsibilities, review participants must be prepared for the meeting(s). This includes being familiar with the products under review and associated collateral products. Significant preparation time prior to the meeting may be necessary. Reviewers should also be familiar with any requirements or standards to which the project or review items are subject.

11.4.2 Technical Reviews

Whereas management reviews focus on planning and reporting efforts, the objects of technical reviews are primarily specification and design documents. The objective of such reviews is to determine whether:

- The software product conforms to its technical specifications.

- The software product adheres to regulations, standards, guidelines, plans, and procedures applicable to the project.

- Changes to the software product are properly implemented and affect only those system areas identified by the change specification.

Other objectives of technical reviews include these:

- Ensure that the subject of the review is traceable to its appropriate requirements.

- Provide insight and feedback for the technical effort.

- Maintain ongoing communication between the customer's technical staff and that of the developing organization.

- Verify that technical commitments are being met.

IEEE Standard 1028-1997 makes a clear distinction between technical reviews and inspections. This is not always the case in the general literature of reviews, which often uses the terms interchangeably. Both technical reviews and inspections evaluate similar types of documents (although inspections routinely examine code, whereas code is not usually the subject of technical reviews). Technical reviews can be held to provide insight to management so that decisions about the project and its products can be made. Likewise, technical reviews can be used to evaluate alternative technical solutions. Aspects of a subcontractor's technical effort can the subject of a technical review.

Finally, the subjects of technical reviews are often larger design artifacts of the product under development and often span multiple groups and levels of technical involvement. Inspections, on the other hand, are peer reviews. There is no management participation and the primary goal is to find anomalies and verify product quality. The subjects of inspections are usually smaller design entities. Also, although management may utilize reports based on inspection results, there is no direct management participation in inspections.

11.4.2.1   Objectives and Scheduling of Technical Reviews

Similar to management reviews, technical reviews often occur at the completion of a development phase and ultimately provide evidence to management that the product is or is not ready to proceed to the next development phase. Technical reviews concern both in-process and final products. These products include specification documents, design documents, and procedural documents including, but not limited to, the following:

- Software requirements specification (SRS).

- Software design descriptions including software architectural or preliminary design (SPD) and software detailed design (SDD),

- Software test documentation,

- Software user documentation,

- Technical trade studies and white papers,

- Maintenance manual,

- System-build procedures,

- Installation procedures, and

- Release notes.

11.4.2.2   Technical Review Participants

Technical reviews are conducted by the technical leadership of the project in concert with other staff qualified to assess the subject of the review. Management staff may also participate in technical reviews. At least three reviewers should be present, but, as with management reviews, the size of the technical review group should be determined by the size and nature of the subject of the review. This can range from a simple document to multilevel documentation requiring the resources of several different engineering skill groups.

For preplanned reviews, the review participants should be identified in the relevant project documents, such as the project management plan, software quality assurance plan, and/or the software verification and validation plan. In many such documents positions are defined rather than specific persons. It is the review leader's responsibility to ensure that the correct individuals are at the meeting. This can be a daunting task for large projects or projects that impact several distinct entities, such as networking products.

11.4.2.3 Responsibilities of the Participants

The review leader (who may be the customer) must publish the meeting agenda for the review in advance and must ensure that the participants are provided with sufficient background information, including any documents that are the subject of the review. It is the responsibility of all review participants to study the subject of the review prior to the review meeting and be prepared to actively contribute. Lack of proper preparation is one of the major causes of ineffective reviews. During the review, anomalies and other issues should be documented as action items. At the end of the review, the action items should be assigned to individuals who will be responsible for their disposition.

If the subject of the technical review is one of the key intermediate products of the selected software life cycle model, the review should be prepared for and conducted with great care. When reviewing such structured documents, checklists can be of material assistance to the reviewer, both to ensure that important topics are not omitted and to structure and speed up the review process.

The project process and standards documentation should include or reference these checklists, although unplanned reviews may require the creation of specialized checklists. Remember that checklists are not a replacement for reading and thinking; they serve to remind the reviewer to look for problems and topics and to stimulate thought.

11.5 Walkthroughs and Inspections

Peer reviews are technical reviews of work in progress; their objective is to find errors of two types. The first are actual errors in the item being reviewed. The second are systemic or process issues that will cause recurring problems if not corrected.

Two types of peer reviews exist: inspections and walkthroughs. Inspections are the most popular as of the early 2000s. Inspections are also the most cost-effective process for identification of errors and software work products. The space shuttle flight software used inspections as their primary tool for finding errors.

The application of walkthroughs to software is credited to Gerald Weinberg. Dr. Weinberg is famous for writing a book called *The Psychology of Computer Programming* [Weinberg 1971]. Weinberg pointed out that one of the issues in eliminating the errors in a software system is the attachment programmers develop to their code. He observed that programmers often become defensive if an attempt is made to check a code module for errors. In response he developed the concept of an egoless review. An *egoless review* (now called a *walkthrough*) is a review of a module of code by peers of the author. A reviewer explains the basis for the code while "walking" through the system. Contemporary reviewers (i.e., other programmers) point out areas of possible errors. They make no attempt to fix these errors during a walkthrough. The investigation and subsequent correction of possible errors is left to the module's implementer outside of the review environment.

Subsequently, Michael Fagan [Fagan 1976] developed the concept of inspections. He believed walkthroughs to be too informal, and suggested that often the implementer did not follow up on the findings of the walkthrough. In response the concept of *inspections* was developed. When conducting an inspection, specific roles are assigned to individuals who assume specific responsibilities: a moderator, the author(s), readers, and recorders.

The moderator is tasked with facilitating or conducting the meeting, ensuring that the focus does not stray from the primary objective. The author of the document—a piece of code, a software requirements specification, a test plan—is present to answer questions. A reader paraphrases the document to the benefit of the review team. The recorder documents the errors found by the team.

As discussed earlier, one of the key issues of both walkthroughs and inspections is that managers do not attend walkthroughs or inspections. It is felt that the person(s) whose work is being reviewed is less likely to become defensive if management is not present. A defensive confrontation would hinder the error-finding process.

Various opinions exist regarding who may attend a walkthrough or an inspection. Some companies permit SQA people to attend, others permit testers to attend, and yet others send their newest employees for training purposes.

11.5.1   Walkthroughs

A walkthrough is a type of peer review, a systematic evaluation of a software product. It provides the author with valuable, timely feedback about her or his work. It is an effective way to improve the quality of software source code and the documents that describe the design, architecture, or functional requirements of the system [Yourdon 1985]. A walkthrough may also be held for the purpose of educating an audience about a software product. The major objectives of a walkthrough are to (1) find anomalies and (2) evaluate conformance to standards and specifications.

Whereas technical reviews tend to handle large volumes of material, walkthroughs generally deal with small, self-contained segments of a larger entity. For example, for code, no more than 100 to 200 lines should be reviewed in at a single session. Requirements specifications and design documents should be similarly limited. Certainly no more material should be reviewed than can be carefully examined within a 1- to 2-hour meeting time.

11.5.1.1   Objectives and Scheduling of Walkthroughs

In contrast to management and technical reviews, the number of participants and the volume of material covered are limited. Walkthroughs are most commonly associated with reviews of source code, but walkthroughs can and should be conducted for other types of software products, including these:

- Operational concept documents;

- Requirements specifications;

- Software design descriptions, especially detailed module-level designs;

- Software source code;

- Software test documentation;

- Software user documentation;

- System-build procedures;

- Installation procedures; and

- Release notes.

Walkthroughs of many of the above items would naturally be limited to a portion of the complete item. Thus, the full operational concept document would not be reviewed in a single walkthrough, but a single operational scenario or a small set of related scenarios might be. Typically, walkthroughs are limited to a 2-hour duration. The limit placed on the volume of material being reviewed also implies that the review group is limited. IEEE Standard 1028-1997 recommends that walkthrough teams consist of between two and seven people.

The timing of a walkthrough is important, because if it is conducted too early or too late, it may be ineffective. Walkthroughs are more cost effective in catching errors in logic and data flow than is testing, so they should be conducted prior to the more expensive testing process. For other categories of software items, walkthroughs are appropriate whenever logical sections of the document are completed. As a result the project plans should, in most cases, describe the conditions that should be met when the walkthrough is to occur and what further developmental processes are dependent on the completion of a walkthrough and the closure of its action items. Thus walkthroughs are usually event-driven, rather than time-driven, reviews. The SLCMP, SPMP, or other plan(s) should describe the conditions that must have been satisfied prior to conducting walkthroughs of various classes of software items or products.

The configuration management practices of the project should be carefully considered when establishing the conditions for walkthroughs. For example, some organizations require that the review item be entered into a developmental configuration library "owned" by the development group prior to holding the walkthrough. This is done to ensure that the item being examined is indeed exactly the same as that which will be passed onto the next stages of development after the review.

11.5.1.2   Walkthrough Participants and Roles

The composition of the walkthrough team typically includes project staff drawn from the immediate development group, along with peers working on other parts of the system that interact with the item being reviewed. If, for example, the item being reviewed were the specification for a TCP/IP protocol implementation for a network device, the walkthrough participants could consist of the author of the specification, the engineer who will be implementing the specification, and any engineers who are working on other modules or protocols that interface with the TCP/IP module.

The observations and action items are the primary products of a walkthrough. It has been said that "a product review without action items is a fraud." If a substantial number of walkthroughs fail to produce substantive action items it is probable that something is seriously wrong and management action is required.

11.5.1.3   Implementing Effective Walkthroughs

When implemented correctly walkthroughs are effective tools for assessing software products. The following guidelines should help the project manager establish a successful walkthrough process:

- For each hour of meeting time, participants should spend at least an hour of preparation time studying the product under review and any associated documents, such as regulations, standards, guidelines, plans, and procedures against which the software product is to be inspected.

- Walkthroughs should be scheduled to be brief and to the point: 15 minutes to no more than 2 hours. The efficiency and accuracy of the review team diminishes over time. For this reason also avoid scheduling consecutive walkthroughs involving the same participants.

- Review only complete sections of documents or code. Otherwise time is ill spent because the evaluation of fragments often leads to participant frustration and can generate poor data.

- Use standards to avoid disagreements over style, to increase readability and understanding, and to avoid the tendency to focus on style rather than content.

- Ensure that the team respects the role of the walkthrough leader. It is easy within peer groups to let arguments get out of hand. Make sure that everyone agrees to respect the leader's request to end arguments.

- Require that the participants sign walkthrough reports. Although management does not attend such peer reviews the results of the walkthrough and the impact on the product are visible. By acknowledging their role in reviewing the item, the participants will be reminded of the importance of the walkthrough process.

11.5.2 Inspections

As mentioned earlier, inspections are a more formal type of walkthrough. The rise in influence and popularity of the software inspection process can be traced to the mid-1970s, when Michael Fagan published his influential article titled "Design and Code Inspections to Reduce Errors in Program Development" in the *IBM Systems Journal* [Fagan 1976]. That article first introduced the term software inspections into the published literature. An inspection is performed following a five-step process:

1. *Overview.* The author of the work product presents an overview of the purpose and scope of the item being inspected.

2. *Preparation.* Peers of the author study the work product with the goal of understanding it thoroughly and detecting any possible defects.

3. *Inspection meeting.* The inspection team meets and, as a reader presents the work product, points out defects.

4. *Rework.* The author uses the defect list generated during the inspection meeting and revises the work product. The defect list should be included as part of the action items; in fact, it often makes up the entire list of action items.

5. *Follow-up.* The inspection leader verifies the quality of the author's rework and determines if reinspection is necessary.

IEEE Standard 1028-1997 is based on the *Fagan inspection* process with additional requirements, including a planning step together with recommending the collection of defect data for analysis and improvement of software engineering procedures. The express objectives of the inspection process are to:

- Identify specific errors in the document or system.

- Identify systemic errors in the development process.

- Identify deviations from standards and specifications.

- Collect software engineering data (for example, anomaly and effort data).

- Use the collected software engineering data to improve the inspection process itself and its supporting documentation (for example, checklists) (optional).

The use of inspections can materially improve the quality, cost, and schedule performance of an organization and project. Of the review types discussed in this chapter, the software inspection is the most studied, analyzed, written about, and utilized. It has been shown that correct use of the software inspection process provides significant cost and schedule savings to a project's efforts [Grady & Van Slack 1994].

11.5.2.1   Objectives and Scheduling of Inspections

The products that can benefit from an inspection are the same as those listed for walk-throughs. Also, similar to walkthroughs, inspections are limited in the number and composition of participants and the volume of material to be covered. Inspections differ from walkthroughs in the degree of formality, the focus of the process, and the handling of data generated from the review.

The classes of items that will be inspected, together with the conditions that must be met for the inspection to occur, should be listed in one of the major planning documents. If the project is producing an SLCMP it would be the best choice, otherwise the SPMP, the SQAP, or the SCMP will serve, in that order of preference. Inspections and walkthroughs are the classic examples of multiple-occurrence, event-driven reviews.

11.5.2.2   Inspection Participants

Inspections are peer reviews, with the roles of the participants strictly defined, including inspection leader, recorder, reader, author, and inspector. The author is prohibited from acting as inspection leader, reader, or recorder. The leader may also act as recorder. All participants are inspectors, each chosen to represent different viewpoints pertinent to the product under review. Some types of and reasons for selecting specific viewpoints were discussed in the section on walkthroughs.

11.5.2.3   Implementing Effective Inspections

Prior to the meeting, each participant is required to study the work product and check for anomalies. Studying the work product is not restricted to reading the subject of the inspection. Any other work products that are related to it should be cross-checked. For example, if the document under review is an element of the architectural design, then it is necessary to check the corresponding requirements specifications to ensure traceability and consistency. This may require cross-checking against a third-party interface or standard documents. Optimum checking rates have been reported to be approximately 1 page per hour with a deviation of 0.9 pages [Gilb 1998]. Notice that this corresponds roughly to 100 to 200 lines of code.

Inspectors should focus on finding critical defects or anomalies, that is, defects that would be significantly more costly to fix later in the product life cycle or that, if not caught, could cause loss of life or major financial loss. Too much attention paid to minor defects can lead to inspection process inefficiency. The project should have written guidelines describing the characteristics of what constitutes critical anomalies to ensure consistency in the review process. IEEE Standard 1012-1998 provides a basic set of such guidelines.

The general suggestions made to improve the effectiveness of walkthroughs are likewise valid for inspections.

11.6   Audits

An *audit* is an independent evaluation of a process and/or product. The subject of the audit is compared to a set of procedures or standards that have been previously established for the subject. The purpose is to ensure that the process is actually being followed, that proper documentation is being produced, and that reports accurately reflect actual activities. Audits can be preplanned or unscheduled. Audits may be required because certain conditions have occurred or they may be contractually required. Company staff performs some audits, while others may involve customer representatives or independent third parties.

The scope of an audit can include the entire software project development effort or may focus on one particular software configuration item or process. Here are some common types of audits that deal with software:

- *Project audit.* This type of audit is associated with the evaluation of a project's progress and performance compared to its planned progress and performance and/or compared to the progress and performance of similar projects. It is a tool used by management to detect and evaluate risks to the project; assess cost, schedule, and performance relationships within the project; assess the effectiveness of management processes; identify activities and processes that hinder performance; and provide information to the project's client.

- *Post-project audit.* This type of audit is designed to fulfill a legal or contractual requirement, to provide feedback to management about the successes and failures of a project that can be used for future project improvement, and to account for expenditures and property associated with the project.

- *Functional configuration audit (FCA).* This type of audit verifies that a software product's actual functionality and performance are consistent with its requirements specifications. This audit is held prior to software delivery to verify that all requirements specified in the software requirements specification have been met. The requirements specification, test results, and any validation and verification reports typically are the basis of the FCA. The audit also verifies that associated operational and support documents are complete and satisfactory. Any discrepancies are identified and recorded.

- *Physical configuration audit (PCA).* This type of audit provides an independent evaluation of a software product configuration item to confirm that components in the built version map to their specifications. It provides a means of establishing the product baselines. The audit verifies that the software as built is consistent with its design documentation.

  To clarify the difference between the FCA and the PCA it is helpful to visualize them in terms of an automobile radio. The FCA verifies that the radio plays. The PCA verifies that the radio in the automobile is the actual radio ordered.

- *In-process audit.* This type of audit provides management with a "live view" of the software product as it evolves through the software life cycle so that appropriate and timely decisions can be made. Critical items to audit include the following

  - *Hardware and software interfaces:* Should be consistent with the design requirements in the SRS.

  - *Functional requirements of the SRS:* Should be fully validated by the SVVP.

  - *Product design:* Should always satisfy the functional requirements of the SRS.

  - *Code:* Should be consistent with the detailed design documents.

  - *Processes:* Should be consistent with organizational and customer requirements, as expressed in the contract and in published plans and documents.

- *Independent or external audit.* This type of audit is conducted by external auditors who are not part of and do not have allegiance to the audited organization. It is usually called by the software acquirer to provide an independent opinion about the work in progress.

11.6.1   Objectives and Scheduling of Audits

Almost every aspect of a software project can be the subject of an audit, from project plans and reports to project documents and code. IEEE Standard 1028-1997 gives a detailed, but not exhaustive, list of software products subject to audit. Some examples of items suitable for audit include the following:

- The SPMP, SLCMP, SQA, and SCMP, to verify that they implement the desired requirements (Depending on the audit scope, these could be contractual requirements or the technical or business requirements of the organization.);

- Developmental items to verify that only approved changes, and no other, have been made to them;

- Minutes and action items of reviews to verify that they have been conducted in compliance with the project's published procedures;

- Reports and logs of testing to verify that the correct testing and anomaly reporting procedures have been followed;

- Configuration management records, to verify that they are complete and consistent and conform with applicable policies or standards;

- Build sheets or files used for final product preparation, audited to ensure that the delivery has the required components and only those components; and

- Schedule and cost records, to ensure the project is implementing the policies and procedures documented in the SPMP, along with other requirements imposed by regulatory and contractual vehicles.

A common theme in all of the preceding examples is that some item or process is examined to determine its compliance with one or more contractual or regulatory obligations or some requirement listed in an organizational standard, such as IEEE Standard 1012-1998 or IEEE Standard 730-1998. Planned audits often occur on life cycle phase boundaries. Audits may also be conducted based on indications of problems within a project, such as lack of progress or quality concerns. NASA's *Manager's Handbook for Software Development* [NASA 1990a] recommends audits be triggered one or more of the following events occurs:

- Deviations of greater than 25 percent from planned staffing, resources, or schedule;

- An increasing number of failed tests in the late phases of system or acceptance testing;

- Missing critical capability in a software system; or

- Slippage of the delivery schedule.

We should mention that audits can be disruptive and expensive. When they are necessary they should be taken seriously, performed faithfully, and any findings addressed promptly. However, they should not be conducted excessively.

11.6.2 Audit Participants

Auditors differ from review, walkthrough, and inspection participants in that they must be totally free from any bias and influence that would inhibit objectivity. This requires that the auditors come from outside the organization being audited and that they precisely respect the scope of the audit. The reason for the audit, who requested that the audit be performed, and any relevant contractual obligations will determine if this means auditors come from totally separate organizations or from other groups within the same organization. At a minimum, auditors must not report directly to or be responsible to the same management as the project managers of the audited group. Three entities are involved in an audit:

1. *The entity authorizing the audit (initiator):* May be a manager in the audited organization, a customer or user representative of the audited organization, or a third party.

2. *The audit organization (lead auditor, auditors, recorder):* May be a separate organization or members of the project organization who are not directly involved with the development group. The audit organization is responsible for the audit process and providing resources to do the audit. For successful audits, the auditors' expertise and experience must be at least on a par with, and preferably greater than, that of the developers and managers of the audited process/product.

3. *The audited organization:* Responsible for providing all relevant information needed by the audit team and also is responsible for correcting or resolving all deficiencies turned up by the audit.

11.6.3   Understanding and Supporting Audits

The program manager must respond positively to any and all audits. Although they may appear to be immediately disruptive to the project they usually ultimately have a positive influence. The program manager should remember that audits are a fact of life in every business and should not allow a negative attitude toward the audit to be communicated to the project staff. This requires that the project manager have an appreciation of what auditors do and why they do it.

Auditors collect data either through document review or interviews with development personnel. The goal of checking documents is to verify that the document conforms to the standards established for the project. If omissions or deviations are encountered, a reasonable explanation should be forthcoming. The auditor must be careful to avoid examining the technical correctness of documents or decisions. It is not the auditor's job to judge the solutions proposed or implemented by the document. That is properly the function of the V&V process.

Audits produce observations and findings. *Findings* are serious discrepancies that are material to the audit subject between what was expected and what was in fact found. *Observations* are minor or immaterial discrepancies. Findings should be treated with great seriousness and should be addressed promptly. Observations may or may not require action. In some cases an observation from one audit may become a finding in another. As a result, observations should be examined carefully to determine if they require action as well.

Auditors watch for a number of "red flags" when conducting an audit:

- Inconsistencies within a document or between documents;

- Code that manifestly does not comply with the project's published standards;

- Repeated instances of minor but undocumented discrepancies;

- Any artifact whose prerequisite (according to the project's processes) artifacts do not exist; The classic example is delivered code for which there are no design documents, reviews, or test documents;

- Absence of ownership for any artifact of the development process;

- Absence of ownership for any development processes;

- Repeated expressions of cynicism toward the project processes; and

- Reports documenting completed activities without appropriate authority.

Performing an audit usually requires interviews to be conducted with both individuals and groups. This is done to obtain an understanding of process issues that may not appear in printed documents. Auditors usually utilize checklists for document inspection, together with structured questionnaires, for use when interviewing.

Some red flags that auditors will watch for when interviewing personnel are:

- Disagreements among project personnel on matters of fact, with disagreements among more senior personnel, managerial or technical, being the most serious;

- Reticence of audited personnel to divulge information; and

- Disagreement with customer on technical or contractual requirements.

Other problems that might show up through a combination of interviews and document reviews include:

- Status that is inaccurately reported,

- Frequent changes to plans and schedules,

- Key personnel leaving the project in an unplanned manner,

- Critical items not being tracked,

- Increasing numbers of defects appearing late in the product life cycle, and

- Too many or too few defects found for the type of project being audited.

It is often not possible to completely inspect all of the desired documents in their entirety. Likewise it is often not possible to interview all personnel involved in a particular project. In such cases sampling should be used. If sampling is used the audit team should include persons who are knowledgeable about statistical methodologies.

11.6.4 Responding to Audit Findings

On completion of the initial audit, the lead auditor customarily debriefs the immediate group whose activities or products are being audited. In this forum the preliminary findings and observations identified in the course of the audit are discussed. Beyond the requirements of common courtesy, this meeting gives the audited organization an opportunity to clarify any misunderstandings that may have occurred prior to the release of the audit results to third parties. This includes the initiator of the audit.

In addition, the preliminary debrief allows the management of the audited organization or project to prepare its response to the audit results, which can be discussed with the audit team, assuming the actions described within the response lie within management's realm of authority.

The primary objective of these preliminary post-audit discussions is to reduce the likelihood that disagreements of fact remain. (Note that differences of opinion are allowed.)

After these preliminary discussions, the audit team will prepare the final report and findings for delivery to the initiator of the audit. The audit response will likewise be forwarded through the appropriate management chain.

11.7 Summary

The proper use of reviews will help a software project deliver products that meet user requirements in terms of quality, schedule, and cost. IEEE Standard 1028-1997 describes five different types of reviews—management reviews, technical reviews, walkthroughs, inspections, and audits—that make up a comprehensive review process for a software project.

Management reviews are formal evaluations of a project-level plan or the project's progress relative to a plan. The management review monitors the status of schedules, confirms that requirements are being met, and evaluates the effectiveness of project management approaches used to achieve project goals.

Technical reviews examine specification and design documents with the objective of providing management with evidence to confirm whether the software product conforms to its specifications, that changes are properly implemented, and that items are traceable to requirements.

Walkthroughs are an evaluation of a software product or a completed segment of a software product conducted by a group of peers, including the author of the document. The purpose of a walkthrough is to find anomalies and improve the software product.

Inspections are a more formal, structured process than walkthroughs, but, like walkthroughs, inspections are conducted by a group of peers. Primary reasons for conducting an inspection are to identify deviations in the product so they can be corrected, to identify the sources of errors so that they can be corrected or eliminated, and to collect data that can be used to improve the software development process.

Audits are an independent evaluation of a process or product that compares the process or product to established requirements, procedures, and standards. The purpose is to ensure that the process is actually being followed, that proper documentation is being produced, and that reports accurately reflect actual activities. The scope of an audit can include the entire software project development effort or may focus on one particular software configuration item.

Reviews are one of the most basic and effective tools at a project manager's disposal to gain valuable feedback about the progress of the project, to help control costs and quality, to help conform to applicable standards and regulations, and to improve the software development process.

Applicable Standards

IEEE Std 610.12-1990. *IEEE Standard Glossary of Software Engineering Terminology.*
    IEEE, New York.

IEEE Std 730-1998. *IEEE Standard for Software Quality Assurance Plans.* IEEE, New York.

IEEE Std 828-1998. *IEEE Standard for Software Configuration Management Plans.* IEEE, New York.

IEEE Std 829-1998, *IEEE Standard for Software Test Documentation.* IEEE, New York.

IEEE Std 830-1998. *IEEE Recommended Practice for Software Requirements Specifications.* IEEE, New York.

IEEE Std 1012-1998. *IEEE Standard for Software Verification and Validation.* IEEE, New York.

IEEE Std 1016-1998, *IEEE Recommended Practice for Software Design Descriptions.* IEEE, New York.

IEEE Std 1028-1997. *IEEE Standard for Software Reviews.* IEEE, New York.

IEEE Std 1058-1998. *IEEE Standard for Software Project Management Plans.* IEEE, New York.

IEEE Std 1061-1998. *IEEE Standard for a Software Quality Metrics Methodology.* IEEE, New York.

IEEE Std 1063-1987(R1993). *IEEE Standard for Software User Documentation.* IEEE, New York.

IEEE Std 1074-1997. *IEEE Standard for Developing Software Life Cycle Processes.* IEEE, New York.

IEEE Std 1219-1998. *IEEE Standard for Software Maintenance.* IEEE, New York.

IEEE Std 1220-1998. *IEEE Standard for the Application and Management of the Systems Engineering Process.* IEEE, New York.

IEEE Std 1228-1994. *IEEE Standard for Software Safety Plans.* IEEE, New York.

IEEE/EIA Std 12207.0-1996, *IEEE/EIA Standard: Industry Implementation of International Standard ISO/IEC 12207:1995 Standard for Information Technology—Software Life Cycle Processes.* IEEE, New York.

Additional References

[Fagan 1976]   Fagan, M. (1976). "Design and Code Inspections to Reduce Errors in Program Development." *IBM Systems Journal*, March, vol. 18, no. 3, pp. 182–211.

[Gilb 1996]   Gilb, T. (1996). "Inspection Failure Causes." *Testing Tech-niques Newsletter*, Online Edition, October.

[Gilb 1998]   Gilb, T. (1998). "Inspection Team Leader Training Course." Microsoft Power Point Slides, http://www.stsc.hill.af.-mil/SWTesting/gilb.html.

[Grady & Van Slack 1994]   Grady, R. B., and Van Slack, T. (1994). "Key Lessons in Achieving Widespread Inspection Use." *IEEE Software*, July, vol. 11, no. 4, pp. 46–57.

[Holland 1996]   Holland, D. (1996). "Document Inspection: An Agent of Change." Primark Investment Management Services Limited, http://ourworld.compuserve.com/homepages/KaiGilb/UNICOM.pdf.

[Johnson 1998]   Johnson, P. M. (1998). "Introduction to Formal Technical Re-views." http://www.ics.hawaii.edu/ johnson/.

[Johnson et al. 1993]   Johnson, P. M., Tjahjono, D., Wan, D., and Brewer, R., (1993). "An Instrumented Approach to Improving Software Quality through Formal Technical Review." *Proc. Pacific Northwest Software Quality Conf.*, Portland, Oregon.

[Kelly 1993]   Kelly, J. (1993). "Inspection and Review Glossary, Part 1." *SIRO Newsletter*, vol. 2, April.

[Knight & Myers 1993]   Knight, J. C., and Myers, E. A. (1993). "An Improved In-spection Technique." *Communications of the ACM*, November, vol. 36, no. 11, pp. 51–61.

[Livson 1998]   Livson, B. (1998). "Best Practise SQA, Auditing and Reviews." http://www.bal.com.au/AUDITING.htm.

[Marciniak 1994]   Marciniak, J. J., ed. (1994). *Encyclopedia of Software Engi-neering.* John Wiley and Sons, New York.

[Meredith 1989]   Meredith, J. R. (1989). *Project Management—A Managerial Approach*, 2nd ed. John Wiley and Sons, New York.

[NASA 1990a]   National Aeronautics and Space Administration. (1990a). *Man-ager's Handbook for Software Development*, SEL-84-101. Au-thor, Washington, DC, http://sel.gsfc.nasa.gov.

[NASA 1990b]   National Aeronautics and Space Administration. (1990b). *Software Quality Assurance Audits Guidebook*, SMAP-GB-A301. Author, Washington, DC, http://satc.gsfc.nasa.-gov/assure/assuregb.html.

[NASA 1993a]   National Aeronautics and Space Administration. (1993a). *Software Formal Inspections Guidebook*, NASA-GB-A302. Author, Washington, DC, http://satc.gsfc.nasa.gov/fi/fipage.html.

[NASA 1993b]   National Aeronautics and Space Administration. (1993b). *Software Formal Inspections Standard*, NASA-STD-2202-93. Author, Washington, DC, http://satc.gsfc.nasa.gov/fi/fipage.html.

[Porter & Johnson 1997]   Porter, A. A., and Johnson, P. M. (1997). "Assessing Software Review Meetings: Results of a Comparative Analysis of Two Experimental Studies." *IEEE Trans. Software Engineering*, March, vol. 23, no. 3, pp. 129–145.

[Porter & Siy 1998]   Porter, A.A., and Siy, H. (1998). "Understanding the Sources of Variation in Software Inspections." *ACM Trans. Software Engineering and Methodology*, January, vol. 7, no. 1, pp. 41–79.

[Wallace et al. 1992]   Wallace, D. R., Peng, W. W., and Ippolito, L. M. (1992). *Software Quality Assurance: Documentation and Reviews*, NISTIR 4909. National Institute of Standards and Technology, Gaithersburg, MD.

[Weinberg 1971]   Weinberg, G. (1971). *The Psychology of Computer Programming*. Van Nostrand Reinhold, New York.

[Wheeler et al. 1997]   Wheeler, D. A., Brykczynski, B., and Meeson, Jr., R. N. (1997). "Software Peer Reviews." *Software Engineering Project Management*, 2nd ed., R. H. Thayer, ed. IEEE Computer Society Press, Los Alamitos, CA, pp. 454–469.

[Yourdon 1985]   Yourdon, E. (1985). *Structured Walkthroughs*. Yourdon Press, Englewood Cliffs, NJ.

Part III

Project Planning and Management

Part III, Chapters 12–15, describes the activities needed to plan and manage a software development project, from the initial cost and schedule estimates, through the detailed planning and execution of the project, and concludes with the maintenance of the product after its development has been completed. It presents both structural and quantitative methods for performing these tasks, including the range of possible project organizations used to perform the project activities, methods for estimating the scope of activities, how those activities relate to one another, metrics that can be used to gain visibility into the efforts, and methods for evaluating the risks the project is subject to.

Chapter 12, *Software Cost and Schedule*, describes methods for developing and documenting the initial estimates most commonly needed when first evaluating the feasibility of projects. It presents the tools and techniques needed to perform the detailed, day-to-day scheduling required to execute a software development project in a predictable manner and clarifies the relationship between the software life cycle model and the schedule. It then describes how individual tasks of the project should be evaluated, or statused, when determining the overall health of the project. In particular, it describes the concept of earned value and the role it plays in managing the technical, financial, and time performance of a project.

Cost and schedule are, however, only two aspects of successful software project management. In order to give coherence to the totality of the effort, the implementation, quality, managerial, cost, and schedule aspects of the project must be coordinated. Chapter 13, *Software Engineering Project Management*, describes what the software engineering project manager must do to successfully coordinate the many activities of a software systems development project. Chapter 13 uses the software project management plan (SPMP) as the vehicle for this description. The outline of the SPMP, as presented in IEEE Standard 1058-1998, is used as the framework to express the coordination tasks.

Key to the success of any development project is the approach used to manage risks as they arise during the conduct of the project. Proper risk management requires first and foremost that the risks be accurately and faithfully identified. This requires that the activities of the project, their interactions, and their relationships to external events are well understood by the project team. This implies in turn a clear understanding of the software development life cycle, the product, the project schedule, and how they interact. Chapter 14, *Software Risk Management*, describes the technical and managerial methods available for controlling and responding to risks. While IEEE Standard 1540-2000 does not stipulate a particular format for the risk management plan, this chapter concludes with a description of the content and scope of such a plan.

Visibility into the status of risks, as well as visibility into the status of items under development and the activities used to build those items, are provided by software metrics, the topic discussed in Chapter 15, *Software Metrics*. A properly designed software metrics program provides the software engineering project manager with invaluable insight into the project. A large range of various types of metrics is available, many more than any individual project can use or need. Selecting the set of metrics that are most important and appropriate to a given project is one of the most important decisions the software project manager will make when planning the project.

Chapter 12

Software Cost and Schedule

12.1 Introduction

The reliable management of any activity, especially those involving creative developmental efforts, is founded on three fundamental activities:

1. Initially plan the work in a structured, organized, and logical manner into a series of well-defined interrelated, bounded tasks.

2. Monitor, or status, the work as the tasks are performed, ensuring that resources are available as required.

3. Control, by applying corrective action when tasks are not performed as or when planned.

The application of inadequate energy, insight, and intelligence to these three tasks is at the root of many problems encountered in development projects. This is especially the case with software development, where the nature and full scope of the work that needs to be performed is often poorly understood, either technically or managerially, by the parties involved.

Why is this so? A reason commonly given, citing no less of an authority than Fred Brooks [Brooks 1987], is that "software is invisible." One rationale for this statement is that software, unlike hardware, has no distinct physical embodiment. Thus a circuit card, chip or gate array, is a product of a series of intellectual processes of specification, design, and test not unlike software. In fact, increasingly so as some types of hardware as digital circuits are often designed using specification languages, such as VHDL. The difference is that these activities culminate in a concrete artifact. As a result, once the need for a hardware item is identified, virtually everyone involved has a general expectation of what is intended and how it will be produced.

Software, on the other hand, never leaves the region of intellectual processes until it finally makes its presence known indirectly, manifesting itself (correctly or not) through the operation of the system on which it is executing. In addition, only a small portion of the population is aware if a chip design requires rework, necessitating another iteration of design and fabrication at the foundry, whereas virtually the entire population becomes aware of and may well be impacted by developmental problems with major software systems.

In a materialistic culture the above discussion is, on the face of it, compelling. This is especially the case if the observer knows nothing of the processes of software specification, design, implementation, and test. However, claims of "invisibility" should not be accepted from anyone who is familiar with these processes and how their products (the design) are represented. The effort (cost) expended when performing the tasks needed to develop a software product, once expended, is gone forever. If a task was not specified or performed correctly, then it must be performed again. In the meantime the schedule clock is ticking. The customer(s) want the product or there would be no project in the first place. The project staff will want to see the fruits of their labors in use.

So we, as software engineering project managers, owe it to the customer, our staff, and ourselves to understand the work, to plan it in a logical, organized manner, and to manage it actively. We should make our software visible to all. If we do not, the lack thereof will be self-evident. This is not an easy task because many software development projects are very complex, requiring the completion of many interrelated activities. Dependencies on external events and data often exist. Any particular project will have unique tasks that depend on and influence other tasks in the project. Many of these specific circumstances do not and cannot appear in the textbook development models. Compounding all of the above is the fact that obtaining an accurate picture of the instantaneous status of some tasks can be very difficult. Projecting their future status can be even more difficult. Making changes to the project plan, either by reorganizing the plan or by reorganizing an individual task, can be complex and must often be done in an emotional charged environment.

But all of the above should be and must be done. Without an organized project plan, founded on a clear understanding of what is needed, why it is needed, and when it is needed, a project will, at best, be completed by accident.

This chapter describes the activities that should be performed to:

- Create the initial estimate for the cost and schedule needed to produce a software product based on its specific requirements.

- Identify the sources of project level requirements.

- Build and structure the list of all tasks needed to accomplish the project (e.g., to satisfy the product and project requirements).

- Identify the interrelationships between those tasks.

- Create a time-ordered network of those tasks. This is the project schedule.

- Develop estimates for the schedule and resource requirements (including cost) for the tasks.

- Assign resources, especially people, to the tasks.

- Create or apply the systems used to monitor the performance of the project as the tasks are performed.

- Monitor the execution of the tasks.

- Apply corrective action when things do not develop according to the plan, including making changes to individual tasks as well as restructuring the task network.

As extensive as the above list is, this chapter does not include every possible situation that can arise in performing the above steps. Instead it strives to describe the principles behind them, as well as pointing out the most common errors made in performing them.

Because there is no single IEEE standard that directly describes cost and schedule estimation and management, this chapter will refer to other standards. In particular, IEEE Standard 1058-1998, *IEEE Standard for Software Project Management Plans*, and IEEE Standard 1045-1992, *IEEE Standard for Software Productivity Metrics*, should both be referenced, along with the Chapters 13 and 15 of this book.

12.2   Objectives

In this chapter you will learn:

- The importance of cost and schedule estimation and management.

- The causes of cost and schedule estimation errors.

- How to specify what is to be estimated.

- What a work breakdown structure is.

- What work packages are and how they are specified.

- How to estimate the cost and schedule of a software project.

- The methods available for use in preparing estimates.

- The advantages and disadvantages of each of those methods.

- How to estimate the size of products using diffferent methods.

- The techniques available for representing project schedules.

- What a critical path is and its importance in project management.

- What earned value is and how it is used to manage project cost and schedule.

12.3   Initial Software Cost and Schedule Estimates

In most software development projects the bulk of the cost and the majority of the schedule are expended on specifying, designing, implementing, integrating, testing, and delivering

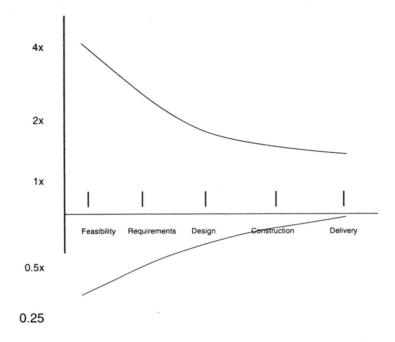

Figure 12.1: Range of Error in Estimates as a Function of Phase

the software products stipulated in the project's authorizing documents (e.g., the contract). Furthermore, at the time the project is initially planned only the most general characteristics of the product are often known: The first substantive work product of most projects is the software requirements specification (SRS).

As a result, initial cost and schedule estimates must be developed based on the most general characteristics of the products. These initial estimates are usually accurate to no more than 120 percent [Stutzke 1997]. In practice, estimates are often much less accurate. Therefore, the process of estimation and scheduling should be repeated after the SRS is approved and accepted. Figure 12.1, adapted from a work of Boehm et al. [Boehm et al. 1995], shows the range of possible errors in the estimates of cost at various points in a product's development. Thus when the concept of the software is being developed (the feasibility phase), the estimate can be low or high by factors of 4 (that is, $4\times$ to $0.25\times$). In other words, a total range of 16:1! Later, during the design phase, the range narrows to a factor of 1.5 on each side of the nominal, representing a total range of 2.25:1. As would be expected, for projects that more or less repeat the processes of prior projects, developing similar products with stable technology and personnel would be expected to operate closer to the middle of the range (the region of greatest predictability), while novel products, being produced with unstable staff and untried technologies, would be subject to much greater variability.

Initial estimates are primarily based on the requirements, formal or not, of the product and the capabilities of the organization performing the work. They also depend on project requirements, such as are often found in the statement of work (SOW). However, many SOW requirements, along with other project-level requirements, are unique and hence not represented in the models. Estimates of such activities must be prepared at a more detailed, discrete level. This is described in later sections of this chapter. Chapter 3, on software requirements, describes what requirements should and should not be contained in the SRS and what should be placed into the SOW.

Notwithstanding these limitations, such initial estimates are useful. They bound the effort and risk of the program and serve as the basis from which the more detailed and accurate estimates are derived. They are often the only estimate available at the time the project is proposed to the customer. If the project is similar to another recent effort, or if the SRS was developed prior to the proposal, then the initial estimate can be much more accurate.

Cost and schedule estimates can influence whether or not a project is undertaken at all. Questions that should be considered in determining whether or not to initiate a project include the following:

- Can the project be completed within the allotted time?

- What personnel, capital, and information resources are required to complete the project?

- Are these resources readily available or will more be required?

12.3.1 Methods for Preparing Initial Estimates

Three major categories of systematic methods are used to develop initial software cost and schedule estimates. In order of increasing sophistication they are as follows:

1. *Analogy:* The actual cost and schedule of one or more specific, similar projects are used to develop the estimates.

2. *Rules of thumb:* Institutional or individual (expert) experience or guidelines are used, often derived from a broad base of projects, usually within a single organization.

3. *Parametric models:* These use properties of the product, like lines of code, as a parameter (or input) for a model, producing a prediction of some other property, such as cost and schedule. These models are derived and calibrated using a broad experience base derived from many projects at multiple organizations.

The project manager should consider the following questions when preparing a cost and schedule estimate and when selecting the method to be used for the current project:

- What type of project is this? What are its deliverables and activities?

- Is the type of this project similar to some previous projects?

- What kind of estimation techniques will be appropriate for this project?

- What are the risks that will affect the success of this project?

Historical cost and schedule data (sometimes called *past actuals* or a *project database*) describe how much one or more previous projects actually cost and how much time they actually required to complete each deliverable. The estimation team should consider the following questions when examining candidate projects, their products, development histories, and their historical cost and schedule data:

- Are the products similar?

- Are the technologies similar?

- Are the magnitudes of the project similar?

- Are the contract terms similar?

- Is the organization now more or less mature in its developmental practices?

- How much did this (the past) project really cost to develop?

- How long did this project really take to develop?

- How did the actual project cost compare to the budgeted cost?

- How did the actual project schedule compare to the estimated schedule?

- Was the past project underbudget/schedule?

- Was the past project overbudget/schedule?

- What areas experienced cost/schedule overruns?

- Why were there cost/schedule overruns in those areas?

In practice, most software projects are estimated primarily by one of the methods and then cross-checked, wherever possible, by the other two. The estimation is usually performed in an iterative manner, with an initial estimate based on the most generic characteristics of the project and subsequent estimates becoming more refined as the peculiar requirements of both the product and the project are included in the estimate.

There are, of course, variants to these methods. For example, as a matter of business strategy the project may be bid based on the funding available. In that case the methods listed above can be used to bound the risk to the customer (will they get all their desired features?) or to the developer (will they experience a one-time loss on the development?).

12.3.2 Common Estimation Problems and Risks

Some common difficulties and sensitivities are inherent in all of the techniques discussed above. The following sections discuss each of these in turn.

12.3.2.1 Sensitivity to Requirements

The first issue is fundamental, namely, that the requirements of the project and the product must be known with a degree of certainty commensurate with that desired from the estimate. This one issue produces more problems than any other. For an in-depth discussion of many of the problems with capturing and documenting requirements the reader is directed to Chapter 3.

12.3.2.2 Diseconomy of Scale

The second issue is likewise fundamental, namely, that software development suffers from diseconomies of scale. That is, a 20 percent larger product (measured in lines of code) can easily require 35 percent more effort (labor hours) to produce. Hence the larger product costs 12.5 percent more hours per line of code to produce. This applies to all lines of code produced and not just to the additional 20 percent. This is contrary to experience in many other areas of economic activity. It is a consequence of the high level of coordination and communication necessary throughout the software development process.

Making the situation worse is the fact that this diseconomy of scale effect usually compounds the uncertainty in requirements, producing a highly nonlinear effect on the error in costs and schedule estimates. This effect has been noted for more than 25 years. The parametric models discussed in the next section show this feature explicitly. Rules of thumb derived from experience will usually show this sensitivity as well. Similarity methods will only do so if the products being compared are of nearly equal size.

12.3.2.3 Brooks Law

Fred Brooks observed a third effect in the 1970s [Brooks 1975], when it was noted that there is an optimal staffing profile for any given project. That is, as a function of time or development phase, there is an optimal number of qualified personnel that can be productively applied to any given project. Adding more people usually does not make the project complete sooner and all too often serves to increase costs. Worse, because of the difficulty in managing and training additional staff, the project may well complete later.

Thus, at any given level of implementation technology, product complexity, and organizational capability there is an optimal staffing curve. Significant deviations from this curve, regardless of the cause, will often result in increases to the project's cost and schedule. The parametric models also represent this fact. As with any other rule, of course, there are always exceptions.

For example, if a project will require 200 labor-months the parametric models (which are based on and calibrated using program experiences) would predict it would require something like 20 months of schedule, for an average staffing of 10 people. It would be extremely unreasonable to expect that 30 people could be applied to the project and that a schedule of 7 months would result. It is more likely that the project will finish in 24 months instead of 20 and that it would cost 400 percent more to complete.

The classical case of this optimality phenomenon is referred to as *Brooks law:* Adding more staff to a project that is late just makes it later. As with any other rule there are exceptions. Thus the paper of Stutzke [Stutzke 1994] describes specific conditions under which adding staff to a project will in fact produce useful results.

12.3.2.4 Sensitivity to Staff Skills and Experience

A fourth difficulty is the absolute criticality of obtaining the very best technical staff. Many program managers recognize this instinctively. The parametric cost and schedule estimation models highlight this fact, with personnel excellence having a greater impact than any other group of factors, excluding the sheer size of the product.

12.3.2.5 The Optimal Staffing Level Is Not Uniform

A fifth difficulty is that the average staffing of a project, obtained by dividing the total effort by the months of schedule, is at best a general indicator of the staffing level of a project. For the first and last quarters of many projects the staffing level may be less than one-third of the average, while during the middle half of the schedule the staff may rise to 150 to 200 percent of the average. The parametric models show this effect clearly.

Because the early phases of a project are spent performing analysis and design activities, while the later are spent integrating and testing the product, this is intuitive. Only so many individuals can productively perform design activities, especially at the architecture level. Likewise, only so many individuals can productively integrate and test a product, since this is often a serial process. Finally, the available pool of individuals skilled in analysis, design, and integration tasks imposes further constraints on the staffing level that can be productively employed in the earlier and later phases of a development project.

12.3.2.6 Many Factors Are at Work

The estimation process, regardless of how it is performed, should be approached with due care and rigor. The parametric models have many parameters, each of which may impact the cost estimate by 10 percent or more. The compounded effect of selecting five parameters incorrectly can easily exceed 60 percent. Likewise, selecting an inappropriate prior project for a similarity analysis can result in major errors in the estimation of a new project. The best way to avoid this is to use experienced estimators.

An important part of any estimation process is the evaluation of the risk of the project and the establishment, depending on the degree of uncertainty in the estimate, of some degree of margin. While a margin of 20 percent is reasonable, circumstances may argue for values as high as 50 percent. Competitive or management pressures often result in much lower values as a matter of practice. It is worth noting that the profit margin for many enterprises is between 15 and 30 percent, so the risk margin (or *pad*, or *risk allowance*, as it is sometimes known) can often exceed the expected profit. This important business issue is beyond the scope of this volume but software estimators should realistically represent the uncertainty in their estimates so that the appropriate business decisions can be made by their own and the customers' organizations.

Finally, keep in mind that motives and reality are different. That is, just because something, such as lower cost or a shorter schedule, is desired, does not make it possible. Likewise, technical feasibility does not always equate with economic possibility.

12.3.3   Parametric Models

Parametric estimation models produce, with varying degrees of refinement, estimates of the cost and schedule using parametric inputs. Typically the inputs describe:

1. The expected size of the product,

2. The nature of the product,

3. The capabilities of the organization, and

4. Properties of the project.

Models of this type have been developed by performing statistical analysis of hundreds of previous projects, with periodic recalibration as the software industry has evolved.

These are the principal models [Stutzke 1997]:

- The COnstructive COst MOdel (COCOMO) was developed by Barry Boehm. The latest version, COCOMO II, is readily available at no cost from the University of Southern California via their Web site (http://sunset.usc.edu/research/cocomoII). Commercially supported versions are also available.

- PRICE S is a commercial, software-specific version of the PRICE cost and schedule originally developed by Frank Freiman and Robert Park of RCA.

- SLIM, an effort estimation method developed by Larry Putnam, is based on the Rayleigh-Norden distribution [Pillai & Nair 1997].

- SEER-SEM was developed by Randall Jensen of Hughes Aircraft (http://www.galorath.com).

Because the COCOMO models are widely available and nonproprietary, they are very commonly used. Software tools and user guides can be obtained free of charge from the University of Southern California Web site (http://www.usc.edu).

12.3.3.1   COCOMO II

This is an evolution of an earlier model developed and released by Barry Boehm in 1981. It was described in great detail in his book *Software Engineering Economics*. There were several subsequent commercial implementations of COCOMO 81 in the period from 1985 to 1995. There were also commercial implementations with extensions, such as COSTAR (http://www.softstarsystems.com), which supports several versions of the COCOMO models (1981, 1984, Ada COCOMO, and COCOMO II) using both traditional and incremental development methods.

In addition, because the equations and rationale for COCOMO 81 were openly published, many individuals implemented their own models of COCOMO 81 using spreadsheets in the early and late 1980s. After rejoining the University of Southern California, Dr. Boehm and his colleagues undertook a research program, the purpose of which was to update and revise the original work. In 1997–1998 the first versions of COCOMO II were released. There have been periodic releases since then.

The original COCOMO 81 equations were derived by fitting curves to the log-linear data sets. This produced equations of the form:

$$\text{Effort in labor months}(E) = C(KDSI)^a$$

where $KDSI$ is the number of thousands (K) of delivered source instructions, C is a multiplier whose value depends on the nature of the project and ranges from 2.4 to 3.6, and exponent a ranges from 1.05 to 1.20.

$$\text{Schedule in months} = 2.5E^b$$

where exponent b depends on the nature of the product and ranges from 0.28 to 0.32.

Based on the project histories used to create the model, Boehm and his associates were able to further decompose the schedule into the classical phases, allocating spans of time and effort to each phase. This allows the estimator to develop time phased effort expenditure (staffing) curves, much as is done with the SLIM model.

The critical factor used to select the multipliers and exponents in the first versions of COCOMO 81 was the degree to which the project must operate under tight constraints imposed on both the product and the development effort, on the one hand, or whether the developers have latitude to develop a product with considerable design freedom in a familiar environment.

A custom, hybrid hardware/software (a so-called "embedded" system) product intended to control a mission-critical function in a constrained (throughput and memory) environment is the classical example of the more difficult class of systems. A small database application written for personal or casual use would be an example of a less difficult system.

Instead of taking this approach COCOMO II uses variations of its equations that directly select the exponents and multipliers based on the user-selected scale attributes, discussed below. They are described in detail in the COCOMO II documents.

In addition, COCOMO II can be used to model a broader variety of circumstances than did the original COCOMO 81 model. It does this by supporting two models:

1. *Early design:* This would typically be the one applied when performing initial estimates when relatively little is known about the desired product.

2. *Postarchitecture:* This would usually be applied after the requirements and early design phases have been completed.

As mentioned above, COCOMO II introduced the concept of the scale attributes, consisting of five factors. The factors included in the scale attribute group are as follows:

1. The degree of novelty of the product, called *precedentedness*. The more novel the project is, the higher the cost will be. Precedentedness is an inverted scale: Higher degrees of precedentedness mean lower novelty and lower cost.

2. The degree of flexibility afforded the development team. The less flexible the project (more constrained), the higher the cost. Both SRS and SOW constraints can contribute to this factor.

3. The degree of risk present in the architecture. This is distinct from the novelty of the application, which is intrinsic and independent on the architecture.

4. The degree of cohesion and mutual support possessed by the development team.

5. The process maturity of the organization(s) performing the development.

These attributes all serve to modify the difficulty of the project.

The primary input to the model is the size of the product being developed. COCOMO 81 used only human-generated, nonblank, noncommented, source lines of code. In COCOMO II the size of the product effort can be expressed in any one of the following three forms:

1. Source lines of human-generated, noncommented code. This is the measure of product size directly supported by the original COCOMO 81 model;

2. Unadjusted function points, which are in their turn estimated using another parametric model, briefly described later in this chapter; and

3. Adaptation, which is used when an existing product is being modified to operate under new conditions or environments. For example, an application is being adapted to a new operating system. When this mode is selected a whole range of product and project attributes must be entered. Among these is the human-generated, noncomment, nonblank equivalent line-of-code count for the product being adapted, as well as the effort to integrate autotranslated code.

Likewise, in common with the COCOMO 81 model, COCOMO II has 16 individual attributes that impact the cost and schedule of a project. Each of the individual attributes has between three and five possible settings. The combined impact can easily be 100 to 200 percent, so care must be taken when selecting the values for each of the attributes. The COCOMO II user's manual describes the criteria that should be applied in selecting the settings for each of the attributes.

Depending on which of the two models is chosen, there are 7 early design or 17 postarchitecture effort multipliers. For the early design model the 7 factors are as follows:

1. *Personnel capability:* A global assessment of the proposed project personnel and how well their skills match the projects technical needs is needed.

2. *Product reliability and complexity:* This is an evaluation of how complex the product and its development are, together with how reliable it must be.

3. *Required reuse:* How extensively will parts (or all) of the product be reused in the future?

4. *Platform difficulty:* How much will the development or delivery computing platform change, together with any execution time or memory challenges posed by it?

5. *Personnel experience:* This is an assessment of the experience levels of the project staff.

6. *Facilities:* The extent to which the project will be impacted by distributed development and software tool issues is a factor.

7. *Schedule:* This is an evaluation of the criticality of achieving a specific schedule objective, with cost being a secondary concern.

In the postarchitecture model, most of these 7 factors are further broken down into 17 attributes and organized into four groups. Because the postarchitecture estimation model is intended for use later in the development history, much more should be known than would be the case during the early design phase.

These are the four postarchitecture attribute groups:

1. The nature of the product,

2. The capabilities of the personnel,

3. Certain attributes of the project, and

4. The stability and limitations of the developmental and execution (target) computing environments.

To give a sense of the model, the individual attributes are listed below for each of these groups. For full details the reader is referred to the COCOMO Web page.

For the product attribute group:

1. *Reliability:* How reliable must the product be when operating?

2. *Data:* How much data does product functionality require?

3. *Complexity:* How much logic is required to perform the functions?

4. *Documentation:* How much documentation is required?

5. *Reuse:* How heavily will the components or products being developed be expected to be reused later?

For the personnel attribute group:

1. *Analyst experience:* How many years of experience do the project analysts have performing requirements and design activities?

2. *Analyst capability:* What is the intrinsic capability of the analysts?

3. *Programmer capability:* What is the capability level of the programming staff (detailed design through integration)?

4. *Platform experience:* What level of experience does the programming staff have with the execution (the target) and the development environments?

5. *Language experience:* What level of experience does the staff have with the programming language and development tools and environment?

6. *Personnel continuity:* How much staff turnover is expected?

For the project attribute group:

1. The degree of use of software tools,

2. The extent to which the development effort is distributed across multiple sites, and

3. The degree of schedule compression desired, with cost being a secondary concern.

For the platform attribute group:

1. The degree to which the execution time of the product will stress the computing power of the target platform,

2. The degree to which memory usage (RAM, ROM, or disk) of the application will stress the target platform, and

3. The stability of the target and development platforms hardware and software.

COCOMO II allows the project to be broken down into a series of subsystems or modules. This allows more accurate adjustment of the attributes on a module-by-module basis. This facility will be essential as the cost and schedule estimation process transitions to the detail phases of development.

12.3.4   Estimating Product Size

All of the methods described above are based in one way or another on measures of product size, usually reduced to the common denominator of human-generated, nonblank, noncomment lines of source code. This should not be surprising, as the source code of the system (or its earlier representations in the form of requirements or design documents) is the primary product of the human activity of building the system through the processes of design, code, and test. The labor costs of the project staff, in turn, dominate all other costs of developing the system, with the obvious exception of those systems (such as spacecraft) whose testing requires the expenditure of vast sums of money. Hence the amount of code required should, assuming some aggregate rate of production (that is, lines of code per staff-month or staff-hour), largely determine the cost of developing the product.

The principal limitation with basing cost and schedule estimates for a new product on its size in lines of code is that the uncertainty in that metric can be large early in the project's evolution. There are two causes of this uncertainty. First and foremost is the uncertainty in the requirements. This is a fundamental limitation of all methods. Second, even if the requirements are stable and well known, the volume of code needed to implement those requirements can be uncertain. Irrespective of these drawbacks there is sometimes no readily available alternative.

12.3.4.1   Lines of Code Estimation

If a direct estimate of product (or component) lines of code is desired, it can be developed using either the analogy or rule-of-thumb methods. Estimating the size of the entire product at once is referred to as *top-down estimation*, while decomposing the product into a series of smaller components and then summing them is referred to as *bottom-up estimation.*

These methods can also be applied to individual components. For example, if a major portion of the product is similar to an existing one then it can be used directly (top-down) on a similarity basis, with the rest of the product's functionality being broken down into smaller pieces (bottom-up), which in turn could be individually estimated using the analogy or rule-of-thumb methods.

Implicit in the above discussion is the assumption that both a list of initial requirements and an initial architecture are available to guide the estimation process.

Finally, the project must be carefully examined to ensure that no lines of code are omitted. For example, if a program generator is used to develop a reporting subsystem, then the lines of text used to specify that subsystem in the language of the program generator must be included. Likewise, if the product requires a database, then the lines of text used to specify the scheme must be included. Finally, if the user interface is implemented using a dialog specification language then the lines of code for that part of the product must be included. The *IEEE Standard for Software Productivity Metrics* (IEEE Standard 1045-1992) defines criteria that should be applied to this task.

Experience has shown that the accuracy of estimates ultimately depends on the skill of the estimator and the estimation database available to them. Depending on the novelty of the product, the skill and experience of the estimator, and the breadth and depth of documented organizational experience, these methods will work more or less well. In an effort to reduce these dependencies other methods have been developed. The principal methods are function points and object points. The accuracy of both of these methods will ultimately rely on the development of an estimation database. The advantage of these methods is that they provide an organized process for doing so prior to developing the actual code.

12.3.4.2 Function Points

Function points attempt to measure the functionality of the software product in standard units, independent of the language and technology used to implement the product. Alan Albrecht of IBM first developed the Function Point method in 1979 [Albrecht & Gaffney 1983]. The method consists of accessing the essential external and internal functions required of the product and then scaling them based on complexity factors, called *weights*, to produce a final measure of product size. This measure can then be used directly or converted to lines of code using a scaling factor.

The primary advantage of using function points is that the method is based on a structured assessment of the delivered functionality rather than on any architectural or technological artifacts. In addition it is openly documented by the International Function Point Users Group (IFPUG), which produces and maintains the *Function Point Practices Counting Manual*. Although the method is structured, the determination of the weights can be somewhat subjective. In addition, the estimator must take care to map the requirements onto the categories of external and internal behaviors. Double counting and overlaps must be avoided.

The number of function points (a measure of size) represented by a set of requirements is estimated by enumerating the number of each of four categories of external system behaviors or transactions, together with the number of internal logical files. The complexity of each of component of the five categories is then evaluated as being low, medium, or high. These weighted values are then totaled to produce the *unadjusted function count* (UFC) of the product.

The five categories of external and internal items are shown in Table 12.1, together with their weights based on the complexity of the data being passed by each of the transactions or internal files.

	LOW	MEDIUM	HIGH
EXTERNAL INPUTS	3	4	6
EXTERNAL OUTPUTS	4	5	7
EXTERNAL INQUIRIES	3	4	6
EXTERNAL INTERFACES	5	7	10
INTERNAL FILES	7	10	15

Table 12.1: Function Point Count Weights for Complexity [Garmus & David 1996]

Inspection of Table 12.1 reveals a number of things. First, for a given complexity level an external inquiry produces the same function count as does an external input, whereas an external output of the same complexity produces a function count value that is between 20 and 33 percent greater than either of them. Displaying an external output implies that something worth displaying was generated, so a higher weight (and subsequent count) should be expected.

Likewise, because interfacing to external systems usually carries with it the burdens of protocol, data conversion, and cooperative processing the weight is higher. Finally, the use of internal files implies that the processing is of a certain complexity because the retention of internal information is necessary in the first place. Hence internal files carry with them the greatest weights.

The next step in the calculation of function points is to determine the value adjustment factor by assessing the impact of 14 factors that affect the functional size of the system. The 14 factors are listed in Table 12.2. Each adjustment factor is then scored on a scale that ranges from 0 to 5. The descriptions of the values for the adjustment factors are shown in Table 12.3.

Factors
1.   Data communications
2.   Distributed functions
3.   Performance
4.   Heavily used operational configuration
5.   Transaction rate
6.   Online data entry
7.   Design for end-user efficiency
8.   Online update (for logical internal files)
9.   Complex processing
10.   Reusability of system code
11.   Installation ease
12.   Operational ease
13.   Multiple sites
14.   Ease of change

Table 12.2: Function Point Value Adjustment Factors [Garmus & David 1996]

Final Complexity Factor: $TCF = 0.65 + 0.01 \sum_{i=1}^{14} F_i$

The function point user's manual gives full details of how to apply the method and should be consulted for further details, together with the Web site of the IFPUG.

Note that there are 14 value adjustment factors and their individual ranges go from 0 to 5. As a result, any systematic bias in their selection will introduce considerable error

Adjustment	Description
0	Not present or has no influence
1	Insignificant influence
2	Moderate influence
3	Average influence
4	Significant influence
5	Strong influence

Table 12.3: Function Point Adjustment Factors [Garmus & David 1996]

into the results. Since the selection of the values is somewhat subjective, this is usually the single largest source of error encountered when using the function points method.

To appreciate the meaning of the function point value, it is useful to convert it into lines of code. Table 12.4 shows expansion rates (the number of lines of code that one function point represents) for a variety of languages. This table is derived from empirical studies.

Function Point Calculation: $FP = UFC \times TCF$

LANGUAGE	FI
ASSEMBLY	320
C	150
COBOL	105
FORTRAN	105
PASCAL	91
ADA	71
PL/1	65
PROLOG/LISP	64
SMALLTALK	21
SPREADSHEET	6

Table 12.4: Function Point-to-Line of Code Conversion [Garmus & David 1996]

12.3.4.3 Object Points

In the 1990s Watts Humphrey of the Software Engineering Institute described a new method for estimating the size of a software product based on objects [Humphrey 1995]. In this method, called PROBE, the estimators or their organization develops a historical database of the lines of code needed to implement objects and their methods of varying types and complexity. Although each organization should develop its own table, Humphrey provided initial tables for C++ and Object Pascal. Table 12.5 shows the initial table for C++:

Method Category	Very Small	Small	Medium	Large	Very Large
Calculation	2.34	5.13	11.25	24.66	54.04
Data	2.60	4.79	8.84	16.31	30.09
I/O	9.01	12.06	16.15	21.62	28.93
Logic	7.55	10.98	15.98	23.25	33.83
Setup	3.88	5.04	6.56	8.53	11.09
Text	3.75	8.00	17.07	36.41	77.66

Table 12.5: C++ Object Size in LOC by Method and Complexity [Humphrey 1995]

The goal of the PROBE method is thus, based on the product requirements, to develop counts of each of the six method categories of the five complexity classes listed in Table 12.5. In other words, a matrix of the same form as Table 12.5 is created, except the object counts are entered into the 30 cells. The values in those cells are then multiplied by the values in the matching cells of Table 13.5. Finally, these products are summed to create a total line of code estimate. The following equation illustrates the calculation.

$$TOTAL\_LOC = \sum_{i=1}^{5} \sum_{j=1}^{6} LOC_{ij} CNT_{ij}$$

where LOC is the matrix shown in Table 12.5 and CNT is the matrix of object counts for each of the 30 method types and complexities.

The matrix of object counts (CNT) is created as follows:

1. Using the product requirements an architectural, or conceptual, design is created.

2. Walk through the design for each class of inputs and interactions, identifying what objects of each of the seven method categories are needed.

3. Estimate the complexity of each method identified above.

4. Tally the results into the cells of the matrix CNT.

As with the other methods of estimating the size of a software product, experience and historical data are essential. In particular, accurate use of the PROBE method requires that the estimator develop the ability to accurately judge the number of methods and their complexities and how those complexities relate to the lines of code needed to implement such methods.

Finally, Humphrey goes on to describe how the historical data can also be used to develop a prediction, or confidence, interval for the line of code estimate.

For more details on the PROBE method his book [Humphrey 1995] should be consulted.

12.4 Detailed Costing and Scheduling

In the previous sections the methods available for the estimation of the cost and schedule for a project's classical software development activities were discussed. As mentioned at the outset of that section, those estimates are macroscopic in nature. That is, the software cost and schedule is broken down into a relatively small number of activities following the classical waterfall model of requirements, design, implementation, and test. For each of the subsystems being modeled, the cost and schedule for each of these serial activities is estimated.

For a project of any reasonable size or complexity, this macroscopic information provides a starting point for the detailed costing and scheduling that make up the actual planning of the project. The detailed planning effort described in this section can be thought of as "microscopic" in comparison to the earlier estimation work.

12.4.1 Planning Activities

The following activities should be performed when developing detailed plans for a software development project:

- Determine the project objectives, requirements, and activities. The technical requirements of the project are only part of this. The contract and SOW should be carefully reviewed as well. Any dependencies on external events or data (such as a decision by the customer, or externally provided test data) should be identified.

- Identify all project deliverables. Again, the software items being delivered are usually a subset of all the deliverables. For example, user's manuals or postdelivery support is often required. Likewise, periodic status reports may be required.

- Partition the project requirements, dependencies on external events, deliverables, and activities into work packages. Guidelines for creating work packages are given in later subsections. The work packages should be cross-checked against the project requirements for completeness.

- Identify and describe any essential dependency among work packages. For example, requirements should be completed prior to the start of the design.

- Sequence the work packages, either in series or in parallel. The software activities should follow the project's selected software life cycle processes plan. Using this sequencing, which must satisfy the dependencies identified earlier, the scheduling network for the project should be created using a modern network scheduling tool. See Appendix B for a description of network scheduling.

- Estimate the resources needed to perform each work package. The methods discussed in Section 12.3.4 should be used to estimate the labor component.

- Estimate the schedule needed to perform each work package. These time spans should be entered into the network schedule. In this way the dates at which deliverables will be completed can be evaluated.

- Estimate the budgets needed to perform the work packages and the project. The budgets will usually include labor, capital, and expenses. The labor budget will usually be dominated by the software development activities.

- Evaluate the resulting cost and schedule and determine if further iteration or refinement is needed.

Software costing and scheduling, therefore, is the process of determining the activities necessary to complete a given software development project and developing estimates of the time and cost it will take to complete them.

Software budgets and schedules are developed iteratively and in tandem, since each provides information that is helpful in preparing the other. The time spent in preparing a software budget or schedule is dependent on the size and complexity of the project. In can be as low as 2 percent of the total project cost and schedule but can easily exceed 10 percent.

Thus one of the major project planning tasks, and a primary responsibility of the software engineering project manager, is the identification and sequencing of all project work packages and the preparation of a detailed project budget and schedule that can be understood by the project as well as by the parent organization's financial and managerial organizations. The project budget and schedule are documented representations of the activities needed to develop the project deliverables. In other words, they are predictive models of how the project is expected to proceed.

The Estimation Team

For anything larger than the most trivial of projects, a cost and schedule estimation team should be assembled. The team should consist of the software engineering project manager, the requirements engineer, the chief software designer, the architect of software life cycle processes, and other appropriate project personnel.

For larger projects the work of this team may continue for several weeks or months. As part of its deliberations the team must identify the risks that may affect project cost, schedule, or quality. The likelihood of each risk factor eventuating must be considered. For more on the topic of risk management, see Chapter 14.

For a schedule or budget to be effective, it must possess several major characteristics. The budget and schedule must be:

- Understandable to the software engineering project manager, the project staff, and the customer;

- Complete and consistent with the project contract, SOW and technical specifications;

- Sufficiently detailed to provide a basis for measurement and control of the project over time;

- Capable of highlighting critical tasks;

- Robust and tolerant of the expected risks;

- Flexible and easily modifiable and maintainable;

- Based on reliable time and cost estimates;

- Consistent with the organization's accounting and management methods;

- Realistic and specify only resources that are truly needed and available; and

- Compatible with plans for other projects that share resources.

12.4.2 Determining Project Objectives

First and foremost, the objectives of a software development project must be established. The cost and scheduling team must determine what is to be delivered by the project (e.g., software products, documentation, training), assess the "goodness" of the requirements for those deliverables, and identify what other activities must be performed beyond those needed to satisfy the technical requirements. Requirement documents of high quality are critical to the accuracy of cost and schedule estimates since unclear, ambiguous, or unstable (creeping) requirements will render the budget and schedule meaningless. To increase the accuracy of cost and schedule estimates, the team must realistically evaluate other project attributes. The attributes that should be considered include the size of the project, external dependencies to which the project is subject, the desired and expected completion dates, as well as other costs such as unique hardware, facilities, subcontracts, and travel.

The importance of correctly identifying and categorizing costs is discussed in a later section.

12.4.2.1 Nontechnical Requirements and Objectives

Most projects have requirements that do not directly appear in the technical requirements of the product. The statement of work, work breakdown structure (WBS, discussed in Appendix A), contract, and the minutes of meetings with the customer will often contain such programmatic or program-level requirements. Of course, not all projects will use all of these documents.

As an example, the SOW may require periodic travel to customer sites for reviews or consultation. The travel costs should be included in the appropriate budget line, as should the labor required to prepare for the trip, to attend the meetings, and to answer follow-on questions arising from the meeting. The scope of the meeting and its objectives will determine exactly how much effort must be expended in these areas.

12.4.2.2 Documenting Project Requirements

As the relevant documents are reviewed the project requirements should be entered into a table that includes the following:

- A unique identifier for the requirement,

- A specific reference to the source of the requirement,

- A description of the requirement,

- References to any related or potentially conflicting requirements, and

- A list of product deliverables whose creation the requirement impacts.

This table should be reviewed periodically by the estimation team and by the software engineering project manager. The review should address the completeness, consistency, and verifiability of the requirements. Just as the SRS is used to initiate the project design process, this list of project requirements is used to initiate the project scheduling process. In particular, this table should be used as the starting point for subsequent traces of the project requirements into the project work packages.

12.4.3   Identifying and Creating Work Packages

12.4.3.1 Work Packages

A *work package* is a discrete task that must be performed in order to achieve the objectives of the project. When first created the specification of a work package consists of the following:

- A description of the task to be performed;

- A list of preconditions that must be satisfied in order to initiate the task (a precondition may be an item or a state);

- A list of postconditions that will be satisfied on completion of the task (a postcondition may also be an item or a state); and

- A list of the project objectives whose completion this work package contributes toward. This should consist of references to the table described in the previous section.

This concept is illustrated in Figure 12.2. As the cost and schedule estimation process proceeds the time, effort, and resources needed to perform the work package are added to this list, together with the method to be used in evaluating its status.

A work package must possess the following attributes:

- It is necessary. In particular, it can be logically and causally related to other tasks and, eventually, to one or more project objectives. The ultimate proof of this will come when the full network schedule is created.

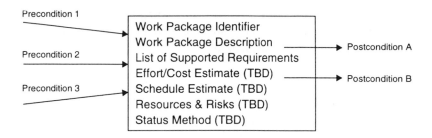

Figure 12.2: Draft Work Package

- It is coherent and of reasonable size. That is, it should not be a collection of unrelated tasks. It should not, as a general rule, exceed either 5 percent of the total project effort, or more than 2 staff-months of effort. For typical projects this translates to the work of two or three people over a 2- to 3-week time span. In other words, between 160 and 360 hours of effort.

- All preconditions must be satisfied at the beginning of the task. If one of the preconditions can only be satisfied after the task has begun, then the work package should be decomposed into one work package containing the activities that do not depend on that precondition and another that cannot start until that precondition can be satisfied. Depending on the activities contained in the initial work package, this may produce a pair of serial or parallel work packages.

- All postconditions should occur at the end of the task. Thus if one postcondition of a work package (say, the release of a document) is achieved earlier than other postconditions, then the work package should be decomposed into two or more smaller work packages.

- It is clearly defined. The objective of the work package should be written in a simple declarative sentence.

- The effort and time required to perform the work package task are bounded. It has clear completion criteria. The method used to periodically evaluate (status) the percentage of the work package that is completed must be clearly defined.

- The effort required to accomplish the task's objective must be understood. The technical approach, along with the methods and tools required to perform the work, must be understood and realistic. Those methods must be consistent with the selected software life cycle model, methods, and processes.

- It does not replicate or overlap another work package of the project. Such replication or overlap will make it all but impossible to create a coherent scheduling network.

- The effort and schedule can be estimated using only one or two distinct methods.

- It must be possible to monitor the work as it is being performed and to apply corrective action in the event of deviations and to adapt to external changes. In other words, the work packages must be manageable.

As the work packages are identified and documented, keep in mind that the objective is to create a set of tasks that can be "strung" together to create the project scheduling network. As a result, it is both useful and customary to create preliminary schedule networks as the work packages are being created. This iterative process allows the scheduling team and the software engineering project manager to gauge the realism of the work packages and the schedule together.

Indeed, for large, multiyear programs, it is usually a waste of effort to plan the entire network at this fine level of detail at the start of the program. Instead, the schedule first should be laid out using larger blocks of related activities and then those activities whose start dates lie within some manageable time window (forward from the current date) are elaborated using the above guidelines. Six to nine months is a reasonable planning window.

Figure 12.3 provides an example of a completed work package specification for a software development activity.

Work Package Specification

Activity number: 3.3.2

Activity name: ARCH-SS-XYZ
Activity description: Specify the architectural structure of subsystem XYZ
Project requirement: Deliverable prime software, WBS 5.6
Estimated duration: 5 weeks
Earned value status method: Incremental in 6 steps. See attached status plan.
Resources needed:
Personnel: 2 senior telecomm designers
Skill: Designers familiar with X2 protocol
Tools: 1 Sun workstation with IDE; 1 VT100/DEC 785
Travel: One 3-day design review in San Diego
Work product/postconditions: Architectural specification for SS-XYZ
Test plan for subsystem XYZ
Baselined?   Yes for both
Risks: Availability of senior designers
Preconditions: An approved architectural concept for the total system
Completion criteria: PDR sign-off for subsystem XY

Figure 12.3: Example of a Work Package Specification

12.4.4 Sequencing the Work Packages

When the initial list of work packages has been completed and each one documented, it should be reviewed for completeness. That is, the work packages must, when completed together, satisfy the project objectives. This should be done by performing a review of the work packages using the above criteria to create a checklist. In addition to the criteria used to evaluate the individual work packages, the network as a whole should be evaluated. Entering them into a suitable scheduling tool helps do this. The preconditions and postconditions of the work packages implicitly determine a minimal or essential scheduling network, with the postconditions of one or more work packages becoming the preconditions of others.

When the initial network has been created the result must be reviewed to determine the following:

- How consistent are the tasks? Are there any preconditions that cannot logically be satisfied? Are there any postconditions that connect to a later precondition or final project deliverable or objective?

- How complete is the network. Are all desired project objectives achieved? Are all constraints and criteria satisfied?

- Are there opportunities to further decompose some of the work packages, thereby creating better visibility into cost or schedule performance?

- Is the schedule network robust? That is, can it withstand reasonable external and internal perturbations? Does it have more than one critical path or a single critical path with multiple subcritical paths that are within a few days or weeks of being critical?

The last two areas of evaluation can only be performed when the schedule of and the resources needed to perform each work package have been identified. The cost and schedule for each work package must be estimated before this can be done.

12.4.5 Estimating the Cost and Schedule of Work Packages

Estimating a software project's cost and schedule is not easy for either experienced or novice project managers. The software engineering project manager, working with the estimation team should:

- Define and standardize the estimating process that will be used for each work package.

- Cross-check estimates with more than one estimation technique.

- Calibrate the estimation techniques and models with experience and models.

As the cost and schedule estimate for each work package is developed, the estimation team should consider the following factors, together with the relationships between them:

- *Work package product attributes:* The scope of the work package and any required quality attributes should be evaluated. The quality attributes include those that are implicit to activity as well as those that are explicitly required by the contract, SOW, or WBS. For example, large systems requiring high degrees of quality and security are more expensive and take longer to develop than small software products requiring very little quality. This should be reflected in the individual work packages.

- *Resource constraints:* The available calendar time must be considered. The schedule must reflect the time available to work on the project excluding vacations, holidays, sick time, and the potential for staff turnover. The generic factors (sick time, vacations, turnover, staff meetings) can be reflected in the work hours available per employee per week or month for each work package, while the impact of vacations and holidays can only be evaluated when the work packages are scheduled against the calendar. For projects whose development activities span several nations or regions, it will be necessary to consider multiple holiday and vacation calendars.

- *Assumptions:* This refers to conditions that must be true if the estimate is to be correct but whose truth the estimators are unable or unwilling to ascertain.

- *Assets:* Assets are the corporate resources that include personnel (engineers, managers, and other technical staff), technology, development process models, supporting processes, and infrastructures (hardware, software and communications, etc.) needed to complete or verify the work packages.

- *Budget:* Budgets (allocated funding) are needed to procure assets not already available.

- *Risks:* Risks may develop into potential problems that can affect the outcome of the software project's success.

The format for the cost and schedule estimate of each work package should contain:

- Name(s) of the estimator(s).

- Amount of time and effort expended producing the estimate.

- A clear statement of the basis for the estimate. This includes both the method as well as the scope of the activities in the work package.

- A description of any cost and schedule drivers and assumptions that were made.

- A description of the risks associated with the work package and the estimates.

- A range of estimates for effort, schedule of task completions, and resources with associated probabilities. Typically a three-point scale of high, medium, and low likelihood is used. The effort and task completion estimates should be presented as functions of time using curves or tables. Figure 12.4 gives an example of these curves, with the solid line representing the nominal predicted effort (in staff-months) and completion (in percent complete) and the dotted lines representing the range of acceptable behavior.

- The estimator's level of confidence in the accuracy of the estimate (0–10: low, medium, or high).

- What it would take to develop an improved estimate.

This information is then appended to the work package specification described earlier.

As the cost and schedule estimates for each work package are developed, the estimation team should document any assumptions on which the estimates are based. For example, the estimate should include whether or not a V&V contractor will be used to monitor the work package activities. Likewise, if it is assumed that the estimate is based on stability of the requirements, that assumption should be stated. Documented assumptions clarify and justify the estimate, and, as those baseline assumptions change, the estimate must be evaluated and revised as necessary.

Risk assumptions also should be included in the cost and schedule estimate. The probability that each risk will in fact come into being should be assessed, together with the impact of the risks to the cost, schedule, and quality. Some of these risks will be generic to several work packages, while others will be unique to a single work package. Chapter 14, Software Risk Management, describes the risk management process in more detail.

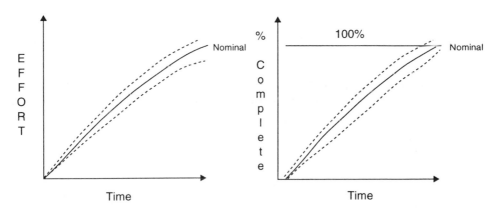

Figure 12.4: Sample Work Package Effort and Completion Curves

12.4.6   Creating Budgets

Depending on the company's accounting system, the precise budget category (called a budget line) that each of these estimated costs is assigned to will vary. Some costs are automatically included in the labor rate, such as general depreciation and expense. Thus if no special facility costs are required then the depreciation of the existing facilities will usually be included. Other costs, such as those associated with unique capital, depreciation, or expenses, may be included explicitly. Travel costs are typically charged directly to the contract, most often in a budget line called "Other Direct Costs" (ODC).

When preparing the budgets the estimating team, and most of all the PM, must be familiar with the company's rules of accounting to ensure that costs are assigned to the correct budget category. This can have a material effect on overhead costs so due care should be exercised. The costs for each work package should be broken down into those categories. By totaling these categories the total cost of the project can be computed.

In projects spanning multiple years any inflation factors, such as salary increases or escalation to expense or capital costs, must be included. This is typically done by the accounting or finance function. If it is not, then the software project manager must ensure that this fact is highlighted to management and addressed.

12.4.7   Reviewing the Schedule and Cost

When the cost and schedule of all the work packages of the project have been estimated and the schedule network has been created and the budget categories created and tallied, the program's total cost and schedule can be reviewed. The review should be conducted following the guidelines described in Chapter 11. In particular, it should address the following points:

- Is the schedule logically complete? That is, does it confirm to the list of project requirements?

- Is the schedule minimal? That is, is it trying to do too much by, say, attempting to deliver "nice-to-have," but not really essential items? Is the network too complex?

- Is the schedule reasonable? That is, when compared to the predictions of a top-down schedule and cost estimate based on the product requirements are the project's cost and time to deliver reasonable? Are they consistent with past experiences? Are any deviations reasonable and explainable?

- Does the project have too many critical or near-critical paths? If so, then the schedule is unforgiving and will break under even slight external or internal stresses.

- Is the schedule consistent with the project software life cycle process and management approaches?

- Most importantly, does the schedule conform to the project delivery and cost objectives?

Invariably the first versions of the network schedule fail one or more of these evaluation criteria. When this occurs the network must be "debugged," much like a computer program.

The following general approaches can be used to track down the source of the problem on a case-by-case basis:

- If the schedule omits certain project requirements, the existing work packages should be reviewed to see if the omitted requirements fit naturally into one of those packages. If not, then it is better to create new work packages that do satisfy the requirements. The reason for the omission should also be examined.

- If the schedule is not minimal then the nice-to-have requirements should be removed completely or moved off the main path of the program. If the network is too complex, it should be simplified until the project objectives and processes are self-evident with all tasks accounted for. Excessive (or coincidental) complexity usually results in the objectives and processes of the project being hidden by the network instead of being highlighted by it.

- If the network is complete but fails the reasonableness tests at some point, then the work packages that contribute to the variance should be examined critically. It may well be that the network is complete. In any case the reasons must be intrinsic to the project and product, not coincidental.

- When schedule networks are first created, it is common for the project cost and schedule budgets to be exceeded. It is completely possible and indeed likely that this is correct. However, it may not be and so the cost and schedule estimates of individual work packages must be examined to ascertain if they should be reestimated. This must be done with care and discretion to avoid forcing the estimates downward to match the available schedule and funds. Doing so invariably introduces more risk. It is usually at this point that the most productive members of the staff are assigned to the most critical tasks.

- If differences are discovered between the logic of the network and the project life cycle processes, then both must be examined to determine which is, in fact, the most reasonable approach for the current project. This should be done pragmatically, not dogmatically.

- If the network fails to achieve one or more of the primary project objectives, the anomaly should be traced backward through the network until the reason for the variance is discovered. It should be addressed at that point, either by modifying an existing work package or by adding others.

12.5   Monitoring Project Performance

As the project team performs the tasks described in the schedule network the status of the work packages must be actively and continuously monitored to ensure that their individual and collective objectives are achieved. Ideally, such active monitoring would not be required. If everything were ideal and perfect, including the requirements, the cost and schedule estimates of the work packages, and the technical methods and staff, such active monitoring would not be required. As each work package is completed, it will produce perfect work products on time, cheerfully passing them onto the next activity.

12.5.1   Status Reporting

Of course, the scenario described above almost never happens. Work package estimates are incorrect, requirements change, software tools or methods break in new or novel circumstances, facilities and resources are not available when needed, design and implementation errors occur, and employees get sick, have personal problems, or resign.

Without active monitoring of the execution of the project tasks, the negative impacts of these and other common circumstances will not become visible until it is too late to recover from their effects. At the same time, the monitoring of performance should be reasonable so that it does not itself become a major consumer of resources. For smaller projects in informal organizations the software project managers themselves may do the bulk of the work. In larger projects in more formal organizations specialized project schedulers, controllers, and accounting personnel will provide critical assistance to the project manager.

In any case the individual responsible for each active work package typically produces a weekly status report to the project manager. This status report should include the following:

- The hours worked on the work package. Depending on the organization's time-recording practices these data may actually come from the finance or accounting functions or from the individuals performing the work.

- The task leader's informal assessment of the group's activities. The productivity metrics described in IEEE Standard 1045-1992 and the metrics chapter of this book (Chapter 15) give examples.

- Any issues that have arisen during the past week that have impacted or will impact the cost, schedule, or quality of the work package.

- An analysis of the root cause of the issues and what options are available to offset their impacts.

These informal status reports represent one of the major opportunities for the team leader to positively impact the effectiveness of the project. The first two items are critical to obtaining a clear picture of the projects instantaneous status, while the last two are essential in anticipating problems and fixing them before they become visible in the formal status system.

12.5.1.1 Formally Statusing the Schedule

On a periodic basis, perhaps weekly but certainly no less often than monthly, the status of each active task in the project network schedule should be formally assessed, the complete scheduling network updated, and new schedule and cost predictions generated.

The exact frequency with which this is done depends on the total duration and magnitude of the project, together with costs of performing the periodic update, as well as the penalties associated with failing to deliver within the project's cost and schedule objectives. In any case weekly status reporting of the type described above will greatly simplify the task of formally updating the project network. This formal assessment, especially for larger projects, is where the project schedulers, controllers, and accounting support organizations become critical members of the management team supporting the project manager.

The precise methods and the schedule for such status reports and subsequent schedule reviews should be described in the project's software engineering project management plan (SEPMP), as described in Chapter 13. Included in this plan should be the thresholds that, when exceeded by a group of related work packages, constitute a *variance*. These variance thresholds are usually expressed as a percentage of aggregated cost and schedule, but are sometimes absolute quantities. When a variance occurs the individual responsible for the work must analyze the problem and develop a recovery plan for the group of packages.

When the project schedule review has been completed, it should produce an overall assessment of the project's final cost and schedule, including any incremental deliveries, as well as a list of variances that identifies the work packages that are under- or overrunning their allocated time or cost budgets by more than the defined thresholds.

12.5.1.2 Dealing with Variances

The SEPMP should describe the general categories of corrective actions that should be used when unacceptable cost or schedule variances occur. The general forms of corrective action available are:

- Reduce the requirements of one or more work packages. This may or may not be desirable or even legal, in the case of contract efforts. In any case the customer must be consulted before making such a change. Of course, if the requirements have "crept" upward, the reduction could simply return them to their correct, contracted condition.

- Break one or more work packages into parallel efforts. Earlier in the project this might have been considered and rejected because of the higher level of management required or because of perceived increased risks created by the additional tasks. When faced with a choice between slipping schedules or applying some more management effort or incurring an increment of risk, the decision may be different.

- Apply more staff to the problem areas. This may or may not work, depending on the specific circumstances and the individuals involved. Applying one or two higher caliber individuals to a few very specific tasks that they have experience in is one thing; sprinkling dozens of people across a whole project is another.

- Change the technical approach. You may determine that the processes or tools selected for the work package were inappropriate. In some cases the original selections were totally wrong and must be changed. The question has to be, given the work already accomplished, which is the best option: to continue or to change? The project personnel must realistically evaluate the cost, schedule, and quality impacts of any options. Making a change of this type can result in considerable rework. On the other hand it may be the only viable solution in some circumstances.

Exactly when these corrective actions are applied is another matter. It may or may not be optimal to apply them to the work packages that are currently experiencing difficulty. The decision of where to apply changes to the project plan must bear in mind:

- The current completion status of all active work packages, especially any collections of work packages experiencing difficulty (which might already be unrecoverable);

- The likelihood that the corrective actions will be successful if implemented in one or another part of the network;

- The negative effects of any unsuccessful corrective actions and the likelihood of that happening; and

- The global impacts of any of the corrective actions (successful or not) to the entire project network.

In complex situations corrective actions are often developed iteratively, using scheduling tools to evaluate the effectiveness of the candidate changes.

12.5.2   Assessing the Completion Status of Work Packages

The assessment of the cost and schedule status of work packages is a critical and difficult subject. Without an accurate picture of the status of each active work package, the view of the project as a whole is compromised. The subject is a difficult one because it requires that a clear picture be formed of what activities are being performed in each work package and how those activities relate to the accomplishment of the work package objectives. Over time the program management community has settled on a small number of approaches for evaluating the status of work packages.

The most common methods used to assess work package status are (1) subjective, (2) objective, and (3) level of effort. Each of these methods of statusing a work package is appropriate under some conditions, while under others any one of them may be wildly inappropriate. In particular, the use of the subjective method should be avoided unless no other option is available. The following sections describe each of these methods. When selecting the method for an individual work package the following factors should be considered:

- Is it feasible to apply the method to this work package?

- Is the effort required to apply the method reasonable?

- Is it clear how the method will be applied to this work package?

- What is the impact of incorrectly evaluating the status?

- What is the likelihood that the status will be evaluated incorrectly using this method?

The approach to be used in evaluating the status of each work package must be determined at the time the project schedule is being created. In addition, the related groups of work packages should be identified so that their aggregated status can be reported. The classical example of this is the status of all design or coding activities.

12.5.2.1 Subjective Methods

In this method the status of the work package is rated on a scale of 0 to 100 percent at each reporting period. When the work package is first activated (that is, work has started) the status is 0 percent. Upon completion (deactivation) of the work package the status is 100 percent. At intermediate points the evaluation is subjective. Excessive use of this method classically results in the notorious condition where "the last 10 percent of the work requires 50 percent of the schedule and cost."

The subjective method can be used for activities whose status cannot be evaluated using any objective means. This should not be the case for major software development activities: Objective methods are available for use in those cases. In addition, the use of this method along the critical path or for large work packages is always a danger sign and should be avoided at all costs. Use of this method for short-duration work packages off the critical path, which together total less than a few percent of the total program cost, and for which there is no other reasonable status method, may be acceptable. However, when the status of such a work package remains stagnant (classically at a 90 percent+ level) for several reporting periods it is time to "point the moving finger" at the work package.

12.5.2.2 Objective Methods

This is the most reliable method of all to apply. In its simplest and preferred form, the individual work package has only two status values: 0 and 100 percent. When the work package is activated the status is 0 percent. When the task described in the work package is completed and objectively verified, the status is 100 percent and the work package is deactivated. If the work packages are small and produce products (such as design artifacts, test plans, code, and similar items) that can be objectively evaluated. this method is strongly recommended. This method is also called *binary reporting*.

Use of this method for large work packages should be avoided. If it must be used for large tasks, the individual responsible for the work package must vigorously manage it and report on risk studiously. If, for some reason, the work packages must be longer in duration than a few weeks, then intermediate status values can be used, assuming that they are themselves based on objective criteria. Finally, the work packages should bear a clear relationship to the project's developmental processes so that a clear and consistent picture can be formed of the health of products and processes of the project.

12.5.2.3   Level of Effort Method

The level of effort (LOE) method of statusing a work package is most applicable to support activities that produce no concrete end items. When planning such work packages the work package is assigned a fixed duration and constant expenditure rate, called the *level of the effort*. In this method the planned and actual rates of expenditure, or "burn," of the work package are compared to determine the status. If 20 percent of the work package funds have been expended on a given date and if the schedule (as measured by the date) calls for 19 percent to have been expended, then the work package is (within 5 percent, that is 1 part in 20) progressing per the plan.

Examples of work packages for which LOE statusing may be applicable are as follows:

- Clerical support;

- Routine project management and oversight tasks, such as quality assurance;

- Maintenance of the project configuration libraries; and

- Routine, periodic staff meetings.

LOE statusing should not be used for work packages that generate a specific, major deliverable. Nor should it be used for large, project-critical tasks. Because LOE tasks generate no concrete deliverable, which can be used to verify that value has actually be received from the expenditure, they should always be examined carefully to ensure the estimated level of effort is accurate. In addition, when other parts of the schedule cause slips to occur, most LOE tasks will be extended as well, because they typically support the ongoing activities of the project.

12.5.2.4   Aggregate Reporting

In the previous sections the application of the binary reporting method to short-duration tasks was strongly advocated. The sole defect of this method is that it is difficult to detect systematic trends in the project and its processes. This defect can be easily remedied by identifying groups or aggregates of work packages and then reporting on their cumulative status.

For example, the status of the coding tasks required to implement a software configuration item could be aggregated. This would produce a set of graphs similar to those shown earlier in Figure 12.4, where the effort expended to date and completion status of each of the coding tasks of the individual modules is combined. If a significant number coding work packages experience difficulty, this will be reflected in the aggregated metric and will usually be a sign that there are systematic problems in this area early in the process.

12.5.3 Earned Value

Once the instantaneous status of a work package or aggregation of work packages is known, we can determine if the tasks represented by them are proceeding according to the cost and schedule estimates. It is also possible to forecast the performance of the project on those work packages into the future. To achieve this in a systematic manner, the concept of *earned value* (EV) was developed by the DoD community in the 1960s and 1970s [USAF 1978]. A current, detailed description is given by Fleming [Fleming 2000].

12.5.3.1 Three Basic Metrics of EV Systems

A project management system using earned value, generally referred to simply as the *earned value system*, is based on three fundamental metrics, which are simultaneously evaluated at a given point in time (usually the date of the most recent status update of the project):

1. *How much effort was (according to the plan or schedule) to have been expended working on the work package by the date of status.* This is usually measured in labor-hours or dollars. It is referred to as the budgeted cost of work scheduled ($BCWS$).

2. *How much effort was actually expended on the work package as of the status date.* This should be measured in the same units as the planned expenditures to date. It is referred to as the actual cost of work performed ($ACWP$).

3. *The planned effort needed to achieve the observed level of completion of the work package as of the status date.* In other words, given the actual level of completion, how much effort was planned to have been expended, irrespective of the date. This is referred to as the budgeted cost of work performed ($BCWP$). This is also known as the earned value.

The meaning of the first two metrics, along with how they are evaluated, is obvious. $BCWS$ is how much effort was to have been expended on the activities of the work package on the status date, while $ACWP$ is how much effort has actually been expended as of that date.

Evaluating $BCWP$ requires a slightly more subtle process. To evaluate $BCWP$, it is necessary to know the planned relationship (or curve) between the planned completions (status) and the planned expenditures. In other words, to achieve a given level of status, how much money or time should have been expended according to the plan? To facilitate this, the work package description must include curves or tables showing both the planned expenditure of effort and the planned percent complete as functions of time.

Evaluating $BCWP$ then becomes a matter of first reading the status versus time curve or table backward, to find the date at which the current status was expected to be have been achieved. Second, using the effort versus time curve or table, the effort planned to have been expended on that date is found. This is the $BCWP$. It represents how much effort was to have been expended to achieve the current status. Figure 12.5 illustrates this concept. For clarity only the nominal plan lines are shown.

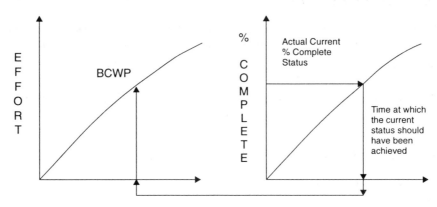

Figure 12.5: Evaluating $BCWP$

The remainder of the discussion is written from the viewpoint of a single work package. If multiple work packages are being analyzed together, then the $BCWS$ and $ACWP$ values of the component packages are simply summed, while the $BCWP$ must be evaluated by weighting the task completions of the various work packages according to their effort content, thereby creating a composite curve or table of completions versus time.

12.5.3.2 Variances

Using the three metrics just discussed ($BCWS$, $ACWP$, and $BCWP$), it is possible to evaluate how well the effort expended on the work package(s) is following the plan. The basic concept behind all earned value systems is that if the effort (cost) is being expended as planned (both in time and efficiency) then $BCWP = ACWP$, which means that the effort required to achieve the actual status ($BCWP$) is the same as the effort planned to achieve that level of completion.

Likewise, if $BCWS = BCWP$, then effort is being expended at the planned rate. That is, as scheduled.

If both equalities are true, then the work package will complete on schedule and on budget. In the event of variances (one or both of the equalities are false, within a given tolerance) these metrics can be compared and combined in different ways.

To approach the analysis of project status systematically, most earned value systems make use of four metrics derived from the three already discussed:

1. *Cost variance:* $CV = BCWP - ACWP$;

2. *Schedule variance:* $SV = BCWP - BCWS$;

3. *Cost performance index:* $CPI = BCWP/ACWP$; and

4. *Schedule performance index:* $SPI = BCWP/BCWS$.

The first two of these, CV and SV, are used to detect problems. If the magnitude of CV exceeds a threshold, usually expressed as either an absolute number or as a fraction of $BCWP$, then effort is being expended slower or faster than planned. If the magnitude of SV exceeds another threshold, then the completion of tasks is taking more or less effort than planned, which, assuming there is no cost variance, implies that the work package will be finished late.

The second two derived metrics, CPI and SPI, are used to perform more detailed analyses of problems detected using SV and CV. Because the values of each of the two indices can fall into three distinct regions (less than 1, 1, greater than 1), there are nine possible conditions, as described in Table 12.6.

Case	CPI	SPI	Cost	Schedule	Typical Actions
1	1	1	On budget	On schedule	No action required.
2	1	> 1	On budget	Ahead of schedule	Examine impact of early release of resources.
3	1	< 1	On budget	Behind schedule	If tasks impact critical path, take action to correct.
4	> 1	1	Under budget	On schedule	No action required.
5	> 1	> 1	Under budget	Ahead of schedule	See case 2.
6	> 1	< 1	Under budget	Behind schedule	See case 3. Determine if personnel being diverted.
7	< 1	1	Over budget	On schedule	Evaluate global impact to cost. Consider improving technical methods and/or personnel.
8	< 1	> 1	Over budget	Ahead of schedule	Evaluate global impact to cost. Consider improving technical methods and/or personnel.
9	< 1	< 1	Over budget	Behind schedule	See discussion in text.

Table 12.6: Cost and Schedule Performance Indices Triage

Of the nine possible conditions for SPI and CPI, case 9 is the worst of all possible worlds. It is also the most common: The collection of work packages is behind schedule and over budget. If the magnitude of the variances is large and has real impact to the project, then the only course of action is to investigate in detail. It may be that the initial estimate was defective. It may be that the requirements have changed. It may be that the methods and procedures used to perform the work are badly matched to the problem or the level of expertise of the staff. Or it may be that the method used to evaluate status is inappropriate to the task.

Finally, near the end of a project (as measured by completions, not time) the performance indices will be of little use, because only a few tasks should be active at the end of a project and those should be managed in a detailed, focused manner, not using aggregate metrics such as SPI or CPI.

12.5.3.3 Limitations of the Performance Indices

When using the earned value metrics, especially the CPI and SPI, the user must appreciate that their values may be of limited accuracy early in the life of any given work package even if the method of evaluating status is perfectly matched to the task. This phenomenon has two distinct origins. First, when work is initially started on a work package it is not uncommon for the work to progress slightly less effectively than planned. This is a result of the staff orienting themselves ("gearing up") toward the activities of the work package. This effect should be planned for when the work package is initially estimated but invariably it is not done quite right.

The second effect magnifies the first and is intrinsic to the formula for both SPI and CPI. For example, in the formula for the latter metric,

$$CPI = BCWP/ACWP$$

the variable $ACWP$ appears in the denominator. Early in the life of a work package $ACWP$ is small, as is $BCWP$. Because $ACWP$ is in the denominator, a relatively small absolute uncertainty in either its value or in the value of the status used to evaluate the $BCWP$ can introduce large uncertainties into the value of CPI. As work continues $ACWP$ and $BCWP$ grow and the relative sizes of the uncertainties are diminished, making CPI more reliable.

As a concrete example, suppose both $BCWP$ and $ACWP$ are scaled to the interval (0, 1) and that each is accurate to within 0.05. Then a direct calculation of the maximum and minimum values shows that the value of the CPI might actually be anywhere between:

$$Max\_CPI = (BCWP + 0.05)/(ACWP - 0.05)$$

and

$$Min\_CPI = (BCWP - 0.05)/(ACWP + 0.05)$$

In the formula for the maximum possible value CPI might actually have, the numerator is as big as it can be, while the denominator is as small as it can be. Reversing the signs produces the minimum value that the CPI might actually have.

If the measured values of $BCWP$ and $ACWP$ are both 0.1 (in other words, the work package is 10 percent complete), then

$$CPI = 0.1/0.1 = 1$$

but

$$Max\_CPI = 0.15/0.05 = 3$$

and

$$Min\_CPI = 0.05/0.15 = 0.3333$$

So the relative uncertainty in the CPI can be as high as 200 percent. Although this exact circumstance may not ever occur, it demonstrates the nature of the problem.

Later, when $BCWP$ and $ACWP$ are both 0.5 (the activities being reported are 50 percent complete), the estimates become,

$$CPI = 0.5/0.5 = 1$$
$$Max\_CPI = 0.55/0.45 = 1.22$$
$$Min\_CPI = 0.45/0.55 = 0.82$$

So the CPI becomes more accurate as the work progresses. The problem is that now 50 percent of the effort has been expended. This limitation is a fundamental one. The only solutions are to:

1. Make the status accounting system as accurate as possible, eliminating systematic measurement errors such as the absolute error of 5 percent in the example above.

2. Use the indices on larger collections of work packages. In that way nonsystematic errors will tend to cancel, even early in the life of the work packages.

3. Ensure that the team leaders for the work packages clearly understand the work being performed; monitor the work closely; support their staff; perform their own analysis of any issues that arise, along with options for action; and include this information and recommendations in their regular status reports.

4. The software engineering project manager must support the team in these efforts, keep asking questions, understand the work, and use the scheduling system to manage the work in a meaningful way.

Finally, the earned value system should be used as an indicator of problems, not as an absolute predictor of future status.

12.5.3.4 Evaluating Future Status of Work Packages

As described earlier, the three basic metrics of an EV system can be used to detect variances in the cost or schedule performance of a project. However, the possible implications of those variances can be estimated by computing secondary metrics from the basic three, together with the planned duration of the work package, the current completion status, and the time the work package has been active.

The most commonly used predictive metrics are (1) the estimate at completion (EAC) metric, that is, the final total cost of the work package; and (2) the estimate to completion (ETC) metric, that is, the cost of completing the work package. Each of these can be derived using the current status of the work package.

Based on slightly different assumptions, it is possible to derive various estimates for the total costs to complete a work package. For packages statused using anything other than the LOE approach, the estimate of the cost to complete is given by this formula:

$$EAC = BAC/CPI$$

where BAC is the original budget at completion of the activities, excluding any reserves. This formula simply rescales the entire budget of the activities based on the cost performance index. This assumes that whatever is currently impacting the cost performance will continue to do so for the remainder of the effort. If the work package collection is homogeneous in content (that is, the processes and methods used to complete the work are the same), then this may be a reasonable assumption, but the estimate is still subject to the limitations described above. More often, an EAC computed this way serves to "flag" the problem and give a rough indication of its magnitude.

The corresponding formula for the ETC is:

$$ETC = EAC - ACWP$$

Finally, the quantity

$$ACWS/AS$$

where AS is the current actual status (that is, percent complete) of the work package, is sometimes referred to as the *burn rate*, namely, how much effort is required to improve the completion status by 1 percent. In this case it is the actual burn rate, while

$$BCWP/AS$$

would be the budgeted burn rate at the same current completion status, AS.

It is important to realize that these secondary metrics will suffer from any inaccuracies present in the primary ones. In addition, they should be used as diagnostics tools or flags, not as absolute predictors. The best way to predict the future cost and schedule status of the work package is to:

1. Use the earned value and scheduling systems, together with technical metrics, to develop an understanding of why the work package(s) is not progressing as planned.

2. Apply corrective actions to the work package(s), both to improve performance and predictability as appropriate.

3. Use that knowledge and experience to develop a new, more accurate project schedule.

12.6 Summary

Accurate, disciplined cost and schedule estimates are the foundation of any successful development project. They provide the mechanisms for creating a project schedule that can be used to manage and guide the project. Just as importantly, the requirements of the project and the product must be clearly understood so that they can be translated into the activities that make up the project schedule. A clear and comprehensive system for collecting and analyzing the status of the project must be created and used vigorously.

Several tools and methodologies are available for use in estimating the cost and schedule of software development projects on a macroscopic scale. The estimates produced by these tools will most often be the only ones available at the time a project is proposed. Estimates of this type can later be used as the starting point for the detailed cost and schedule estimates needed later when a full scheduling network is created.

The accuracy of the estimates of project costs and schedules will be significantly improved if the actual, detailed cost and schedule data from previous programs are collected and analyzed over time. To improve the estimates of future projects, historical project data should be collected and analyzed. The accuracy of estimation models will be materially improved if they are calibrated with actual data from previous programs.

The software engineering project manager is ultimately responsible for preparing the cost and schedule estimates and the activity network that makes up the complete project schedule, but he or she should involve other members of the development team in this activity. The estimates will benefit from the involvement of experienced individuals with a variety of insights and viewpoints. Finally, the project team will have a greater sense of ownership in and commitment to the schedule if the members have actively participated in its creation.

The project schedule network is the key tool used to manage the project and to judge its progress. Accurate budgets and schedules place the entire project statusing system on a firm foundation and will significantly contribute to the success of a software development project.

Finally, it must be said that the people performing the tasks of the project are the ultimate key to success. The project schedule is a means to ensure that their efforts are directed in the right directions at the right time.

Applicable Standards

IEEE Std 1045-1992. *IEEE Standard for Software Productivity Metrics.* IEEE, New York.

IEEE Std 1058-1998. *IEEE Standard for Software Project Management Plans.* IEEE, New York.

Additional References

[Albrecht & Gaffney 1983]   Albrecht, A. J. and Gaffney, J. J., Jr. (1983). "Software Function, Source Lines of Code, and Development Effort Prediction: A Software Science Validation." *IEEE Trans. on Software Engineering*, vol. SE-9, no. 6, November, pp. 639–648.

[Bennatan 1992]   Bennatan, E. M. (1992). *On Time, Within Budget, Software Project Management Practices and Techniques.* John Wiley & Sons, New York.

[Boehm 1996]   Boehm, B. (1996). "Anchoring the Software Process." *IEEE Software*, July, pp. 73–82.

[Boehm 1981]   Boehm, B. W. (1981). *Software Engineering Economics.* Prentice-Hall, Upper Saddle River, NJ.

[Boehm et al. 1995]   Boehm, B., et al. (1995). "Cost Models for Future Life Cycle Processes: COCOMO 2." *Annals of Software Engineering*, vol. 1, pp. 57–94.

[Brooks 1975]   Brooks, F., Jr. (1975). *The Mythical Man Month.* Addison-Wesley, Reading, MA.

[Brooks 1987]   Brooks, F., Jr. (1987). "No Silver Bullet: Essence and Accidents of Software Engineering." *Computer*, vol. 20, no. 4, pp. 10–19.

[Chang & Christensen 1999]   Chang, C. K., and Christensen, M. J. (1999). "A Net Practice for Software Project Management." *IEEE Software*, vol. 16, no. 6, pp. 80–88.

[Cori 1997]   Cori, K. (1997). "Fundamentals of Master Scheduling for the Project Manager." *Software Engineering Project Management.* IEEE Computer Society Press, Los Alamitos, CA, pp. 218–229.

[Fenton & Pfleeger 1997]   Fenton, N. E., and Pfleeger, S. L. (1997). *Software Metrics, A Rigorous & Practical Approach*. PWS Publishing Company, Boston.

[Fleming 2000]   Fleming, Q. (2000). *Earned Value Management*. Project Management Institute, Newtown Square, PA.

[Gaffney 1997]   Gaffney, J. E., Jr. (1997). "How to Estimate Project Schedule." *Software Engineering Project Management*. IEEE Computer Society Press, Los Alamitos, CA, pp. 257–266.

[Gaffney & Cruickshank 1997]   Gaffney, J. E., Jr., and Cruickshank, R. D. (1997). "How to Estimate Software System Size." Software Engineering Project Management. IEEE Computer Society Press, Los Alamitos, CA, pp. 246–255.

[Garmus & David 1996]   Garmus, D., and David, H. (1996). *The Software Measuring Process: A Practical Guide to Functional Measurements*. Yourdon Press, Upper Saddle River, NJ.

[Humphrey 1995]   Humphrey, W. (1995). *A Discipline for Software Engineering*, SEI Series in Software Engineering. Addison-Wesley, Reading, MA.

[Jones 1997]   Jones, C. (1997). "By Popular Demand: Software Estimating Rules of Thumb." *Software Engineering Project Management*. IEEE Computer Society Press, Los Alamitos, CA, pp. 267–269.

[Legg 1997]   Legg, D. B. (1997). "Synopsis of COCOMO." *Software Engineering Project Management*. IEEE Computer Society Press, Los Alamitos, CA, pp. 230–245.

[Parkinson 1957]   Parkinson, G. N. (1957). *Parkinson's Law and Other Studies in Administration*. Houghton-Mifflin, Boston.

[Pillai & Nair 1997]   Pillai, K. and Nair, V. S. Sukumaran Nair, "A Model for Software Development Effort and Cost Estimation." *IEEE Transactions on Software Engineering*, vol. 23, no. 8, pp. 485–497.

[Putnam & Myers 1982]   Putnam, L., and Myers, W. (1982). *Measures for Excellence*. Prentice-Hall, Upper Saddle River, NJ.

[Stutzke 1994]   Stutzke, R. D. (1994). "A Mathematical Expression of Brook's Law." *Proc. 9th Int'l. Forum on COCOMO and*

                                    Software Cost Modeling, Center for Software Engineering,
                                    University of Southern California, Los Angeles, 1994.

[Stutzke 1997]   Stutzke, R. D. (1997). "Software Estimating Technology:
                                    A Survey." *Software Engineering Project Management.*
                                    IEEE Computer Society Press, Los Alamitos, CA, pp.
                                    218–229.

[Thayer 1997]   Thayer, R., ed. (1997). *Software Engineering Project Man-
                                    agement*, 2nd ed. IEEE Computer Society Press, Los
                                    Alamitos, CA.

[Thayer & Fairley 1998]   Thayer, R., and Fairley, R. (1998). *Software Project Cost
                                    and Schedule.* Project management course presented by
                                    The Professional Development Group of the IEEE Com-
                                    puter Society.

[USAF 1978]   U.S. Air Force (1978, November). *Cost-Schedule Man-
                                    agement of Nonmajor Contracts*, AFSCP 173-3. Andrews
                                    AFB, MD: U.S. Air Force Systems Command.

Chapter 13

Software Engineering Project Management

13.1 Introduction

The software engineering project manager (PM) plays a critical role in every software development project. The importance of software project management is best illustrated in the following paragraphs extracted from two Department of Defense (DoD) reports:

> A report from the STARS initiative (STARS: Software Technology for Adaptable, Reliable Systems) states, "The manager plays a major role in software and systems development and support. The difference between success or failure—between a project being on schedule and on budget or late and over budget—is often a function of the manager's effectiveness." [DoD 1982].

> A *Report to the Defense Science Board Task Force on Military Software* states that " . . . today's major problems with software development are not technical problems, but management problems." [DoD 1987]

In recognition of this situation, the key process areas that make up the first two, most basic levels of the software engineering capability maturity model (CMM) consist almost entirely of management activities. Although the most well-known studies, such as those cited above, have drawn their information largely from government contracting (where the data are available and subject to public scrutiny), the reality is that the same situation pertains in the private, commercial sector as well, where the data are largely hidden from view behind layers of commercial interest. It has been repeatedly reported in trade magazines that in excess of 50 percent of recent major information technology projects are over budget by nearly a factor of 2 [Hoffman & King 1997]. The fact that commercial companies recognize the importance of this is reflected in the fact that fully 60 percent of recent CMM assessments have been conducted by commercial companies working outside of the government sector [SEI 2000].

The specification, design, implementation, integration, testing, fielding, and maintenance of software systems are complex tasks, requiring the planning, coordination, and execution of a multitude of diverse and yet interrelated activities. The software engineering PM is the individual responsible for this planning, coordination, and execution. The precise form the project manager's role takes depends largely on:

- The structure and capabilities of the developing organization itself (the organizational context);

- The nature of the relationship with the acquiring organization (the contractual context);

- The nature of the product and the underlying technologies (the product context);

- The project's existing infrastructure and company policies (the process context);

- The background and skills of the project team (the staffing context)

- The background and skills of the individual assigned PM responsibilities (the personal context); and

How these factors impact the PM's role is explained in subsequent sections. In general, they do not operate in isolation. That is, the structure and capabilities of the developing organization may interact with the technology of the product to produce a different set of demands on the PM than would the simple sum of the two factors separately.

In all cases, being the PM for a major project is a difficult task. The job consists of more than merely passing out assignments, collecting status, reporting to upper management and acquirers, and demanding performance from staff, although all of these things are required at one time or another. It is not a cost accounting job, but costs must always be borne in mind. For large projects supported by specialized schedulers, the PM must understand the logic behind the schedule and how the scheduling tools operate.

In the case of smaller projects and organizations the PM will often act as scheduler as well. The SEPM function is not a technological one but the impact of technology cannot be ignored. It is not a process improvement function but the role of processes and their life cycle must be considered. It is not a software quality assurance (SQA) or software configuration management (SCM) role, but these and similar systems must be understood and used to the advantage of the project. Finally, the PM task is not a human resources function, but the PM must be able to relate to, work with, lead, and inspire people.

Although the job of project manager is a difficult one, it is also rewarding. The PM is privileged to have broad visibility into the interactions of the many internal and external forces at work in a software development project, as well as broad influence over the key factors that determine the progress of the work. There is no better vantage point from which to learn the technical, managerial, and business lessons and skills that experience has to teach, provided the PM "steps up to the plate."

The following sections describe the objectives and activities of software engineering project management, the steps that should be followed in planning a software project, the guidelines that should be applied when designing and establishing the organization, how these activities relate to the other management activities of a program, and finally how the project should be "worked" on a day-to-day basis.

13.2   Objectives

In this chapter you will learn:

- The importance of software engineering project management (SEPM).

- The role of the software engineering project manager (PM). The five main functions and activities of project management.

- The planning necessary for software projects. The contents of a software engineering project management plan (SPMP).

- The relationship of the SPMP to other project plans.

- How to identify the critical factors of the project.

- How to monitor and control the critical factors.

- How to run the project while technology inexorably moves forward.

- The tools and techniques available for scheduling and tracking.

- How to decompose the project into manageable activities and tasks.

- How to select an effective team structure.

- How to map tasks onto the team structure.

- How to select the team leaders.

- How to select key technical staff.

- How to define a training plan and how to execute it.

- What motivational techniques are available and effective.

- How to assign responsibility.

- How to delegate authority.

- How to follow up on assignments and tasking.

13.3   Software Engineering Project Management Functions and Objectives

13.3.1   Universal Functions of Management

Management can be defined to be those activities and tasks undertaken by one or more persons for the purpose of planning and controlling the activities of other persons in order to achieve objectives that cannot otherwise be accomplished. Figure 13.1 depicts the classic management model as portrayed by such well-known authors in the field of management as Koontz and O'Donnell [Koontz & O'Donnell 1972] and others [Rue & Byars 1983, Cleland & King 1972, MacKenzie 1969].

The discipline of management science has recognized for some time that the five functions shown in Figure 13.1 are universal [Koontz & O'Donnell 1972, Fayol 1949]. How these functions are implemented will vary with the nature of the activity being managed, the technologies available to perform the work and manage it, the industry or profession within which it is occurring, the specific content of the work, regulatory factors, and social climate.

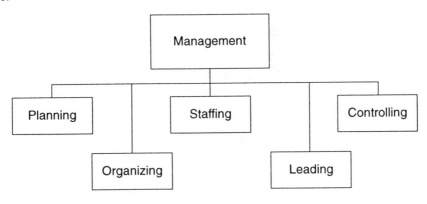

Figure 13.1: Classic Management Model

13.3.2   Definitions

Project management is thus a system of the procedures, practices, technologies, skills, and experience necessary to implement the five functions required to manage a project. If the product of a project is software, then the act of managing the project is called software engineering project management (SEPM). The manager of a software engineering project is called the software engineering project manager, the software project manager (SPM), or just plain project manager (PM).

Software engineering projects are sometimes part of larger, more comprehensive projects that include—in addition to the software—equipment (computing and otherwise), facilities, personal, training and procedures. Examples include aircraft systems, accounting systems, radar systems, inventory control systems, telecommunication systems, and e-commerce systems. These systems engineering projects are typically managed by one or more system project managers (sometimes called program managers) who manage projects composed of engineers, domain experts, scientific specialists, programmers, support personnel, and others. If the software to be delivered is a "stand-alone" software system (a system that does not involve development of other nonsoftware components), the software engineering project manager may be called the system project manager.

Note that many development projects require the functions both of a system project manager and a software engineering project manager. Thus even if no custom hardware is delivered, the project may require, in addition to the development of the software itself, that installation be accomplished, as well as the development of training materials and procedures. The scale and nature of the project, together with the capabilities of the individuals, will determine if distinct individuals are needed to satisfy these two roles.

13.3.3 Objectives of Software Engineering Project Management

Distinct from the functions for management and the methods used to perform them are the objectives of the PM. In their simplest, idealized form, these are the delivery of a product that reliably performs specified functions and is developed within stipulated cost and schedule parameters. The reality is often more complex. First, in some cases there is no explicit performance specification, whereas in others the "contract" may be informal, depending on the relationship between the product's supplier and the acquirer. Second, even when there is a specification of performance and a contract for the cost and schedule, there is usually room for different views of the relative importance of those items, along with their specific meanings. Third, one or more of the specification, cost, or schedule will change during the lifetime of the activity. Fourth, the immediate contract may not embody all of the organization's tactical or strategic objectives. Examples of these would be creation or penetration of a business market, or developing the capabilities and reputation needed to win new projects. Finally, there are the objectives of the individual PMs, which are usually a mixture of professional and personal goals.

It is manifestly impossible to enumerate all possible interactions between and within the above listed categories of objectives. Therefore, this chapter adopts the view that, in the aggregate, all of the above classes of objectives are best served by delivering a good-quality, functional product for a reasonable cost and schedule. Further, this should be done in a manner that is coherent and understandable to the developing and acquiring organizations. It rarely happens that a specification and contract are perfect. Problems arise in every development. The issue is what is done about the problems and how it is done.

Planning for and responding to problems in a way that does not unnecessarily impact the goals of quality, functionality, cost, and schedule should be the fundamental objective of the PM. Or as a wise man once said to one of the authors: "If you're late, they will be angry.

If you're over budget, they'll shout. But if you don't deliver they will never forgive you." There will, of course, be exceptions to this rule but exceptions should be recognized and treated as such. It is easier to spot the exceptions when they are framed within the context of this generic objective.

13.4   Software Engineering Project Management Functions

13.4.1   The Universal Management Functions

As discussed before, the functions of the PM fall into one of the five major categories common to all management efforts. The five categories are planning, organizing, staffing, leading, and controlling. Table 13.1 expands on the functions performed in each of the categories.

Function	Discussion
Planning	Determine the course of action, including the activities and the processes by which they will be accomplished, together with the schedule, for achieving the project objectives.
Organizing	Determine the work to be done, partition the tasks into work units, and assign work units to organizational units. Assign responsibility and authority necessary to execute the tasks.
Staffing	Select, mentor, and train people to perform their tasks.
Leading	Lead the project in a positive, open manner. Create an atmosphere that will motivate people to achieve the project objectives.
Controlling	Measure and evaluate accomplishment of tasks. Apply corrective action by application of the other four management functions.

Table 13.1: Major Management Functions

All of these functions are performed on an ongoing basis throughout the life cycle of the project. Some of them, however, are performed at greater levels of intensity at the beginning, the middle, or the end of the project. For example, the planning function dominates early in the program life cycle, when the schedule and resource requirements are developed, the project life cycle processes are defined, the software quality and configuration management plans are developed, and the software program management plan is written.

Subsequently, as deviations to the plan arise (as determined by the measurement and evaluation activities of the controlling function), elements of the project must be replanned and restructured. Likewise, the organizing function is performed most intensely early in the project but must be performed on an ongoing basis as required by the project life cycle or as an element of corrective action when adverse trends emerge.

Note that the organizing function involves the definition of tasks, the sizing of tasks, and the grouping of tasks into like activities. It does not involve people; that is a function of *staffing*.

13.4.2 Planning

Planning a software engineering project consists of the management activities that lead to selection, among alternatives, of future courses of action for the project and a plan for completing those actions.

Planning thus involves specifying the *goals* and *objectives* for a project and the *strategies*, *policies*, *plans*, and *procedures* for achieving them. "Planning is deciding in advance what to do, how to do it, when to do it, and who is to do it" [Koontz & O'Donnell 1972]. Table 13.2 reflects the details of the planning activity.

Activity	Definition or Explanation
Set objectives and goals.	Determine the desired outcome for the project.
Develop policies.	Make standing decisions on important recurring matters to provide a guide for decision making.
Forecast future situations.	Anticipate future events or make assumptions about the future; predict future results or expectations from courses of action.
Conduct risk assessment.	Anticipate possible adverse events and problem areas; state assumptions; develop contingency plans; predict results of possible courses of action.
Determine possible courses of action.	Develop, analyze, and/or evaluate different ways to conduct the project.
Make planning decisions.	Evaluate and select a course of action from among alternatives.
Plan for contractors/ subcontractors.	Establish formal agreements between project acquirers and contractor suppliers.
Prepare budgets.	Allocate estimated costs to project functions, activities, and tasks.
Develop project plans.	Establish policies, procedures, rules, tasks, schedules, and resources necessary to complete the project.

Table 13.2: Planning Activities for Software Projects

Planning functions typically occur in three contexts:

1. During the proposal or feasibility study phase,

2. At the beginning of the project, and

3. Throughout the course of the project life cycle.

The reader should appreciate that each of these three contexts impose different requirements on the PM. Thus, during the proposal phase the objective is to demonstrate to the acquirer (customer) of the software system that the candidate supplier (developer) of the system:

- Understands the technical problem and risks and what kind of management actions are necessary to reach the project goals;

- Knows and understands the statement of work (or the memorandum of understanding between the acquirer and supplier if both are in the same organization) and the product requirements, and any external events and dependencies that may impact the project;

- Has identified the required resources and has a plan to obtain them; and

- Has the discipline and capabilities to plan and execute the project on an ongoing basis.

Internal to the supplier these same considerations will allow management to gauge the risks in bidding and performing on the project.

13.4.2.1 Set Objectives and Goals

The first planning step for a software engineering project is to determine:

- The identification of what tasks are to be performed,

- How they are to be performed,

- When they are to be performed, and

- What resources are required to perform them.

13.4.2.2 Develop Policies

Policies are predetermined management decisions. The project manager may establish policies for the project to provide guidance to supervisors and individual team members in making routine decisions. For example, it might be a policy of the project that status reports from team leaders are due in the project manager's office by close of business each Thursday.

Policies can reduce the need for interaction when making decisions and provide a sense of direction for the team members. In many cases, the project manager does not develop new policies for the project, but follows the policies established at the corporate level, ensuring that the staff are aware of this decision.

13.4.2.3   Forecast Future Situations

Determining future courses of action will be based on the current status and environment as well as the PM's vision of the future. The project manager is responsible for forecasting situations that might impact the software project.

Forecasting can be broken down into two steps. In step 1 the future environment of the project is predicted, and in step 2 the response of the project to that environment is predicted. Step 1 involves prediction of future events such as availability of personnel, the inflation rate, availability of new computer hardware, and the impact these future events will have on the project. In step 2 the impact on the project, such as the specification of future expenditures of project resources and funds on the future environment, is projected. As part of this activity, the project manager is also responsible for estimating risks and developing contingency plans for countering those risks.

13.4.2.4   Conduct a Risk Assessment

Risk is the likelihood of a specified hazardous or undesirable event occurring within a specified period or circumstance. The concept of risk has two elements: the frequency, or probability, that a specified hazard might occur and the consequences of it. Risk factors must be identified and forecasts of situations that might adversely impact the software project must be prepared [Fairley & Rook 1996]. For example, serious doubt might arise that the software can be developed for the amount specified in the contract. Should this occur, the results would be a loss of profit for the company.

Contingency plans specify the actions to be taken should a risk (a potential problem) become a real problem. The risk becomes a problem when a predetermined risk indicator metric crosses a predetermined threshold. For example, the budget has been overrun by 12 percent at software specification review (SSR). The preset threshold metric was 10 percent; therefore, the appropriate contingency plan must be put in effect. Risk management is discussed in more detail in Chapter 14.

13.4.2.5   Determine Possible Courses of Action

In most projects, there is more than one way to conduct the project—but not with equal cost, equal schedule, or equal risk. It is the project manager's responsibility to examine various approaches that could achieve the project objectives and satisfy the success criteria.

For example, one approach might be very costly in terms of personnel and capital resources yet reduce the schedule dramatically. Another approach might reduce both schedule and cost but take the severe risk of being unable to deliver a satisfactory system. A third approach might be to stretch the schedule, thereby reducing the cost of the project. The manager must examine each course of action to determine advantages, disadvantages, risks, and benefits. See Chapter 7 of this book for descriptions of iterative life cycle models that are tailored to dealing with risks of this kind.

13.4.2.6   Make Planning Decisions

The project manager, in consultation with higher level management, the customer, and other appropriate parties, is responsible for selecting the best course of action for meeting project goals and objectives. The project manager is responsible for making trade-off decisions involving cost, schedule, design strategies, and risks.

The project manager is also responsible for approving the methods and tools, both technical and managerial, by which the project will be managed and the product developed. For example, will the requirements be documented using structured analysis methods or Coad's object-oriented analysis charts? Will testing be done top-down, bottom-up, or both? Which tools, techniques, and procedures will be used in planning the development schedule: PERT, CPM, workload chart, work breakdown charts, or Gantt charts [Cori 1985]?

13.4.2.7   Plan for Contractors/Subcontractors

Finally, the software management plan (SMP) must identify any elements of the project that will be performed by contractors (for projects being done in-house) or subcontractors (for project being done by a prime contractor). *This does not include individuals working as contract labor.* Rather it refers to specific, measurable, work packages whose development will be turned over to external organizations.

The relationship between the acquirer and the contractor and/or the prime contractor and the subcontractor is a formal one. It should be documented as a contract with a specification and a statement of work (SOW) for the work to be performed by the contractor/subcontractor.

Here are some typical reasons for using a contractor/subcontractor:

1. The contractor/subcontractor has specialized knowledge of either the application domain or a critical technology. They may even have an existing product that can be quickly modified to form a major component of the final system being developed.

2. The acquiring organization or the prime contractor does not have adequate staff or facilities to perform the work, while the candidate contractor/subcontractor has staff and facilities readily available.

3. The acquirer may have directed the use of the subcontractor.

4. Management may believe that managing a contractor/subcontractor through a contract, specification, and SOW is easier than managing the details internally.

5. Management may believe that managing an external contractor/subcontractor is easier than dealing with internal company personnel and resources.

The first two items are often the most appropriate reasons to use a contractor/subcontractor. However, even in these cases the contract, SOW, and specifications must be crafted with great care.

If a contractor/subcontractor is being considered because the acquirer directed it, this is usually a danger sign. If the acquirer directs that a particular subcontractor be utilized, then the PM must carefully evaluate the situation and should ensure that their company is protected under the contract. In addition, the PM must ensure that all parties apply appropriate discipline in reporting status using contractually correct channels. The foundation should be set down in the terms and conditions of the subcontract but it must be followed up on a regular basis.

Under most conditions items 4 and 5 are illusions on the part of the PM or company management: Managing a contractor or a subcontractor on a development project is usually more difficult than managing internal resources. The PM will usually have less direct authority and visibility when dealing with a contractor/subcontractor as compared to internal resources.

Among all the tasks associated with contracting, the selection of the contractor is the most critical task. If at all possible the contract should be competed between two or more firms. In preparing the terms and conditions of the subcontract the following guidelines should be applied:

- The terms and conditions of the subcontract should be consistent with those of the prime contract and the role the subcontractor will play in the program. This includes quality, configuration management, and monitoring prov .ions, as well as business requirements. Thus if the prime contract is fixed price, then so should be the subcontract.

- In particular, the reporting provisions of the subcontract, although no less stringent than those of the prime contract, must also be sufficient to control the risk that is intrinsic to the effort itself, irrespective of the acquirer's reporting requirements.

- The SOW of the contract/subcontract must clearly identify what items are to be delivered by the contractor and subcontractor and when. The prime contractor must make certain that these are consistent with and supportive of his or her own detailed schedule.

- Any items (requirements, data, equipment, etc.) needed by the contractor or subcontractor should be clearly identified, along with when they are needed.

- The acquirer or prime contractor should build in schedule reserve (e.g., setbacks) in the dates given to the contractor or subcontractor. The setbacks should not be excessive but they should be at least 10 percent of the total lapsed time.

- The contracted/subcontracted activity should be subjected to a special risk review and identified in the program's risk management plan. This may appear to be excessive or unfair to contractors/subcontractors, but it is a valid need.

- In addition to the contract and the contract SOW, a formal set of testable requirements for the subcontracted items must be in place.

- The items being subcontracted must be subjected to formal testing procedures to ensure that they satisfy the requirements.

- Adequate follow-on support should be negotiated into the subcontract as a discrete activity. This should begin during the integration of the subcontracted item into the larger system and should continue through system sell-off and installation. These items should be priced separately from the development effort.

13.4.2.8   Prepare Budgets

Budgeting is the process of identifying the cost and schedule elements of the project plan. The project manager is responsible for determining the cost and schedule for the project and allocating the budget and schedule to project tasks. Cost is the common denominator for all elements of the project plan. Requirements for personnel, computers, travel, office space, equipment, and so forth can only be compared and cost trade-offs made when these requirements are measured in terms of their monetary value. The cost and schedule estimation processes themselves are discussed in Chapter 12 of this book.

13.4.2.9   Documenting the Project Plans

In addition to other specified or required elements of the project plan, it often useful to describe the methods and technologies to be followed and used during the project. Some software system acquirers will, in fact, require that a draft version of the SMP be submitted as part of the proposal. This plan is sometimes called the software development plan (SDP). It is recommended that a draft SMP be developed during the proposal development process even if the acquirer does not require it that be submitted as part of the proposal. Doing so starts the risk management process early.

Once the contract has been awarded or the memorandum of understanding agreed to, the SPMP or SDP should be finalized or, if necessary, created. The SPMP should be a controlled document. That is, either the acquirer or the management of the supplier organization should have visibility into it and should approve any changes.

The SMP must be written with great care to ensure that:

- It contains the essential information needed to guide the management of the project.

- Both the project staff and the acquirer and the management of the supplying organization can read it so that they can share a common view of the project.

- It does not contain inappropriate levels of detail that will be subject to frequent changes during the normal course of executing the project.

- It is consistent with other documents and plans that the project will be operating under.

- It does not needlessly duplicate information in other controlled documents.

- It sets the stage for and provides a framework for the detailed execution of the project.

Section 13.5 of this chapter provides more guidance on creating the SMP. The need for consistency between the SMP and other documents and plans merits special mention at this time, in particular, the life cycle, configuration management, quality assurance, risk management, and verification and validation plans. These plans contain major elements of "how" tasks will be performed, whereas the SMP is the integration point for all of these plans. The PM must ensure that these other plans are consistent with each other and the SMP. Thus the SMP will contain a schedule for the development program, which must implement the life cycle model described in the SLCMP. Likewise, the SMP will specify certain types of technical reviews and should describe the roles of the developing, quality assurance, configuration management, and verification and validation functions in those reviews. For smaller projects and organizations these other plans can be included within the SMP.

13.4.2.10 Planning beyond the SMP

In addition to the planning that is documented in the SMP, a great deal of additional, detailed planning is necessary to execute the activities described in the SMP. Thus the SMP contains a top-level schedule showing major development phases, reviews, external dependencies, and deliveries. In the mind of acquirers this is *the* schedule. It is often contractual.

To achieve this schedule, however, a much more detailed working-level schedule is needed so that the project can be managed on a day-to-day basis. Likewise, the SMP will contain a general staffing plan, whereas the SPM and other project leaders will need a much more detailed view of staffing on an ongoing basis if the project is to succeed.

The relationship between the top-level plans in the SMP and the day-to-day, detailed, plans is simple: The SMP lays out the fundamental requirements, constraints, and strategy for the development effort. The working-level plans must comply with and implement the plans in the SMP. The SMP contains macro-plans, whereas the working plans are micro in their level of detail.

For example, the SMP would typically show the detailed design phase as one or two lines on a schedule charts, with one or two major milestone reviews of the detailed design indicated. The micro-level schedule would give visibility into the activities of individual engineers on a weekly basis as they design their software component. It would also stipulate a peer review for this component on a specific date.

Planning at this level of detail gives visibility into the progress of the project and allows the SPM to apply corrective action to problem areas before serious schedule and cost impacts develop. However, it requires that the schedule be regularly and periodically replanned as events unfold. The administrative burden of revising a formal document would make this impossible.

Thus on an ongoing basis the project must be planned and replanned. This day-to-day planning is necessary because:

- Much detailed planning (such as detailed integration planning) cannot be done until the earlier tasks have been completed (in the example of integration planning, it is necessary to know the product design to the lowest levels).

- Unplanned external events can occur.

- Unforeseen technical or personnel problems can occur inside of the program.

In other words, human foresight is incomplete and imperfect: Planning can be information limited. Therefore, detailed planning of an activity often cannot be done too far in advance. As a general rule of thumb the detailed planning of a phase of activity (such as detailed design) can be done on a preliminary basis when the immediately previous and necessary (in the sense of PERT or CPM) activity(s) starts. When those same activity(s) are between 50 and 75 percent complete, a more detailed plan of the next activity can be created. It can then be finalized when the immediately previous activities are 90 percent complete.

These are general guidelines and, like everything else, should be modified to suit the situation. For example, if the next block of activities requires specialized resources that take significant time spans to obtain, then the planning timetable should be modified so that the resources can be made available. If the resources take a long time to acquire, then the project will have to accommodate the risk of having too many or too few resources: Just because plans are needed early will not make them more accurate than the available information allows. Our motives do not change the underlying realities. On the other hand we should do the best possible with the available information.

The fact that we do not have perfect information, together with the inevitability of change, should not deter us from planning. The fact that circumstances change makes planning all the more important: The plan is a model of how the program will develop over time and, as such, is often the best instrument by which to evaluate and represent the impact of such changes.

It is also inappropriate to not change plans when it is necessary. Refusal to change a plan will often result in a serious disconnect between the plan and the reality. Of course, not all plans should change at the same rate. In particular, changes to certain plans should be viewed as major program events. It is one thing to reschedule the details of integration testing on a daily basis as problems are found. It is quite a different matter if a future staffing curve changes weekly by 10 percent. In particular, revisions to the controlled SMP should be rare, perhaps three to six during the life of a multiyear program. If not, then it is a sign that the program is writhing in agony, or that the SMP was written at too fine a level of detail—or both.

The following factors should be considered in developing and assessing the detailed project plan and schedule:

- Is the effort required to perform the tasks reasonable? First, is the amount of labor specified realistic? Second, does any single task encompass too much effort with no further decomposition when, in fact, the available knowledge would allow it to be further decomposed? The total effort of the project should determine the number of tasks identified in the plan. During initial planning these tasks might be as large as 500 hours of effort, whereas during detailed planning they should be of the order of 100 hours or less.

- Is the plan too simple or too complex? That is, is the number of interrelationships between the project tasks excessive or are key dependencies being ignored, resulting in too simplistic a plan? Are there more external dependencies than is absolutely necessary? A graphical representation (such as is provided by the CPM or PERT methodologies) of the project plan is often the best way to visualize the complexity of the plan.

- Does the plan address the key program technical and risk issues? Are they clearly represented in the plan?

- Does the plan clearly show the fundamental process activities? Will the process issues be manageable using the plan?

13.4.3 Organizing

Organizing a software engineering project involves developing an effective and efficient organizational structure for assigning and completing project tasks and establishing the authority and responsibility relationships among the tasks. Table 13.3 provides an outline of the activities that must be accomplished by the project manager in organizing a project.

Activity	Definition or Explanation
Identify and group project functions, activities, and tasks.	Define, size, and categorize the project work.
Describe organizational responsibilities and interfaces.	Describes the project organization's internal and external interfaces and dependency on external groups.
Select project structures.	Select appropriate structures to accomplish the project and to monitor, control, communicate, and coordinate.
Create position descriptions.	Establish titles, job descriptions, and job relationships for each project role.
Define responsibilities and authority.	Define responsibilities for each organizational position and the authority to be granted for fulfillment of those responsibilities.
Establish position qualifications.	Define qualifications for persons to fill each position.

Table 13.3: Organizing Activities for Software Projects

13.4.3.1 Identify and Group Project Function, Activities, and Tasks

Equal to the activity of planning—which defines the tasks to be done, establishes the amount of effort required to complete the task, and produces a schedule sequencing the project tasks and events—is the activity of determining the project organization or structure.

The placement or recruiting of the staff to fill the project organization is referred to as *staffing*, which is covered in a later section.

The purposes of the project structure are as follows:

- To focus the efforts of many on a specific set of goals;

- To facilitate communication between organizational entities;

- To create a positive, supportive environment in which the project staff can work; and

- To provide visibility into the activities, status, and needs of the project.

The factors that influence the structure of the project organization include these:

- The structure of the parent organization,

- The nature and architecture of the product itself,

- The personnel available,

- The contract,

- The duration and scale of the project,

- The cost accounting and other management systems of the parent organization, and

- The life cycle processes of the project.

13.4.3.2 Describe Organizational Relationships and Interfaces

Most projects have a very large number or separate but interrelated actives, tasks, and entities. (See Figure 13.2 for an example of some of the large number of possible internal and external interfaces.)

These interfaces have various degrees of authority associated with them. For example, configuration management control when and under what circumstances a controlled item can be modified. Another example might be that system engineering provides the top-level requirements to the software system engineering. And technical support provides the final "say so" on the customer documentation.

In this regard it is important to distinguish between two views of the project team structure: the *operational* and the *administrative*. In the operational view, the team and the other project resources (computers, buildings, and so on) form a machine that executes the project schedule, accepting requirements and needs at its input and delivering a product at its output. It implements the project life cycle model.

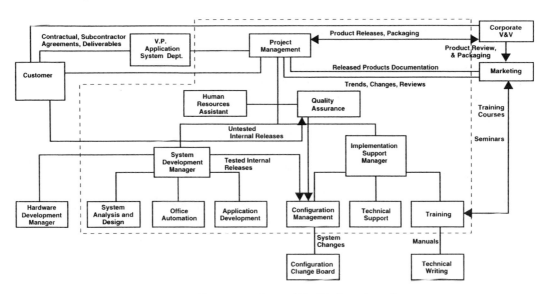

Figure 13.2: Example of Possible Project Interfaces

In the second view the team is an authority structure, often represented by an organization chart, in which tasking flows down from the top and the results of completed tasks flow up. The situation is directly analogous to viewing a software system from either a data flow or a structure chart perspective. Both views have validity but the informed PM, as a leader, knows when to use each view to maximum advantage at any point in the project's development.

Because software development projects are often performed within the context of larger organizations, which may rely heavily on the administrative view in their operation and support systems, there may be a natural tendency to view the structure of the project team solely from the perspective of authority. This can generate needless friction between the project management personnel and the company infrastructure groups and can divert attention from the true purposes of the project and the parent organization. This should be avoided by clearly showing the relationship between the organization of the project and its purposes, and those of the parent organization.

For example, if the project is being executed within a large, multiproject organization, the PM will often have to structure the team around preexisting company structures and resources. The PM may come from one of the business areas or from engineering. The choice made often depends on company culture. The operational project staff, in any case, will come from engineering, quality assurance, and configuration management departments, whereas the management support staff would come from accounting and scheduling departments.

It is easy to become confused about the relationship between the company organization and that of the project team, since the same type of graphic, an organization chart, represents both structures. If you keep in mind that the structures are used to perform very different processes on an operational basis then the confusion is lessened.

The company organizational chart is used to manage the parent organization on a continuing basis, beyond the life of any single project. Depending on the maturity and size of the organization the functions of technology and new business development, training, and such activities that are necessary for the long term success of the operation and its programs will often be performed outside of any particular project.

Normally an individual program manager is not responsible for the administrative operation of the company infrastructure. In anything but the smallest projects, guiding and leading a project to completion is a full-time job. Likewise, the management of the parent organization "backbone" (sometimes called functional or resource management) is a full-time job as well. This approach is often called the matrix project organization.

The relationship between project and functional management is critical, no matter how responsibilities are partitioned. Without successful projects there is no reason to have a parent organization. Likewise, without a parent organization the projects will be starting from scratch, with increased costs, stresses, and delays in obtaining resources. A mature parent organization should also provide systems that satisfy human resources, accounting, and other infrastructure needs of the projects. Ideally, the parent organization should provide institutional development processes.

Hence the PM must seek the active support of the functional managers, so that the required resources can be applied to the project. In their turn, the functional managers must support projects consistent with the organization goals. Finally, the executive management of the company must ensure that those goals are correctly identified, implemented, and communicated within the organization. Whether or not this ideal is achieved, the PM must be an effective advocate for the interests of their program, in addition to their other duties. In order to be an effective advocate the PM must:

- Adopt a direct, professional attitude;

- Be an effective communicator;

- Understand the project technology, business objectives, and risks;

- Understand the broader organizational objectives and infrastructure systems; and

- Understand the role his or her program plays in the company.

13.4.3.3 Select a Project Structure

After identifying and grouping project tasks, the project manager must select an organizational structure. A software development project can be organized using one of several different and overlapping organizational types including these examples:

- *Conventional organization structure:* line or staff organization;

- *Project organization structure:* functional, project, or matrix; or

- *Team structure:* Egoless, chief programmer, or hierarchical.

The project manager may not have the luxury of selecting the best project organizational type, since this may be determined by policy at the corporate level. Regardless of who determines the organizational structure, the chosen structure should match the needs and goals of the project with an environment that facilitates communication between the organizational entities. The following paragraphs describe these organizational considerations.

Conventional Organizational Structures

A *line* organization has the responsibility and authority to perform the work that represents the primary mission of the larger organizational unit. In contrast, a *staff* organization is a group of functional experts that has responsibility and authority to perform special activities that help the line organization do its work. All organizations in a company are either line or staff in this model. (See Figure 13.3 for an illustration of a line organization.)

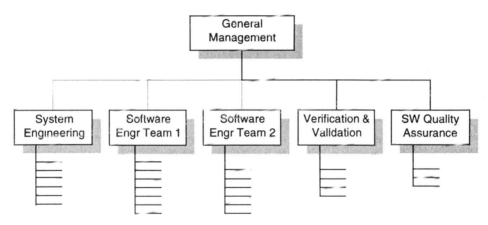

Figure 13.3: A Line Organization in a Software Development Organization

Project Organization Structures

A project structure is a temporary organizational form that has been established to develop and build a system that is too big to be done by one or, at most, a few people. In a software engineering project, the system to be built is a software system. A project structure can be superimposed on a line or staff organization.

- *Functional project organization:* One type of project organization is a *functional* organization. This is a project structure built around a software engineering function or group of similar functions. A project is accomplished either within a functional unit or, if multifunctional, by two or more functional units. The project is accomplished by passing the work products from function to function as the project passes through

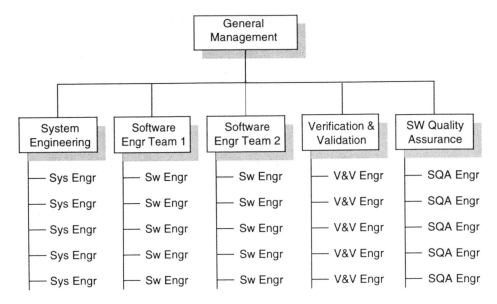

Figure 13.4: Functional Project Organization

the life cycle phases. (See Figure 13.4 for an illustration of a functional project organization.)

- *Project organization:* Another type of project organization is built around each specific project; a project manager is given the responsibility, authority, and resources for conducting the project [Middleton 1967]. (The project organization is sometimes called a *projected* or *projectized* organization to get away from the term "project project organization."). The manager must meet project goals within the resources of the organization. The project manager usually has the responsibility to hire, discharge, train, and promote people within the project. Note that the software project manager has total control over the project and the assigned software personnel. (See Figure 13.5 for an illustration of a project organization.)

- *Matrix project organization:* The third project organization type is the *matrix* organization (sometimes called matrix project organization), which is a composite of the functional organization and the project organization [Stuckenbruck 1981]. The project manager is given responsibility and authority for completing the project. The functional managers provide the resources needed to conduct the project. In a matrix organization, the project manager usually does not have the authority to directly hire, discharge, train, or promote personnel within his project. Because each individual worker is "supervised" by two separate managers, the system is sometimes called the "two-boss" system. (See Figure 13.6 for an illustration of a matrix project organization.)

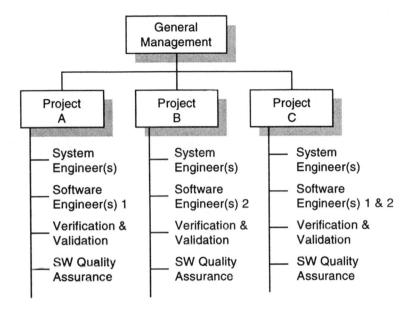

Figure 13.5: Project Organization

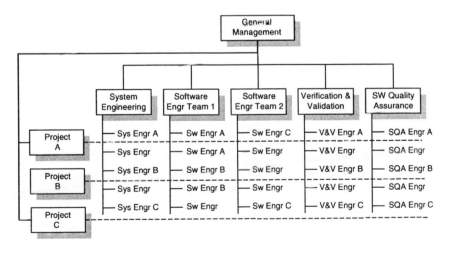

Figure 13.6: Matrix Project Organization

Team Structures

Within the larger organizational structures discussed above, a software development project is typically organized around a number of software engineering teams. These teams usually consist of five to seven members. Examples of structures for these teams include *egoless programming teams*, *chief programmer teams*, and *hierarchical teams* [Mantei 1981].

13.4.3.4 Create Position Descriptions

Once the tasks are identified, sized, and grouped, and the organizational structure has been specified, the project manager must create job titles and position descriptions specific to the project. These should not be confused with more general titles and descriptions used by the organization's human resources function. Developing the position descriptions of the project team and filling those positions must be done with great care and attention to detail. Personnel skills are usually recognized as being the single greatest influence on software productivity. There are two parts to optimizing this influence, namely, developing project position descriptions that appropriately reflect the needs of the project and then filling those positions with the best possible staff.

The needs of the project are derived from the project plans, in particular, the software life cycle process plan and the detailed project schedule. The software life cycle process plan determines the technical skills and experience needed to perform the project tasks. The detailed project schedule describes the timing and numbers of personnel needed to perform those tasks.

When developing the position descriptions for the project, inappropriate specificity must be avoided. Thus for a project with a 2-year projected schedule, it is not productive to specify experience with a tool for which any journeyman software engineer can be trained to operate in 4 days. The basic capabilities of the engineer are more important than such a skill: The learning curve for such a tool can be planned for. On the other hand, if the project has a 2-month schedule, this is a different matter. Either an engineer who is already facile with the tool should be selected or an engineer must be trained and become facile in advance of the project need.

Finally, the PM must not create organizational confusion. Thus the position or job descriptions for the project team must be consistent with and, indeed, leverage to the maximum extent possible, any institutional position or job descriptions. In particular, care must be taken not to transgress any legal constraints imposed by government entities having jurisdiction over human resource issues.

As an example, consider a hypothetical networked project whose acquirer is in the airline parts distribution business. Specimen position descriptions are presented below. They will have generic components as well as project-specific ones. The generic components are more typical of those a multiproject, functional engineering organization would utilize. The generic elements are, with modification, drawn from the Volume 13, No. 1, February/March 1996 issue of *High Technology Careers* magazine.

- *Project managers:* Responsible for system development and implementation within major functional areas. Direct the efforts of software engineers, analysts, programmers, and other project personnel.

- *Software system engineers:* Design and develop software to drive computer systems. Develop firmware, drivers, and specialized software such as graphics, communications controllers, operating systems, and user-friendly interfaces. Work closely with hardware engineers and applications and systems programmers; requires understanding of all aspects of the product.

- *Scientific/engineering programmers, programmer-analysts:* Perform detailed program design, coding, testing, debugging, and documentation of scientific/engineering computer applications and other applications that are mathematical in nature. May assist in overall system specification and design.

- *Software verification and validation engineers:* Able to develop independent V&V plans, procedures, and tools. Able to develop test procedures and develop test cases for both real-time and non-real-time software systems.

- *Software quality assurance engineers:* Able to develop software development procedures and standards. Conducts audits of software systems and overview tests. Will work closely with independent V&V teams.

13.4.3.5 Define Responsibilities and Authority

Responsibility is the obligation to fulfill commitments. *Authority* is the right to make decisions and exert power. It is often stated that authority can be delegated, but responsibility cannot. Koontz and O'Donnell [Koontz & O'Donnell 1972] support this view by defining responsibility as "the obligation owed by subordinates to their supervisors for exercising authority delegated to them in a way to accomplish results expected."

Responsibility and authority for organizational activities or tasks should be assigned to the organizational position at the time it is created or modified. The project manager is assigned and in turn assigns the responsibilities and the corresponding authorities to the various organizational positions within the project.

13.4.3.6 Establish Position Qualifications

Position qualifications must be identified for each position in the project. Position qualifications are established by considering issues such as these: What types of individuals do you need for your project? How much experience is necessary in the area of the application? How much education is required: BS in computer science, MS in artificial intelligence? How much training is required, either before or after the project is initiated? Does the applicant need to know C, C++, Java, or some other programming language? The establishment of proper and accurate position qualifications will make it possible for the manager to correctly staff the project.

Some short examples of typical position qualifications for software engineering titles and positions are illustrated here:

- *Project managers:* Background in successful systems implementation, advanced industrial knowledge, awareness of current computer technology, intimate understanding of user operations and problems, and proven management ability. Minimum requirements are four years of significant system development and project management experience.

- *Software system engineers:* Seven years of experience in aerospace applications designing real-time control systems for embedded computers. Experience with Ada preferred; BS in computer science, engineering, or related discipline.

- *Scientific/engineering programmers, programmer-analysts:* Three years of experience in programming aerospace applications, control systems, and/or graphics. One-year minimum with FORTRAN, assembly, or C programming languages. Large-scale or mini/micro hardware exposure and system software programming experience desired. Minimum requirements include undergraduate engineering or math degree.

- *Verification and validation engineer:* Minimum of three or more years of experiences in one or more aspects of V&V for real-time systems. Must be able to work independently of the development teams. MS degree in software engineering preferred. Salary commensurate with experience.

- *Software quality assurance engineer:* Minimum of three years of experience working in software QA environment. Some CM experience desirable; BS or MS in computer science with specialty in software engineering. Travel required.

13.4.4 Staffing

Staffing a software engineering project consists of all of the management activities that are required to fill (and keep filled) the positions that are defined in the project organizational structure. This includes selecting candidates for the positions and training or otherwise developing them to accomplish their tasks effectively. The staffing activity includes terminating project personnel when necessary.

Staffing is not the same as organizing; staffing consists of filling the roles specified in the organizational structure through selection, training, and development of personnel. The objective of staffing is to ensure that project roles are filled by personnel who are qualified (both technically and temperamentally) to occupy them. Table 13.4 provides an outline of the activities and tasks that must be performed when staffing projects.

The selection of project personnel is one of the most critical management activities. Depending on the parent organization structure and the size of the project, the PM will either directly select the personnel or will task others to do so based on project needs. In either case the parameters used to guide the selection of the project personnel must be determined. These parameters are most commonly:

Activity	Definition or Explanation
Fill project positions.	Select, recruit, or promote qualified people for each project position.
Assimilate newly assigned personnel.	Orient and familiarize new people with the organization, facilities, and tasks to be done on the project.
Educate or train personnel.	Make up deficiencies in position qualifications through training and education.
Provide for general development.	Improve knowledge, attitudes, and skills of project personnel.
Evaluate project personnel.	Record and analyze the quantity and quality of project work as the basis for personnel evaluations. Set performance goals and appraise personnel periodically.
Compensate project personnel.	Provide wages, bonuses, benefits, or other financial remuneration commensurate with project responsibilities and performance.
Terminate assignments.	Transfer or separate project personnel as necessary.

Table 13.4: Staffing Activities for Software Projects

- The years of experience,

- The technical skills required,

- The educational background required, and

- The personal skills required.

Together these parameters, along with others, make up what is commonly referred to as a *position description* (or *job description*). This term is usually used within the human resources function of medium to large sized companies, in the context of more generic positions within the company's structure. Hence confusion is possible between the personnel requirements of a particular project and the generic, institutional position requirements. Care must be taken to clarify the distinction between positions in the company administrative structure and those in the project team: The position descriptions of a project must be immediately applicable to the project goals, whereas the position descriptions of the institution are usually used to document career progression as the employee "moves up the ladder" in a career that will, in all likelihood, span multiple programs over time.

To avoid this problem, the program manager must understand the company's human resources (HR) systems and their nomenclature. If the term *position descriptions* is already used within HR it may be advisable to use the term *program task requirements* or something similar that captures the intent without creating confusion.

It is not enough to specify that an individual have experience with a certain tool, method, or process. To specify the ability required in the critical skills, a required number of years of experience in the application of the skill is often stated. This is, at best, an indirect indicator but it is the simplest way to specify the expected ability of the individuals who are being considered for the position. Three to five years of experience is a very common requirement for most technical jobs.

Finally, the personality attributes required for the position must be considered. These depend very much on the position and its relationship to other groups. Thus a requirements engineer must be able to communicate effectively and openly with the acquirer and the project designers. A software application engineer may have to work in a small group but is primarily performing solitary tasks that require the ability to work alone for extended periods. In that case the person chosen must be able to accept tasking and deliver results on a reliable basis.

13.4.4.1 Fill Project Positions

The project manager is responsible for ensuring that the positions that were established during organizational planning for the project are filled in a timely manner. In staffing any software project, the following factors should be considered.

- *Intelligence:* Does the candidate have the capability to learn, to take on challenging tasks, to find creative solutions, and adapt to changing environments? This factor often drives all others.

- *Education:* Does the candidate have the necessary minimum level of formal education for the job? For more senior individuals this is often offset by experience.

- *Skills:* Do the candidates have an acceptable level of experience? Is it of the right type and variety? Have they worked on similar projects before? Did they see those projects through and learn from their mistakes? Are they experienced or trained in the language, methodology, and equipment to be used, and the application area of the software system?

- *Character:* Is the candidate motivated to do the job, work for the project, work for the company, and work honestly and openly while working on the assignment? Does the candidate demonstrate loyalty to the project, the company, and to the decisions of management?

- *Personality:* Is the candidate a self-starter, willing to carry a task through to the end without excessive direction? Does the candidate fit in with the current staff? Are there conflicts that need to be resolved?

Obviously, the relative importance of these factors will vary with the position being filled. Also, what is expected from a freshly graduated engineer should be different from what is expected from someone with five years of applicable experience.

Deficiencies in any of these factors can be offset by strengths in other factors. For example, deficiencies in education can be offset by experience, a particular type of training, or enthusiasm for the job. Serious deficiencies mean the individuals should be utilized only if there is no other option, and then only if their performance can be improved in a timely manner.

This discussion of staffing would be incomplete without a discussion of two important topics: the use of part-time project staff and contract labor. Members of the project staff are part time when their efforts are spread across multiple projects. In general this should be avoided, because it tends to dilute commitment and effort available to each of the projects. It often results in two or more PMs being unhappy and the employee feeling uncomfortable.

Such spreading of staff across multiple projects is generally unfair to the projects and to the staff involved and should be avoided. Like any other rule, however, on some occasions it is appropriate to break it. For example, if a highly specialized skill is needed on an occasional, non-time-critical basis on several projects then "spreading" the staff member across multiple projects can work but still requires extra management attention. A better option would be to schedule each projects' tasks over a shorter time period (assuming this can be done realistically) so that it can be completed by someone working full time rather than part time. Doing so gives the employees a sense of having fulfilled their obligations professionally and simplifies the management task. However, this may not be achievable in all situations.

In other words, treat such multitasking of staff as a necessary evil. But if needed, do it right. If done right, it can give staff a broader range of project experience quicker, although that should usually not be a reason to do it.

Last, staff hired under contract labor agreements (sometimes called consulting, body shopping, agency labor, or temporary labor) can be used to satisfy staffing needs. Classically the reason for using such outside, temporary staff is some combination of two factors: (1) Highly specialized skills are needed that are not available in-house, or (2) inadequate numbers of personnel are available for a short-term need.

When utilizing temporary, contract staff other factors must be considered:

- Does the work to be performed by the temporary staff require excessive training in procedures and processes that are specific to the company or project? If so, it may not be economic. It may still be necessary.

- Will the project duration and the outlook for the company allow the contract labor to be replaced with permanent company staff later? If so, who will train and mentor the new employees? Is the schedule used to make this judgment realistic?

- Is the relationship between the company and the contractor well understood and appropriate under the local labor laws? Have agreements protecting the companies' proprietary data and the intellectual property rights of both parties been executed, consistent with applicable laws?

- Are the total compensation packages of the contract and permanent staff reasonably consistent? Without exposing private information the PM must be able to defend this decision. Usually contractors earn more on an hourly basis but do not receive many of the other forms of compensation provided to regular employees.

- If the position of the contracted individual is especially critical, can a retention clause be inserted in the agreement? If the individual is contracting through an agency does the agreement allow, assuming both the individual and the company are in agreement, for the individual to be converted to a regular employee? Are the terms financially reasonable?

- Is the termination clause explicit and consistent with local law, given all of the above considerations? Contract labor can normally be terminated at the convenience of the hiring company but a compromise may be needed if a retention clause is required for other reasons.

Finally, in the event that an external agency is used to hire temporary staff, the PM must ensure that the project/company retains the right to interview the individuals proposed by the agency, as well as making the final selection of individuals.

13.4.4.2 Assimilate Newly Assigned Personnel

The manager must ensure that the staff are familiarized with the project objectives and schedules, and with any project procedures, facilities, and plans necessary to ensure their effective integration into the project. For staff who are already part of the parent organization this is usually all that is required.

In many companies, usually one or more general orientation programs are available for assimilating new hires. These are commonly the responsibility of a functional organization outside of the project. The human resources organization usually performs a very general orientation, while the functional department will train and orient new hires in their processes and practices. Arrangements should be made for suitable orientation of any contract personnel as well.

13.4.4.3 Educate or Train Personnel

Education and training are different concepts. *Education* teaches basic principles, theory, and the underlying concepts of a discipline, thereby establishing a long-term foundation for current and future work. *Training* teaches a skill or the knowledge necessary to use, operate, or make something. The skill is typically needed in the near future. Indeed, if not used in the near term the skill will atrophy.

It is not always possible to recruit or transfer employees with exactly those skills needed for a particular project. Therefore, the manager must ensure that the staff are (most commonly) trained and (sometimes) educated so that they meet the project requirements. Training methods include on-the-job training, formal courses developed in-house or by vendors, courses available through local universities, colleges, or schools, or self-study.

Individual projects are more likely to have training rather than education needs, while functional organizations, whose personnel will support many projects during their career, will usually be responsible for education activities. As always, however, exceptions are dictated by circumstances. In many large organizations education and training in general company procedures, policies, processes, and common toolsets are provided to all staff by a functional organization.

Project-specific training may also be provided by these organizations but it may not be, depending on circumstances. In the case of contract labor, the training should be that which is needed precisely to perform the function for which the contract staff were contracted. Ideally, this should be restricted to the applicable processes, processes, and procedures. The individuals who are contracted should already be familiar with the necessary tools and technical methods.

Many organizations as part of International Standards Organization (ISO) or Software Engineering Institute (SEI) initiatives require that each individual have a *training plan* that specifies career education and training goals and the steps each person will take in achieving those goals.

13.4.4.4 Provide for General Development of Project Staff

In addition to education and training, the organization must ensure that general capabilities of the project staff improve. Allocating the time to perform general development will often conflict with immediate project goals. The company management team, including the PM, must balance the value of the general improvement of the organizational capability with the needs of the program. The PM may require assistance from other managers within the parent organization in dealing with this smoothly. Of particular concern is the initiation of a general development activity midstream in a project with a short, critical schedule. Counterbalancing this immediate concern is that, if the long-term needs of the staff and the organization are not met, the capabilities needed for any individual project will erode.

One of the purposes of providing general development for the employee is to improve overall organizational effectiveness. For example, courses and degree programs at the local university in appropriate disciplines, funded by the company, will broaden the skill base available to the company and improve employee morale, thereby aiding in employee retention.

In companies organized functionally the ultimate approval of such arrangements is usually not within the authority of the PM, but their support will be critical in arranging the time to execute the development program. In return, the functional organization may have to supply additional staff so that the participating employee can commit the time necessary to the general development activity.

Contract labor is usually specifically excluded from general development training, due to the long-term intent of such training.

13.4.4.5   Evaluate Project Personnel

The project manager must periodically evaluate the performance of personnel working on their project. This occurs in two ways. First, in the course of normal, day-to-day work the PM, together with any intermediate managers or group leaders, should provide continuous feedback to the project staff on their performance and that of their groups. This should occur naturally as part of the controlling activity. Each layer of management should communicate directly and clearly to those individuals who report to them on an objective, project-oriented basis. This ensures that the people are reminded of the importance of their work to the project and that performance problems are noted early. Individuals working as contract labor should be treated the same as regular employees in this regard.

Second, depending on the structure and culture of the parent organization, the PM will provide observations on the performance of the staff to their "home" organizations. The management of the home group then develops the formal performance appraisal and 'delivers' it to the employee in an interview. In some cases the PM, again dependent on the parent organization's structure, policy, and procedures, will develop and deliver the performance appraisal. In either case the appraisal provides feedback to staff members concerning the positive and negative aspects of their performance.

Appraisals should be done at regular intervals as required by company policy. The PM should exercise care to comply with any applicable labor law requirements. The human resources function of the parent organization should be aware of any constraints in this area and should be consulted.

Individuals working as contract labor are usually not given an annual review by the project manager but are evaluated by their own immediate project supervisor.

13.4.4.6   Compensate Project Personnel

Compensation is commonly made up of three components:

1. *Wages and benefits:* Wages are the direct payment to the employees in return for their labor. They may be paid on an hourly or salaried basis. This is largely determined by local labor laws. Benefits are typically made up of such items as medical insurance, company contributions to savings plans, and disability insurance. The PM should expect to have limited influence over benefits, because they are usually a fixed multiplier of the employee pay within a given labor grade, with the exception, in some locales, of small, single-project organizations. The other exception is contract labor, which usually does not receive benefits directly from the organization using their services.

2. *Incentive compensation:* The most common forms of incentive compensation are bonuses and stock options. In some cases overtime pay can be given to employees

who do not normally receive it, again, depending on labor laws. Incentives may be offered to contract labor but this must be clarified in their agreement and, of course, must be consistent with any relevant laws.

3. *Perks (the abbreviation of perquisites):* Perks include such items as a reserved parking spot, a better office, education at the local university, or involvement in an industry-wide activity. The PM may have considerable latitude in this area, especially if the substance of the perk benefits the program. Otherwise the scope of action of the PM will depend on the culture of the parent organization.

The exact degree of influence the PM can exercise over each of these areas will be determined largely by the structure, policies, and procedures of the parent organization. In general, the PM will have more influence over the last two items. In the case of individuals working under labor contracts, the PM may have more latitude over the rate of pay but the total compensation should be reasonably consistent with that of regular employees having similar skills and experience.

13.4.4.7 Terminate Project Assignments

Because project managers are responsible for assigning tasks, they must also be responsible for the termination of tasks. Termination of tasks occur naturally as the work of the project is completed. Sometimes, however, tasks are terminated before they are completed. This can happen if the acquirer decides the project should cease working on certain tasks and, as a result, issues a so-called "Stop Work" notice, or if the individual assigned the task is unable to complete it.

In the former case the PM must clearly communicate to the project staff the reasons for the Stop Work order. Failure to do so can result in serious morale problems. In the latter case of an individual who is unable to complete a task, it should be assigned to someone else who can. It may be that the task was unsuitable for the original individual but if a pattern of failure emerges such failures should be documented when they occur and the matter dealt with promptly. Individuals who are unable to perform useful work on a project should be removed from the project. Depending on the situation their ultimate fate may range from reassignment to a more suitable project, downgrading of their position within the company, or separation. The direct involvement of the PM may be limited in the case of outright separation but at the very least the PM has the responsibility to document the nonperformance.

One of the advantages of the matrix project organizational structure is the support it provides the project manager in moving individuals between jobs, as well as providing continuity of knowledge between similar projects. Unsatisfactory individuals can be sent back to their function manager with very little justification and a recommendation that the individuals be reassigned to a different project that can make better use of their skills. On the other hand, this can also be one of the major disadvantages of the matrix organizational structure. A very valuable worker can be removed from a project by the functional manager to work on a project that the matrix manager (correctly or not) perceives as more important with a minimum of justification.

Usually, contract workers can be terminated at any time but this must be done consistent with their agreement. The reasons should be the same (that is, the work is done or the individual does not perform) as for regular employees, but when the current project work is completed the company has no obligation to place the individual elsewhere in the organization. Likewise, if the contracting individuals do not perform, the company has no obligation to try to improve their performance.

13.4.5 Leading

Leading a project consists of motivating and guiding project personnel so that they come to understand and contribute to the achievement of project goals. Once subordinates are trained and oriented, the project manager has a continuing responsibility to clarify their assignments, guide them toward improved performance, and motivate them to work with enthusiasm and confidence toward project goals. As a result, leading relies heavily on interpersonal skills.

Leading is sometimes considered to be synonymous with directing. Compare, for example, Koontz and O'Donnell [Koontz & O'Donnell 1972] with Koontz, O'Donnell, and Weihrich [Koontz et al. 1984]. Leading a project involves providing leadership to the project, providing day-to-day supervision of the project personnel, delegating authority to the lower organizational entities, coordinating activities of the project members, facilitating communications between project members and those outside the project, resolving conflicts, managing change, and documenting important decisions. Table 13.5 provides an outline of the project management activities that must be accomplished by project managers to lead their projects.

Leadership is one of the most important functions performed by the PM. Without good leadership the most carefully planned program will miscarry. Leadership has two primary components: substance and style. *Substance* is what the PM does about problems and issues. *Style* is the environment the PM creates as he or she goes about attacking the problems.

13.4.5.1 Provide Vision and Direction

There are similarities and differences between these two related concepts. Vision usually refers to a strategic view of where the project is going and how it will get there, whereas direction is the tactical assignment of staff to perform specific tasks. Vision helps to motivate the staff and provides them with a global conceptual framework in which to perform their assigned tasks. Direction provides the staff with their immediate tasks.

Common elements of vision are:

- The importance of the customer's needs,

- The value of the product being built,

Activity	Definition or Explanation
Provide vision.	Provide a conceptual or strategic view of where the project is going and how it will get there.
Provide direction.	Provide day-to-day instructions, guidance, and discipline to help project members fulfill their assigned duties.
Provide leadership.	Create an environment in which project members can accomplish their assignments with enthusiasm and confidence.
Supervise personnel.	Provide day-to-day instructions, guidance, and discipline to help project members fulfill their assigned duties.
Motivate personnel.	Provide a work environment in which project personnel can satisfy their psychological needs.
Coordinate activities.	Combine project activities into effective and efficient arrangements.
Delegate authority.	Allow project personnel to make decisions and expend resources within the limitations and constraints of their roles.
Facilitate communication.	Ensure a free flow of correct information among project members.
Resolve conflicts.	Encourage constructive differences of opinion and help resolve the resulting conflicts.
Manage changes.	Stimulate creativity and innovation in achieving project goals.
Document directing decisions.	Document decisions involving delegation of authority, communication and coordination, conflict resolution, and change management.

Table 13.5: Leading Activities for Software Projects

- The correctness of how it is being built, and

- The fit of the product into broader company strategy.

These elements should all be familiar, because this information should be present in the detailed project schedule and plan in either their original or revised forms. What is direction then? It is nothing less than issuing the final orders to perform the tasks that have been defined and scheduled as part of the planning function. Thus vision provides the "big picture" motivation and goals, while direction keeps the program moving forward on a day-to-day basis.

13.4.5.2 Provide Leadership to the Project Team

The project manager provides leadership to the project team by interpreting plans and requirements to ensure that everybody on the project team is working toward common goals. Leadership results from the power of the leaders and their ability to guide and influence individuals. The project managers' power can be derived from their leadership position; this is called *positional power*. The project managers' power can also be derived from their own "charm," sometimes called *charisma*; this is called *personal power*.

A good leader is able to align the personal goals of subordinates with organizational goals of the project. Problems can arise when the project manager who has only positional power comes into conflict with a subordinate who has personal power over the project members. For a discussion of different uses of power by managers, see Boyatzis [Boyatziz 1971].

13.4.5.3 Supervise and Motivate Personnel

After the project personnel have been assigned and begun their tasks, they must be supervised and motivated. *Supervision* is largely an administrative and mechanical function, whereas *motivation* is a personal and emotional one. *Motivation* is the individuals' drive to satisfy their psychological needs

The tasks of supervision are:

- Following up on assignments,

- Recording status,

- Giving advice to assist the staff in overcoming difficulties, and

- Redirecting staff as required overcoming difficulties.

The tasks of motivation are:

- Keeping the staff focused on the project and product,

- Ensuring that the staff understands that their efforts are important and valued,

- Continually updating and communicating the project schedule to the staff,

- Providing a vision for the product and project, and

- Ensuring that the goals of the project and the individual are in harmony and communicate that fact to the staff.

13.4.5.4 Coordinate Project Activities

In the ideal condition project tasks, once set in motion, would each be performed independently of one another. This would allow each work group or individual engineer to perform clear-cut, well-defined tasks with maximum efficiency. Under this condition no coordination would be required: Just working through the detailed program plan and schedule would ensure completion. The reality, of course, is very different.

Project tasks are almost always interrelated in subtle ways that may or may not be represented on the detailed project schedule. The schedule network will show the primary dependencies between tasks, such as between the design and implementation of an item. The project team should have visibility into the schedule. There are also secondary but important dependencies. Whether the relationships between tasks are explicitly recognized or not they must be dealt with. This is the simplest, clear-cut form of coordination. Finally, unexpected events occur. In this mode the PM must exercise considerable leadership by clarifying the problem, identifying technical and programmatic options, replanning the relevant parts of the program with the staff, and launching the new efforts. This must be done while not disrupting other parts of the project that could otherwise continue as planned

13.4.5.5 Delegate Authority

To complete tasks, subordinates need appropriate levels of authority. The PM must ensure that individuals have enough authority to do their work effectively and creatively. Such authority may be temporary or permanent. Some individuals may be delegated authority because of their position. This is usually done through their position description. If the authority is being delegated on a medium-term basis, a letter delegating the authority should be written and circulated inside and, as required, outside of the project. If the authority span of the authority is short term and is localized to a small part of the project organization, then it can be done verbally, although this should be done with care.

The following considerations should be applied to the delegation of authority:

- When done appropriately and positively it usually motivates personnel. It shows the project staff that management trusts them.

- If done inappropriately, it can demotivate personnel. If done excessively or communicated inadequately, the staff may perceive that management does not understand the project or, worse, is dodging its responsibility.

- The authority should be delegated consistent with the life cycle processes of the project.

Successful managers will:

- Delegate everything that they possibly can to their subordinates.

- Have confidence in both their own abilities and those of their subordinates.

- Follow up with subordinates and assist them as needed to accomplish their tasks.

Many software development managers came up "through the ranks" and were former software engineers or programmers. It can be very difficult for these former designers and implementers to recognize that they are now managing those activities and are not directly building the product. However, by adopting the proper mind-set and with coaching from more senior managers they can soon learn the importance of *delegation of authority*.

13.4.5.6 Facilitate Communication

Communication is the key to keeping the project moving in the right direction; that is, progressing per the plan in accordance with the life cycle processes. Communication must be actively maintained between the following groups:

- The management of the project,

- The project staff,

- The acquirer,

- Any support groups within the parent organization,

- The management of the parent organization, and

- Any subcontractors or suppliers.

The available forms of communication are as follows:

- *Personal contact and dialog:* This is most effective in maintaining project morale and motivation.

- *Staff meetings:* This gives the PM an opportunity to communicate to all staff.

- *Regular activity reports:* These are often done weekly by each subordinate and should identify issues and problems as well as report on sheer activity.

- *Newsletters and announcements:* These should be reserved for major events or issues.

- *Program and technical reviews:* These are opportunities to communicate with the project staff.

- *Formal, contractual letters and notices:* These should usually be a reserved for significant issues that have already been discussed using other, less formal, communication methods.

Whenever the PM communicates with anyone the following questions should be borne in mind:

- Can the information help the persons do their immediate tasks?

- Will the information impact motivation negatively or positively?

- If the impact is intrinsically negative, can it realistically be offset?

- Is it too early to communicate the information? That is, is it likely to change quickly?

In some cases the information may be intrinsically negative and there is nothing that realistically will completely offset it. The only recourse then is to alert the staff, focus them on fundamental project objectives, and, as appropriate, enlist their aid in finding the best possible response to the situation.

13.4.5.7   Resolve Conflicts

Conflicts usually arise out of either technical, schedule, or personality problems. Conflicts are usually manifested by disagreements over how best to proceed with the project and often arise when events do not proceed according to the plan. The goal of the PM must be to lead the team to a resolution, maintaining the focus on the problem to be solved in the context of the overall project objectives. Effective communication and a clear vision of where the project and product are going are the keys to achieving this goal.

Personality problems are often inflamed by technical or schedule pressures. In the event that a personality conflict cannot be resolved in a more general context the PM should arrange a meeting with the individuals involved and directly address the issue objectively. If this still fails to resolve the issue, then the PM may need to seek assistance from the company's functional organizations, in particular human resources. Ultimately, if one or more individuals refuse to adopt a positive attitude they may have to be removed from the situation.

13.4.5.8   Manage and Adapt to Changes

Changes come from either inside or outside of the project. Internally driven changes usually arise when things do not go according to plan. Externally driven changes can arise as changes to acquirer requirements or as changes to project tools and facilities, such as the unexpected revision of a major software tool by the tool vendor. The most serious situations arise when a major portion of the product design is impacted during or after coding. At that point up to 50 percent of the program effort may have been expended, perhaps more.

A considerable revision to designs and code may be necessary, with attendant cost and schedule impacts.

When the need for a change has been identified the following steps should be taken:

1. Clearly understand the proposed change and its root causes.

2. Inform the project staff that a change may occur.

3. Perform a preliminary technical analysis impact of the change. This includes both impact to the design and implementation as well as to performance.

4. Assess the cost and schedule impact of the change.

5. Assess any contractual implications of the change in light of the above.

6. Verify that the change is really needed. If required by contract, notify the acquirer of the preliminary cost, schedule, and performance impacts.

7. As appropriate, ensure that the acquirer and other relevant parties approve of the change.

8. Identify any project tasks that need to be stopped immediately.

9. Communicate to the staff that the change will in fact occur.

10. Issue Stop Work notices for any activities that should definitely be stopped.

11. Perform a full replanning activity as quickly as possible. Inform the staff.

12. Restart the project efforts.

This sequence may need to be modified, depending on the project's contractual and logistical arrangements.

When working through changes with the project staff, the PM should always keep the focus on objective issues and producing a result that is as positive as circumstances allow. Sometimes, changes will result in the project realizing an opportunity to improve the cost, schedule, or quality by making a change. The PM must then assure himself that the opportunity is indeed real. If it is then the relevant management plans should be changed accordingly.

13.4.6 Controlling

Controlling is the collection of management activities used to ensure that the project goes according to plan. Performance and results are measured against plans, deviations are noted, and corrective actions are taken to ensure conformance of plans and actual results.

The PM should ask these questions: Is the project on schedule? Is it within cost? Are there any potential problems that will cause delays in meeting the requirement within the budget and schedule? Control provides the plans and approaches for eliminating the difference between the plans and/or standards and the actuals or results. Table 13.6 provides an outline of the project management activities that must be accomplished by project managers to control their projects.

Activity	Definition or Explanation
Develop standards of performance.	Set goals that will be achieved when tasks are correctly accomplished.
Establish monitoring and reporting systems.	Determine necessary data, who will receive it, when they will receive it, and what they will do with it to control the project.
Measure and analyze results.	Compare achievements with standards, goals, and plans.
Initiate corrective actions.	Bring requirements, plans, and actual project status into conformance.
Reward and discipline.	Praise, remunerate, and discipline project personnel as appropriate.

Table 13.6: Controlling Activities for Software Projects

To control a project two things must occur: (1) The current state, or status of the project must be known with adequate accuracy, and (2) decisions must be made based on the desired state, the current state, and the objectives. The management functions discussed in the preceding subsections are then used to implement these decisions. The planning function is most commonly used but the others may be needed. In many cases this must be done iteratively, by assessing several possible decisions options before arriving at a final decision. The decision is then implemented using the management functions.

The analytical ability, experience, and intuition of the PM will determine the quality of the decisions. The quality is usually, however, information limited. That is, an optimal decision cannot be produced with flawed or missing data on the state of the program. The key elements of the program state are:

- The current status of each of the activities in the project plan;

- The labor expended on each task. If the organization maintains a time recording or cost accounting system with sufficient granularity then this data should be readily available;

- Using the status of each task and the labor expended on that same task, the actual performance of the organization can be compared to the planned performance. This is referred to as earned value;

- The technical stability of the product as indicated by change requests, test anomalies, processing, bandwidth and memory reserves, and other performance and quality metrics;

- The status of any subcontractors;

- The integration of the above to form a clear picture of the project trends; and

- Ongoing evaluation of project risks.

The above data can then be compared to the planned state of the program. Variances between the plan and actual states would then be cause for action as outlined above.

13.4.6.1 Develop Standards of Performance

The project manager is responsible for developing and specifying standards of performance for the project. The project manager either develops standards and procedures for the project, adopts and uses standards developed by the parent organization, or uses standards developed by the customer or a professional society. See, for example, the 1999 four-volume set titled *IEEE Software Engineering Standards Collection*.

13.4.6.2 Establish Monitoring and Reporting Systems

The project manager is responsible for establishing the methods of monitoring the software project and reporting project status. Monitoring and reporting systems must be specified in order to determine project status. The project manager needs feedback on the progress of the project and quality of the product to ensure that everything is going according to plan. The type, frequency, originator, and recipient of project reports must be specified. The use of status reporting tools to provide visibility of progress—not just resources used or time passed—must be implemented.

Any and all software methods, procedures, tools, and techniques must also be specified. Some tools that aid in controlling of a software engineering project are PERT, CPM, workload charts, and Gantt charts [Cori 1985]. A paper by Howes [Howes 1984] presents the earned-value method of tracking a software engineering project. This concept is also discussed in Chapter 12 of this book.

13.4.6.3 Measure and Analyze Results

The project manager is responsible for measuring the results of the project both during and at the end of the project. For instance, actual phase deliverables should be measured against planned phase deliverables. The measured results can be management (process) results and/or technical (product) results.

An example of a process result would be the status of the project schedule. An example of a product result would be the degree to which the design specifications correctly interpreted the requirement specifications.

13.4.6.4   Initiate Corrective Actions

If standards and requirements are not being met, the project manager must initiate corrective action. For instance, the project manager can change the plan, add staff, use overtime or other procedures to get back on plan, or change the requirements.

The project manager might change the plans or standards if apparently the original plans or standards cannot be met. This might involve requiring a larger budget, more people, or more checkout time on the development computer. It also might require reducing the standards (and indirectly the quality) by reducing the number of walkthroughs or by changing from reviewing all software modules to only reviewing the critical software modules.

13.4.6.5   Reward and Discipline the Project Members

The project manager should reward people for meeting their standards and plans, and discipline those who without good reason do not. This should not be confused with the rewards and discipline given to workers for performing their assigned duties; that is a function of staffing. The system of rewards and discipline discussed here is a mechanism for controlling ability to meet a plan or standard. In many organizations, the PM will need to enlist the support of the functional organizations to accomplish this.

13.5   Creating the Project Plan

The SPMP, or software project management plan, was repeatedly mentioned in the preceding sections. In some environments it is referred to as the software development plan. Regardless of the name, the SPMP is a critical document. If correctly prepared, it will assist in generating a more realistic cost estimate and will give everyone on the program a clear vision of where the project is headed and, in conjunction with other plans, how it will arrive there. If done wrong it will, at best, be ignored and, at worst, engender cynicism and actually get in the way of progress.

When creating the SPMP the author(s) should always bear the following in mind:

- Why is the plan being written? The author(s) must view the plan as something that will be of use to themselves as program managers, not just something they are doing to "check a box." It should also be intelligible and useful to the project staff.

- Is the information sufficient for the intended purpose? That is, can the program be executed using the plan as a strategy document? If the level of detail is insufficient to guide the project then, if not addressed directly, the program direction may become ad hoc.

- Is the information excessive? That is, is it not essential? Adding excessive detail can result in too little freedom of action to address problems as they arise. The level of detail should be sufficient so that the plan, in conjunction with the current program status, can be used to make important decisions. If the plan has to be consulted on a day-to-day basis, the program may become paralyzed.

- Is the plan consistent with other management plans? If the SPMP overlaps with, for example, the software life cycle management plan, the author(s) should ask themselves "Is this necessary?"

- Finally, does it satisfy any acquirer or company requirements?

Achieving the correct level of detail in the SPMP is usually difficult. As with writing requirements, there is a natural human tendency to write down whatever we know, whether it is essential or not. Add to this the brutal reality that we cannot foresee all possible circumstances and it is easy to see how a SPMP can end up with too much detail in some areas and too little in others.

The solution is usually to write the SPMP with adequate detail to ensure that the project's essential goals are achieved and constraints not violated, supplemented with such information as is needed to direct the program strategically, and then stop. Depending on what other plans are being developed, more information than this may be needed. For example, if there is no separate software configuration management plan, then more detail would be appropriate in that area.

Finally, the SPMP should be reviewed by the management of the company to ensure that they are familiar with the commitment the company is making. For example, if the start-up plan includes a schedule for acquiring resources, such items may be funded from company capital funds and must be planned in advance.

IEEE Standard 1058-1998 provides a format for the SPMP. The outline of the substantive sections is given below. The reader is referred to the standard for the full outline format.

Clause 1: Overview.

Clause 2: References.

Clause 3: Definitions.

Clause 4: Project Organization.

Clause 5: Managerial Process Plans.

  Subclause 5.1: Start-up plan.

  Subclause 5.2: Estimation plan.

  Subclause 5.3: Work plan.

  Subclause 5.4: Control Plan.

  Subclause 5.5: Risk management plan.

  Subclause 5.6: Project closeout plan.

Clause 6: Technical Process Plans.

> **Subclause 6.1:** Process model.
>
> **Subclause 6.2:** Methods, tools, and techniques.
>
> **Subclause 6.3:** Infrastructure plan.
>
> **Subclause 6.4:** Product acceptance plan.

Clause 7: Supporting Process Plans.

Clause 8: Additional Plans.

Clause 9: Plan Annexes and Indices.

13.6 Summary

Managing a software development project is a demanding and satisfying task. It requires that the PM exercise good judgment, be knowledgeable of the product technology and processes, be able to communicate effectively with the acquirer, the project staff, and company management, be able to plan the activities of the project, be able to respond positively to change when it happens, and be able to document work appropriately. It also provides the incumbent with excellent visibility into business, technical, and personnel management opportunities.

This chapter has described the major activities needed to perform these functions and also provided practical advice on performing those functions. It has described the format and content of the software management plan following the IEEE standard. Just remember to keep your eye on the ball . . . and keep swinging.

Applicable Standard

IEEE Std 1058-1998. *IEEE Standard for Software Project Management Plans.* IEEE, New York.

Additional References

[Boehm 1989]   Boehm, B. W. (1989). *Tutorial: Software Risk Management.* IEEE Computer Society Press, Los Alamitos, CA.

[Boehm 1988]   Boehm, B. W. (1988). "A Spiral Model of Software Development and Enhancement." *Tutorial: Software Engineering Project Management.* IEEE Computer Society Press, Los Alamitos, CA.

[Boyatziz 1971]   Boyatzis, R. E. (1971). "Leadership: The Effective Use of Power." *Management of Personnel Quarterly*, Bureau of Industrial Relations, pp. 1–8. Reprinted in 1997 in *Tutorial: Software Engineering Project Management*, 2nd ed. R.H. Thayer, ed. IEEE Computer Society Press, Los Alamitos, CA.

[Cleland & King 1972]   Cleland. D. I. and King, W. R. (1972). *Management: A Systems Approach*, McGraw-Hill Book Company, New York.

[Cori 1985]   Cori, K. A. (1985). "Fundamentals of Master Scheduling for the Project Manager." *Project Management Journal*, June, pp. 78–89.

[DoD 1982]   Department of Defense (1982). *Strategy for a DOD Software Initiative*, DoD Report, 1 October 1982. Washington, DC. (An edited public version was published in *Computer*, November 1983.)

[DoD 1987]   Department of Defense (1987, September). *Report on the Defense Science Board Task Force on Military Software*. Office of the Undersecretary of Defense for Acquisition, Department of Defense, Washingon, DC.

[Fairley & Rook 1996]   Fairley, R. E., and Rook, P. (1996). "Risk Management for Software Development." *Software Engineering*, M. Dorfman and R.H. Thayer, eds. IEEE Computer Society Press, Los Alamitos, CA.

[Fayol 1949]   Fayol, H. (1949). *General and Industrial Administration*. Sir Isaac Pitman & Sons, Ltd., London.

[Hoffman & King 1997]   Hoffman, T. and King, J. (1997). "Project management ills cost businesses plenty." *ComputerWorld Magazine*, September 22. International Data Group, Inc.

[Howes 1984]   Howes, N. R. (1984). "Managing Software Development Projects for Maximum Productivity," *IEEE Transactions on Software Engineering*, Vol. SE-10, No. 1, January, pp. 27–35. Reprinted in 1997 in *Tutorial: Software Engineering Project Management*, 2nd ed. R.H. Thayer, ed. IEEE Computer Society Press, Los Alamitos, CA.

[Koontz & O'Donnell 1972] Koontz, H., and O'Donnell, C. (1972). *Principles of Management: An Analysis of Managerial Functions*, 5th ed. McGraw-Hill, New York.

[Koontz et al. 1984]   Koontz, H., O'Donnell, C., and Weihrich, H. (1984). *Management*, 8th ed. McGraw-Hill, New York.

[MacKenzie 1969]   MacKenzie (1969). "The Management Process in 3-D," *Harvard Business Review,* vol. 47, no. 6, pp. 80–87. Reprinted in Tutorial: *Software Engineering Project MAnagement,* edited by R. H. Thayer, IEEE Computer Society Press, Washington D.C., 1988.

[Mantei 1981]   Mantei, M. (1981). "The Effect of Programming Team Structures on Programming Tasks." *Communications of the ACM*, Vol. 24, No. 3, March, pp. 106–113. Reprinted in 1997 in *Tutorial: Software Engineering Project Management*, 2nd ed. R.H. Thayer, ed. IEEE Computer Society Press, Los Alamitos, CA.

[Middleton 1967]   Middleton, C. J. (1967). "How to Set Up a Project Organization." *Harvard Business Review*, November–December, pp. 73–82. Reprinted in 1988 in *Tutorial: Software Engineering Project Management*, R.II. Thayer, ed. IEEE Computer Society Press, Los Alamitos, CA.

[Rue & Byars 1983]   Rue, L. W., and Byars, L. L. (1983). *Management: Theory and Application.* Richard D. Irwin, Homewood, II.

[SEI 2000]   Software Engineering Institute (2000). *Process Maturity Profile of the Software Community 1999 Year End Update,* Pittsburgh, PA. (Available from SEI Web site, http://www.sei.cmu.edu.)

[Stuckenbruck 1981]   Stuckenbruck, L. C. (1981). "The Matrix Organization." *A Decade of Project Management*, Project Management Institute, pp. 157–169. Reprinted in 1997 in *Tutorial: Software Engineering Project Management*, 2nd ed. R.H. Thayer, ed. IEEE Computer Society Press, Los Alamitos, CA.

Chapter 14

Software Risk Management

14.1   Introduction

Risk management is an organized set of processes used to identify risk factors, develop and select options to be used in handling risks, and then mitigate risks if they in fact occur. The primary goals of risk management are to identify potential problems and plan responses to them that can be implemented early enough to avoid a crisis. If it is to be effective, a risk management strategy must be established early in the life cycle of a software project. Likewise, the risk factors must be continually monitored and addressed throughout the product life cycle. This chapter defines and explains the various components of effective risk management. It also clarifies the difference between risk management and project management.

This chapter is based on IEEE Standard 1540-2001, *Standard for Software Life Cycle Processes—Risk Management*, together with the authors' experience in project management and the material drawn from Chapter 15, "Risk Analysis and Management," of *System Engineering Management Guide* [DSMC 1990] with additional information from *Risk Management: Concepts and Guidance* [DSMC 1989] and from Fairley [Fairley 1994] and [Fairley & Rook 1997].

14.2   Objectives

In this chapter you will learn:

- The difference between project management and risk management.

- How to identify a project risk.

- Where to look for risks in a project.

- How to separate management risk from technical risks.

- What kind of schedule risks exist.

- What kind of cost risks exist.

- What kind of requirement risks exist.

- What kind of quality risks exist.

- What kind of operational risks exist.

- How to perform a risk analysis.

- How to compute risk exposure.

- How to compute risk leverage.

- How to compute the optimum cost of a risk solution.

- How to develop and use a "Top Ten" risk tracking list.

- How to prepare a risk management plan.

- How to perform risk management.

- The major issues in implementing a good risk management program and how to recognize them.

- How to apply a risk handling technique.

- How apply risk avoidance.

- How to apply risk assumption.

- How to apply problem control.

- How to apply risk transfer.

14.3   Elements of Risk Management

Risk management is the umbrella term used to describe the processes used to control risk. It is an organized set of methods used to:

- Identify risk factors and their impacts (risk identification).

- Develop and select the options for dealing with those risks (risk analysis).

- Mitigate those risks if and when they become problems (risk handling).

The primary goal of risk management is to identify and respond to those potential problems with sufficient lead time to avoid a crisis. An organized risk management strategy must be developed and put in place early in a software project's life cycle. Risks must then be continually monitored and addressed throughout the system life cycle.

IEEE Standard 1540-2001 defines a *risk* to be "the likelihood of an event, hazard, threat, or situation occurring and its undesirable consequences; a potential problem."

14.3.1   Project Risks

As stated above, a project risk is a potential problem that would be detrimental to a project's success should it in fact materialize. The major components of a risk are (1) the probability that something undesirable might happen, and (2) the resulting consequences to the project should that event occur. For example,

- The requirements for a product might grow (the risk),

- Resulting in a schedule overrun (the immediate consequence),

- Which in turn will (almost always) result in some combination of delayed delivery of the product and a cost overrun or delivery of an unsuitable product (an impact to quality);

- All of which would result in customer and user dissatisfaction and stress in the developing organization.

Risk is present in some form and degree in most human activities. It is certainly present in software engineering projects. It is generally characterized by the following:

- Uncertainty is involved, often expressed as a probability or likelihood.

- A loss is associated with it, such as life, health, money, property, reputation, or opportunity.

- It is manageable—in the sense that human action can be applied to change its form and degree.

A problem is a risk that has materialized. A problem arises when the undesired event has occurred and a potential loss is now real. Risk exposure is the product of the probability and the potential loss caused by a problem should it occur.

When dealing with risk in this general sense it is not always easy to distinguish between single events, multiple events, continuous events, and interdependent events, or between cause and effect. In planning a project, many risks may be identified. Systematic risk management requires that initial concerns be isolated to specific root causes, and that the probabilities of the root causes and potential losses associated with the effects be determined. A key tool in the systematic management of risk is the risk management plan (RMP), which is described below. To be effective, the specific outcomes to be avoided by the risk management plan must be explicitly stated in order to identify possible courses of action for risk reduction.

14.3.2   Issues Impacting Risk Management

The proper management of risk is often limited or restricted by a number of issues, some of which are intrinsic to the problem, while others arise from how project staff and management respond to risks.

- Risk management is complex and must often deal with subtle issues, such as probability and decision trees.

- Human insight and foresight are limited. Crystal balls are rarely found on sale.

- Projects often operate in survival mode, leaving little energy or enthusiasm for worrying about things that haven't gone wrong . . . yet, resulting in a "pay to fix problems, not avoid them" mentality.

- The culture of the development organization, or the customer, or both, may operate on the basis of (1) risk denial or (2) excessive optimism.

- Sometimes risk management is viewed as a bad influence on the development team. Any individual who identifies a risk, whether it is a large risk or a small risk, may be deemed a "troublemaker" and is often shunted aside or ignored by both management and other members of the staff.

- The solution to a major risk can be beyond the capabilities and resources of the individual who first identifies it. Organizational attitudes that convey the attitude "Don't bring me a problem unless you bring me a solution" result in management being uninformed about potentially severe risks, with a resulting failure to implement appropriate risk mitigation strategies.

Very often the intrinsic difficulty of foreseeing risks and planning for them interacts with the cultural and organizational factors.

14.3.3   Risk Management and Project Management

There is a basic difference between risk management and the traditional tasks associated with project management. The goal of traditional project management is to systematically control the common risks that have, over many years, been identified as being intrinsic to virtually all development projects. In contrast, risk management is concerned with identifying and managing the unique threats to a specific project that might prevent delivery of a suitable product on time and within budget.

Software project management deals with risks common to all software projects. Over time, methods of managing common and pervasive risks have become institutionalized in the tools and techniques used to develop software or any other technical item. For example, project planning and scheduling, configuration management, and verification and validation are all proven risk reduction techniques. In this sense, traditional project management can be viewed as a systematic approach to controlling such generic risk factors.

Examples of such common risks and their generic solutions include:

- *Costly late fixes*—Mitigated by early verification of requirements and the design.

- *Error-prone products*—Mitigated by the use of verification, validation, and incremental testing and technical (peer) reviews throughout the life cycle.

- *Uncontrolled development processes*—Mitigated by developing and following well-defined processes.

- *Uncontrolled product*—Mitigated by configuration management and quality assurance practices.

- *Poor communications*—Mitigated by regular status, documentation, acquirer-supplier reviews, and technical interchange meetings.

Used alone traditional project management usually becomes a recipe for "problem management"; difficult problems that cannot be managed using the above standard processes are only addressed when problems actually arise. In this sense, *project management is reactive when problems occur outside the scope of its traditional processes, whereas risk management strives to address these problems proactively.*

Risk management deals with potential problems unique to a specific software project. Risk management allows developers, managers, and customers to make informed decisions based on a systematic assessment of what might go wrong, the associated probabilities, the severity of the impacts, and the range of potential solutions. Risk management is also concerned with developing strategies and plans to abate the major risk factors, to intelligently respond to those risks that do become problems, and to continually reassess risk.

Risk management is effective when significant decision making, planning, resources, money, and effort are expended to reduce the probabilities and/or impacts of the identified risk factors. The effort invested in these processes will determine whether risk management is performed successfully, over and above traditional project management.

Thus, risk management is not synonymous with project management, nor is it a replacement for project management, nor is it something entirely separate. Rather, it is an explicit augmentation and extension of traditional project management processes, and it is closely intertwined with the information-gathering and decision-making functions of project management. The phrase "When a project is successful, it is not because there were no problems but that the problems were overcome" [Rook 1986] captures the essence. Risk management does not guarantee success, but has the primary goal of identifying and responding to potential problems with sufficient lead time to avoid crisis situations, so that it becomes possible to conduct a project that meets its goals to the maximum extent possible.

14.3.4 Steps of Risk Management

An effective program of risk management is conducted in a series of specific steps:

1. Identification of risk factors, which can impact the project and then categorizing them according to how they would impact the project;

2. Analysis of the identified risks on an ongoing basis to evaluate the likelihood of the risk factor actually occurring, as well as quantifying the impacts, thereby developing a profile of the risk over time;

3. Developing and implementing approaches (or treatments) for handling or responding to the risks; and

4. Implementing mechanisms to monitor the risks on an ongoing basis.

Each of these topics should be addressed in the RMP and are discussed in the following sections. IEEE Standard 1540-2001 adds to these operational tasks the overarching management activities of (1) planning and implementing risk management and (2) evaluation of the risk management process itself. Because these tasks are generic to the management and software improvement processes described in other chapters of this book, the remaining sections focus on the four tasks unique to risk management.

14.4   Identifying Risks

The first step in managing the risks to a project is to identify them. Risks cannot be analyzed or handled until they are identified and described in an understandable way. *Risk identification is an organized, thorough approach to seeking out the real risks associated with a program.* It is *not* an open-ended process of dreaming up highly improbable combinations of unlikely events in an effort to discover every conceivable whim of outrageous misfortune. At the same time, risks should not be ignored simply because the consequences are too severe to contemplate. Risk identification, together with the other risk management steps, must be performed periodically throughout all phases of a project.

14.4.1   General Approaches to Risk Identification

Some degree of risk exists in all programmatic, technical, engineering, quality, logistics, and distribution and operational activities. Viewed from this perspective these areas can be examined in an effort to discover and identify risks at their root causes.

- *Programmatic risks* include restricted or untimely funding, mandated schedules, excessive contractual constraints, or political risks.

- *Technical and engineering risks* may involve the risk of meeting a performance requirement or a safety or security requirement, and may also include risks in the feasibility of a design concept or the risks associated with using state-of-the-art hardware or software.

- *Quality risks* usually occur when the development practices that were to be used to develop a product are not actually followed. This can result in a product that does not satisfy requirements.

- *Logistical risks* commonly include reliability, maintainability, operability, and suitability concerns. These typically impact the product after delivery.

- *Distribution and operational risks* (also called *deployment risks*) can result in improper installation and use of the product, which can, in turn, impact its use by customers.

Most programs, of course, involve activities from each of these categories and hence can be vulnerable to problems in these areas that may, in turn, impact other aspects of the development or use of the product.

An alternative approach to identifying risks is to examine where the risks have their primary impact and then trace back to the root causes. Five common, interrelated areas that are impacted by risks are schedule, cost, requirements, quality, and operation. It is common to refer to risks according to the primary area that they impact, even though the actual source of the risk may lie in another area. Hence an unexpected growth in requirements will usually be viewed as (primarily) a schedule risk, while some might argue that, in fact, it is a contractual risk since the requirements are part of the contract. In either case the root cause is the requirements.

Hence risks can be identified either directly or inversely. Direct identification is performed by first identifying likely root causes (such as requirements growth) and then determining the areas impacted. Inverse identification proceeds by first determining the areas of impact to which the program is vulnerable and then working backward through the cause-and-effect chain to find the likely root causes.

Identifying risks in either the direct or inverse mode is a complex task requiring both judgment and experience. As a result, it is best done using a team approach. The membership in the team should include personnel with a reasonable range of experience and viewpoints. The team members should be drawn from the ranks of senior software designers, product integrators, quality assurance, configuration management, and project management. The team should be encouraged to openly seek all risks that are likely to have material impacts to the project, with specific guidelines as to what constitutes "material" and "likely." The team must approach their task iteratively, refining their knowledge of the candidate risks and their likely impacts as they learn more about the project and its risk.

The team will have many sources of information and methods for identifying risks, either directly or inversely. Any source of information that allows recognition of a potential problem can be used for risk identification. Some of these include:

- Life cycle cost and schedule analysis,

- Requirements documents,

- Prototyping and simulation models,

- Lessons-learned files that distill the experience of previous projects,

- Cost and schedule estimates and actuals from previous projects,

- Parametric cost and schedule models,

- Trade studies and analyses,

- Statements of work, work breakdown structures (WBS), and

- Schedule networks.

14.4.2 Identifying Schedule Risks

Techniques for identifying schedule risks include sensitivity analysis using parametric models and network representations of the schedule, such as CPM and PERT. These tools are described in the chapter on cost and schedule estimation, Chapter 12. Probabilistic techniques, such as a Monte Carlo[1] simulation, or the intrinsic capabilities of tools such as PERT can be used to produce the distribution[2] functions for various project milestones. The use of parametric models will be discussed under the category of cost risks in the next section. PERT and CPM are discussed in Chapter 12 of this book.

Such simulations can be used, first and foremost, to evaluate the likely range of the values for the completion date of critical events. For example, Figure 14.1 shows the distribution function for the completion date of an event whose desired completion date is 50 days after the start of the project. According to this graph the network predicts that the nominal (that is, the 50 percent likelihood point) completion date of the event will indeed satisfy the schedule objectives of the program. However, the simulation predicts that a 25 percent probability exists that the date might be 15 days or more beyond that. If this is unacceptable then the logic of the network must be examined, together with the distributions of the time spans of the individual tasks, in order to identify the exact cause of the problem. Several popular network scheduling tools either have this capability or it can be obtained as an "add-on" capability to data exported to spreadsheets or other commonly available tools.

Another way in which networks can be used to detect and identify risks is by examining the logic of the network, looking for cross coupling of tasks (or sequences of tasks), as well as looking for complexity. This is best done using a graphical display of the network: Humans are good at grasping such complexities when the whole can be perceived visually. When examining the logic nodes or junction points, those with a high degree of fan-in (see Figure 14.2, node 8, which has a fan-in of 3) and those with a high degree of fan-out (see Figure 14.2, node 3, which has an fan-out of 3) are potential high-risk areas.

A node with a high degree of fan-in has many tasks that must be completed before the milestone can be achieved. Thus, no subsequent tasks can be initiated until all tasks fanning into the node are completed; delay in any one will delay the task with the high fan-in. Conversely, a node with a high degree of fan-out implies that many other (successor) tasks are dependent on the completion of this one task. Hence there are many other chains

---

[1]Monte Carlo simulations are used to compute the distribution functions of complex quantities whose value depends on many parameters, which are not deterministic but whose probabilities are known. The technique was first developed to compute the path of neutrons in nuclear reactions by S. M. Ulam [Ulam 1976]. This was one of the first applications of the MANIAC computer.

[2]The cumulative distribution of a quantity is the likelihood that a quantity will have a value less than or equal to a given value.

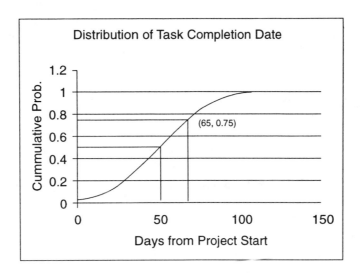

Figure 14.1: Distribution Function of the Date of a Critical Event

of tasks through which the delay will ripple, magnifying the impact of a delay to the single task with a high fan-out.

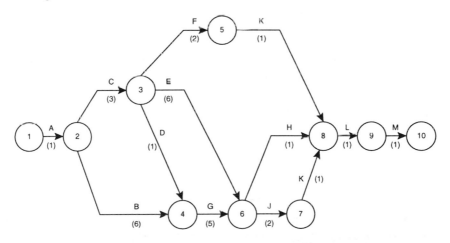

Letters = Activities; Numbers = Milestones; (X) = Activity duration

Figure 14.2: An Example Activity Network

Finally, nodes (activities or external events) that lie along the critical path will also impact the schedule seriously if they slip: By definition a slip of the completion date for any activity on the critical path will result in a slip to a critical program event. For an example, see path ABGJKLM in Figure 14.2. In addition, if all of the slack time is consumed along a noncritical path, this path will also become critical. This means that now the project staff must juggle resources in an effort to minimize the impact of two sets of schedule slips, which makes the management task even more complex, thereby increasing risk elsewhere in the project. As a result, tasks that lie along near-critical paths should be examined.

14.4.3   Identifying Cost Risks

Techniques for identifying cost risks include use of algorithmic cost models to evaluate the sensitivity of project cost to the assumptions used when the project cost was estimated [Boehm 1981]. The sensitivity of the project costs to changes in the values of the attributes used to estimate project can be explored by performing a series of "what-if" evaluations using, for example, the COCOMO II model.

COCOMO II and other parametric cost and schedule prediction models are discussed in Chapter 12, the chapter on cost and schedule estimation. Such models typically produce both cost and schedule estimates and hence can be used to evaluate the sensitivity of their predictions (in either an absolute or a relative sense) to changes or errors in the attributes of the project, the product, or the personnel. This can be done in either the direct or inverse mode: The models may show that the project cost (or schedule) is sensitive to a combination of factors, such as the experience of the analysts and the reliability of the application. If both of these attributes change, a new risk would be generated.

Conducting such sensitivity analysis of the project cost (and schedule) will show if the project is sensitive to attributes that are in fact subject to change. Of necessity this type of analysis deals with cost risks on an aggregate basis and even then will only identify risks that lie within the span of the model's parameters and the activities it includes. Projects typically have other activities and dependencies that can generate risks that are not represented in such generic cost models. To identify risks arising from those activities a different approach must be taken. For example, an external dependency (such as the delivery of a new version of a commercial operating system) critical to the continued progress (and hence impacting cost and schedule) can be best detected by reviewing the project schedule and statement of work.

In the chapter on cost and schedule estimation the concept of a work breakdown structure (WBS) was introduced. The WBS provides a hierarchical decomposition of project processes and deliverables. When the project cost and schedule estimates are created, the WBS is used to create a matching hierarchical representation of the project costs. Using this hierarchy a matching risk hierarchy can be created, which will then provide a model for how the risks and their costs propagate through the products and processes of the project [Fairley & Thayer 1997]. Because project scheduling networks also contain many elements of the WBS organized in the sequence in which they occur, examination of the WBS directly provides an alternative view of the project.

When performing such a systematic analysis of project cost and schedule risks, it is useful to bear in mind some of the classical causes of such risks. Budgets are usually expressed in terms of effort (people × time). At first blush it would seem that a schedule could be reduced by increasing the staff assigned to the project. However, as discussed in the chapter on cost and schedule estimation, people and time are not interchangeable in practice, even if they are in the above expression [Brooks 1975, Brooks 1974]. The nonlinear increase in cost that results from attempting to reduce the schedule below its natural minimum (e.g., such as is predicted by COCOMO or past experiences with similar projects) may result in a very high risk that the project cannot be completed within the budget. Hence, the natural response to a schedule risk may result in the creation of a cost risk.

Other factors that influence cost and schedule risks include these:

- *Uncertain requirements*—The requirements of the project are initially not known or well understood. This can result in very large cost (and schedule) estimation errors being built into the project.

- *Incorrect cost estimates*—Even if the requirements are well understood, errors can occur during the estimation process. These can be as simple as bookkeeping errors or as complex as using unrealistic factors in the estimation model or not compensating for inflation.

- *Creeping requirements*—Project requirements slowly increase without a corresponding increase in the budget (or the schedule).

- *Schedule compression*—Brought about by either incorrect initial schedule estimates or commitments before the project starts, or by pressures from marketing, upper management, and the customer. This creates schedule risks and usually results in a non-linear increase in costs [Boehm 1981, Gaffney 1997].

- *Unreasonable budgets*—Budget estimates might be based on incorrect assumptions or analyses or on a decision that the project will be bid for the price necessary to satisfy the market, upper management, and/or the customer rather than what is necessary to satisfy the essential technical requirements.

14.4.4   Identifying Requirement Risks

Many risk factors for software projects result from requirements that are inadequate in one or more of the following ways:

- *Incorrect requirements*—Requirements that attempt to state user needs and customer expectations but contain outright errors. Rework will be the result.

- *Incomplete requirements*—Requirements that do not state desired product features or particular aspects of desired product features. Cost and schedule will both grow.

- *Inconsistent requirements*—Requirements that conflict with other requirements in the same specification. The results is likely to be rework (raising cost) and a loss of quality.

- *Unexpectedly hard requirements*—Requirements that result in a technically difficult or complex product that is either difficult to design or to implement. Cost, schedule, and quality are all put at risk.

- *Infeasible requirements*—Requirements that cannot be achieved using current available people, tools, or technology. The very existence of the project will be at issue.

- *Unclear requirements*—Requirements that have more than one semantic interpretation. Rework is the likely result, or customer dissatisfaction.

- *Unverifiable requirements*—Requirements for which no finite process exists to verify that the product meets the requirements. Effort will be misdirected.

- *Untraceable requirements*—Requirements for which there is no audit trail from requirements to tested code and back. Unnecessary effort will be expended.

- *Volatile requirements*—Requirements that are constantly changed as some requirements are added, while others are subtracted and others changed or reinterpreted. Cost, schedule, and quality are all likely to suffer.

Any correction to the software requirements to correct the unexpected incomplete requirements, inconsistent requirements, unclear requirements, and so forth will result in an unbudgeted increase in cost and schedule, removal of desired features, or reduction in product quality. As observed in the chapter on software requirements, the later in the program that these problems evidence themselves the worse the impact will be.

Identifying requirements risks in the direct mode can be done by explicitly verifying and validating the contents of the requirements documents. Of course, if there is no requirements document, then the risk is potentially unbounded. In addition, the requirements can be probed for sensitivity. That is, are there requirements (for example, performance) that, if changed slightly, will require a radically different technical approach to the solution? Or are there requirements that, if modified, will change which third-party software package is used, for example, to provide a database capability. If so, then a change in those requirements late in the project can result in massive rework to the product design or implementation.

Hard to implement or infeasible requirements can be difficult to detect. A set of requirements may be logically complete, they may be logically consistent, and they may be traceable. They may have all the properties specified in this book and all others. Yet they may be very difficult or impossible to implement, either because of a phenomenological problem or because of constraints in the state of the art. An independent review of the requirements and the preliminary or conceptual design by technically experienced staff is one of the few ways in which risks of this type can be identified.

A particular risk is the inadvertent creation of a death spiral driven by interactions between schedule or cost problems and increases in requirements. For example, it sometimes happens that the schedule is incorrect because of, say, an estimation error, while the cost budget still has margin in it. In an effort to address the problem, the developer offers new features to the customer to compensate for the projected late delivery of the product. These new features, however, will cause the schedule to slip even more, exacerbating the schedule problem and, because the new features consume the cost margin, causing the cost projections to exceed the budget. Now the developer goes to their own upper management and, in an effort to resolve the cost issue, suggests that the product capabilities be expanded to serve additional customers. Their management accepts this proposal and marketing goes to work. Financial commitments from several new customers are obtained, resolving the previous cost problem but, in the course of the negotiations, even more capabilities are added to the product, resulting in an even greater cost and schedule problem.

While all this is going on, the original customer sees nothing but a series of schedule slips, one after the other, and because of the conflict between their and the developer's interests created by the addition of the new customers, the developers may not fully expose the causes of the secondary problems. This serves to lower the confidence of the original customer in the developers, resulting in yet more problems. And so it goes.

Notice that in this example the origin of the initial risk was not requirements, but that the initial smaller cost risk triggered a much worse problem in requirements.

14.4.5   Identifying Quality Risks

Many risk impacts can result from the delivery of unexpectedly poor software quality:

- *Unreliable software* —The software does not perform its intended functions under specified conditions for stated periods of time.

- *Unusable software*—Unreasonable effort is required to use the software or to train software users.

- *Unmaintainable software* —Extraordinary effort is required to locate and fix errors in the software or to upgrade it for future use.

- *Nonportable software*—Extreme difficulty is encountered in converting the software for use in a different operating environment.

- *Nonexpandable software*—Software capability or performance cannot be increased by enhancing current functions or adding new functions/data.

Any correction to the software product to fix such unplanned poor quality will result in an unbudgeted increase in cost and schedule or a decrease in desirable features. In addition, before the quality problem is explicitly recognized it will consume budget and schedule during the test and integration process.

Quality risks can be identified by examining the organization's processes and background in order to evaluate their consistency with the maturity and experience assumptions used in the proposal and implicit in the development of the product. Thus if the organization has never built a product even one-half of the size of the current effort, then, unless specific steps have been taken to improve the organization's processes, it is highly likely that quality problems will be encountered. Similarly, if the current project has reliability requirements levied on it but the organization has no experience with the quality management of such requirements, then risk arises.

In addition, quality risks associated with all suppliers must be considered. For example, if a commercial database is being used in an application that requires continuous operation, then there is risk that the database product will have a "memory leak" (that is, it does not correctly free up dynamically allocated memory). Such potential quality problems in the supplier software represent risks.

Finally, quality risks, which might otherwise be unlikely, can become virtual certainties when the project is placed under stress when other problems occur. The classical example is taking procedural shortcuts in response to schedule problems. The result is often the creation of product quality risk. Hence, quality risks can often be identified by assessing and reducing the impact other risks will have if they occur.

14.4.6 Identifying Logistical and Operational Risks

An operational risk is one that results in the project producing a product that does not satisfy operational needs. That is, the product does not possess the functional, performance, or quality attributes the customers and users want and need even if the product does satisfy its stated requirements. Thus the product may well work properly when operating in a laboratory setting, but when used in the operational environment at the time of its delivery does not operate in a satisfactory manner. The causes of this could range from avoidable sensitivities of the product to its operational environment to the introduction of other systems or processes into the operational environment that are fundamentally incompatible with the product as specified. This can very easily happen if the product to be developed is large. In such cases, delivery may occur years after the development is initiated. The underlying operational environment can easily change during that period.

Logistical risks can sometimes overlap with other risks. Here are some examples of logistical problems and some overlaps:

- The product has a technical requirement for reliability. Failure to achieve this particular technical requirement may well create a logistical problem when the product is installed, requiring unplanned support.

- The product is unduly sensitive to its installation process, or the installation process might not be documented correctly or in sufficient detail.

- The Help function of the product and the customer's approach to managing their in-house Help Desk are incompatible. This results in an insupportable product.

- The approach to updating the product in the field requires dedicated, high-speed network connections when in fact the market for the product is largely that of home offices.

The reason logistical and operational risks often overlap with the other categories is that they are usually detected late in the project life cycle. Because operation and logistical support are the last phases of most developmental life cycles this is hardly surprising. The reality, however, is that the seeds of such risks are often sowed much earlier in the project, very often in the requirements phase.

Operational and logistic risks do not include the risk of the product creating a hazard when it is in operation. Hazard is an intrinsic property or condition of a system that has the potential to cause an accident. See Chapter 5, Software Verification and Validation, for a formal definition of hazards and the associated concept of criticality.

Techniques commonly used to identify operational or logistics risks include performance modeling, reliability modeling, analysis of quality factors, and examination of industry trends. Individuals with experience in supporting and fielding products should be included on the risk assessment team specifically to identify risks of these types.

14.5 Risk Analysis

Risk analysis is the second step in the risk management process. Performing risk analysis requires that the identified risks be examined to determine the probabilities of their actually occurring and the resulting consequences. The purpose of risk analysis is to discover the causes, effects, and magnitude of identified risks, and to provide the insight needed to subsequently develop and examine alternative options for managing the identified risks in the risk treatment process. Many tools, such as schedule network models and life cycle cost models, can aid the analysis.

The ultimate product of risk analysis is a *watch list* or a *risk registry*, which captures the prioritized risk factors, consequences of those risks, and indicators and corresponding thresholds that provide warning of the onset of a problem; that is, the events that indicate that a potential problem has become a real problem, together with the individual assigned to monitor or address the risk. A typical watch list includes the following:

- The trigger events or metrics (for example, externally supplied item delayed more than 2 weeks), together with any thresholds which, when crossed, should activate the risk treatment plans;

- The related areas of exposure (for example, development schedule delayed);

- As they are developed, the actions that are to be taken to avoid or minimize the impact of the risk becoming a problem. In other words, how the risk is to be treated or handled; and

- The individuals responsible for planning and executing the plan used to treat the risk.

A common form of a watch list is that of a "Top Ten" risk-tracking list (see Table 14.1 for an example). The project manager and the development staff periodically assess the 10 greatest technical and/or managerial risks and list them in priority order. If the project uses

Rank This Week	Rank Last Week	No. of Weeks on List	Problem	Risk Handling Approach	Responsible Individual
1	1	3	Projected project scope exceeds cost and schedule allocated	Scope requirements to fit schedule and budget	Project lead software engineer
2	–	1	Errors in C++ compiler and/or run-time library	Short term: Update project coding standard to avoid Long term: Resolve problems with compiler vendor	Short term: Lead SW process engineer Long term: Computing resources manager
3	3	3	More engineers in hiring plan than workstations in capital plan	Obtain management support for emergency update to capital plan	Project software manager
4	7	2	SQA plan not completed	Short Term: Prioritize generation of plan so sections needed to support immediate/ critical project processes done first Long term: Evaluate staffing profile of SQA to determine if problem will continue; due in 5 working days	Short term: Project SQA engineer Long term: Director SQA
5	4	2	Staff not familiar with workstation and Java	Obtain training on the Sun workstation and Java by June 15	Project software architect
6	NA	0	Insufficient/ inexperienced software engineers	Plan needed by June 10	Director of software engineering

Table 14.1: "Top-Ten" Risk-Tracking List (in this case n = 6)

weekly status reports, as is recommended in Chapter 12, then the risks can be evaluated weekly. This list becomes the key in deciding where to focus managerial and technical effort. Of course, the list does not have to contain *exactly* 10 problems. Ten has been selected over the years as a reasonable number that can be tracked on a frequent basis by a skilled project manager,

As the watch list is periodically reevaluated (weekly at the working level, monthly at the management and customer levels), items are added, modified, or deleted as appropriate. This creates the profile of each risk over time and will aid the risk management team in detecting trends in individual risks as well as systematic issues in the risk management process.

The key step in risk analysis is the assessment of the impacts (or exposures) represented by the risks. The areas of exposure were determined in the process of risk identification, while the same tools and methods used to identify many of the risks (parametric models, schedule networks, for example) can be used to quantify their impact. In the course of quantifying the exposure, it is often observed that the value obtained depends on the severity of the problem. Uncertainty is often associated with the exact severity of the problem, which leads to uncertainty in the precise level of exposure.

For example, suppose a project has a cost budget of $2 million and a schedule of 16 months. Using records of earlier projects, the organization believes that there is a 40 percent chance that the growth in the final product lines of code estimate will between 0 and 5 percent. The 5 percent represents the budget reserve allocated to this cost. By reviewing prior project histories and carefully reviewing the requirements of the current project, the team estimates that there is a 25 percent chance that the size will increase between 5 and 10 percent. Similarly, they estimate that there is a 15 percent chance that the growth will be between 10 and 15 percent, and that there 10 percent chance that the increase could total between 15 and 20 percent. This distribution is shown in the first three columns of Table 14.2.

Growth (%)	Probability of Occurrence (%)	Total Product Size	Cost Exposure ($000s)	Schedule Exposure (month)
0–5	40	25,000 LOC	0	0
5–10	25	26,250–27,500	110–220	0–0.5
10–15	20	27,500–28,750	220–340	0.5–1
15–20	15	28,750–30,000	340–460	1–1.5

Table 14.2: Distribution of Software Growth and Resulting Exposures

In Table 14.2 the cost exposures have been expressed as ranges to represent the fact that, as is often the case, two sources of uncertainty actually exist: the probability that the risk will eventuate and the uncertainty in the exposure.

Using either parametric models or historical data on productivity, the impact of each of these exposures (the growths in cost and schedule) can be evaluated. These are shown in the last two columns of Table 14.2. From this table the average, median, and worst case cost and schedule exposures can be estimated. Thus the median cost impact is between $110K and $220K, with a median schedule impact of about 0.5 month. The average cost impact is similar at around $160K, while the worst case impact is $460K, more than double the median and average. Notice in this example that the probability of some exposure is 60 percent.

Since the risk was that the lines of code would grow, this example exhibits the classical behavior predicted by COCOMO and other models when the product size increases over time: The cost is impacted much more than is the schedule on a relative basis. However, if the growth in the product size occurred as the result of a discrete event late in the project life cycle, then the schedule exposure would be much greater. Similarly, if the exposure had arisen from a discrete event (such as late delivery of a component developed by a subcontractor) then the relative schedule exposure might be much greater than that of the cost. Thus each risk must be analyzed in light of its exposure impact on the project's activities and products.

By developing a similar table for each of the identified risks it becomes possible to rank them. Invariably the uncertainty in the data and the assessment of the risks is initially high so individual and collective judgment must be applied to the available data. Over time the project manager should work to reduce the shortfalls in the information necessary to evaluate the risks.

14.6   Risk Treatment

Risk treatment (or handling) is the third step in the risk management process and is composed of implementing techniques and methods to reduce the likelihood and impact of risks. Risk management is incomplete if there are no provisions for treating the identified and quantified risks.

Techniques for treating risks fall into five categories:

1. Risk avoidance,

2. Risk acceptance (or assumption),

3. Problem control (prevention),

4. Risk transfer, and

5. Refinement of knowledge.

Risk treatment methods are constrained only by the ingenuity and skills of the project manager and the project staff. Treating any specific risk will often require the application of two or more of these techniques. While an explicit decision to ignore (or accept) a risk is a viable option, an implicit decision to do the same is not. A documented action with supporting rationale is required for all risk treatment options. Table 14.3 gives examples of these techniques applied to everyday circumstances.

Risk	Avoidance	Acceptance	Control	Transfer	Knowledge Refinement
Vehicle and/or occupant injury in an auto accident while driving to work	Live close to work and walk / Ride rapid-transit systems	Drive to work and hope for the best	Reduce speed limits / Wear seatbelts / Strengthen side panels / Go with a safe driver	Carry auto insurance / Operate good emergency medical systems / Sue other driver	Determine safest automobiles through crash tests / Determine safest route to work
Developing cataracts from microwave oven radiation	Use gas or electric oven / Don't cook food	Use microwave oven only when you are in a hurry	Provide users with Faraday shielding / Design ovens with door interlocks	Carry health insurance / Provide free cornea transplants	Measure radiation for different ovens / Evaluate good cooking practices
Getting shot by someone with a handgun	Eliminate handguns / Don't live in Washington DC	Assume it will happen to the other guy	Stay away from high-crime areas / Be constantly vigilant / Buy bullet-proof glass for car	Carry health insurance / Operate good emergency medical systems / Sue shooter	Determine areas to avoid / Establish warning signs of impending danger
The hard disk on your computer crashes	Don't use a hard disk	Keep using the disk and promise yourself to back it up tomorrow	Periodically back up the disk	Use a disk-recovery software utility	Determine frequency of failures for different hard disks

Table 14.3: Risk Treatment Techniques [Morgan 1981]

14.6.1   Risk Avoidance

Risk avoidance is performed by selecting a lower risk approach to satisfying a requirement instead of a higher risk solution. The statement "I will not accept this risk; I will look for a less risky solution to the problem" reflects the intent of risk avoidance. Selecting a low-risk solution is not always appropriate; a higher risk solution may be deemed more appropriate because of increased design flexibility, potentially lower cost, or potentially early delivery of the product. The alternatives should be examined with care and all risks and benefits carefully assessed.

To avoid risk means to avoid the probability and/or consequences of an undesired event happening. Risk avoidance may be reflected, for example, in the choice of system architecture or in the criteria applied to the selection of a subcontractor. Not every risk can be avoided. Note that avoiding risk in one area of a project might increase risk in another area.

14.6.2   Risk Acceptance

Risk acceptance or assumption implies that a conscious decision has been made to accept the consequences should the undesired event occur. The statement "I am aware of the risk, and I choose to accept it because of the potential benefits of this approach" typifies risk acceptance. Some amount of risk assumption is always present in software development programs. The problem is that too often risks are accepted by default, not by an act of volition. The project manager must determine the appropriate level of risk that can safely be assumed in each situation as it is identified and evaluated.

Risk acceptance acknowledges the existence of risk and results in an explicit decision to accept the consequences if the risk eventuates. The process of identification, analysis, and selection of risk treatment techniques allows the project manager to accept the "right" risks, such as those with low probability, low impact, or both. Those that are too risky to accept may be avoided by adopting a lower risk approach through risk avoidance or risk control.

14.6.3   Risk Control

The statement "I am aware of the risk, and I will develop options to reduce the potential of the problem occurring and/or to reduce its effect should the problem occur" describes this method of handling risk. Exercising risk control requires that project status be regularly monitored and that alternative solutions be developed if the risk becomes a problem. This often involves the use of reviews, verification and validation, development of fallback positions, and similar management actions. Implementing a program of risk control requires that a risk management plan be developed and that the risk control effort be tracked according to that plan. A program of risk control must integrate not only the traditional cost and schedule plans but also the technical performance plans. It must also identify a collection of alternative courses of action should risks eventuate. These alternatives are commonly called contingency plans.

For example, solutions include developing alternative sources for commercial-off-the-shelf (COTS) software, parallel development of critical components, or increasing the budget and/or personnel assigned to specific areas. The creation, evaluation, and selection of contingency plans require a deep understanding of the project products, processes, and risks. It also requires that the cost of the alternatives be evaluated along with their paybacks and the costs of the risks themselves. This topic is discussed in detail in a later section.

14.6.4 Risk Transfer

Risk transfer involves transferring potential problems to other areas of responsibility. For example, transferring some data processing functions from the client to the server may mitigate risk of poor client performance in a client/server system. The risk of developing inadequate training materials for a new system that will be integrated into a complex preexisting environment might be best reduced by transferring the primary responsibility for developing those materials to the customer, who understands the environment best. Of course, risk transfer is only appropriate if all parties agree to the approach. In addition, care must be exercised that the transfer of a risk factor includes transfer of the responsibility for a successful outcome; transferring a difficult technical issue to a subcontractor does not eliminate the risk of failure by the prime contractor: The customer will still hold the prime contractor responsible because failure of the subcontractor will still result in failure of the overall product.

Risk transfer is most appropriate when it reduces either the likelihood or the exposure of the risk better than any other risk treatment option.

14.6.5 Refinement of Knowledge

Although this is not a "true" risk handling technique, uncertainty can be reduced by improving the project team's knowledge about the product, the processes used to build it, and the capabilities of the staff, the facilities, and the tools. The knowledge acquired over time can be used to refine the assessment of risks already identified, as well to identify new risks and develop new contingency plans. This is a continuous process that enables the participants to perform risk management with greater confidence.

Knowledge acquisition techniques include the following:

- Prototyping,

- Benchmarking,

- Simulation and modeling,

- Incremental development, and

- Collection and analysis of metrics.

The refinement of knowledge should be viewed as an ongoing activity performed throughout the project life cycle.

14.7   Estimating Risk Impacts and Avoidance Costs

The identification, analysis, and handling of risks are not free; however, they can be cost effective. Risk management is similar to buying insurance: If a potential problem does not occur, management can be subjected to criticism for having wasted time and money on problems that did not materialize. Paradoxically, the very effort expended on risk management should reduce the likelihood of the problems occurring. The real question should be what is the correct amount of time and effort to expend performing the activities of risk management?

One method of calculating the cost effectiveness of risk management is to follow these steps:

1. Determine the probability of an undesired event. This may be a single number or a range (as in Table 14.2 in an earlier section).

2. Determine the cost of the loss if the risk becomes a problem. This is the exposure expressed in economic terms. Again, this can be a single number or a range.

3. Finally, for each value of the exposure, compute its contribution to the risk exposure (RE):

$$RE = (\text{probability of loss}) \times (\text{amount of loss})$$

In the example shown in Table 14.2, the four values of the probability and corresponding ranges of the cost loss would result in the ranges of values for the risk exposure shown in Table 14.4.

Growth (%)	Probability of Occurrence (%)	Size	Cost Impact ($000s)	Risk Exposure ($000s)
0–5	40	25,000 LOC	0	0
5–10	25	26,250–27,500	110–220	27–55
10–15	20	27,500–28,750	220–340	44–68
15–20	15	28,750–30,000	340–460	51–69

Table 14.4: Cost Risk Exposure Arising from Software Growth

From Table 14.4 the following summary conclusions can be drawn:

• The worst-case risk exposure is $69K.

• As a result, no more than $69K should be expended to control this risk, because this is the largest possible risk exposure, assuming the probabilities in the first column are reasonably accurate.

- Although it is conceivable that there will be no loss (the first row), it seems reasonable to expend no less than $27K attempting to control this particular risk.

All of this assumes, of course, that a rationale way exists to expend these funds that will reduce the likelihood of the software growth actually occurring. One method of evaluating the potential effectiveness of a specific risk handling technique is to compare the risk exposure before and after the technique is applied against the cost of planning and performing the risk handling.

A metric that does this comparison systematically is called *risk leverage*. Risk leverage (RL) is computed by the following formula:

$$RL = \frac{[(\text{RE before mitigation}) - (\text{RE after mitigation})]}{(\text{cost of risk mitigation})}$$

Risk mitigation activities may reduce the probability of the risk or the potential loss or both. Higher values of risk leverage indicate the areas for investing in risk management. A value of 1 indicates that the cost of mitigation equals the expected savings. Because of the uncertainties involved, organizations typically require that the value of the risk leverage be at least 2 before committing to the mitigation effort.

In the example discussed previously, suppose the project team develops a staged risk mitigation plan that reduces the likelihood of a size of the growth of the product to zero. Here are the steps of the plan selected by the project:

Phase 1: Accept the risk of a growth of between 0 and 5 percent because this is within the reserves established for this cost element.

Phase 2: Expend $5K for a source code license for a small package of specialized software components. Expend a further $5K in on-the-job training in it use by two engineers. The mathematical functions represent about 5 percent of the expected product lines of code.

Phase 3: Defer a desirable but not critical capability that represents a further 5 percent. Whereas there are no direct costs associated with this change, a special trip to corporate headquarters may be necessary to explain the situation. Between preparing for the meetings and the travel costs this is estimated to require an expenditure of a further $10K.

Phase 4: Expend $30K in training funds to incrementally improve the coding practices of the project staff. It is believed that this will reduce product size by a further 5 percent.

Notice that the Phase 2 and 3 actions, if accepted by the project, must be committed to early in the project. If they are not, effort will be expended on designing a feature that might be eliminated or on designing components that could be replaced. Committing to Phase 4 could be deferred until after the design is completed and before the coding begins. In

Growth (%)	Probability of Occurrence (%)	Risk Exposure Before Mitigation ($000s)	Cumulative Cost of Mitigation ($000s)	Risk Leverage
0–5	40	0	0	NA
5–10	25	27–55	10	2.7–5.5
10–15	20	44–68	20	2.2–3.4
15–20	15	51–69	50	1.0–1.4

Table 14.5: Risk Leverage Arising from Software Growth

that case an indicator and threshold should be established, such as the number of defects detected in code reviews early in that phase of development.

The four phases of risk mitigation in the example given in Table 14.5 are all independent and could be performed in any combination or order. In this example the leverage metric suggests that unless another risk mitigation approach can be found the best strategy is to commit to Phases 2 and 4 and invest $20K in those risk mitigation efforts. While this incremental, near-term strategy is being implemented, the project should seek other approaches to combating the risk of larger growths in the software size. For example, the components of the cost of implementing the next step in the plan (which raises the cost from $20K to $50K) should be carefully examined.

This example can be used to illustrate another point: Evaluating the effectiveness of a particular risk mitigation strategy can be complex. Suppose, for example, that the incremental strategy is adopted to control the growth of the product discussed in Tables 14.2 through 14.5. As part of the normal risk management process this risk is monitored. After a few months an increase of 5 percent occurs. Does this mean that the mitigation strategy has failed? Here are two of several possible answers to this question:

- If the growth occurred in areas of product design or project processes that the incremental strategy was attempting to address. then the answer is probably "yes."

- However, a more detailed examination of current circumstances may show that had the strategy not been in place the growth would have been 10 percent, which would imply that the strategy worked by reducing the actual growth from 10 to 5 percent, so the answer would probably be "no."

When performing evaluations the phenomena of "analysis paralysis," wherein a situation is analyzed in greater depth than is required or the available data allow, should be avoided. This requires that the project manager exercise appropriate control over the risk management and analysis processes, both encouraging the staff to explore and evaluate risks as the project progresses and simultaneously keeping the team focused on the objective: To help build and deliver products.

14.8 Monitoring and Controlling Risks

One of the most common errors made in implementing risk management is a refusal to acknowledge that a risk has become a problem and that a risk treatment or handling plan must be implemented. It is easy to say, "Let's look at this situation again next week and see if corrective action is still warranted." This approach, if repeated, usually results in major cost and schedule problems for the program. In turn, once the problem can no longer be denied, the resulting pressures on the project staff will usually result in quality problems. As Fred Brooks [Brooks 1975] said in his famous book, *The Mythical Man-Month*, "How does a project get to be a year late? . . . One day at a time." One of the primary objectives of all project management techniques is to avoid such "schedule drift."

As risks are monitored the watch list, or risk registry, should be updated, producing the profile of each risk over time. Risks that have not yet eventuated are known as *inactive risks*, whereas risks that have eventuated are known as *active risks*. In addition, the status of any active risk treatment plans should be reviewed periodically. Thus risk monitoring and management consists of three tasks:

1. Monitoring of inactive risks so that if they do become active prompt action can be taken. Proper selection of indicators and thresholds is critical to effective monitoring.

2. Review of the status of risks currently being actively mitigated.

3. Reevaluation of inactive risk mitigation plans to verify that they are still appropriate to the changed circumstances and, as appropriate, revision of those plans.

Each of these activities has its own tasks and review requirements:

1. Risks identified and accepted in the risk identification and analysis phases should be monitored consistent with the risk of loss and the project's normal review processes. Particular attention should be paid to the risk thresholds or triggers, which can either be values of metrics or discrete events that have been previously identified as "sounding the alarm" that a potential problem has either has become or has a high probability of becoming a real problem.

2. Risks whose mitigation or treatment plans are currently active should be reviewed on a regular basis (weekly, as suggested earlier) and immediately prior to any major milestone of the mitigation plan if the regular review does not fall within 2 days of the milestone. The purpose is, of course, to maintain focus on handling the risk. Reviews of active risk handling plans should include not only how the plan is progressing but also an examination of any circumstances that influence the underlying processes impacted by the risk.

3. Reevaluation of inactive risk treatment plans should be performed in advance of any of the events that are deemed likely to cause the risk or when an assumption made in the plan is invalidated. It is also reasonable to review all risk handling plans on a

periodic basis; because of the sheer effort involved in doing so, however, such global reviews of all inactive plans must be done less frequently than weekly. Monthly or even quarterly should be sufficient, provided the data needed to trigger the reviews listed above are included in the plans.

14.9   Planning a Risk Management Program

Proper management of a complex activity such as risk management requires that it be organized and documented using a plan. The two major components of the risk management plan are as follows:

1. A description of the general approaches used to identify, analyze, and manage risks; and

2. The specifics of any risks that have been identified at the time the plan is being written or updated.

The risk management program plan should describe the following:

- The project's approach to risk identification, risk analysis, risk handling/mitigation, and risk monitoring;

- The role of risk assessment in design reviews, technical performance evaluation, supplier management, staffing, facilities, and change control processes;

- The general methods of risk reduction, monitoring, and handling that will be used for each assessed risk; and

- The roles of key staff and organizations in the risk activities of the risk management activities.

All risks identified at the time the plan is being created or revised together with their risk handling plans should be described. The risk management program plan should require that a separate risk handling plan be prepared for each high-risk item, identify the timing for its development and citing review responsibilities. The plan should also specify that a risk reduction report be prepared for each item classified as medium or high risk. The risk management plan (RMP) should contain, for each identified risk, the following:

- Statement and assessment of the risk factor;

- Probability of the risk becoming a problem;

- Estimated consequences and/or cost of the problem;

- Assumptions that impact the risk, its impact or its reduction/mitigation plan;

- Alternatives considered with risk level, cost, and schedule identified for each;

- Recommended risk reduction/mitigation method;

- Impact statement for implementation of plan (cost/schedule/technical);

- Responsible individual(s) and organization;

- Risk indicator metrics to be tracked;

- Risk trigger thresholds;

- Criteria for declaring closure of the problem should it occur;

- Reviews and decision points; and

- Recommended backup/fallback approaches, including estimated cost and schedule.

The development of the plan should always bear in mind the objectives of risk management:

- Eliminate risks wherever possible,

- Minimize the direct impact of risks,

- Isolate the impact of risks so they do not ripple into other project activities,

- Develop alternate courses of action, and

- Establish schedule and cost reserves to cover risks that are not known (commonly referred to as "unknown unknowns").

The purpose of risk management planning is simply to focus organized, purposeful thought on the subject of eliminating, minimizing, or containing the effects of undesired events and then capturing the results so the project team can monitor the identified risks, act to ameliorate those risks, and to identify new risks as the project progresses.

Annex A of IEEE Standard 1540-2001 provides a useful example of a risk management plan in outline form that is a good framework for structuring the RMP of many projects. Figure 14.3 presents an annotated version of this outline. The use of this outline is not mandatory for a project to assert compliance with the standard because the annex is considered informative, not required.

1. Overview

    1.1 Date of Issue and Status—Date of the most recent revision, as well as its released status. That is, Draft, Approved, or other states relevant to the organization.

    1.2 Issuing Organization—Who has created this document.

    1.3 Approval Authority—Any approvals required for this plan to go into effect.

    1.4 Updates—A brief revision history of the plan in list form.

2. Scope—Describe what projects and products this RMP applies to. Discuss any constraints or limitations relevant to the risk management effort.

3. Reference Documents—Any documents referred to within the document or which otherwise may be required to understand the background of the document.

4. Glossary—Any special terms or acronyms used in the document.

5. Risk Management Overview—Describe the specific approach of this project and organization to risk management.

6. Risk Management Policies—Describe the general policies and guidelines used by the organization in implementing risk management.

7. Risk Management Process Overview—At a summary level (sufficient to allow the reader to understand the subsequent sections) describe the processes and procedures used to implement the policies.

8. Risk Management Responsibilities—Identify the organizations and individuals responsible for performing risk management.

9. Risk Management Organization—Identify how the responsible parties work together to implement the policies and processes.

10. Risk Management Orientation and Training—Describe any training required to effectively implement the risk management approach described in this plan.

11. Risk Management Cost and Schedules—Identify the unique costs associated with implementing this plan. Identify scheduling relationships between the activities of this plan to one another or to external events.

12. Risk Management Process Description—This is a more detailed description of that described in item 7.

Figure 14.3: Outline of Example RMP (Annotated from IEEE Standard 1540-2001)

12.1 Risk Management Context—Describe any risk management approaches used in the parent organization, together with any adaptations used by the current project. Describe the relationship to the other management activities of the project and organization.

12.2 Risk Analysis—Describe the specific processes and procedures used by the project to perform risk analysis.

12.3 Risk Monitoring—Describe the specific processes and procedures used by the project to monitor the risks.

12.4 Risk Treatment—Describe the approaches to be used to treat risks on this project.

13. Risk Management Process Evaluation—Describe how the risk management process will itself be monitored and evaluated as an element of process improvement.

13.1 Capturing Risk Information—Describe the sources of information on the operation of the risk management effort and how that information will be obtained and recorded.

13.2 Assessing the Risk Management Process—Describe the procedures and methods that will be used to evaluate the efficacy of the risk management effort.

13.3 Generating Lessons Learned—Describe how useful information (lessons learned) generated by the evaluation of the risk management will be identified and documented.

14. Risk Communication—Describe what reports and other instruments will be used to deliver the results of risk analysis, monitoring, and profiling to the parties involved.

14.1 Process Documentation and Reporting—What documents will be produced and reported, including the frequency.

14.2 Coordinating Risk Management with Stakeholders—Describe what information will be provided, what meetings will be held, and how often with the principals directly involved in performing the risk management effort.

14.3 Coordinating Risk Management with Interested Parties—Describe what information will be provided, what meetings will be held, and how often with other parties who have an interest in the risk management effort but are not directly involved in its implementation.

15. Risk Management Plan Change Procedures and History—Describe the policy and procedures to be applied in managing the RMP. If appropriate, the Configuration Management Plan of the project can be referenced. At greater length describe the revision history of the document.

Figure 14.3: Outline of Example RMP (Annotated from IEEE Standard 1540-2001) (continued)

14.10   Summary

The risk factors for every software project should be identified, analyzed, and monitored and strategies for their mitigation developed and implemented as required. Every project should have a risk management plan, and every project manager should keep an up-to-date list of the "Top Ten" project risks. Risk indicators and metrics should be collected, analyzed, and heeded; and preplanned risk handling activities should be implemented when the project metrics indicates that a risk has become a problem.

Applicable Standards

IEEE Std 610.12-1990. *IEEE Standard Glossary of Software Engineering Terminology.* IEEE, New York.

IEEE Std 1540-2001. *IEEE Standard for Software Life Cycle Processes—Risk Management.* IEEE, New York.

Additional References

[Boehm 1981]   Boehm, B. W. (1981). *Software Engineering Economics.* Prentice Hall. Upper Saddle River, NJ.

[Boehn 1989]   Boehm, B. W. (1989). *Tutorial on Software Risk Management.* IEEE Computer Society Press, Los Alamitos, CA.

[Brooks 1974]   Brooks, F. P. (1974). "The Mythical Man-Month." *Datamation*, vol. 20, no. 12, December. Reprinted in *Software Engineering Project Management*, 1997, 2nd ed., R. H. Thayer, ed., IEEE Computer Society Press, Los Alamitos, CA.

[Brooks 1975]   Brooks, F. P., Jr. (1975). *The Mythical Man-Month: Essays on Software Engineering.* Addison-Wesley, Reading, MA.

[DSMC 1989]   Defense Systems Management College. (1989, March). *Risk Management: Concepts and Guidance.* Superintendent of Documents, U.S. Government Printing Office, Washington, DC.

[DSMC 1990]   Defense Systems Management College. (1990, January). Chapter 15 in *System Engineering Management Guide.* Superintendent of Documents, U.S. Government Printing Office, Washington, DC.

[Fairley 1994]   Fairley, R. E. (1994). "Risk Management for Software Projects." *IEEE Software*, vol. 11, no. 3, May.

[Fairley & Rook 1997]   Fairley, R. E., and Rook, P. (1997). "Risk Management for Software Development." *Software Engineering*, M. Dorfman and R. H. Thayer, eds. IEEE Computer Society Press, Los Alamitos, CA.

[Fairley & Thayer 1997]   Fairley, R. E., and Thayer, R. H. (1997). "Work Breakdown Structure." *Software Engineering Project Management*, 2nd ed., R. H. Thayer, ed. IEEE Computer Society Press, Los Alamitos, CA.

[Gaffney 1997]   Gaffney, J. E. (1997). "How to Estimate Software Project Schedules." *Engineering Project Management*, 2nd ed., R.H. Thayer, ed. IEEE Computer Society Press, Los Alamitos, CA.

[Morgan 1981]   Morgan, M. Granger (1981). "Table 1: Risk-Abatement Strategies Fall into Four Major Categories: Choosing and Managing Technology-Induced Risk." *IEEE Spectrum*, December, p. 56.

[Rook 1986]   Rook, P. (1986). "Controlling Software Projects." *Software Engineering*, January, pp. 7–16.

[Ulam 1976]   Ulam, S. M. (1976). *Adventures of a Mathematician*. Charles Scribner's Sons, New York, p. 196.

Chapter 15

Software Metrics

15.1   Introduction

Software metrics help project personnel, their customers, and their management make better decisions during the product life cycle and also provide an objective basis for specifying attributes of a software product or a development process.

Currently more than 500 individual metrics have been proposed for use in understanding the operation and development of software products during the last few decades. Such a large number of candidate metrics suggests two things. First, it is an indicator of both rapid progress and, correspondingly, immaturity. Second, selecting a manageable number of useful metrics for any given organization or project is more challenging than it would be were there, for example, only a few dozen candidates.

A final consequence of this wide diversity is that the effort of the research community has been spread more or less thinly in its study of a large number of metrics rather than concentrating on more in-depth studies of a smaller number of more practical metrics.

When planning a metrics effort the candidates should be evaluated for their utility in the following areas of application:

- Tracking project and product progress,

- Determining product and project complexity,

- Determining when a desired state of quality has been achieved,

- Analyzing defects,

- Validating project processes, and

- Providing a basis for estimating future projects.

Software measurement, measures, and metrics have been active areas of software engineering for more than 30 years. The overall objective of the work in these areas has been to describe and quantify software and its development in terms that are meaningful to software practitioners, researchers, and their customers. Early practice and research in software measurement concentrated on the areas of software cost and schedule, errors and reliability, and size and complexity. The community continues to explore these topics, as well as these more general questions:

- What is to be measured and why?

- What units of measurement should be used?

- How should it be measured?

- What is the nature of the data available?

- How should it be collected?

- How should it be analyzed and used?

- How should the data and measures be validated?

These questions, when taken together with the earlier list of desired applications and the lists of candidate metrics given later in this chapter, form a useful conceptual framework for establishing the metrics program of a project with known metrics and will help when conducting research into new ones. The emphasis of this chapter is, of course, the application of known metrics to projects.

The complexity of the task, together with the large number of potentially useful metrics, renders the task of establishing a software metrics program for a new project or organization rather daunting. To help the reader, this chapter provides an introduction to software metrics and the issues involved in establishing a software metrics effort and in using the data produced by it. It also provides the reader with a road map to the available literature and lists of recommended metrics. These lists were developed to improve the management of software development projects by various governmental agencies responsible for developing and acquiring software products.

The IEEE standards provide additional support to this effort. Specifically, the standards provide a framework for the definition and use of metrics in the areas of software project management, configuration management, life cycle modeling, quality assurance, maintenance, and validation and verification through the plans described in the applicable standards. Metrics can be used to manage each of these activities. Conversely, many of the activities listed will generate information used in the project metrics program. Thus the IEEE standards provide a basis for selecting, measuring, and using metrics in a software development program.

The IEEE standards listed below should be used in developing the plans listed above. While there is no separate standard for the format of the plan for the metrics program, there is a section reserved for planning the metrics program in the software project management plan (SPMP). Use of the standards listed here will aid software engineering project managers and other personnel in planning and performing the activities of a comprehensive metrics program and in preparing the metrics section of the SPMP:

- IEEE Standard 1061-1998, *IEEE Standard for Software Quality Metrics Methodology*, provides guidance on selecting and implementing software quality metrics.

- IEEE Standard 1045-1992, *IEEE Standard for Software Productivity Metrics*, provides guidance on selecting and implementing software productivity metrics.

- IEEE Standard 982.1-1988, *IEEE Standard for Dictionary of Measures to Produce Reliable Software*, and IEEE Standard 982.2-1998 describe various measures for use in different life cycle phases to aid in building reliable software.

15.2 Objectives

In this chapter you will learn:

- What software measurement is.

- What software measures and software metrics are.

- Why and how a software metrics program can aid software engineering project management.

- The primary reasons for using software metrics.

- The activities of a software metrics program.

- How to plan and implement a software metrics program.

- How to write a software metrics plan.

- How to define a good software metric.

- How software metrics are classified.

- The definitions of process and product metrics.

- What quality, productivity, and management metrics are.

- Why some metrics are classified as reflective and others as predictive.

- Why software metrics is more than just data collection.

- Why and how to use historical data.

- What metrics frameworks are available and how to use them.

- What the Goal-Question-Metric paradigm is.

- How to use the paradigm for defining goals.

- How to validate software metrics.

- Why the selection of software metrics should be qualitative, not quantitative.

- Examples of core metrics that have been used successfully.

- What measurement scales are.

- The differences and similarities among the nominal, ordinal, interval, and ratio scales.

- The characteristics of each scale and what statistics are appropriate for each scale.

- How to measure staff-hours, source statements, and documents.

- The measures used to produce reliable software.

- What metrics activities can be carried out as part of software quality assurance, verification and validation, and maintenance.

- What a software anomaly is.

- The categories available to classify software anomalies.

15.3 Measurement and Metric Concepts

15.3.1 Software Metrics, Measures, and Measurement

Measurement is the act or process of measuring. *Measurement* is the process of assigning numbers or symbols to selected attributes of an entity. An *attribute* is a feature (or property) of an entity. An *entity* can be a physical object or it can be an event or process occurring in the real world. The assignments must be carried out following clearly defined rules. Thus, the act of measurement creates a mapping from the real world to a formal, mathematical world. More formally, the process of measurement maps entities in our world into a formal mathematical domain in which well-understood, structured operations can be performed and the results clearly comprehended.

An important objective of the measurement process is to create mappings that preserve any observed relationships among the attributes. Performed correctly, measurement assists in the quantification of concepts and attributes in order to objectively examine and analyze them. Measurement is the fundamental process used to create and maintain measures and metrics.

A *measure* is also defined as a unit of measurement—the extent, dimensions, capacity, and so on—of anything, especially as determined by a standard; a result of measurement. A universal or local standard must be established for each measure. An example of a measure would be lines of code (LOC). Because no *a priori* standard exists to determine what a LOC is, an organization must define a local standard as to what constitutes a LOC. Such a local standard can be adopted from existing literature (such as the IEEE standards) or could be produced by local research. The selection or definition adopted must preserve relationships with other properties, such as cost or schedule.

A *metric* is defined as a calculated or composite indicator based on two or more measures. An example of a metric would be defects per thousand lines of code (KLOC). Thus a measure is the result of a direct measurement, whereas a metric is the result of a computation using two or more measurements.

Although metrics and measures have different formal definitions, in practice they are used synonymously and interchangeably. The direct result of a measurement (such as cost) is often used operationally in much the same manner as a metric (such as lines of code produced per hour of effort). Thus, in the literature and practice of software engineering, the terms *software metrics*, *software measures*, and *software measurement* are used interchangeably to refer to many activities including:

- Productivity models and measures,

- Quality models and measures,

- Reliability models and measures,

- Performance models and evaluation,

- Cost and schedule estimation,

- Data collection,

- Structural and complexity metrics,

- Management by metrics, and

- Methods and tools evaluation.

15.3.2 Uses of Metrics

Metrics can be used to quantify characteristics or attributes of entities in order to understand them, to predict their future behavior, and, ultimately, to control them. Properly used metrics can provide visibility into causal relationships that would not otherwise be possible.

Characteristics of a software item can be measured to obtain quantitative evidence of the consistency and completeness of requirements, of the quality of the design, and of the readiness of an item for test. Attributes of processes and products can be measured to determine if a product is ready for delivery, or if the schedule will be achieved, or if cost targets have been met. Properties of the final product are measured to determine if it fulfills contractual requirements.

Properly understood and defined metrics can be invaluable in all of the above scenarios. Without suitable metrics, unreliable, subjective opinion would have to be used. Ultimately expert judgment will always be called on to make decisions, but such judgments are always more effective if they are based on well-understood data.

The three primary reasons for using software metrics are usually held to be (1) understanding, (2) predicting, and (3) controlling. This order follows the natural order in which control systems are developed and is a common feature of control systems, whether they are used to manage a project or control the temperature of a refrigerator.

First, the entity to be controlled, or managed, must be understood at the appropriate level of detail. In control theory this phase is referred to as *system identification*. A model of the entity's essential responses (outputs) to changed (and measured) inputs or controls is developed. In other words, metrics are used as both the outputs (responses) and inputs (controls) of the entity. This understanding is then used to extend the model to a predictive one, wherein the specific effects of changes in the values of controls on the model responses are determined.

Such models are usually not fully deterministic, nor are they necessarily complete. That is, there is uncertainty as to the specific effect of an input change to the outputs, as well as inputs and controls that are not accounted for. The solution to this uncertainty regarding the entity's response is to implement *feedback*. A feedback process examines the desired output, the input applied, and the actual output and then, based on the understanding of the entity being controlled, produces a new, modified input. This process is applied iteratively and, if successful, produces a useful degree of control.

In applying this control system model to software development and metrics, the ultimate objective has to be to obtain a useful degree of insight and control into the process and its products. The definition of "useful" will be different as a function of the organization, project, and the point in time involved. Thus when metrics are first introduced "useful" may mean simply that the project can foresee major problems in advance and offset the impacts of those problems but cannot reduce the severity of the problems. Later, as the understanding of the process and the metrics improves, "useful" may mean that projects can apply corrective action to reduce the severity of the impacts themselves.

15.3.2.1 Understanding

The understanding of software development processes and the resulting products can be increased when suitable metrics are identified. Indeed, the effort to identify and measure metrics itself inevitably increases the understanding of those undertaking the effort. In their simplest forms metrics can be used to establish which situations are typical and which atypical. Metrics can be used to calculate estimates of cost, effort, and schedule expenditures for various products or processes. Metrics can assess the status of an ongoing project, track potential risks, uncover problem areas before they become crisis areas, adjust work flow, and evaluate the ability of project personnel to control the quality of work products.

This understanding, however, does not come automatically. It can only be developed by working with the metrics over a period of time. As each candidate metric is evaluated, a key question is the degree to which the metric is a control (input to the entity) or a response (output from the entity). Depending on the entire set of metrics selected, some will naturally stand out as inputs, while others will recommend themselves as outputs. Thus the number of lines of code in a product is usually an input, with a total cost as an output. Studies have shown, however, that they are related, so cost could be used as the controlling input, so that its development consumes no more than the available funding and time.

15.3.2.2 Prediction

Metrics can help predict qualities that the product and its associated development process will exhibit in the future. Based on historical norms, predictions can be made about what might happen on current or future products and projects. Historical information from an organizational metrics database can be used to estimate cost, schedule, or resource requirements on similar projects. Metrics database information can also be used to predict the likely number of defects remaining in code and estimate the amount of testing needed before product release. Such studies will usually result in predictive relationships between metrics, such as these:

- Cost,

- Schedule,

- Effort,

- Quality,

- Size,

- Testing,

- Reuse,

- Quality, and

- Reliability.

The essential model of the entity (product or processes) will usually reveal relationships between these and other metrics. From this understanding predictions of the effect on the outputs can be made based on changes to the inputs. Organizations need not start this effort from scratch. Numerous tools and methodologies are available, for example, that predict cost and schedule based on organizational, project, and product attributes. Likewise, several tools and methodologies are available for estimating error rates. Before establishing a metrics program the current state of the practice should be reviewed by consulting the literature and the Web sites of the IEEE Computer Society, the Software Engineering Institute, and those of software engineering research centers of several universities.

15.3.2.3 Controlling

The ultimate objective of any metrics program is to improve the quality of the product and the efficacy of the processes that produce it. Once the predictive relationships have been established, they can be used to control the project. In particular, by using predictive metrics the changes to control (input) metrics needed to achieve a specific result (as indicated by desired output metrics) can be computed. The effect of the changes can then be monitored using the selected output (response) metrics. The measured and predicted values can then be used to further refine the control process.

Three complications must always be kept in mind when using predictive relationships:

1. The uncertainty as to the exact values of the input and output metrics. That is, no measurement is perfect.

2. The uncertainty in the relationship between the inputs and outputs metrics. That is, our knowledge of the model is not perfect.

3. The delay between the time an input is changed and the time the resulting change is seen in an output. That is, there is a time delay or lag between the changes of the input and the resulting change to the output.

In the software development process the lag between cause and effect (as defined by a particular metric changing) can be many months. If these effects are not understood, the result will be an overcontrolled condition, wherein product and process changes are made faster than the system can respond. Such overcontrol usually produces wild swings in behavior, inducing chaos in a program. The dual effects of lack of visibility (that is, lack of suitable understanding of the process and metrics) and the sheer complexity of software projects and products can produce an unstable situation. Dorner [Dorner 1997] describes several situations in which overcontrol of complex situations can produce catastrophic results.

The answer is, of course, not to merely control (or manage) the problem, but rather to do so insightfully. In this effort establishing a metrics program plays two roles. First, it provides insight into the process being controlled: software products and their developmental processes. Second, as the organization's understanding and use of metrics matures, the metrics can be used to control the projects more effectively.

15.3.3 Classes of Metrics

It is often useful to classify measures and metrics according to the measurable entity on which the measure or metric is based, the intended usage of the measure or metric, and the time period, project phase, or process represented by the measure or metric. Two major categories of measurable entities that are of interest to project personnel are product and process metrics. Product metrics quantify characteristics of the software being developed. Process metrics quantify characteristics of the environment or the process being employed to develop the software.

Product metrics measure an attribute of the software product at some state of development, from requirements to maintenance. The range of products measured includes the software source code, object code, documentation, and other by-products of the software production process including requirements and design specifications, test plans, and user manuals. Some common product metrics measure the size and complexity of the item. A size metric for each work product can be defined. The number of requirements, the number of design components, the number of code modules, and the number of test cases are size measures for products. The complexity of requirements, of design, of the code itself, and of the test procedures can be measured as well.

Process metrics measure properties of the software development process used to produce the product. The processes measured can span one or more phases of the software development life cycle including requirements development, design, code generation, configuration management, change control, testing, maintenance, reengineering and reuse, and quality assurance. The processes measured can include any specific activity, set of activities, or time period within the project.

Two common classes of metrics used to evaluate processes are progress and defect metrics. Progress metrics measure how tasks within a process or set of processes are being completed. This is commonly done by comparing the actual date of completion of, or of effort required to perform, a process task with the planned date or effort. By comparing the actual and planned completion dates, the trend of the overall phase or project schedule can be inferred. Likewise, an analysis of the actual and planned effort needed to perform tasks can reveal process cost trends.

During the performance of a process task, as well as during subsequent tasks that use the results of that task, defects or anomalies are found. Thus an error or oversight in design may be discovered during the design phase itself, or later during the coding of the design, during a code review, or during testing. The percentage of defects introduced during a specific process step that are discovered at each later step is often used as a measure of the effectiveness of the processes. Such data can indicate which processes should be improved. How to improve the process will usually require the examination of much more specific information.

In addition to the above, process metrics can be based on measures of reuse, methodology, tools, and techniques used, as well as objective information about personnel experience and training.

Metrics can also be categorized into quality, quantity/productivity, and project control categories, depending on how the metric will be used. Software quality metrics measure the degree to which software possesses a given attribute that reflects its quality. Common examples include reliability, maintainability, and portability. Software quantity/productivity metrics measure some physical attribute of software. Examples include lines of code, function points, and pages of documentation. Project control metrics include budget or schedule expended, earned value, and similar properties.

Metrics can be further categorized into reflective metrics and predictive metrics. Reflective metrics measure attributes of entities at the present moment. Thus they capture the results of events up to the present. Predictive metrics extrapolate attributes using the current, reflective data out to a future point in time. Thus, a rate of module design completion can be used to predict the future net productivity of the project when all coding and testing are completed.

Keep in mind that these categories are not mutually exclusive. Thus a metric may be a quality metric but may also be a predictor used by the project control function. Likewise, the product metrics are influenced by the process metrics, since the processes being measured produce the product. Table 15.1 illustrates this concept with four common metrics according to how a particular organization views the primary uses of several metrics.

Software Metric	Primary Measured Entity		Primary Usage			Time Period	
	Process	Product	Quality	Quantity/ Productivity	Project Control	Reflective	Predictive
Planned LOC	X			X			X
Actual LOC		X		X	X	X	
Defects/ KLOC	X	X	X	X		X	X
Number of requirements changes	X		X		X	X	X
Number of schedule changes	X	X			X	X	X

Table 15.1: Sample Common Metrics Classifications

Thus, *actual LOC* is a product measure that provides reflective information about the size of the product, whereas *planned LOC* is a predictive measure used to establish the size of the project (quantity). Defects per thousand lines of code (defects/KLOC, sometimes called the defect density) is a product metric that provides information about the quality of the software product and developmental processes. It can be reflective and, if historical data are available, can be used to predict the latent defect rate. In the hypothetical organization that developed Table 15.1 such data were not available. The defect density is also a reflective process metric because it measures the net effect of the processes used to develop the software. It can be used to evaluate the effectivity of changes to processes.

The number of requirement changes is usually used as a process metric. It is generally used as a measure of process stability and, hence, affects quality. It is a reflective metric in that it measures the current number of changes to requirements, but it can also be used to predict schedule/budget changes. The number of schedule changes is both a process metric and product metric that is used to assess the current state of a project and to predict the likelihood of further schedule changes.

15.3.4   Measurement and Metric Scales

When working with metrics it is important to remember what scale is associated with a given measure or metric. Most obviously, the difference between days and weeks of schedule is significant. More subtly, the scales used for some metrics will limit the analysis and decision processes that can be based on the information represented by the metric. The selection of a scale for a metric is not an arbitrary matter: It must be based on an understanding of the underlying attribute the measurement represents and what analytical operations can be meaningfully performed on the measured data.

Formally, a measurement scale is a mapping from the observable states for an attribute to a numerical range. The mapping in turn determines the type of the scale and the types of operations that can be performed on the metric and the kinds of meaningful statements that can be made about the metric. Five types of scales are used: nominal, ordinal, interval, ratio, and absolute.

The five types of scales are hierarchical, with each higher level possessing all the properties of the lower ones. The higher the level of measurement, the more complex the analysis that can be applied to the data. In the software metrics planning process, emphasis should be placed on selecting metrics that can take advantage of the highest levels of measurement. A higher level measurement can always be reduced to a lower one. Table 15.2 summarizes the hierarchical characteristics of the nominal, ordinal, interval, ratio, and absolute scales. For more details on the metrics scales, the reader is referred to the work of Fenton and Pfleeger [Fenton & Pfleeger 1997].

15.3.5   Direct and Derived Measurement

For each of the measurement scales discussed above, there are two possible methods of obtaining a specific metric: (1) direct measurement or (2) derived, or computed, measurement. Both of these methods have considerations that must be kept in mind when applying the metrics:

- Direct measurements may be objective or subjective. If subjective, it may be difficult to duplicate a particular measurement. Explicit measurement rules are critical.

- Derived measurements are related more indirectly to the reality. In addition, computational errors may be introduced.

These issues should be addressed when validating that each metric means what the developer thinks it means.

15.3.6   Graphical Representation of Metric Data

15.3.6.1   Utility of Graphics

Metric data usually become more meaningful when displayed graphically. This is especially true if these situations hold true:

- The data should or does exhibit trends—and they are important to managing the project and its processes.

- Both planned and actual data values are displayed.

Scale Type	Scale Level	Appropriate Operations	Appropriate Statistics	Characteristics
Nominal	Lowest	$=, \neq$	Mode Frequency	Mutually exclusive No order
Ordinal		$=, \neq,$ $<, >$	Mode Frequency Median Percentile	Mutually exclusive Order
Interval		$=, \neq,$ $<, >,$ $+, -$	Mode Frequency Median Percentile Mean Standard deviation	Mutually exclusive Order Equal intervals
Ratio		$=, \neq,$ $<, >,$ $+, -,$ $\times, \div$	Mode Frequency Median Percentile Mean Standard deviation Geometric mean	Mutually exclusive Order Equal intervals Absolute zero
Absolute	Highest	$=, \neq,$ $<, >,$ $+, -,$ $\times, \div$	Mode Frequency Median Percentile Mean Standard deviation Geometric mean	Mutually exclusive Order Equal intervals Absolute zero

Table 15.2: Characteristics of Measurement Scales

- More than one set of numbers must be examined simultaneously to assess the meaning of the data.

To be useful, graphical displays of data should:

- Be easily and unambiguously traceable to their sources.

- Be easy to update. Nothing inhibits the use of metrics more than a long, drawn-out update process. Ideally, the graphs should be generated automatically using spreadsheets and the data provided by normal project status.

- Avoid the use of color unless it is truly beneficial—printing and e-mail are still not free.

Graphs of progress metrics should also show the following:

- The past history (planned versus actual) for each progress metric used,

- The current status of planned versus actual progress during the reporting period,

- A forecast of likely future progress based on actual progress to date, and

- An identification of any product version numbers and the date of issue of the report.

The following sections give some examples of metrics and their graphical presentation.

15.3.6.2 Software Change Trend Line

One of the common measures of the maturity or stability of a software product is the cumulative number of changes made to the product over time. Figure 15.1 shows an example of this metric from the time a product is released to a single site for alpha testing. The number of changes was defined to be zero at the beginning of this process. The testing of the product went through the following stages:

- During alpha testing, numerous changes were applied to the product.

- At the end of alpha testing, the product was deemed sufficiently stable, or mature, to support beta testing at multiple customer sites. The product configuration was "frozen" (that is, no changes were applied after the completion of the alpha test) and the product was sent to the customer for beta testing.

- During beta testing, the customer identified many significant problems. No changes were made during this period because the product configuration was frozen.

- The product was withdrawn from the field and returned to the laboratory.

- Using the beta test reports, a stress test environment was developed and used for post-beta laboratory testing. Based on empirical data, the developers believed it was one-tenth as stressful as the actual field environment, in the sense that errors were 1/10th as likely to appear per unit of time. As a result the test duration was extended by a factor of 10. Changes were made to the product as a result of this testing.

- The product was then returned to the field for a second round of beta testing. This time it was a success.

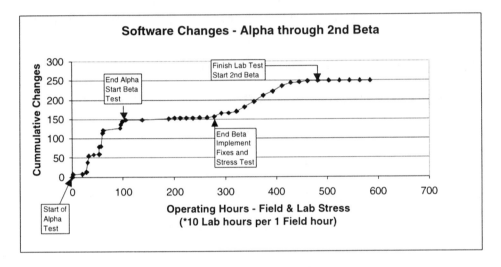

Figure 15.1: Software Maturity

The graph of Figure 15.1 displays a common phenomenon, namely, the failure of a test (in this case the beta test) caused by insufficient product maturity. Looking at the 100-hour point on the graph (that is, the end of alpha testing), we can clearly see that the number of changes has not stabilized. In other words, had the alpha testing been continued, more changes would have been made. Instead, the software was frozen and distributed to the field prematurely. At the 280-hour point, because of the large number of problems seen, which are not shown on this graph, developers recognized that the beta testing had been started prematurely. The product was returned to the laboratory for rework as described earlier. At the end of the laboratory testing period, the product was exhibiting the classical signature of stability in a given test environment. The project could now return the product to beta testing with a higher level of confidence in the ultimate success of their efforts.

The use of the count of changes was valid in this case because the developer's software engineering procedures ensured that the granularity of the changes was fairly constant. Had it not, a graph showing impacted or changed lines of code would have been more appropriate.

15.3.6.3 Graph of Schedule Plan with Control Limits

Figure 15.2 is an example of a plan line with control limits. The plan and actual lines represent the cumulative completions of the code and unit testing of 100 modules. The estimated total schedule for this is 100 days. It is also expected that the size of the product could grow by 5 percent, and that the schedule could extend by 10 percent. The developers and the customer determine that variability within these bounds is acceptable. Based on these assumptions, the historical productivity, and the expected variability of the size of the modules, upper and lower control limits are derived. As modules are completed they are totaled and the result plotted on the graph.

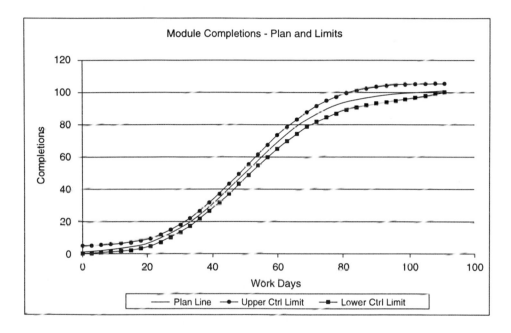

Figure 15.2: Module Completions with Limits

15.3.6.4 Estimated Versus Actual Average Module Size with Control Limits

Figure 15.3 shows a plot of the planned (100 lines of code) and actual average size of completed modules for a project. This metric is commonly used to ensure that the project's development processes are compliant with quality standards. Based on historical records, the project staff determined that the expected variance for the modules should be 50 lines of code. Based on this assumption, and the project's planned module completion schedule, which determines $N(d)$ the number of modules that are completed on or before a given date

d, the upper and lower control limits were set at:

$$\text{Upper limit} = 100 + \frac{50}{\sqrt{N(d)}}$$

and

$$\text{Lower limit} = 100 - \frac{50}{\sqrt{N(d)}}$$

Note that this example illustrates the use of a metric computed using two separate measures, whereas the first two examples were each based on a single measure. It also shows the all-too-common problem of not achieving a goal.

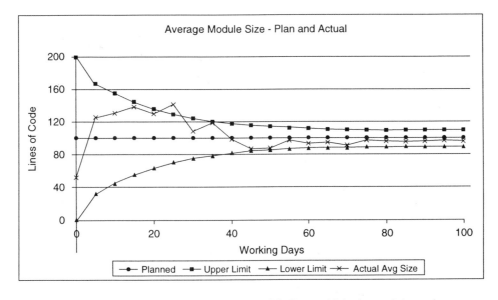

Figure 15.3: Average Module Size with Control Limits and Actuals

15.3.6.5 Frequency of Real-Time Diagnostic Messages: A Pareto Chart

Figure 15.4 illustrates an application of a pareto chart; that is, a frequency distribution which has been sorted in order of decreasing frequency. The data shown represent the number of occurrences for each type of diagnostic message recorded by a real-time, multithreaded system. By examining the relative frequency of the messages observed with that expected (the so-called "operational profile"), the general health of the system can be determined. In addition, if error codes occur frequently, then the areas of the code that emit those messages can be examined for latent defects.

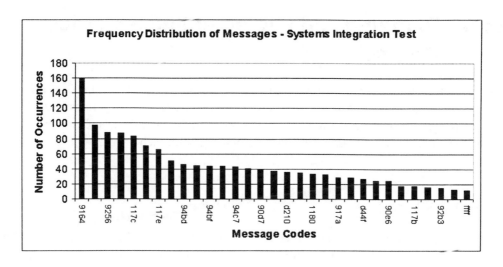

Figure 15.4: Pareto Chart of Diagnostic Messages

15.3.6.6 Histogram of Module Complexity

Figure 15.5 shows an example of an unsorted histogram; in this case the number of modules have a given cyclomatic complexity. Data of this type can be used to manage the developmental processes and to evaluate the adequacy of the projects testing plans.

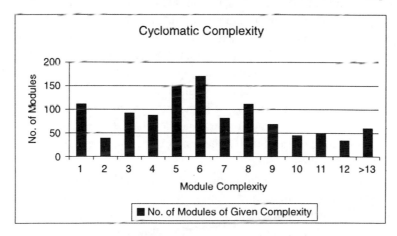

Figure 15.5: Histogram of Module Complexity

15.4 Planning and Implementing a Metrics Program

The key activities of a software metrics program are planning the effort, implementing and using the metrics, and improving or refining the metrics program. Prior to establishing the metrics program, the first two are performed sequentially. Once the metrics program is established, these activities are no longer strictly serial, with each providing feedback to the other.

15.4.1 Planning

Planning can be broken down into three tasks: (1) defining the objectives and goals of the effort, (2) selecting metrics that support the achievement of those objectives and goals, and (3) then defining the policies and procedures needed to make the necessary measurements, compute the required metrics, and deliver them to the entities who need them.

When defining the objectives and goals of the metrics program, the existing software development processes and projects should be described. This "as is" statement establishes a baseline of what data are already available, what the detailed project processes are, and what the project objectives are. If the projects have a software life cycle model plan, a specification, and a statement of work, much of this information will be readily available and need not be duplicated in the metrics planning documentation. In addition, any improvement goals the organization wants to pursue should also be documented.

Having defined the objectives, a metrics set is then selected that measures the degree to which the objectives and goals are being met. The selection must be realistic. That is, the data that must be collected in order to compute the metrics must be available already or readily made available. Thus, when selecting a metric, the data needed to compute the metric must be clearly understood, along with how the metric is to be calculated from those data. Any limitations in the accuracy or timeliness of the data must likewise be understood if the planning is to be realistic. Finally, the scales to be used for measuring and recording the data should be identified.

As mentioned before, hundreds of metrics are available but it generally wise [Jones 1991, Kan 1995] to select a small, meaningful set of metrics. The visibility the metrics provide into key project issues, not quantity, should be the guiding factor in selecting metrics. Ideally a selected metric should possess all of the following characteristics:

- *Simple:* The definition of the metric is simple and understandable.

- *Objective:* Different people using the metric will obtain identical values.

- *Easily collected:* The cost and effort required to obtain the data are reasonable.

- *Robust:* The metric is insensitive to irrelevant changes.

- *Relevant:* The metric relates to the process or product in a meaningful way, as well as to the intent of the metrics effort.

- *Valid:* The metric measures what it purports to.

Both objective and subjective data should be considered when selecting metrics. Objective data consist of actual counts of items (e.g., LOC, staff hours, changes, errors) that can be verified without reference to opinion. Subjective data are based on project personnel's feeling or understanding of a characteristic or condition (e.g., level of difficulty of the problem being solved, degree of new technology involved, stability of requirements). Subjective data can provide critical information for validating and analyzing the objective data. Objective data can indicate inaccuracies in subjective data.

If the metrics program is intended to support a single project, then the metrics selected, together with the data to be measured and their scales, should be documented in the software project management plan (SPMP). If the metrics program is designed to support multiple projects, then the common information can be placed in a single, organizational metrics plan to avoid duplication. It should then be referenced in the SPMP. Next, the procedures to be followed should be defined and documented in the SPMP or organizational plan, as appropriate.

The metrics procedures that should be defined include the following:

- When and how frequently measurement will occur and data will be collected;

- Subsequent time lines for recording and reporting results;

- Sources of the measured data;

- Any forms and procedures for collecting, extracting, and recording data;

- How the data will be stored and accessed;

- Who will be responsible for designing the metrics database and for entering, retaining, and overseeing the metrics effort;

- Who has responsibility for collecting the metrics data;

- Who will use the metrics data;

- How the data will be validated, analyzed, and reported; and

- Any support tools that must be acquired and maintained to support the process.

The use of standardized forms and procedures to record data will significantly increase the accuracy of the reported information and decrease the associated costs. Ideally, manual collection will not be required. Thus, the list of problem reports being worked should be extracted automatically from the project configuration management system. Likewise, the hours worked on a task may come from the organization's cost control system. While planning the initial effort the number of new data collection activities should be minimized. Once the metrics program has proven its worth, the effort can be expanded.

For many organizations, the sources of key metrics data are:

- The project configuration and change management systems;

- Inspection, review, and test results, if not present in the above; and

- The cost accounting and scheduling systems.

15.4.2 Implementation

Implementing the metrics program includes the activities of collecting the data, validating the data and metrics (do they represent what we think they do?), and finally analyzing data and reporting the metrics.

The project managers of small projects may be wholly responsible for performing metrics activities. On large projects, separate metrics personnel are often designated. In either case, project managers must oversee the metrics activities and ensure that accurate metrics data are collected and reported, and that potential problem indications are appropriately analyzed and acted on.

15.4.2.1 Collecting Metrics

To the absolute maximum extent possible, the metrics collection activities should be integrated into the project's software development processes. The goal should be to seamlessly integrate collection within, or as a direct by-product of, the existing software process. Automating collection procedures can significantly decrease metrics program costs and increase the accuracy and timeliness of the data collected. For example, a LOC counting tool can be automatically invoked whenever a module is checked into the software library.

15.4.2.2 Metrics Validation

Demonstrating validity of a metric consists of showing that, to the degree expected and needed for its intended usage, it is predictive, has content and construct validity, and is reliable.

- Predictive validity is demonstrated by showing that suitable correlation exists between the estimated value of a metric and the actual value at some later point in time. In other words, the metric can be used to predict its own future value with a suitable (for the planned usage) degree of accuracy.

- Content validity is demonstrated by showing that the central tendency, variation, and scale of the metric values are consistent with those for the measured values of the real property. In other words, the metric represents or means what it is advertised to. Again, this must be done to the degree required by the intended uses.

- Construct validity is demonstrated by showing that each of the variables that contribute to the indirect measurement of an attribute bears the expected relationship to the attribute. In other words, when one or more metrics are being used to indirectly estimate a property, then the influence of those metrics on the estimated value must correlate with what actually happens. For example, suppose a project needs to track the maintainability of a software item. The project staff elects to use lines of code per module, the number of comments per line of source, and a measure of complexity as the primitive measures, to compute a maintainability index. Validation of the construct (the index) then reduces to showing (by historical data or by reference to other field studies) that the three metrics selected do indeed influence the maintainability in the way implemented.

- Finally, the reliability of a metric is demonstrated by showing that a number of measurements taken using the same measurement method on the same subject produce consistent data. In some cases this is called *repeatability*.

In all four of these validation efforts, keep in mind that the degree of validation required is determined by how the metrics will be used. Inadequate correlation will result in incorrect actions, while needless effort may be expended seeking needless precision or correlation. Furthermore, all four need not be valid for a given metric. For example, a directly measured LOC metric has no construct to validate. It can and should be validated for reliability and content. Depending on how it will be used it can also be validated for its predictive ability.

15.4.2.3 Analyzing Metrics

The primary reason for analyzing software metrics is to draw conclusions and make predictions that can be used to guide the project technical and managerial processes. Therefore, understanding the underlying reality and how the metric relates to it is the fundamental requirement of meaningful and accurate analysis. This understanding is initially developed using industry-wide, institutional, project, and personal history. It is subsequently refined during the planning and usage stages.

As the staff gain experience working with the data, they will develop additional insights. In addition, understanding will be gained into what analytical methods should and should not be used while working with the data. The scales of the metrics form the baseline of what operations are appropriate for the different metrics.

One of the most basic analysis activities is the plotting of measures and metrics over time, looking for features and trends as the project progresses. In some cases these plots have both planned (predicted or desired) and actual curves. Classic examples of this are cost and schedule data, lines of code produced, or projections of memory usage. Establishing appropriate control limits or uncertainty regions is an important activity in the analysis process. A simple example will illustrate how control limits can vary over time.

- Suppose a project is developing 1,000 units, with the average unit size estimated to be 200 lines of code, resulting in an estimated product size of 200,000 lines of code.

This size has cost, schedule, and memory usage implications.

- Early in the project 25 units are completed, with an average size (for this sample) of 240 lines of code.

- A straight extrapolation of this limited sample (which represents only 1 percent of the ultimate product) would yield a new estimate of product size of 240,000 lines of code.

- This would imply that the memory usage will grow by 20 percent, with an even larger relative growth in cost and a smaller relative increase in schedule, based on standard cost/schedule prediction models.

- However, if a detailed inspection of the 25 completed modules shows that the standard deviation of this sample is 50 lines of code, then the original 200 line of code average lies within one sigma $(240 - 50, 240 + 50)$ limits of the observed data.

- So there is reason for concern but caution should be exercised in making any changes. Later, however, when 50 modules are completed the picture could change, because the larger data set should produce a smaller standard deviation.

- Finally, it is also possible that the first 25 modules selected were implemented first because it was believed that they were more complex and hence of higher risk. The fact that the resulting modules were larger than the expected average would not be shocking in that case. Examination of other data (such as number of requirements or subjective complexity assessments) would verify if this were the case or not.

As this simple example shows, it is only by maintaining an ongoing analysis of the project and product data, together with the resulting management decisions, that interpretations of the data can be made with any confidence [Humphrey 1995].

15.4.3   Improving the Metrics Program

Improvement activities consist of distributing the metrics reports, evaluating progress toward the objectives/objectives of the measurement program, and recommending improvements in the measurement process being used. Recommendations come from feedback to the reports and from the other metrics activities.

The creation, use, and maintenance of an organizational project history database can significantly benefit an organization's metrics program. The availability of project and product metrics is of little or no value unless personnel also have access to models of metrics that represent what should be expected. Software metrics data must be collected across all projects and over long periods of time by organizations in order to provide information that can lead to long-term software process improvement.

Database use can ensure that the scope of measurement information includes an entire project's product data at all levels and also its process data. Using information from an organizational history database, personnel can gauge whether measurement trends in the current project differ from similar past projects.

Three classes of data for each past project should be archived in the database: cost/schedule, process, and product data. Cost data should be confined to measures of effort that remove the effects of labor. Process data should include information about the project (such as methodology, tools, and techniques used) and information about personnel experience and training. Product data should include size, change, and error information.

15.4.4 Section Summary

This section can only give the most general guidelines and suggestions for instituting a metrics program for a project or organization that does not already have one. Implementing a software metrics program can be both challenging and demanding. It can also be extremely rewarding for the products, the organization, and the individuals involved. Issues that commonly arise are:

1. Too many metrics are included in the initial effort.

2. The relationships between the metrics, the products, and the processes are poorly understood.

3. Too much is expected of the metrics effort too soon.

4. Staff skills and training are not adequate to the tasks.

5. The data needed to perform the effort are not available.

6. The implicit limitations of the data are not understood.

7. The configuration management practices of the organization are not adequate to the task. Software items change faster than measurements can be made.

For more details on implementing metrics programs, the reader is referred to Grady's book [Grady 1992], which describes the experiences of the Hewlett-Packard company in establishing metrics programs. The Ami handbook [Pulford et al. 1996] includes a detailed description of how to implement a metrics effort. Finally, the March 1997 special issue of *IEEE Software Magazine* contains several useful articles on implementing a software metrics program.

15.5 Techniques for Selecting Metrics

Metrics methodologies, also referred to as metrics frameworks, are used as decision aids for organizing, selecting, communicating, and evaluating the required metrics for a given software development project. Two of the most important methodologies that have been developed and are used by many software development organizations are the Goal-Question-Metric paradigm and Practical Software Measurement.

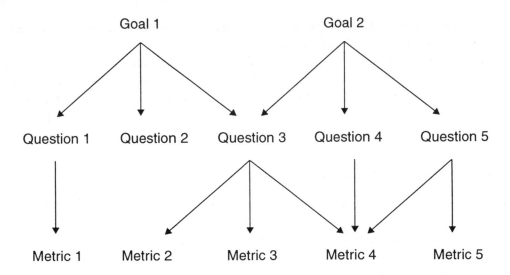

Figure 15.6: GQM Paradigm

15.5.1   The Goal-Question-Metric Paradigm

The Goal-Question-Metric (GQM) paradigm (Figure 15.6) is a mechanism for defining and evaluating a set of operational goals and measures [Basili & Weiss 1984]. GQM was proposed in an effort to provide a systematic approach to the determination of project goals that can be refined into questions that can, in turn, be answered in a quantifiable manner using software metrics. Goals can be defined for any object, for a variety of reasons, with respect to various models of quality, from various points of view, and relative to a particular environment. Applying the GQM paradigm involves these steps:

1. Develop a set of corporate, division, and project goals.

2. Generate questions that define those goals as completely as possible in a quantifiable way.

3. Specify the metrics that need to be collected to answer those questions and to track process and product conformance to the goals.

4. Develop mechanisms for data collection.

Collect, validate, and analyze the data in real time to provide feedback to projects for corrective action, and analyzing the data post mortem to assess conformance to the goals and make recommendations for future improvements.

A template is used to define goals in terms of five parameters:

1. Object,

2. Purpose,

3. Focus,

4. Perspective, and

5. Environment.

The object and purpose define the object or objects of study, what is going to be done, and why it is being done. Any given goal may have several objects and several purposes. A complex goal should generally be divided into smaller, simpler goals. The focus and perspective define the key items of interest and the points of view from which they are evaluated. The environment is a description of the project embedded within its context (business and organizational). This is used to categorize the project together with an appropriate selection of similar projects for comparison purposes. Table 15.3 provides examples and summarizes the five goal parameters.

Parameter	Question	Example
Object	What object?	Processes, products, models, metrics, etc.
Purpose	Why?	Characterizing, evaluating, predicting, motivating, improving, understanding, managing, controlling, certifying, etc.
Focus	What aspect?	Cost, correctness, defects, changes, product metrics, reliability, user friendliness, etc.
Perspective	Who?	User, customer, project, manager, project personnel, developer, corporation, etc.
Environment	Where?	Problem factors, people factors, resource factors, process factors, methods, tools, constraints, etc.

Table 15.3: GQM Goal Parameters

Once the goals have been elaborated using the above templates, the questions and metrics can be derived. Two types of questions are generally formulated: product-related questions and process-related questions. Product-related questions are formulated for the purpose of defining the product, defining the quality perspective of interest, and providing feedback. Process-related questions are formulated for the purpose of defining the process, defining the quality perspective of interest, and providing feedback. After the questions and metrics have been developed, they should be examined together to validate that answering the questions will indeed support achieving the goals. Performing this step can reduce the likelihood of expending effort gathering data only to find out that the question does not truly provide insight into the goals. Table 15.4 summarizes the GQM question guidelines

Question Type	Subgoals	Questions related to:
Product-related questions	Product definition	Physical attributes, cost, changes and defects, context, etc.
	Quality perspectives definition	Major model, validity of the model for the particular environment, validity of the data collected, model effectiveness, substantiation of the model, etc.
	Feedback	Improving the product relative to the quality perspective of interest
Process-related questions	Product process definition	Quality of use, domain of use, etc.
	Quality perspectives definition	Major model, validity of the model for the particular environment, validity of the data collected, model effectiveness, substantiation of the model, etc.
	Feedback	Improving the process relative to the quality perspective of interest

Table 15.4: GQM question guidelines

Once the questions have been framed using these guidelines the set of metrics is determined. Answering a question may require more than one metric. Metrics selected may be objective or subjective. The types of metrics selected in turn determine the mechanisms used for data collection, analysis, and validation. Note that goals are refined top-down into questions and then into metrics, but metrics are interpreted bottom-up in the context of questions and then goals.

Because it is based on the idea that all data collection in a metrics program should be based on a rationale that is explicitly documented, GQM helps identify useful and relevant metrics for a specific project. Developing and documenting a clear, objective rationale for each metric also assists in obtaining the support of project personnel in the metrics program. It also directly supports the development of the metrics section of the SPMP. A current, longer description of GQM is given by Solingen and Berghout [Solingen & Berghout 1999] and can also be found at the GQM Web site at the University of Delft in the Netherlands (http://is/twi.tudelft.nl/gqm/indexframe.html). An additional description can be found at the Software Engineering Institute's Web site (http://www.sei.cmu).

15.5.2 Practical Software Measurement

Practical Software Measurement (PSM) [US Army 2000] is an alternative approach for defining, selecting, implementing, and using software metrics. PSM started from the premise that software measurement, risk management, and financial performance management are three quantitative disciplines that evolved independently and, as a result, are often implemented separately. Integration of these three activities will provide even greater insight and control. Risks, status measures, and financial performance all need to be considered when making project decisions. Risk analysis helps to identify and prioritize issues that drive the definition of the measurement process. In turn the measurement process helps quantify the likelihood and impact of risks. Finally, the measurement process provides an objective basis for reporting financial performance using techniques such as earned value (discussed earlier).

PSM views measurement as a process that must be adapted to the technical and management characteristics of each project and be risk and issue driven. The PSM approach defines three basic measurement activities: (1) tailoring, (2) applying, and (3) implementing.

Tailoring involves selecting an effective and economical set of measures for the project. GQM can be used to perform this activity. Applying involves collecting, analyzing, and acting on the data defined in the tailoring activity. In the final activity, implementing, the cultural and organizational changes necessary to establish an effective measurement process are addressed.

Because the software process itself is dynamic, the measurement process also must change and adapt as a project and organization evolves. As a result the activities of tailoring and applying are performed iteratively. The issues, measures, and analysis techniques must change over time to best meet the project's information needs.

PSM provides nine principles that define the characteristics of an effective measurement process to aid in the tailoring and implementing activities:

1. Project risks, issues, and objectives drive the measurement requirements.

2. The developer's process defines how the software is actually measured.

3. Collect and analyze data at a level of detail sufficient to identify and isolate problems.

4. Implement an independent analysis capability.

5. Use a structure analysis process to trace the measures to the decisions.

6. Interpret the measurement results in the context of other project information.

7. Integrate software measurement into the project management process throughout the software life cycle.

8. Use the measurement process as a basis for objective communication.

9. Focus initially on single project analysis.

One of the primary objectives of software measurement is to help the project achieve its objectives, identify and track risks, satisfy constraints, and recognize problems early in the product life cycle. These objectives can be expressed as risks or, more generally, as issues. PSM emphasizes identifying risks and issues at the start of a project and then using the measurement process to provide insight into them. Issues and risks should often be considered together, rather than individually, to get a true understanding of project status. Issues and risk categories common to most projects include the following:

- Schedule and progress,

- Resource and cost,

- Growth and stability,

- Product quality,

- Development performance, and

- Technical adequacy.

An extensive discussion of this approach is described in the reference [US Army 2000], which can be found at http://www.psmsc.com.

15.6   Sample Core Metrics

The IEEE standards do not require a particular set of metrics to be used. Instead the IEEE requires that the organization analyze its needs and objectives and then select metrics appropriate to its particular product, project, and organization. For organizations beginning a software metrics program, selecting an initial core set of metrics can be difficult. The following sections describe core sets of metrics used successfully by several large organizations and the motivation behind their selection.

15.6.1   NASA Core Metrics

During the testing phase of a space shuttle mission control center upgrade in 1990 and 1991 NASA, initiated a pilot metrics program to improve management visibility into the schedule, risk, and quality of software delivery. Measures were defined for tracking progress and quality on software development projects that are supported by the assistant director for program support (DA3) of the Mission Operations Directorate (MOD) of NASA's Johnson Space Center (JSC). Based on this pilot effort, NASA expanded the pilot metric set to cover the entire software development life cycle.

MITRE Corporation developed the metrics for NASA, which are considered by many to be the best set of management metrics available today. NASA's metrics were selected based on the following criteria:

- The metrics set had to have small data collection and analysis costs.

- Multiple metrics during each life cycle phase were required to provide sanity checks among the metrics and ensure quality data.

- Each metric had to have a proven background for establishing goals and guidelines for indications of possible action.

Table 15.5 summarizes NASA's DA3 MOD core metrics. These metrics have been included in the Software Engineering Laboratory core metrics described below. The MITRE Corporation Web site (http://www.mitre.org/support) includes many related presentations and articles on the use and development of software metrics, including articles from the Software Experience Center at the University of Maryland.

15.6.2 Software Engineering Laboratory Core Metrics

The Software Engineering Laboratory (SEL) is an organization sponsored by NASA that was created for the purpose of investigating the effectiveness of software engineering technologies when applied to the development of application software. In selecting its core metrics, SEL developers focused first on understanding their software development process and then on improving it. The overriding goal of their measurement program is to assess the effects of various methods, tools, and models on the software process, and to identify and apply the best practices.

Tables 15.6 and 15.7 summarize the SEL core metrics and metrics the SEL recommends based on their successful use in practice. The complete source of the NASA SEL guidebook on software measurement can be obtained either from the NAS SEL Web site at http://sel.gsfc.nasa.gov or from the NASA software guidance Web site at http://swg.jpl.nasa.gov.

15.6.3 United States Army Core Metrics

Project managers on U.S. Army software development projects are required to monitor six management issues in order to assess the status of the software projects for which they are responsible:

1. Schedule and progress,

2. Growth and stability,

3. Funding and personnel resources,

4. Product quality,

5. Software development performance, and

6. Technical adequacy.

Metric	Units of Measure	Intended Visibility	Description
Software size	SLOC	Schedule Risk	The number of lines of code in the system that must be tested and maintained
Software staffing	Staff-hours expended per month	Schedule Risk	The number of software engineering and first-line management personnel directly involved with the project development
Requirements stability	Measured in numbers of *shalls* in the project's controlling documents	Schedule Risk	The total number of requirements to be implemented for the project
Development progress	Unit completions	Schedule	The number of modules successfully completed from subsystem functional design through unit test
Computer resource utilization (CRU)	Percent of resource capacity	Risk	The percent of CPU, memory, I/O channel, and disk utilization
Test case completion	Number of test cases planned and successfully completed	Schedule	The percent of test cases successfully completed
Discrepancy report (DR) open duration	Number of critical discrepancy reports open for various periods of time	Schedule Risk Quality	The time lag from problem report initiation to problem report closure
Fault density	Discrepancy reports per KSLOC	Risk Quality	The open and total defect density over time
Test focus	Percent	Risk Quality	The percent of problem reports with a software fix
Software reliability	Units of failure per active test hour for each discrepancy report criticality level	Risk Quality	The probability that software will not fail for a specified time period under specified conditions
Design complexity	Number of paths though a module	Risk Quality	The number of modules with a complexity greater than an established threshold

Table 15.5: NASA Core Metrics

Metric	Usage
Source code growth rate	• Reflects requirements completeness and quality of the software development process • Strong progress indicator during implementation • Stability indicator during testing
Effort data	• Reflects the nature of the project environment and the type of product being developed • Indicator of progress and quality • Replanning aid for future projects
System size estimates	• Reflects requirements stability and completeness • Indicator of system stability
Computer usage	• Use of CPU is directly related to particular process being applied • Progress indicator for design and implementation
Error rates	• Provides insight into product development and process improvement • Indicator of software reliability • Indicator of software quality
Reported/corrected software discrepancies	• Provides insight into software reliability, progress in attaining test completion, staffing weaknesses, and testing quality • Enables personnel to estimate quality and completion dates
Software change rate	• Reflects the software development process and stability of project requirements • Stability indicator
Development activity status data	• Provides insight into the process of individual development activities that comprise a particular phase • Progress indicator • Indirect software quality indicator

Table 15.6: SEL Core Metrics

Metric	Usage
Changes to source	• Quality of configuration control • Stability of specifications/design
Changes to specifications	• Quality of specifications • Need to replan
Classes of changes	• Design instability • Specifications volatility
Computer usage	• Progress • Design instabilities • Process control
Discrepancies reported/open	• Areas of staffing needs • Reliability of software • Reliability of schedules
Effort in total	• Quality of planning • Quality of managing
Effort per activity	• Schedules • Need to replan
Effort to repair/ effort to change	• Quality of design • Cost of future maintenance
Errors per inspection	• Quality of software • Lack of desk work
Classes of errors	• Specific design problems
Errors in total Size of modules planned/designed/ inspected/coded	• Software reliability • Cost of future maintenance • Progress
Manager's estimate of total size	• Stability of specifications • Need to replan
Size of source growth	• Quality of process • Design completeness/quality
Specifications/design items to-be-done	• Level of management control
Planned/executed/ passed tests	• Completion schedules • Progress

Table 15.7: SEL Recommended Metrics

The U.S. Army has identified 14 core metrics to assist project managers in addressing these six management issues. Table 15.8 lists these 14 metrics and their purposes.

15.6.4 Department of Defense Core Metrics

The Software Engineering Institute (SEI) was tasked by the Department of Defense (DoD) to develop a set of basic measures that would help the DoD plan, monitor, and manage its internal and contracted software development projects. The purpose of the metrics was to provide information for three important management functions:

1. *Project planning:* Estimate budgets, schedules, and defect rates.

2. *Project management:* Track and control costs, schedules, and quality.

3. *Process improvement:* Provide baseline data, trace root causes of problems and defects, identify changes from baseline data, and measure trends.

The SEI determined that metrics covering size, effort, schedule, and quality should be used. The SEI recommended the four metrics shown in Table 15.9. These metrics address important product and process issues. The complete text of the SEI report can be found at the SEI Web site [SEI 1992].

15.6.5 USAF Software Metrics Policy

In 1994 the Office of the Undersecretary of the U.S. Air Force [USAF 1994] published a software metrics policy to be applied to all programs producing software items totaling more than 20,000 lines of source code. The objective of the policy is to reduce the risk of lower than desired quality and cost and schedule overruns. The policy mandated that such programs develop and apply a metrics program that addressed the following areas:

- Product size,

- Effort (staff labor),

- Schedule,

- Software quality, and

- Rework.

15.7 Associated IEEE Standards

The metrics-related IEEE standards can aid in planning and performing metrics activities and preparing the metrics section of the SPMP. The standards provide guidance on:

Metric	Usage
1. Cost	Tracks software expenditures ($ spent vs. $ allocated).
2. Schedule	Tracks event/deliverable progress (progress vs. schedule).
3. Computer resource utilization	Tracks percent resource capacity utilized (planned vs. actual size).
4. Software engineering environment	Rates developer's environment (developer's resources and software development process maturity).
5. Manpower	Indicates developer's application of human resources to the development program and the developer's ability to maintain sufficient staffing to complete the project.
6. Development progress	Indicates the degree of completeness of the software development effort. Can be used to judge readiness to proceed to next state of software development.
7. Requirements traceability	Tracks requirements to code (% requirements traced to design, code, and test).
8. Requirements stability	Tracks changes to requirements (user/developer requirements changes and effects).
9. Complexity	Assesses code quality.
10. Breadth of testing	Tracks testing of requirements (% functions/requirements demonstrated).
11. Depth of testing	Tracks testing of code (degree of testing).
12. Fault profiles	Tracks open vs. closed anomalies (total faults, total number of faults resolved, and the amount of time faults are open).
13. Reliability	Monitors potential downtime (software's contributions to mission failure).
14. Design stability	Tracks design changes and effects (changes to design, percent design completion).

Table 15.8: Army Core Metrics

Metric	Usage
1. *Size:* counts of physical SLOC	• Size • Progress • Reuse • Rework
2. *Effort:* counts of staff-hours expended	• Effort • Cost • Rework • Resource allocations
3. *Schedule:* calendar dates	• Schedule
4. *Quality:* counts of software problems and defects	• Quality • Readiness for delivery • Improvement trends • Rework

Table 15.9: DoD Core Metrics

- Required software metrics information to be included in the SPMP,

- Software quality metrics,

- Software productivity metrics,

- Measures to produce reliable software,

- Metrics activities to be carried out as part of software quality assurance,

- Metrics activities to be carried out as part of verification and validation, and

- Metrics activities to be carried out as part of software maintenance.

In creating the plans for a project it is important to achieve consistency and balance without creating needless duplication. Thus, the common processes and objectives of the project's metrics program should be documented in the SPMP, with only that information that is absolutely unique to a particular other plan (say, the SCMP) being inserted in that document. The other plans can then reference the SPMP in their metrics subplan sections.

15.7.1   Software Metrics and the Software Project Management Plan

IEEE Standard 1058-1998, *IEEE Standard for Software Project Management Plans*, specifies the format and content of an SPMP and describes the required software metrics information to be included. The SPMP is the controlling document for managing a software project and defines the technical and managerial processes necessary to develop software products that satisfy the product requirements.

The control plan portion of the SPMP specifies the metrics, reporting mechanisms, and control procedures necessary to measure, report, and control:

- Product requirements,

- Project schedule,

- Project budget,

- Project resources,

- Quality of work processes, and

- Quality of work products.

The SPMP must specify the methods, tools, and techniques to be used in collecting, reporting, and retaining product and project metrics. The plan must identify the metrics to be collected, the frequency of collection, and the methods to be used in validating, analyzing, and reporting the metrics.

It is strongly recommended that as much of the metrics planning information for the project be placed in the SPMP, with the other plans (detailed below) containing descriptions of how those activities will use the metrics in the operation and management of their processes. If the project does not create an SPMP (which is not recommended), then the subordinate plans must carry the full burden of describing their own metrics programs.

15.7.2 Software Productivity Metrics

IEEE Standard 1045-1992, *IEEE Standard for Software Productivity Metrics*, provides guidance on selecting and implementing software productivity metrics. The standard defines a framework for measuring and reporting software productivity. It focuses on definitions of how to measure software productivity and what to report when giving productivity results.

Accuracy and consistency of the data used are essential to the calculation of productivity metrics. Using staff-hours reduces the potential for large errors and increases the accuracy of productivity metrics. Elements of productivity are consistently categorized by using a scheme of primitives and attributes. Attributes are measurable characteristics of a primitive. The standard requires that all attributes be measured for each primitive.

The standard defines measurement primitives for computing software productivity. A primitive is the lowest level for which data are collected. The input primitive for software productivity is the staff-hour actually expended on the project activities. The output primitives are source statements, function points, or documents. Staff-hours (or labor hours) can be further broken down into direct and support hours of various categories.

The standard requires that only source statements written by people be counted and that they be counted only once. Hence, source statements that are expanded within a software module (e.g., macro expansion) or supplied to the program (e.g., by an include statement) are counted only once for all modules being measured. Source statements are counted in one of two ways: (1) as logical source statements (LSS, the number of software instructions) or (2) as physical source statements (PSS, the number of nonblank, noncommented line of source). The primitive unit of measure for a document is a physical page for hardcopy and a screen or page image for electronically displayed documents.

The standard requires measurement of all items whose creation requires more than a predetermined, nontrivial amount of project resources. All items that actively support the development or usage of a software product must be measured. These include requirements, architectural, and design specifications, data definitions, user manuals, reference manuals, tutorials, training guides, installation and maintenance manuals, and test plans. Documents that are produced but not preserved beyond completion of a project should also be measured. These include proposals, schedules, budgets, project plans, and reports.

The standard does not prescribe specific productivity metrics that must be used. It does provide examples of some common productivity metrics which are summarized in Table 15.10.

The standard also lists characteristics that are inherent factors of software development that may have a significant impact on productivity. Whenever data are collected to assess software productivity, these characteristics should be captured and documented in order to ensure consistent comparisons between projects.

The characteristics are divided into three categories:

1. *Project characteristics* describe the people and processes involved in the development effort. They represent factors that the developer may be able to control or alter. Project characteristic information is recorded in one of two main categories: personnel or software development environment. Personnel characteristics to be recorded include education, experience, expert assistance, training, size, and turnover. The software development environment characteristics to be recorded include the tools, techniques, and administration used during the development.

2. *Management characteristics* describe how a project is managed. Management characteristics to be recorded include user participation, stability of product requirements, and constraining factors.

3. *Product characteristics* reflect the nature of the product itself. Product characteristics to be recorded include criticality, degree of innovation, complexity, development concurrency, and a description of the product.

15.7.3 Metrics to Produce Reliable Software

IEEE Standard 982.1-1988, *IEEE Standard Dictionary of Measures to Produce Reliable Software*, provides a set of measures indicative of software reliability that can be applied to

Category	Primitive Measured	Usage	Metric
Productivity ratios	Source statements	Measure staff productivity	Delivered new source statements
			Direct delivered staff-hours
	Documentation		Number of words
			Directly delivered staff-hours
Output-to-output ratios	Source statements	Measure code delivery	Delivered source statements
			Total source statements
		Measure project code reuse	Reused source statements
			Total source statements
	Documentation	Measure density of documents	Number of words
			Number of ideograms
			Number of graphics
	Mixed	Provide insight into software development process	Document pages
			Total source statements
Input-to-input ratios	Direct delivered staff-hours and direct non-delivered staff-hours	Provide insight about effort expended	Direct delivered effort
			Direct nondelivered effort
			Total direct effort
			Total effort
	Support staff-hours		Support effort
			Total direct effort

Table 15.10: Productivity Metrics

the software product as well as to the development and support processes. The standards are designed to assist project management in directing product development and support toward specific reliability goals. The standards include guidance for these tasks:

- Applying product and process measures throughout the software life cycle, providing the means for continual self-assessment and reliability improvement;

- Optimizing the development of reliable software, beginning at the early development stages, with respect to constraints such as cost and schedule;

- Maximizing the reliability of software in its actual use environment during the operation and maintenance phases; and

- Developing the means to manage reliability in the same manner in which cost and schedule are managed.

The standards present a selection of 39 applicable measures, the proper conditions for using each measure, the methods of computation, and the framework for a common language among users.

Errors, faults, and failures serve as primitive units for the majority of the measures presented. The size, type, complexity, or criticality of the software does not restrict applicability of the measures. The 39 measures presented are divided into two functional categories: product and process. The product measures presented address cause and effect of the static and dynamic aspects of both projected reliability prior to operation and operational reliability. The product measures presented are further classified into six subcategories:

1. *Errors/faults/failures:* Count of defects with respect to human cause, program bugs, and observed system malfunctions.

2. *Mean-time-to-failure/failure rate:* Derivative measures of defect occurrence and time.

3. *Reliability growth/projection:* The assessment of change in mean hours of failure-free operation of the product under testing and in operation.

4. *Remaining product faults:* The assessment of residual or latent faults in the product during development, test, or maintenance.

5. *Completeness/consistency:* The assessment of the presence and agreement of all software system parts.

6. *Complexity:* The assessment of complicating factors in a system.

The process measures presented address cause and effect of both the static and dynamic aspects of the development and support management processes necessary for maximizing quality and productivity. The process measures presented are further classified into three subcategories:

1. *Management control:* Assessment of guidance of the development and maintenance processes.

2. *Coverage:* Assessment of the presence of all necessary activities to develop or maintain the software product.

3. *Risk/benefit/cost evaluation:* Assessment of the process trade-offs of cost, schedule, and performance.

15.7.4 Metrics for Software Quality Assurance

IEEE Standard 730-1998, *IEEE Standard for Software Quality Assurance Plans*, provides uniform, minimum acceptable requirements for the preparation and content of software quality assurance plans (SQAPs). It also describe metrics activities to be carried out as part of the software quality assurance function. In addition, the SQAP may include the project software metrics plan if the SPMP does not.

In addition, the IEEE standards in these areas are complementary, with IEEE Standard 1061-1998, *IEEE Standard for a Software Quality Metrics Methodology*, providing a process that can be used to identify and implement software quality metrics.

SQAPs must include a section identifying the standards, practices, conventions, and metrics to be used, together with the phases of the project life cycle to which they apply. The software quality assurance product and process metrics selected must be described. Examples of software quality metrics include the following:

- *Branch metric:* The result of dividing the total number of modules in which every branch has been executed at least once by the total number of modules.

- *Decision point metric:* The result of dividing the total number of modules in which every decision point has had (1) all valid conditions and (2) at least one invalid condition, correctly processed, divided by the total number of modules.

- *Domain metric:* The result of dividing the total number of modules in which one valid sample and one invalid sample of every class of input data items (external message, operator inputs, and local data) have been correctly processed, by the total number of modules.

- *Error message metric:* The result of dividing the total number of error messages that have been formally demonstrated by the total number of error messages.

- *Requirements demonstration metric:* The result of dividing the total number of separately identified requirements in the software requirements specification (SRS) that have been successfully demonstrated by the total number of separately identified requirements in the SRS.

- *Number of procedural noncompliance's observed during monitoring of project processes.*

- *Number of unresolved procedural noncompliances.*

The IEEE software quality metrics methodology given in IEEE Standard 1061-1998 is a systematic approach to establishing software quality requirements and identifying, implementing, analyzing, and validating process and product software quality metrics. The methodology does not mandate the use of specific metrics. An organization can use whatever metrics it chooses as long as the metrics used are validated.

The purpose of these metrics is to take measurements throughout the software life cycle to determine whether the software quality requirements are being achieved. Such metrics provide a quantitative basis for making decisions about the software, thereby reducing subjectivity in its assessment and control. Establishing software quality requirements involves identifying them for a specific product and then assigning them various attributes. The project team must agree on all attributes defining the requirements. Quality and reliability factors that represent management and user-oriented views are then assigned to the attributes.

Metrics are then identified that support each of the desired factors. This is done by decomposing each selected factor into one or more subfactors. The objective is to select quality and reliability subfactors that are concrete attributes of software that are more meaningful to technical personnel. One or more metric is then assigned to each subfactor. Only validated metrics (i.e., either direct metrics or metrics validated with respect to direct metrics) can be used. A target value and range that should be achieved during development are then defined for each assigned metric. A cost-benefit analysis is performed by identifying the costs of implementing and the benefits of applying the metrics. The metrics set is adjusted accordingly to obtain the greatest benefit at the least cost.

15.7.5 Software Metrics and Verification and Validation

IEEE Standard 1012-1998, *IEEE Standard for Software Verification and Validation*, describes the activities used to determine whether development products of a given activity conform to the requirements of that activity, and whether the software satisfies its intended use and user needs. It also describes metrics activities to be carried out as part of verification and validation (V&V). Appropriate metrics should be an integral part of the project V&V approach. The V&V metrics selected should consider the software integrity level (defined in IEEE Standard 1012-1998) assigned to the software and system, application domain, project needs, and current industry practices.

The standards classify V&V metrics into two categories:

1. Metrics for evaluating software development processes and products and

2. Metrics for evaluating V&V task results and for improving the quality and coverage of V&V tasks.

V&V metrics for evaluating software development processes and products that have been found to be useful on most projects include the following:

- Completeness of information (concepts, requirements, design, etc.);

- Software size;

- Requirements traceability;

- Number of changes (requirements, design, code, etc.);

- Logic and data complexity;

- Analysis or test coverage (requirements, code, functional, module, test cases, etc.);

- Control and data coupling;

- Status of actual versus planned progress;

- Number of defects discovered over time;

- Period in the development process where defect is detected;

- Defect category;

- Severity of defect;

- Systemic of repeated errors having the same cause;

- Time to fix a defect (impact to schedule);

- V&V effectivity metrics (e.g., the number of defects identified by a V&V task verses the number of defects identified later); and

- V&V coverage metrics (e.g., the number of software modules verified and validated versus the total number of modules).

15.7.6   Software Metrics and Software Maintenance

IEEE Standard 1219-1998, *IEEE Standard for Software Maintenance*, describes the processes for managing and executing software maintenance activities, including the metrics activities to be carried out during software maintenance. The processes apply to both the planning of maintenance for software while under development, as well as the planning and execution of software maintenance activities for existing software products.

Three major cost drivers dominate the effort expended during the software maintenance process: documentation, communication and coordination, and testing. Maintenance metrics should include metrics that accurately track performance based on these cost drivers. Examples of applicable metrics include document change pages, efforts to negotiate the scope of the work to be included in the change package, and classification of the error rates by priority and type.

The project's software maintenance plan (SMP) must include a section identifying the standards, practices, conventions, and metrics to be applied and how compliance with these items is to be monitored and ensured. The format and contents of the SMP are discussed in Chapter 6.

15.7.7 Software Metrics and Software Anomalies

IEEE Standard 1044-1993, *IEEE Standard Classification for Software Anomalies*, withdrawn in 2001, provided guidance on classifying software anomalies and analyzing the associated data collected. It described the processing of anomalies discovered during any software life cycle phase, and provides comprehensive lists of anomaly categories and related data items that are helpful in identifying and tracking anomalies. As a result, it provided a set of standard definitions that should be used when establishing the metrics program. While it has been withdrawn, it still provides a valid framwork for defining anomalies.

An anomaly is any condition that departs from the expected. This expectation can come from documentation (requirement specifications, design documents, user documents, standards, etc.) or from someone's perceptions or experiences. An anomaly is not necessarily a problem, error, fault, or failure. Anomalies may be found at any time during the project life cycle and especially during the review, test, compilation, or use of software products and documents.

The IEFE standards described a uniform classification process to be applied to anomalies found in software and its documentation. It is expected that users will modify the process based on their organization's procedures. The anomaly classification process is a series of activities, starting with the recognition of an anomaly through to its closure. Four sequential steps are defined:

1. Recognition that an anomaly exists and the documentation thereof;

2. Investigation to confirm that the anomaly exists and what options exist to resolve it;

3. Action planning to map out the activities needed to resolve the anomaly; and

4. Disposition of the anomaly per the action plan.

Eleven categories were needed to establish a common definition for software anomalies. The categories provide common terminology and concepts to communicate among projects, software development environments, and personnel. Application of less than the proscribed set of categories is not recommended because this may result in insufficient data for meaningful data collection and analysis. Table 15.11 summarizes the 11 anomaly categories. Significant information on each anomaly is collected during the classification process.

Collecting the data described in this standard can assist in the evaluation of quality, reliability, and productivity metrics. This information includes the following:

• The environment and activity in which the anomaly occurred,

Process Step	Mandatory Category	Definition
Recognition	Project activity	What were you doing when the anomaly occurred?
	Project phase	In which life cycle phase in the product did the anomaly occur?
	Symptom	How did the anomaly manifest itself?
	Severity	How bad was the anomaly in more objective engineering terms?
	Actual cause	What caused the anomaly to occur?
Investigation	Source	Where was the origin of the anomaly?
	Type	What type of anomaly/enhancement was it at the code level?
	Project cost	What is the relative effect on the project budget to fix?
	Project schedule	What is the relative effect on the project schedule to fix?
Action	Resolution	What action must be taken to resolve the anomaly?
Disposition	Disposition	What actually happened to close the anomaly?

Table 15.11: Anomaly Categories

- The symptoms of the anomaly,

- The software of system cause of the anomaly,

- Whether the anomaly is the result of problem or an enhancement request,

- Where the anomaly originated (by phase and document),

- The resolution and disposition of the anomaly,

- The impact of several aspects of the anomaly, and

- The appropriate corrective action.

By measuring anomalies, data are obtained that will prove useful in managing these aspects:

- *Quality:* Measuring anomalies allows us to quantitatively describe trends in defect or problem discovery, repairs, process and product imperfections, and responsiveness to customers. Anomaly measures are the basis for quantifying several software quality attributes including reliability, correctness, completeness, efficiency, and usability.

- *Cost:* The amount of rework is a significant cost factor in software development and maintenance. The number of anomalies associated with a product is a direct contributor to its cost. Measuring anomalies can help us understand how and where problems and defects occur, thereby providing insight into methods of detection, prevention, and prediction, and keeping costs under control.

15.8 Summary

Software measurement and metrics are recognized as part of software engineering's "best practices." Metrics should be a key management tool for every software project. The extent of the metrics program for a given software development project will vary with the size of the project, the risks, and the resources available. Done correctly, the effort and resources expended in implementing software metrics will be more than paid back by increases in the reliability and quality of software and visibility into the software development process. Because metrics improve the estimation of schedules and budgets, they can significantly contribute to the success of a project by ensuring that it is delivered within acceptable time and budget parameters. In addition to contributing to the success of an individual software development project, the development history and metric information derived from metrics activities can contribute to the long-term well-being of the organization.

Implicit in much of this discussion of software metrics has been the requirement for a modern, reliable, responsive, software configuration management system. Such a system provides a framework within which the measurements necessary to the metrics program can be performed. Without such a system, the measurements of the product and the processes used to produce it will be made against an unknown baseline. As a result those measurements cannot be reliably related to a state of the product at any point in time. Likewise, many of the most fundamental metrics assume the existence of adequate cost and schedule monitoring and control systems.

Software metrics improve the understanding of the software process and software product it produces. Metrics can be used to describe typical situations and to identify unusual situations. Metrics can be used to calculate actual cost, effort, and schedule expenditures for various products or processes. Metrics enable software project managers to assess the status of an ongoing project, track potential risks, uncover problem areas before they become crisis areas, adjust work flow, and evaluate the ability of project personnel to control the quality of work products.

Metrics can help predict qualities that the product and its associated development process will exhibit in the future. By calculating what is typical, predictions can be made about what might happen on current or future products and projects. Information from a metrics database can be used to estimate cost, schedule, or resource requirements on similar projects. Metrics database information can also be used to predict the likely number of defects remaining in the code and estimate the amount of testing needed before product release.

The role of the software engineering project manager in a projects metrics program should be substantial. On many projects, the software project manager will be wholly responsible for performing the software metrics activities, including writing the SCMP, collecting the software metrics data, maintaining the metrics library, and analyzing the software metrics data. On large projects, the software metrics activities are generally handled by a specialized software measurement function staffed by a software measurements manager and support staff. Some portions of the metrics effort may be performed outside of the project itself. In any case the software engineering project manager will be a primary user of much of the metrics data. Knowing and understanding the procedures and activities involved in software measurement can aid a software project manager no matter what is their direct role and responsibilities with regard to software metrics.

Applicable Standards

IEEE Std 610.12-1990. *IEEE Standard Glossary of Software Engineering Terminology.* IEEE, New York.

IEEE Std 730-1998. *IEEE Standard for Software Quality Assurance Plans.* IEEE, New York.

IEEE Std 982.1-1988. *IEEE Standard Dictionary of Measures to Produce Reliable Software.* IEEE, New York.

IEEE Std 1012-1998. *IEEE Standard for Software Verification and Validation Plans.* IEEE, New York.

IEEE Std 1045-1992. *IEEE Standard for Software Productivity Metrics.* IEEE, New York.

IEEE Std 1058-1998. *IEEE Standard for Software Project Management Plans.* IEEE, New York.

IEEE Std 1061-1998. *IEEE Standard for Software Quality Metrics Methodology.* IEEE, New York.

IEEE Std 1219-1998. *IEEE Standard for Software Maintenance.* IEEE, New York.

Additional References

[Basili & Weiss 1984]   Basili, V. R., and Weiss, D. M. (1984). "A Methodology for Collecting Valid Software Metrics." *IEEE Trans. on Software Engineering*, Vol. SE-10, pp. 728–738.

[Dorfman & Thayer 1997]   Dorfman, M., and Thayer, R. H., eds. (1997). *Software Engineering.* IEEE Computer Society Press, Los Alamitos, CA.

[Dorner 1997]   Dorner, D. (1997). *The Logic of Failure: Recognizing and Avoiding Error in Complex Situations.* Addison-Wesley, Reading, MA.

[Fenton & Pfleeger 1997]   Fenton, N., and Pfleeger, S. (1997). *Software Metrics: A Rigorous and Practical Approach.* PWS Publishing Company, Boston.

[Fowlkes & Creveling 1995] Fowlkes, W. F., and Creveling, C. M. (1995). *Engineering Methods for Robust Product Design.* Addison-Wesley, Reading, MA.

[Grady 1992]   Grady, R. (1992). *Practical Software Metrics for Project Management and Process Improvement.* Prentice-Hall, Upper Saddle River, NJ.

[Grady & Caswell 1987]   Grady, R., and Caswell, D. (1987). *Software Metrics: Establishing a Company-Wide Program.* Prentice-Hall, Upper Saddle River, NJ.

[Humphrey 1995]   Humphrey, W. (1995). *A Discipline for Software Engineering.* Addison-Wesley, Reading, MA.

[Jalote 1991]   Jalote, P. (1991). *An Integrated Approach to Software Engineering.* Springer-Verlag, Berlin.

[Jones 1991]   Jones, C. (1991). *Applied Software Measurement.* McGraw-Hill, New York.

[Kan 1995]   Kan, S. (1995). *Metrics and Models in Software Quality Engineering.* Addison-Wesley, Reading, MA.

[Knutson & Bitz 1991]   Knutson, J., and Bitz, I. (1991). *Project Management: How to Plan and Manage Successful Projects.* American Management Association, New York.

[Lyu 1996]   Lyu, M., ed. (1996). *Handbook of Software Reliability Engineering.* IEEE Computer Society Press, Los Alamitos, CA.

[Marciniak 1994]   Marciniak, J. J., ed. (1994). *Encyclopedia of Software Engineering.* John Wiley and Sons, New York.

[Moller & Paulish 1993]   Moller, K., and Paulish, D. (1993). *Software Metrics: A Practitioner's Guide to Improved Product Development.* IEEE Computer Society Press, Los Alamitos, CA.

[Musa et al. 1987]   Musa, J. D., Iannion, A., and Okumoto, K. (1987). *Software Reliability: Measurement, Prediction, Application.* McGraw-Hill, New York.

[Oman & Pleeger 1997]   Oman, P., and Pleeger, S. (1997). *Applying Software Metrics.* IEEE Computer Society Press, Los Alamitos, CA.

[Pulford et al. 1996]   Pulford, K., Kuntzmann-Combelles, A., and Shirlaw, S. (1996). *A Quantitative Approach to Software Management: The Ami Handbook.* Addison-Wesley, Reading, MA.

[Pressman 1997]   Pressman, R. S. (1997). *Software Engineering: A Practitioner's Approach,* 4th ed. McGraw-Hill, New York.

[SEI 1992]   Software Engineering Institute (1992). *Software Measurement for DoD Systems: Recommendations for Initial Core Measures,* CMU/SEI-92-TR-19. http://www.sei.cmu.

[Solingen & Berghout 1999] Solingen, R., and Berghout, E. (1999). *The Goal/Question/-Metric Method: A Practical Guide for the Improvement of Software Development.* McGraw-Hill, London.

[Sommerville 1995]   Sommerville, I. (1995). *Software Engineering,* 5th ed. Addison-Wesley, Reading, MA.

[Thayer 1997]   Thayer, R. H., ed. (1997). *Software Engineering Project Management,* 2nd ed. IEEE Computer Society Press, Los Alamitos, CA.

[Thayer & McGettrick 1993] Thayer, R. H., and McGettrick, A. D., eds. (1993). *Software Engineering: A European Perspective.* IEEE Computer Society Press, Los Alamitos, CA.

[USAF 1994]   U.S. Air Force (1994, February 16). Department of the Air Force letter, Subject: Software Metrics Policy—ACTION MEMORANDUM, ASAF/Acquisition, SAF/AQ, 1060 Air Force Pentagon, Washington DC, 20330-1060.

[US Army 2000]   U.S. Army (2000). *Practical Software and System Measurement: A Foundation for Objective Project Management,* Version 4.0b. U.S. Army, Dept. of Defense, Washington DC.

[Whitten 1990]   Whitten, N. (1990). *Managing Software Development Projects: Formula for Success.* John Wiley and Sons, New York.

[Zuse 1990]   Zuse, H. (1990). *Software Complexity.* de Gruyter, New York.

Appendix A

The Work Breakdown Structure

A work breakdown structure (WBS) partitions a large project into its component activities and products. Each node in a WBS can represent a product, a process, or both in a hierarchical manner. As a result, a WBS is a useful source of, and tool for the organization of, project requirements. An well-organized and complete WBS is one of the best project management tools available, together with a quality SRS and SOW. Two representation methods and three usage modes are commonly used.

A WBS can be represented graphically or with text using either of the following:

- *Hierarchical chart WBS:* A hierarchical chart is used to show the relationships between higher level products/processes and lower level products/processes. The lower level products/processes are contained in the higher level products/processes.

- *Indented list WBS:* The degree of indentations in the list show the relationships between higher level products/processes and lower level products/processes. Items with greater indentation are contained in items with lesser indentation.

Obviously, these representations are logically equivalent. Figures A.1 and A.2 provide examples of a hierarchical chart WBS and an indented list WBS, respectively.

The three most common WBS types are:

1. *Product WBS:* This is a WBS that partitions a large product into its components, thereby more clearly identifying the larger system.

2. *Process WBS:* This is a WBS that partitions a large process into smaller processes whose completion can be assigned to individual project personnel.

3. *Hybrid WBS:* A hybrid WBS includes both product and process elements.

A product WBS displays and defines the products to be developed, and relates the elements of the product to each other and to the final product. The top level of the product WBS identifies the product by name. A product WBS element is a discrete, identifiable item of hardware, software, data, or services. These items of hardware, software, data, and services together define the project deliverables. Figure A.3 provides an example of a product WBS using the indented list representation method.

A process WBS displays the activities to be accomplished and relates the activities and processes to each other and to the project as a whole. The top level of a process WBS also identifies the project by name. The second level identifies the major processes to be

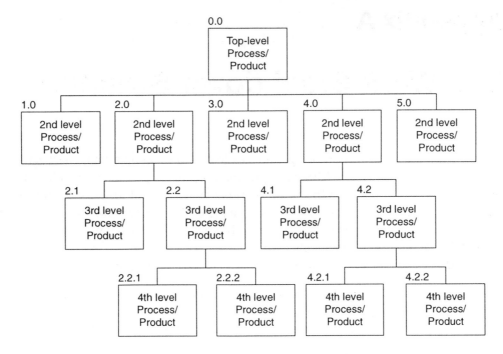

Figure A.1: A Hierarchical Chart WBS

performed (e.g., planning, organizing, requirements analysis, design, coding, testing, and so on). The third level identifies the more detailed activities that must be performed in order to complete the software project. Most process WBSs terminate in tasks. Figure A.4 provides an example of a process WBS using the hierarchical chart representation format. The project (called Project A) is producing an embedded software product with custom hardware.

A hybrid WBS is used in many cases to combine product and process into a single WBS. A hybrid WBS can begin with either processes or products (on the right-hand side), depending on the viewpoint adopted. That is, are the products paramount and the processes the method of implementation, or are the processes central and the product the result of the

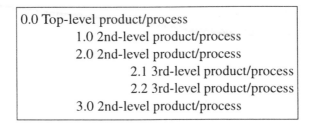

Figure A.2: An Indented List WBS

```
0.0 Air Traffic Control (ATC) System
        1.0 Radar segment
                1.1 Search radar
                1.2 Common digitizer
                1.3 Beacon radar
        2.0 Terminal/tower segment
                2.1 Communications
                2.2 Display
```

Figure A.3: An Indented List Product WBS

execution of them? Alternatively, a hybrid WBS may display both products and processes all on the same level. Figure A.5 provides an example of an indented list hybrid WBS. Note that elements 1.0, 2.0, 4.4, and 4.2.5 are all process elements, while the remainder of the entries are product elements.

Customers may provide a WBS as part of the bid package. Indeed, they may require that their WBS be used in preparing the estimate, with the cost and schedule for each WBS element separately priced and justified. If the customer does not provide a WBS (and many do not), then it is recommended that the project estimation team create one in order to properly organize their work.

If the customer provides a WBS, the developer should realize that it represents the customer's view of the project. Typically it will be product oriented or only contain the most essential (to the customer) processes. Many processes needed by a developing organization will not be present as these will usually vary with the organization. The developer should be clear on which viewpoint is being adopted when the internal WBS is constructed so as not to confuse themselves and the customer.

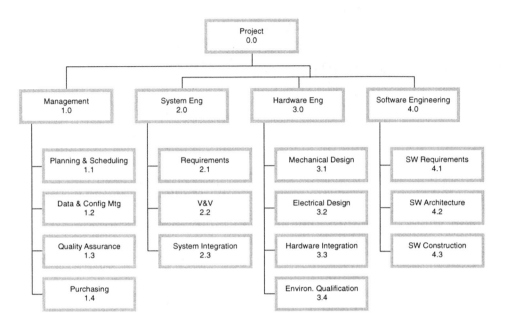

Figure A.4: A Hierarchical Process WBS

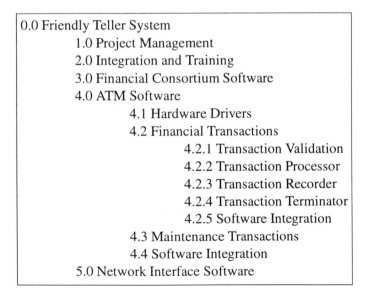

0.0 Friendly Teller System
      1.0 Project Management
      2.0 Integration and Training
      3.0 Financial Consortium Software
      4.0 ATM Software
            4.1 Hardware Drivers
            4.2 Financial Transactions
                  4.2.1 Transaction Validation
                  4.2.2 Transaction Processor
                  4.2.3 Transaction Recorder
                  4.2.4 Transaction Terminator
                  4.2.5 Software Integration
            4.3 Maintenance Transactions
            4.4 Software Integration
      5.0 Network Interface Software

Figure A.5: An Indented List Hybrid WBS

Appendix B

Representing Project Schedules

A project schedule is the conversion of the project plan into an integrated operating timetable. A project schedule is the primary tool used by project managers for monitoring and controlling project activities. In addition, the customer may require a detailed schedule. Management certainly should require that one be created and used.

Schedules should be based on clearly defined work packages. A project schedule provides a graphical representation of the predicted tasks, milestones (major events), dependencies, resource requirements, task duration, and deadlines. It interrelates all project tasks on a common timescale.

A project schedule should be detailed enough to show each task that is to be performed, the name of the person responsible for completing the task, the start and end date of the task, and the expected duration of the task. Other information will be contained in a more detailed work package specification.

Project schedules are most commonly represented by three different techniques: (1) activity lists or spreadsheets, (2) activity/precedence networks, or (3) Gantt charts. Modern software scheduling tools provide support for most of these representations, while some older implementations focus on one or the other.

B.1   Activity Lists

An activity list organizes the activities required to complete a task or project in a sequential form. For each activity, the list should include the activity description, the set of required predecessor activities or other preconditions, and the estimated duration of the activity. An activity list can be generated from the WBS work package specifications. Table B.1 provides an example of an activity list. The postconditions (including the products of each activity) should match the preconditions of any following activities.

B.2   Activity Networks

An activity network is a graphical depiction of an activity list using nodes with interconnecting edges/arrows to represent tasks and their planned sequence of completion. Both preconditions and postconditions are shown explicitly. Two basic types of activity networks exist: (1) *activity on the arrow* and (2) *activity on the node*. Activity on the arrow is

Activity	Description	Preceding Activity	Duration (Weeks)
A	Analyze requirements	–	1
B	Redesign existing components	A	6
C	Design new components	A	3
D	Design interfaces	C, External	1
E	Implement new code	C, External	6
F	Develop integrating plan	C, External	2
G	Modify existing code	B, D	5
H	Finish unit testing	E, G	1
I	Update documentation	E, G	2
K	Develop integration tests	F	1
L	Perform integration tests	H, I, K	1
M	Perform acceptance tests	L	1

Table B.1: Activity List [Thayer & Fairley 1998]

used to represent *activity-oriented* projects, with the activity on the arrows and the relationships between the activities represented by the interconnections at the nodes. Activity on the node was used in the past to represent *event-oriented* projects with the activities on the node and the arrows used solely to represent precedence. The activity on the node form of network is dominant today.

The two most popular forms of activity networks are the Critical Path Method (CPM) and the Program Evaluation and Review Technique (PERT). The differences between CPM and PERT are not fundamental but rather ones of viewpoint. CPM emphasizes activities and PERT emphasizes events. PERT permits explicit treatment of probability for its time estimates, while CPM does not.

These two techniques are most successful when used on projects with activities that:

- Are well defined;

- Can be started, stopped, and performed separately within a given sequence;

- Interrelate with other activities;

- Are ordered in that they must follow each other in a given sequence; and

- Once started, must continue without interruption until completion.

Both techniques are based on the concept of an activity network.

B.3 CPM

CPM was developed by DuPont, Inc., during 1958 and was initially applied to construction projects. CPM uses the activity network representation to highlight the longest duration interconnected path through the network (i.e., the critical path). It determines the earliest possible completion of the work. The critical path must be carefully managed because if a critical path task slips, the entire project will be delayed.

A critical event is formally defined as an event that has identical earliest and latest start times. These two concepts are defined as follows:

1. *Earliest start time (EST):* The EST of an activity is the earliest time an activity can logically begin if all preceding events likewise begin at their earliest times. This is determined by working forward through the network.

2. *Latest start time (LST):* The LST of an activity is the latest time the activity can start without delaying project completions. This is determined by working backward through the network.

If the two times differ then the difference (latest time minus earliest time) is called the *slack time*. *Critical events* have zero slack time.

A *critical path* is a path through an activity network that connects critical events. Every CPM chart has at least one critical path, provided dummy activities are introduced to prevent two activities from starting and ending on the same event. Activities not on the critical path have slack in their start times.

The critical path(s) of a project should be closely examined and monitored during the project, as should those that are nearly critical. For example, the two situations described below are very different:

1. Project A has only one critical path but also has 10 subcritical paths whose slack times are all less than 1 week.

2. Project B has two critical paths and no subcritical paths with slack times of less than 2 months.

From a practical management perspective Project A has 11 critical paths (at least), while Project B has only two. The managers in Project B will have much more latitude to deal with problems than will those of Project A.

Table B.2 provides an example of early and late start and finish times. It will be used in conjunction with the subsequent CPM chart (Figure B.1) using the activity-on-arrow form, although the network can just as easily be represented by the more common activity-on-node form.

Activity	Duration	Earliest Start	Earliest Finish	Latest Start	Latest Finish
A		1	0	1	1
C	3	1	4	3	6
B	6	1	7	1	7
D	1	4	5	6	7
F	2	4	6	11	13
E	6	4	10	6	12
G	5	7	12	7	12
K	1	6	7	13	14
J	2	12	14	12	14
H	1	12	13	13	14
L	1	14	15	14	15
M	1	15	16	15	16

Table B.2: Earliest and Latest Start and Finish Times [Thayer & Fairley 1998]

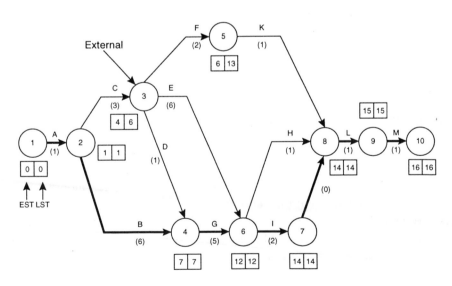

Figure B.1: CPM Chart [Thayer & Fairley 1998]

B.4 PERT Charts

PERT was developed by the U.S. Navy, in cooperation with Booz-Allen Hamilton and the Lockheed Corporation, and was initially applied to the Polaris missile/submarine project in 1958. The goal was to develop a planning and scheduling method for research and development projects.

PERT charts are graphical networks in which the nodes represent activities of the project. PERT charts depict interdependencies between activities and allow project planning to include these relationships. Each node contains information about its predecessors (preconditions), successors (postconditions), and the duration of the task.

Like the CPM method, PERT charts can determine and show the critical path of the project. The PERT method requires three estimates of duration for each activity: (1) the most optimistic time, (2) the most likely time, and (3) the most pessimistic time. Figure B.2 provides an example of a PERT chart.

Note that PERT and CPM charts are topologically similar, with the critical path method being just as applicable to the dominant PERT representation (activity-on-node) as to the CPM (activity-on-arrow) formats. PERT networks are especially adapted to the Resource Loaded Network approach, which can, in turn, be automated [Chang & Christensen 1999]. In the terminology of MS Project, PERT charts are represented by the Project Network Diagram option.

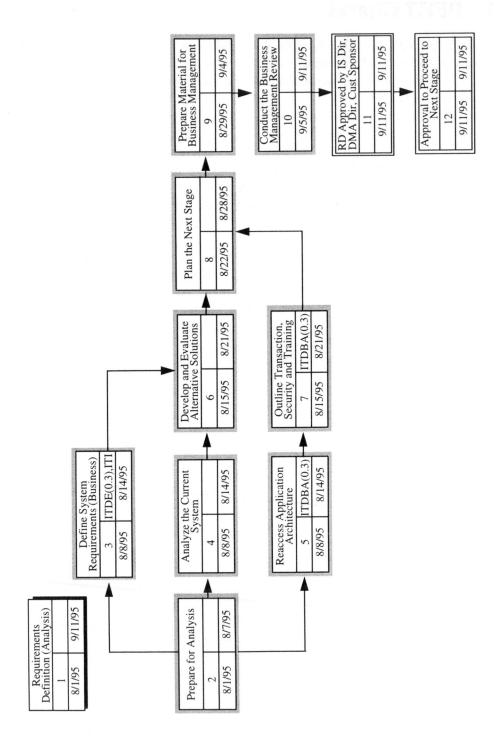

Figure B.2: PERT Chart [http://www.doit.ca.gov]

B.5 Gantt Charts

Henry L. Gantt, a pioneer in the field of scientific management, developed the Gantt chart in 1917. It is one of the oldest and most widely used methods of representing project schedules. Gantt (or bar) charts can be used alone but are often used to display project status, while either CPM or PERT is used to represent the detailed interaction of project activities.

Gantt charts are two-dimensional representations that show the tasks and the time frame for their completion. Each task has a start date, duration time, and end date. Interrelationships are not easily shown on Gantt charts. The planned, actual, and forecast dates at which events occur can be displayed on a single line for each task. The top-level status of the project can be rapidly comprehended as a result but the causes of problems cannot, because the logical relationships are not easily represented in complex projects.

A classical Gantt chart does not explicitly depict the interrelationships among tasks. An example of a linked Gantt chart is given in Figure B.3. MS Project supports this view of project networks as an option.

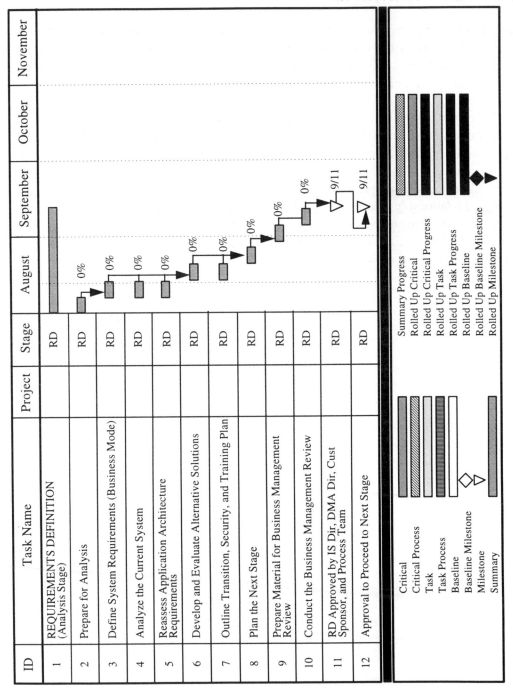

Figure B.3: Gantt Chart [http://www.doit.ca.gov]

B.6   Comparisons

Most projects use more than one method of representing schedules. The Gantt chart, because of its simplicity and ease of understanding, is often used to represent the instantaneous status of a project to project staff, management, and the customer. Several guidelines have been developed to assist in selecting scheduling techniques for projects [Cori 1997]:

1. An activity network should contain at least 20 events/activities. A Gantt chart is generally more appropriate for projects smaller than this.

2. Activity networks that are not computerized should usually be limited to those with fewer than 100 events/activities with 300 events/activities as a practical upper limit. The project manager should realize that the greater the number of events/activities used in the network, the more difficult the network becomes to control and update. Even for 100-node networks the revision of schedule dates is a major chore.

3. Project characteristics that justify the cost and time involved in maintaining activity network representations include projects that are very critical, have high risks or uncertainties, involve many people or organizations, are technically complex, and have activity at diverse geographic locations.

Table B.3 summarizes criteria that can be used by project managers to choose among the CPM, PERT, network, and Gantt methods of representing project schedules.

Finally, the reader should note that modern project tracking tools such as MS Project allow users to select multiple views of the project. Thus a classical Gantt chart representation can be used to depict status, whereas an activity network view can be used for planning, while maintaining a single project schedule database.

Criteria	CPM	PERT	GANTT
Activities versus events oriented	Activity	Event	Activity
Suitability for large projects	Excellent	Excellent	Poor
Suitability for small projects	Poor	Poor	Good
Degree of control	High	Highest	Low
Acceptance by unsophisticated users	Fair	Poor	Excellent
Ease of assembly	Hard	Harder	Easy
Degree of flexibility	High	Highest	Low
Ease of manual calculation	Hard	Hardest	Easy
Accuracy of projections	Higher	Highest	Fair
Cost to prepare and maintain	High	Higher	Low
Vague project scope	Good	Excellent	Poor
Complex project logic	Excellent	Excellent	Poor
Critical completion date	Good	Excellent	Fair
Frequent progress check required	Fair	Hard	Good
Frequent updating required	Hard	Harder	Easy
Frequent logic changes required	Fair	Fair	Poor
Appeal to client	Excellent	Excellent	Good

Table B.3: Schedule Representation Selection Criteria [Cori 1997]

Additional References

[Chang & Christensen 1999] Chang, C. K., and Christensen, M. J. (1999). "A Net Practice for Software Project Management." *IEEE Software*, vol. 16, no. 6, pp. 80–88.

[Cori 1997] Cori, K. (1997). "Fundamentals of Master Scheduling for the Project Manager." *Software Engineering Project Management*. IEEE Computer Society Press, Los Alamitos, CA, pp. 218–229.

[Thayer & Fairley 1998] Thayer, R., and Fairley, R. (1998). *Software Project Cost and Schedule*. Project management course presented by The Professional Development Group of the IEEE Computer Society.

Additional References

Index

About the Authors

Mark J. Christensen, Ph.D.
markchri@concentric.net

Mark J. Christensen, Ph.D., is an independent consultant based in St. Charles, Illinois, USA. Dr. Christensen serves a national client base, offering process and project evaluation services, and project management training. His customers include industrial, governmental, and academic organizations.

From 1988 through 1994 he was the director of software engineering for the Defense Systems Division of Northrop Grumman Corporation. He was responsible for all software development efforts, including customer projects, as well as internal information technology. His IT responsibilities included both management information systems and telecommunications development and operations. He has been involved with process improvement and the Software Capability Maturity Model (CMM) since 1988. He led his product development organization to a CMM level of 3 and his IT group to level 2 in 1993. Both assessments were conducted by an external, independent contractor, who was trained and licensed by the Software Engineering Institute. For two years he developed and taught the software engineering project management module of Northrop Grumman's Program Management Seminar.

From 1996 through 1998 he served as the vice president of Engineering of the Electronic Systems Division of Northrop Grumman Corporation in Rolling Meadows, Illinois. He was responsible for all engineering efforts, covering the full range of technical disciplines, including electronic, software, opto-mechanical, and systems engineering. The management responsibilities included the leadership of 1,200 engineering and technical professionals. He consolidated three geographically diverse engineering organizations in

1997, leading the combined organization to an International Standards Organization (ISO) 9000 certification that same year.

Before joining Northrop Grumman he was an Associate Professor in Mathematics at the Georgia Institute of Technology, where he worked in the areas of computational probability, numerical methods, and computer graphics, and simulation.

Dr. Christensen is a member of the Association for Computing Machinery (ACM) and the IEEE Computer Society (IEEE CS). He chairs the Press Operations Committee of the Computer Society. He is co-author with Dr. Richard Thayer of an upcoming book (1st Quarter 2002) describing how to apply the IEEE Software Engineering Standards to the management of software projects.

He holds a BS degree in physics and mathematics from Wayne State University and an MS in physics from Purdue, where he was a Woodrow Wilson Fellow. His doctorate from Wayne State is in probability theory.

Richard H. Thayer, Ph.D.

Richard H. Thayer, Ph.D., is consultant in the field of software engineering and project management. Prior to this he was a Professor of Software Engineering at California State University, Sacramento, California, United States of America. Dr. Thayer travels widely where he consults and lectures on software engineering, project management, software engineering standards, software requirements engineering, and software quality assurance. He is a Visiting Researcher and Lecturer at the University of Strathclyde, Glasgow, Scotland. His technical interests lay in software project management and software engineering standards

Prior to this, he served over 20 years in the U.S. Air Force as a Senior Officer. His experience includes a variety of positions associated with engineering, computer programming, research, teaching, and management in computer science and data processing. His numerous positions include six years as a supervisor and technical leader of scientific programming groups, four years directing the U.S. Air Force R&D program in computer science, and six years of managing large data processing organizations.

Dr. Thayer is a Fellow of the IEEE, a member of the IEEE Computer Society, and the IEEE Software Engineering Standards Committee. He is a principle author for a Standard for a Concept of Operations (ConOps) document (IEEE std 1362-1998) and a principle author of the Standard for Software Project Management Plans (IEEE std 1058-1998).

He is also an Associate Fellow of the American Institute of Aeronautics and Astronautics (AIAA) where he served on the AIAA Technical Committee on Computer Systems, and he is a member of the Association for Computing Machinery (ACM). He is also a registered professional engineer.

He holds a BSEE degree and an MS degree from the University of Illinois at Urbana (1962) and a Ph.D. from the University of California at Santa Barbara (1979) each in Electrical Engineering.

He has edited and/or co-edited numerous tutorials for the IEEE Computer Society Press:

Software Engineering Project Management (1997), *Software Engineering* (1997), *Software Requirements Engineering* (1997), and *Software Engineering—A European Prospective* (1992). He is the author of over 40 technical papers and reports on software project management, software engineering, and software engineering standards and is invited to speak at many national and international software engineering conferences and workshops.